BUSINESS ETHICS: CASE STUDIES AND SELECTED READINGS

BUSINESS ETHICS: CASE STUDIES AND SELECTED READINGS

THIRD EDITION

MARIANNE M. JENNINGS
Professor of Legal and Ethical Studies in Business
Arizona State University
Director, Lincoln Center of Applied Ethics
Member of the Arizona Bar

WEST **West Educational Publishing Company**
an International Thomson Publishing company I(T)P®

Cincinnati • Albany • Boston • Detroit • Johannesburg • London • Madrid • Melbourne • Mexico City
New York • Pacific Grove • San Francisco • Scottsdale • Singapore • Tokyo • Toronto

Publisher/Team Director: Jack W. Calhoun
Acquisitions Editor: Rob Dewey
Developmental Editor: Mignon D. Worman, Esquire
                          Member, Ohio and California Bars
Production Editor: Sharon L. Smith
Manufacturing Coordinator: Georgina Calderon
Team Assistant: Kristen Meere
Production House: Stratford Publishing Services, Inc.
Cover Design: A Small Design Studio
Cover Illustrator: Warren Gebert
Marketing Manager: Michael Worls

Library of Congress Cataloging-in-Publication Data

Jennings, Marianne.
     Case studies in business ethics / Marianne M. Jennings. — 3rd ed.
          p.   cm.
     Includes bibliographical references and index.
     ISBN 0-324-00404-4
          1. Business ethics—United States—Case studies.   I. Title.
HF5387.J46   1998
174'.4—dc21   98-27453
                                                                          CIP

ISBN: 0-324-00404-4

     3 4 5 6 MZ 3 2 1 0 9

Printed in the United States of America

I(T)P®
International Thomson Publishing
West Educational Publishing is an ITP Company.
The ITP trademark is used under license.

CONTENTS

UNIT IV:
BUSINESS OPERATIONS   *139*

UNIT VI:
BUSINESS AND ITS PRODUCT   *221*

PREFACE

"What is right is right even if no one is doing it. What is wrong is wrong even if everyone is doing it."

Source Unknown

"Goodness is the only investment that never fails."

Henry D. Thoreau
Walden; *Higher Laws*

"Always tell the truth. That way you don't have to remember anything."

Mark Twain

In a 1997 survey conducted for the Ethics Officers Association and the American Society of Chartered Life Underwriters, half of the 1,300 workers from all types of businesses admitted to an unethical or illegal behavior in the past year.[1] Their top two breaches were cutting corners on quality control and covering up incidents.

In December 1997, Marissa Baridis, the compliance officer for Morgan Stanley, Dean Witter, Discover and Co., entered a guilty plea to charges of insider trading. Ms. Baridis was selling sensitive information about pending mergers and other inside business information to friends and former classmates in exchange for cash sums ranging from $2,000 to $10,000.[2]

During 1997 the following events offered some insight into the current issues in business ethics: Tyson Foods entered a guilty plea to charges of making illegal gifts to former agriculture secretary, Mike Espy[3]; Sears, Roebuck and Company[4] agreed to repay funds it had collected from customers while they were in bankruptcy

---

1. Henry Fountain, "Of White Lies and Yellow Pads," *New York Times*, July 6, 1997, p. 7.

2. Dean Starkman, "Five Brokers Indicted for Insider Trades Linked to Ex-Morgan Stanley Officer," *Wall Street Journal*, Dec. 23, 1997, B9.

3. "There's the Outrage," *Wall Street Journal*, Dec. 30, 1997, A10.

4. Chris Woodyard, "Sears to Refund Millions to Bankrupt Customers," *USA Today*, Apr. 11-13, 1997, 1A.

proceedings; Microsoft was ordered to pay $1,000,000 per day for a violation of the conditions established in a consent decree in an earlier antitrust case[5]; Texaco settled a discrimination suit by agreeing to pay $176 million[6]; documents released during litigation with R.J. Reynolds Tobacco Co. revealed that the company's Joe Camel ad campaign was targeted to attract smokers as young as 13[7]; and three executives of the nation's largest for-profit hospital chain, Columbia/HCA Healthcare Corp. were indicted for fraud for overbilling Medicare.[8]

An affidavit from an FBI agent in the Columbia/HCA fraud case included the following description:

> [The investigation] has uncovered a systematic corporate scheme perpetrated by corporate officers and managers of Columbia's hospitals, home health agencies and other facilities in the states of Tennessee, Florida, Georgia, Texas and elsewhere to defraud.[9]

Profits. High returns on investments. Minimizing costs. Fraud. Businesses do exist to make a profit, but business ethics exists to set parameters for earning that profit. This book of readings and cases explores those parameters and their importance.

In 1986, before Ivan Boesky was a household name and Michael Douglas was Gordon Gekko in *Wall Street*, I began teaching a business ethics course in the MBA program in the College of Business at Arizona State University. The course was an elective. I had trouble making the minimum enrollments. However, two things changed my enrollments and my fate. First, the American Association of Collegiate Schools of Business (AACSB) changed the curriculum for graduate and undergraduate business degree programs and required the coverage of ethics. The other event was actually a series of happenings. Indictments, convictions, and guilty pleas by major companies and their officers—from E. F. Hutton to Union Carbide to Beech-Nut to Exxon—brought national attention to the need to incorporate values in American businesses and business leaders.

Whether out of fear, curiosity, or the need for reaccreditation, business schools and students embraced the concept of studying business ethics. My course went from a little-known elective to the final required course in the MBA program.

Application of ethical principles in a business setting is a critical skill. Real-life examples are necessary. Over the past ten years, I have collected examples of ethical dilemmas, poor ethical choices, and wise ethical decisions from the newspapers, the business journals, and my experiences as a consultant and board member. Knowing that other instructors and students were in need of examples, I have taken my experiences and readings and turned them into the cases in this book.

The cases come not only from a dozen years of teaching business ethics, but also from my conviction that a strong sense of values is an essential management skill that can be taught. The cases apply theory to reality; hopefully, they will nurture or reinforce a needed sense of values in future business leaders.

The third edition continues the features students and instructors embraced in the first and the second, including both short and long cases, discussion questions,

---

5. Paul Davidson, "U.S.: Hold Microsoft in Contempt," *USA Today*, Dec. 18, 1997, 1A.

6. "Texaco to Pay $176 Million to End Bias Suit," *Arizona Republic*, Nov. 16, 1996, A1.

7. Milo Geyelin, "Reynolds Aimed Specifically to Lure Young Smokers Years Ago, Data Suggest," *Wall Street Journal*, Jan. 15, 1998, A4.

8. Steven Findlay, "3 Executives From Hospital Chain Indicted," *USA Today*, July 31, 1997, 1A.

9. Id.

hypothetical situations and up-to-the-moment current, ongoing, and real ethical dilemmas. The third edition adds the classic readings in business ethics that provide insight into the importance of ethics in business and how to resolve ethical dilemmas. The organizational structure and indexes, also retained from the first edition, make material easy to locate. A case can be located using the table of contents, the topical index, or the product index, which lists both products and companies by name. An index for business disciplines groups the cases by accounting, management, and the other disciplines in colleges of business. The instructor's manual is updated with more sample test objective- and essay-answer questions of varying lengths and structures. The transparency package, which includes illustrative charts to assist instructors in walking classes through the more complex cases, has been updated and expanded.

This book is not mine. It is the result of the efforts and sacrifices of many. I am grateful to the reviewers for their reviews, comments, and insights. Their patience, expertise, and service are remarkable.

My thanks to Mrs. Kris Tabor for her years of work with me and for her ability to turn notes, inserts, deletions, illegible scratchings, and minute printing into a readable manuscript. Her masterful eye for detail has seen me through three editions of the book and its instructor's manual.

I am fortunate to have a colleague in law, Mignon Worman, as the editor for this edition. Her appreciation for business and morality have been inspirational. I am grateful to Rob Dewey for his continuing support of all my work. All of us are grateful to Sharon Smith for her patient production work and Kristin Meere for her assistance. I am grateful for their tolerance when the phone is answered at my home by toddlers who have little respect for editors. I continue to love editors. Where I see only deadlines, they see both the big picture of the book and its details: they have vision.

I also love my family. They also love editors—they know them by name and by phone calls. I am grateful for their understanding, support, and trips to Kinko's. I am most grateful for their values and the reminder their very presence gives me of what is truly important.

Marianne M. Jennings
Director, Lincoln Center for Applied Ethics
Professor of Legal and Ethical Studies in Business
College of Business
Arizona State University

INTRODUCTION

"The reputation of a thousand years is determined by the conduct of one hour."

———

Japanese Proverb

"A quiet conscience makes one so serene."

———

Byron

"There is no pillow as soft as a clear conscience."

———

Kenneth Blanchard and Norman Vincent Peale
The Power of Ethical Management

"When in doubt, tell the truth. It will confound your enemies and astound your friends."

———

Mark Twain

WHY BUSINESS ETHICS?

A cover story in *Fortune* magazine, entitled "The Payoff from a Good Reputation" (*Fortune*, 10 February 1992), quotes a vice chairman of an advertising agency as saying, "The only sustainable competitive advantage any business has is its reputation." The same could be said about individual business persons. Reputation cannot be found in the annual 10K filing the Securities Exchange Commission requires of a firm and won't be reflected in the net worth recorded on the firm's balance sheet. But its loss can be so devastating that if it were quantifiable, the failure of a firm to disclose that its ethical values were waning would constitute fraud under the federal securities laws. A business lacking an ethical commitment will, eventually, bring about its own demise.

Examining the fates of companies such as Union Carbide, Beech-Nut, E. F. Hutton, Salomon Brothers, Johns-Manville, Exxon, Phar-Mor, Kidder Peabody, Bausch

& Lomb and others whose ethical mishaps resulted in public exposure supports the notion that a lack of commitment to ethical behavior is a lack of commitment to a firm's success.

Many people consider the term "business ethics" an oxymoron. Nonetheless, in keeping with the observation in *Fortune,* compelling reasons support choosing ethical behavior in a business setting. Courses in finance and accounting teach us that the primary purpose and obligation of a business is to earn a profit. The immediate pursuit of the bottom line occasionally can distort even the most conscientious perspective. The fear of losing business and consequently losing profits can lead individuals and companies to make decisions that, while not illegal, raise concerns about fairness, equity, justice, and honesty.

In their 1994 book *Built to Last,* James C. Collins and Jerry I. Porras noted that the common thread among companies with long-term growth and profits was a strong commitment to values. These successful companies had high standards for product quality, concern for employees and employee safety, and reputations for fairness and good service. In short, the ethical components of business were found to be the common thread of success.

A firm must pursue the positive figure for its bottom line with a long-term perspective in mind. Running a successful and ethical business is like running a marathon, not a sprint. Studies show that firms that perform better financially over time are those with a commitment to ethical behavior. For example, in a 1989 study examining twenty-one companies with written codes of ethics and few federal legal and regulatory violations, the Ethics Resource Center found that $30,000 invested in a Dow Jones composite thirty years ago would have been worth $134,000 at the time of the study. If invested in the twenty-one companies, that same $30,000 would have been worth $1,021,861. A study by the Lincoln Center for Ethics at Arizona State University demonstrated that a list of the U.S. corporations that have paid dividends for the past one hundred years coincides with the center's list of companies that make ethics a high priority.

A 1997 study in the *Academy of Management Journal* concludes that firms involved in ethical difficulties (including criminal violations, regulatory citations, and product liability suits) experience earnings declines for at least five years following the public announcement of their problems.[1]

---

1. Melissa S. Baucus and David A. Baucus, *Academy of Management Journal* (1997).

UNIT ONE
FOUNDATIONS OF
BUSINESS ETHICS

WHAT IS BUSINESS ETHICS?

Society recognizes the value of ethics even as it realizes that companies and their employees may not perceive or properly resolve the ethical dilemmas that confront them. Many firms simply adopt a standard of complying with positive law, or any law enacted at any level of government that carries some sanction or punishment for noncompliance. While such compliance promotes many ethical values and moral principles, many actions that comply with positive law raise ethical issues. For example, several border guards formerly stationed at the East German border have been tried for manslaughter for killing East Germans as they attempted to escape into West Germany. In their defense, the former guards argued that they had been ordered to "shoot to kill." However, the judge, in sentencing the men, noted that not all activity that is legal is right. Still, the former guards had faced the dilemma of obeying orders under similar threats to their lives or following their moral standards with respect to the value of human life.

The study of business ethics is thus not the study of what is legal but of the application of moral standards to business decisions. Moral standards are canons of personal behavior that are neither legislated nor changed by legislation. For example, regardless of legislative and regulatory requirements, we all are committed to safety and fairness for employees in the workplace. But what happens when several moral standards conflict? A company that manufactures athletic shoes finds cheap labor in developing nations. The company pays minimum wage for that country, but those wages wouldn't bring enough in one month to allow the workers to buy a pair of the company's shoes. Factory conditions meet that nation's standards but violate nearly all U.S. minimum standards. Without the cheap labor, the shoe manufacturer can't compete. Without the jobs, the nation can't develop, but children are working 50-hour weeks in these third world countries. Fair and just treatment in the workplace is an issue the company must face.

Employees hold moral standards of following instructions, doing an honest day's work for a day's pay, and being loyal to their employers. But what happens when their employers are producing products that, because of inadequate testing, will be harmful to users? To whom do employees turn if employers reject them and their concerns? Other moral standards—of not intentionally harming others and adequately testing products—will present those employees with a dilemma and force them to decide an appropriate course of action.

At one time businesses, consumers, and employees subscribed to the "what's good for GM is good for the country" theory of business ethics. Businesses have now begun to realize that, contrary to Sir Alfred Coke's allegation that a corporation has no conscience, the corporation must develop a conscience. That conscience develops as firms and the individuals within them develop guidelines for their respective conduct.

In the following two readings, economist Milton Friedman and management expert Peter Drucker present different views on the role of ethics in business.

READING 1.1: THE SOCIAL RESPONSIBILITY OF BUSINESS IS TO INCREASE ITS PROFITS[1]

Milton Friedman

When I hear businessmen speak eloquently about the "social responsibilities of business in a free-enterprise system," I am reminded of the wonderful line about the Frenchman who discovered at the age of 70 that he had been speaking prose all his life. The businessmen believe that they are defending free enterprise when they declaim that business is not concerned "merely" with profit but also with promoting desirable "social" ends; that business has a "social conscience" and takes seriously its responsibilities for providing employment, eliminating discrimination, avoiding pollution and whatever else may be the catchwords of the contemporary crop of reformers. In fact they are—or would be if they or anyone else took them seriously—preaching pure and unadulterated socialism. Businessmen who talk this way are unwitting puppets of the intellectual forces that have been undermining the basis of a free society these past decades.

The discussions of the "social responsibilities of business" are notable for their analytical looseness and lack of rigor. What does it mean to say that "business" has responsibilities? Only people can have responsibilities. A corporation is an artificial person and in this sense may have artificial responsibilities, but "business" as a whole cannot be said to have responsibilities, even in this vague sense. The first step toward clarity in examining the doctrine of the social responsibility of business is to ask precisely what it implies for whom.

Presumably, the individuals who are to be responsible are businessmen, which means individual proprietors or corporate executives. Most of the discussion of social responsibility is directed at corporations, so in what follows I shall mostly neglect the individual proprietor and speak of corporate executives.

---

1. SOURCE: *The New York Times Sunday Magazine*, September 13, 1970. Copyright © 1970 by The New York Times Company. Reprinted by permission.

In a free-enterprise, private-property system, a corporate executive is an employee of the owners of the business. He has direct responsibility to his employers. That responsibility is to conduct the business in accordance with their desires, which generally will be to make as much money as possible while conforming to the basic rules of the society, both those embodied in law and those embodied in ethical custom. Of course, in some cases his employers may have a different objective. A group of persons might establish a corporation for an eleemosynary purpose—for example, a hospital or a school. The manager of such a corporation will not have money profit as his objective but the rendering of certain services.

In either case, the key point is that, in his capacity as a corporate executive, the manager is the agent of the individuals who own the corporation or establish the eleemosynary institution, and his primary responsibility is to them.

Needless to say, this does not mean that it is easy to judge how well he is performing his task. But at least the criterion of performance is straightforward, and the persons among whom a voluntary contractual arrangement exists are clearly defined.

Of course, the corporate executive is also a person in his own right. As a person, he may have many other responsibilities that he recognizes or assumes voluntarily—to his family, his conscience, his feelings of charity, his church, his clubs, his city, his country. He may feel impelled by these responsibilities to devote part of his income to causes he regards as worthy, to refuse to work for particular corporations, even to leave his job, for example, to join his country's armed forces. If we wish, we may refer to some of these responsibilities as "social responsibilities." But in these respects he is acting as a principal, not an agent; he is spending his own money or time or energy, not the money of his employers or the time or energy he had contracted to devote to their purposes. If these are "social responsibilities," they are the social responsibilities of individuals, not of business.

What does it mean to say that the corporate executive has a "social responsibility" in his capacity as businessman? If this statement is not pure rhetoric, it must mean that he is to act in some way that is not in the interest of his employers. For example, that he is to refrain from increasing the price of the product in order to contribute to the social objective of preventing inflation, even though a price increase would be in the best interests of the corporation. Or that he is to make expenditures on reducing pollution beyond the amount that is in the best interests of the corporation or that is required by law in order to contribute to the social objective of improving the environment. Or that, at the expense of corporate profits, he is to hire "hard-core" unemployed instead of better-qualified available workmen to contribute to the social objective of reducing poverty.

In each of these cases, the corporate executive would be spending someone else's money for a general social interest. Insofar as his actions in accord with his "social responsibility" reduce returns to stockholders, he is spending their money. Insofar as his actions raise the price to customers, he is spending the customers' money. Insofar as his actions lower the wages of some employees, he is spending their money.

The stockholders or the customers or the employees could separately spend their own money on the particular action if they wished to do so. The executive is exercising a distinct "social responsibility," rather than serving as an agent of the stockholders or the customers or the employees, only if he spends the money in a different way than they would have spent it.

But if he does this, he is in effect imposing taxes, on the one hand, and deciding how the tax proceeds shall be spent, on the other.

This process raises political questions on two levels: principle and consequences. On the level of political principle, the imposition of taxes and the expenditure of tax proceeds are governmental functions. We have established elaborate constitutional, parliamentary and judicial provisions to control these functions, to assure that taxes are imposed so far as possible in accordance with the preferences and desires of the public—after all, "taxation without representation" was one of the battle cries of the American Revolution. We have a system of checks and balances to separate the legislative function of imposing taxes and enacting expenditures from the executive function of collecting taxes and administering expenditure programs and from the judicial function of mediating disputes and interpreting the law.

Here the businessman—self-selected or appointed directly or indirectly by stockholders—is to be simultaneously legislator, executive and jurist. He is to decide whom to tax by how much and for what purpose, and he is to spend the proceeds—all this guided only by general exhortations from on high to restrain inflation, improve the environment, fight poverty and so on and on.

The whole justification for permitting the corporate executive to be selected by the stockholders is that the executive is an agent serving the interests of his principal. This justification disappears when the corporate executive imposes taxes and spends the proceeds for "social" purposes. He becomes in effect a public employee, a civil servant, even though he remains in name an employee of a private enterprise. On grounds of political principle, it is intolerable that such civil servants—insofar as their actions in the name of social responsibility are real and not just window-dressing—should be selected as they are now. If they are to be civil servants, then they must be selected through a political process. If they are to impose taxes and make expenditures to foster "social" objectives, then political machinery must be set up to guide the assessment of taxes and to determine through a political process the objectives to be served.

This is the basic reason why the doctrine of "social responsibility" involves the acceptance of the socialist view that political mechanisms, not market mechanisms, are the appropriate way to determine the allocation of scarce resources to alternative uses.

On the grounds of consequences, can the corporate executive in fact discharge his alleged "social responsibilities"? On the one hand, suppose he could get away with spending the stockholders' or customers' or employees' money. How is he to know how to spend it? He is told that he must contribute to fighting inflation. How is he to know what action of his will contribute to that end? He is presumably an expert in running his company—in producing a product or selling it or financing it. But nothing about his selection makes him an expert on inflation. Will his holding down the price of his product reduce inflationary pressure? Or, by leaving more spending power in the hands of his customers, simply divert it elsewhere? Or, by forcing him to produce less because of the lower price, will it simply contribute to shortages? Even if he could answer these questions, how much cost is he justified in imposing on his stockholders, customers and employees for this social purpose? What is his appropriate share and what is the appropriate share of others?

And, whether he wants to or not, can he get away with spending his stockholders', customers' or employees' money? Will not the stockholders fire him? (Either the present ones or those who take over when his actions in the name of social responsibility have reduced the corporation's profits and the price of its stock.) His customers and his employees can desert him for other producers and employers less scrupulous in exercising their social responsibilities.

This facet of "social responsibility" doctrine is brought into sharp relief when the doctrine is used to justify wage restraint by trade unions. The conflict of interest is naked and clear when union officials are asked to subordinate the interest of their members to some more general social purpose. If the union officials try to enforce wage restraint, the consequence is likely to be wildcat strikes, rank-and-file revolts and the emergence of strong competitors for their jobs. We thus have the ironic phenomenon that union leaders—at least in the U.S.—have objected to government interference with the market far more consistently and courageously than have business leaders.

The difficulty of exercising "social responsibility" illustrates, of course, the great virtue of private competitive enterprise—it forces people to be responsible for their own actions and makes it difficult for them to "exploit" other people for either selfish or unselfish purposes. They can do good—but only at their own expense.

Many a reader who has followed the argument this far may be tempted to remonstrate that it is well and good to speak of government's having the responsibility to impose taxes and determine expenditures for such "social" purposes as controlling pollution or training the hard-core unemployed, but that the problems are too urgent to wait on the slow course of political processes, that the exercise of social responsibility by businessmen is a quicker and surer way to solve pressing current problems.

Aside from the question of fact—I share Adam Smith's skepticism about the benefits that can be expected from "those who affected to trade for the public good"—this argument must be rejected on grounds of principle. What it amounts to is an assertion that those who favor the taxes and expenditures in question have failed to persuade a majority of their fellow citizens to be of like mind and that they are seeking to attain by undemocratic procedures what they cannot attain by democratic procedures. In a free society, it is hard for "good" people to do "good," but that is a small price to pay for making it hard for "evil" people to do "evil," especially since one man's good is another's evil.

I have, for simplicity, concentrated on the special case of the corporate executive, except only for the brief digression on trade unions. But precisely the same argument applies to the newer phenomenon of calling upon stockholders to require corporations to exercise social responsibility (the recent GM crusade, for example). In most of these cases, what is in effect involved in some stockholders trying to get other stockholders (or customers or employees) to contribute against their will to "social" causes favored by the activists. Insofar as they succeed, they are again imposing taxes and spending the proceeds.

The situation of the individual proprietor is somewhat different. If he acts to reduce the returns of his enterprise in order to exercise his "social responsibility," he is spending his own money, not someone else's. If he wishes to spend his money on such purposes, that is his right, and I cannot see that there is any objection to his doing so. In the process, he, too, may impose costs on employees and customers. However, because he is far less likely than a large corporation or union to have monopolistic power, any such side effects will tend to be minor.

Of course, in practice the doctrine of social responsibility is frequently a cloak for actions that are justified on other grounds rather than a reason for those actions.

To illustrate, it may well be in the long-run interest of a corporation that is a major employer in a small community to devote resources to providing amenities to that community or to improving its government. That may make it easier to attract desirable employees, it may reduce the wage bill or lessen losses from pilferage and sabotage or have other worthwhile effects. Or it may be that, given the laws about the deductibility of corporate charitable contributions, the stockholders can contribute more to charities they favor by having the corporation make the gift than by doing it themselves, since they can in that way contribute an amount that would otherwise have been paid as corporate taxes.

In each of these—and many similar—cases, there is a strong temptation to rationalize these actions as an exercise of "social responsibility." In the present climate of opinion, with its widespread aversion to "capitalism," "profits," the "soulless corporation" and so on, this is one way for a corporation to generate goodwill as a by-product of expenditures that are entirely justified in its own self-interest.

It would be inconsistent of me to call on corporate executives to refrain from this hypocritical window-dressing because it harms the foundations of a free society. That would be to call on them to exercise a "social responsibility"! If our institutions, and the attitudes of the public, make it in their self-interest to cloak their actions in this way, I cannot summon much indignation to denounce them. At the same time, I can express admiration for those individual proprietors or owners of closely held corporations or stockholders of more broadly held corporations who disdain such tactics as approaching fraud.

Whether blameworthy or not, the use of the cloak of social responsibility, and the nonsense spoken in its name by influential and prestigious businessmen, does clearly harm the foundations of a free society. I have been impressed time and again by the schizophrenic character of many businessmen. They are capable of being extremely far-sighted and clear-headed in matters that are internal to their businesses. They are incredibly short-sighted and muddle-headed in matters that are outside their businesses but affect the possible survival of business in general. This short-sightedness is strikingly exemplified in the calls from many businessmen for wage and price guidelines or controls or incomes policies. There is nothing that could do more in a brief period to destroy a market system and replace it by a centrally controlled system than effective governmental control of prices and wages.

The short-sightedness is also exemplified in speeches by businessmen on social responsibility. This may gain them kudos in the short run. But it helps to strengthen the already too prevalent view that the pursuit of profits is wicked and immoral and must be curbed and controlled by external forces. Once this view is adopted, the external forces that curb the market will not be the social consciences, however highly developed, of the pontificating executives; it will be the iron fist of government bureaucrats. Here, as with price and wage controls, businessmen seem to me to reveal a suicidal impulse.

The political principle that underlies the market mechanism is unanimity. In an ideal free market resting on private property, no individual can coerce any other, all cooperation is voluntary, all parties to such cooperation benefit or they need not participate. There are no "social" values, no "social" responsibilities in any sense other than the shared values and responsibilities of individuals. Society is a collection of individuals and of the various groups they voluntarily form.

The political principle that underlies the political mechanism is conformity. The individual must serve a more general social interest—whether that be determined by a church or a dictator or a majority. The individual may have a vote and a say in what is to be done, but if he is overruled, he must conform. It is appropriate for some to require others to contribute to a general social purpose whether they wish to or not.

Unfortunately, unanimity is not always feasible. There are some respects in which conformity appears unavoidable, so I do not see how one can avoid the use of the political mechanism altogether.

But the doctrine of "social responsibility" taken seriously would extend the scope of the political mechanism to every human activity. It does not differ in philosophy from the most explicitly collectivist doctrine. It differs only by professing to believe that collectivist ends can be attained without collectivist means. That is why, in my book *Capitalism and Freedom*, I have called it a "fundamentally subversive doctrine" in a free society, and have said that in such a society, 'there is one and only one social responsibility of business—to use its resources and engage in activities designed to increase its profits so long as it stays within the rules of the game, which is to say, engages in open and free competition without deception or fraud."

Discussion Questions

1. How does Dr. Friedman characterize discussions on "social responsibilities of business"? Why?
2. What is the role of a corporate executive selected by stockholders?
3. What analogy does Dr. Friedman draw between trade union wages and corporations' decisions based on social responsibilities?
4. Would Dr. Friedman ever support voluntary actions on the part of a corporation (e.g., conduct not prohibited specifically or mandated by law)?

READING 1.2: THE ETHICS OF RESPONSIBILITY[2]

Peter Drucker

Countless sermons have been preached and printed on the ethics of business or the ethics of the businessman. Most have nothing to do with business and little to do with ethics.

One main topic is plain, everyday honesty. Businessmen, we are told solemnly, should not cheat, steal, lie, bribe, or take bribes. But nor should anyone else. Men and women do not acquire exemption from ordinary rules of personal behavior because of their work or job. Nor, however, do they cease to be human beings when appointed vice-president, city manager, or college dean. And there has always been a number of people who cheat, steal, lie, bribe, or take bribes. The problem is one of moral values and moral education, of the individual, of the family, of the school. But there neither is a separate ethics of business, nor is one needed.

All that is needed is to mete out stiff punishments to those—whether business executives or others—who yield to temptation. In England a magistrate still tends

---

2. SOURCE: *Management: Tasks, Responsibilities, Practices,* by Peter F. Drucker. Copyright © 1973, 1974 by Peter F. Drucker. Reprinted by permission of Harper & Row, Publishers, Inc.

to hand down a harsher punishment in a drunken-driving case if the accused has gone to one of the well-known public schools or to Oxford or Cambridge. And the conviction still rates a headline in the evening paper: "Eton graduate convicted of drunken driving." No one expects an Eton education to produce temperance leaders. But it is still a badge of distinction, if not of privilege. And not to treat a wearer of such a badge more harshly than an ordinary workingman who has had one too many would offend the community's sense of justice. But no one considers this a problem of the "ethics of the Eton graduate."

The other common theme in the discussion of ethics in business has nothing to do with ethics.

Such things as the employment of call girls to entertain customers are not matters of ethics but matters of esthetics. "Do I want to see a pimp when I look at myself in the mirror while shaving?" is the real question.

It would indeed be nice to have fastidious leaders. Alas, fastidiousness has never been prevalent among leadership groups, whether kings and counts, priests or generals, or even "intellectuals" such as the painters and humanists of the Renaissance, or the "literati" of the Chinese tradition. All a fastidious man can do is withdraw personally from activities that violate his self-respect and his sense of taste.

Lately these old sermon topics have been joined, especially in the U.S., by a third one: managers, we are being told, have an "ethical responsibility" to take an active and constructive role in their community, to serve community causes, give of their time to community activities, and so on.

There are many countries where such community activity does not fit the traditional mores; Japan and France would be examples. But where the community has a tradition of "voluntarism"—that is, especially in the U.S.—managers should indeed be encouraged to participate and to take responsible leadership in community affairs and community organizations. Such activities should, however, never be forced on them, nor should they be appraised, rewarded, or promoted according to their participation in voluntary activities. Ordering or pressuring managers into such work is abuse of organizational power and illegitimate.

An exception might be made for managers in businesses where the community activities are really part of their obligation to the business. . . .

But, while desirable, community participation of managers has nothing to do with ethics, and not much to do with responsibility. It is the contribution of an individual in his capacity as a neighbor and citizen. And it is something that lies outside his job and outside his managerial responsibility.

Leadership Groups but Not Leaders

A problem of ethics that is peculiar to the manager arises from the fact that the managers of institutions are *collectively* the leadership groups of the society of organizations. But *individually* a manager is just another fellow employee.

This is clearly recognized by the public. Even the most powerful head of the largest corporation is unknown to the public. Indeed most of the company's employees barely know his name and would not recognize his face. He may owe his position entirely to personal merit and proven performance. But he owes his authority and standing entirely to his institution. Everybody knows GE, the Telephone Company, Mitsubishi, Siemens, and Unilever. But who heads these great corporations—or for that matter, the University of California, the Ecole

Polytechnique or Guy's Hospital in London—is of direct interest and concern primarily to the management group within these institutions.

It is therefore inappropriate to speak of managers as leaders. They are "members of the leadership group." The group, however, does occupy a position of visibility, of prominence, and of authority. It therefore has responsibility....

But what are the responsibilities, what are the ethics of the individual manager, as a member of the leadership group?

Essentially being a member of a leadership group is what traditionally has been meant by the term "professional."... But as a member of a leadership group a manager stands under the demands of professional ethics—the demands of an ethic of responsibility.

Primum Non Nocere

The first responsibility of a professional was spelled out clearly, 2,500 years ago, in the Hippocratic oath of the Greek physician: *primum non nocere*—"Above all, not knowingly to do harm."

No professional, be he doctor, lawyer, or manager, can promise that he will indeed do good for his client. All he can do is try. But he can promise that he will not knowingly do harm. And the client, in turn, must be able to trust the professional not knowingly to do him harm. Otherwise he cannot trust him at all. The professional has to have autonomy. He cannot be controlled, supervised, or directed by the client. He has to be private in that his knowledge and his judgment have to be entrusted with the decision. But it is the foundation of his autonomy, and indeed its rationale, that he see himself as "affected with the public interest." A professional, in other words, is private in the sense that he is autonomous and not subject to political or ideological control. But he is public in the sense that the welfare of his client sets limits to his deeds and words. And *primum non nocere*, "not knowingly to do harm," is the basic rule of professional ethics, the basic rule of an ethics of public responsibility.

There are important areas where managers, and especially business managers, still do not realize that in order to be permitted to remain autonomous and private they have to impose on themselves the responsibility of the professional ethic. They still have to learn that it is their job to scrutinize their deeds, words, and behavior to make sure that they do not knowingly do harm.

The manager who fails to think through and work for the appropriate solution to an impact of his business because it makes him "unpopular in the club" knowingly does harm. He knowingly abets a cancerous growth. That this is stupid has been said. That this always in the end hurts the business or the industry more than a little temporary "unpleasantness" would have hurt has been said too. But it is also a gross violation of professional ethics.

But there are other areas as well. American managers, in particular, tend to violate the rule not knowingly to do harm with respect to:

- executive compensation;
- the use of benefit plans to impose "golden fetters" on people in the company's employ; and
- in their profit rhetoric.

Their actions and their words in these areas tend to cause social disruption. They tend to conceal healthy reality and to create disease, or at least social hypochondria. They tend to misdirect and to prevent understanding. And this is grievous social harm.

The Rhetoric of the Profit Motive

Managers, . . . through their rhetoric, make it impossible for the public to understand economic reality. This violates the requirement that managers, being leaders, not knowingly do harm. This is particularly true of the United States but also of Western Europe. For in the West, managers still talk constantly of the profit motive. And they still define the goal of their business as profit maximization. They do not stress the objective function of profit. They do not talk of risks—or very rarely. They do not stress the need for capital. They almost never even mention the cost of capital, let alone that a business has to produce enough profit to obtain the capital it needs at minimum cost.

Managers constantly complain about the hostility to profit. They rarely realize that their own rhetoric is one of the main reasons for this hostility. For indeed in the terms management uses when it talks to the public, there is no possible justification for profit, no explanation for its existence, no function it performs. There is only the profit motive, that is, the desire of some anonymous capitalists—and why that desire should be indulged in by society any more than bigamy, for instance, is never explained. But profitability is a crucial *need* of economy and society.

Managerial practice in most large American companies is perfectly rational. It is the rhetoric which obscures, and thereby threatens to damage both business and society. To be sure, few American companies work out profitability as a *minimum* requirement. As a result, most probably underestimate the profitability the company truly requires (let alone the inflationary erosion of capital). But they, consciously or not, base their profit planning on the twin objectives of ensuring access to capital needed and minimizing the cost of capital. In the American context, if only because of the structure of the U.S. capital market, a high "price/earnings ratio" is indeed a key to the minimization of the cost of capital; and "optimization of profits" is therefore a perfectly rational strategy which tends to lower, in the long run, the actual cost of capital.

But this makes it even less justifiable to keep on using the rhetoric of the profit motive. It serves no purpose except to confuse and to embitter.

These examples of areas in which managers do not hold themselves to the rule "not knowingly to do harm" are primarily American examples. They apply to some extent to Western Europe. But they hardly apply to Japan. The principle, however, applies in all countries, and in the developing countries as much as in developed ones. These cases are taken from business management. The principle, however, applies to managers of all institutions in the society of organizations.

In any pluralist society responsibility for the public good has been the central problem and issue. The pluralist society or organizations will be no exception. Its leaders represent "special interests," that is, institutions designed to fulfill a specific and partial need of society. Indeed the leaders of this pluralist society of organizations are the servants of such institutions. At the same time, they are the major leadership group such a society knows or is likely to produce. They have to serve both their own institution and the common good. If the society is to function, let alone if it is to remain a free society, the men we call managers will remain "private" in their institutions. No matter who owns them and how, they will maintain autonomy. But they will also have to be "public" in their ethics.

In this tension between the private functioning of the manager, the necessary autonomy of his institution and its accountability to its own mission and purpose, and the public character of the manager, lies the specific ethical problem of the society of organizations. *Primum non nocere* may seem tame compared to the rousing calls for "statesmanship" that abound in today's manifestos on social responsibility. But, as the physicians found out long ago, it is not an easy rule to live up to. Its very modesty and self-constraint make it the right rule for the ethics managers need, the ethics of responsibility.

Discussion Questions

1. How does Professor Drucker see the relationship between business and personal ethics?
2. What problems do leadership groups create for ethics in business?
3. In what three areas does Professor Drucker see managers violating the principle of *primum non nocere*?
4. What is the rhetoric of the profit motive?
5. Does Professor Drucker believe ethical standards vary from country to country?

THE AREAS OF ETHICAL CHALLENGES

The remaining pages of this book present more readings and cases that illustrate ethical dilemmas faced by businesses and business people. The cases require critical examination of one's moral standards and the impact poor ethical decisions can have on individuals and companies. The cases are divided into categories based on The Conference Board's groupings of ethical dilemmas in business. (The Conference Board is a private research and information group that focuses on corporate and business issues.) Each category represents a grouping of the types of ethical dilemmas that were ranked most important by CEOs in a 1991 survey conducted by the Ethics Resource Center. The topics in each category are listed below.

Individual Values and the Business Organization
    Employee Conflicts of Interest
    Inappropriate Gifts
    Security of Company Records
    Personal Honesty
Individual Rights and the Business Organization
    Corporate Due Process
    Employee Screening
    Employee Privacy
    Sexual Harassment
    Affirmative Action/Equal Employment Opportunity
    Employment at Will

RECOGNIZING ETHICAL DILEMMAS

Resolving ethical dilemmas is difficult. So is first recognizing them. Two methods can help you to tell when you are in the midst of an ethical dilemma. First, an ethical dilemma is easy to spot by the language those involved are using. Rationalization begins, and phrases such as the following warn us that we are entering treacherous ethical territory:

"Everybody else does it."

Zoë Baird's nomination for attorney general in early 1993 met with opposition when investigations revealed that Ms. Baird and her husband had employed illegal immigrants as a chauffeur and as a nanny for their child and had failed to pay the Social Security, Medicare, and unemployment taxes required of household employers. The response of many to the issue was that only 25 percent of all household employers paid such taxes; fully 75 percent, or "everybody else," did not. Statistical support is not a valid basis for making ethical choices. The law had been violated. "Everybody else does it" is a rationalization for a poor ethical choice. Everybody else was investing in those risky financial instruments, derivatives. The eventual and catastrophic losses from these instruments to Procter & Gamble, Orange County, Barings Bank, and Gibson Greetings show how "everybody else" is often wrong.

In the following classic reading, Albert Carr compares business to poker and offers a justification for business bluffing.

READING 1.3: IS BUSINESS BLUFFING ETHICAL?[3]

Albert Z. Carr

A respected businessman with whom I discussed the theme of this article remarked with some heat, "You mean to say you're going to encourage men to bluff? Why, bluffing is nothing more than a form of lying! You're advising them to lie!"

I agreed that the basis of private morality is a respect for truth and that the closer a businessman comes to the truth, the more he deserves respect. At the same time, I suggested that most bluffing in business might be regarded simply as game strategy—much like bluffing in poker, which does not reflect on the morality of the bluffer.

I quoted Henry Taylor, the British statesman who pointed out that "falsehood ceases to be falsehood when it is understood on all sides that the truth is not expected to be spoken"—an exact description of bluffing in poker, diplomacy, and business. I cited the analogy of the criminal court, where the criminal is not expected to tell the truth when he pleads "not guilty." Everyone from the judge down takes it for granted that the job of the defendant's attorney is to get his client off, not to reveal the truth; and this is considered ethical practice. I mentioned Representative Omar Burleson, the Democrat from Texas, who was quoted as saying, in regard to the ethics of Congress, "Ethics is a barrel of worms"[4]—a pungent summing up of the problem of deciding who is ethical in politics.

I reminded my friend that millions of businessmen feel constrained every day to say *yes* to their bosses when they secretly believe *no* and that this is generally accepted as permissible strategy when the alternative might be the loss of a job. The essential point, I said, is that the ethics of business are games ethics, different from the ethics of religion.

He remained unconvinced. Referring to the company of which he is president, he declared: "Maybe that's good enough for some businessmen, but I can tell you that we pride ourselves on our ethics. In thirty years not one customer has ever

---

3. SOURCE: Reprinted by permission of *Harvard Business Review*. "Is Business Bluffing Ethical?" by Albert Z. Carr, Vol. 46 (January/February 1968). Copyright © 1968 by the President and Fellows of Harvard College; all rights reserved.

4. *The New York Times*, March 9, 1967.

questioned my word or asked to check our figures. We're loyal to our customers and fair to our suppliers. I regard my handshake on a deal as a contract. I've never entered into price-fixing schemes with my competitors. I've never allowed my salesmen to spread injurious rumors about other companies. Our union contract is the best in our industry. And, if I do say so myself, our ethical standards are of the highest!"

He really was saying, without realizing it, that he was living up to the ethical standards of the business game—which are a far cry from those of private life. Like a gentlemanly poker player, he did not play in cahoots with others at the table, try to smear their reputations, or hold back chips he owed them.

But this same fine man, at that very time, was allowing one of his products to be advertised in a way that made it sound a great deal better than it actually was. Another item in his product line was notorious among dealers for its "built-in-obsolescence." He was holding back from the market a much-improved product because he did not want it to interfere with sales of the inferior item it would have replaced. He had joined with certain of his competitors in hiring a lobbyist to push a state legislature, by methods that he preferred not to know too much about, into amending a bill then being enacted.

In his view these things had nothing to do with ethics; they were merely normal business practice. He himself undoubtedly avoided outright falsehoods—never lied in so many words. But the entire organization that he ruled was deeply involved in numerous strategies of deception.

Pressure to Deceive

Most executives from time to time are almost compelled, in the interest of their companies or themselves, to practice some form of deception when negotiating with customers, dealers, labor unions, government officials or even other department of their companies. By conscious misstatements, concealment of pertinent facts, or exaggeration—in short, by bluffing—they seek to persuade others to agree with them. I think it is fair to say that if the individual executive refuses to bluff from time to time—if he feels obligated to tell the truth, the whole truth, and nothing but the truth—he is ignoring opportunities permitted under the rules and is at a heavy disadvantage in his business dealings.

But here and there a businessman is unable to reconcile himself to the bluff in which he plays a part. His conscience, perhaps spurred by religious idealism, troubles him. He feels guilty; he may develop an ulcer or a nervous tic. Before any executive can make profitable use of the strategy of the bluff, he needs to make sure that in bluffing he will not lose self-respect or become emotionally disturbed. If he is to reconcile personal integrity and high standards of honesty with the practical requirements of business, he must feel that his bluffs are ethically justified. The justification rests on the fact that business, as practiced by individuals as well as by corporations, has the impersonal character of a game—a game that demands both special strategy and an understanding of its special ethics.

The game is played at all levels of corporate life, from the highest to the lowest. At the very instant that a man decides to enter business, he may be forced into a game situation, as is shown by the recent experience of a Cornell honor graduate who applied for a job with a large company:

This applicant was given a psychological test which included the statement, "Of the following magazines, check any that you have read either regularly or from time to time, and double-check those which interest you most. *Reader's Digest, Time, Fortune, Saturday Evening Post, The New Republic, Life, Look, Ramparts, Newsweek, Business Week, U.S. News & World Report, The Nation, Playboy, Esquire, Harper's, Sports Illustrated.*"

His tastes in reading were broad, and at one time or another he had read almost all of these magazines. He was a subscriber to *The New Republic*, an enthusiast for *Ramparts*, and an avid student of the pictures in *Playboy*. He was not sure whether his interest in *Playboy* would be held against him, but he had a shrewd suspicion that if he confessed to an interest in *Ramparts* and *The New Republic*, he would be thought a liberal, a radical, or at least an intellectual, and his chances of getting the job, which he needed, would greatly diminish. He therefore checked five of the more conservative magazines. Apparently it was a sound decision, for he got the job.

He had made a game player's decision, consistent with business ethics.

A similar case is that of a magazine space salesman who, owing to a merger, suddenly found himself out of a job:

This man was 58, and, in spite of a good record, his chance of getting a job elsewhere in a business where youth is favored in hiring practice was not good. He was a vigorous, healthy man, and only a considerable amount of gray in his hair suggested his age. Before beginning his job search he touched up his hair with a black dye to confine the gray to his temples. He knew that the truth about his age might well come out in time, but he calculated that he could deal with that situation when it arose. He and his wife decided that he could easily pass for 45, and he so stated his age on his résumé.

This was a lie, yet within the accepted rules of the business game, no moral culpability attaches to it.

The Poker Analogy

We can learn a good deal about the nature of business by comparing it with poker. While both have a large element of chance, in the long run the winner is the man who plays with steady skill. In both games ultimate victory requires intimate knowledge of the rules, insight into the psychology of the other players, a bold front, a considerable amount of self-discipline, and the ability to respond swiftly and effectively to opportunities provided by chance.

No one expects poker to be played on the ethical principles preached in churches. In poker it is right and proper to bluff a friend out of the rewards of being dealt a good hand. A player feels no more than a slight twinge of sympathy, if that, when—with nothing better than a single ace in his hand—he strips a heavy loser, who holds a pair, of the rest of his chips. It was up to the other fellow to protect himself. In the words of an excellent poker player, former President Harry Truman, "If you can't stand the heat, stay out of the kitchen." If one shows mercy to a loser in poker, it is a personal gesture, divorced from the rules of the game.

Poker has its special ethics, and here I am not referring to rules against cheating. The man who keeps an ace up his sleeve or who marks the cards is more than unethical; he is a crook, and can be punished as such—kicked out of the game or, in the Old West, shot.

In contrast to the cheat, the unethical poker player is one who, while abiding by the letter of the rules, finds ways to put the other players at an unfair disadvantage.

Perhaps he unnerves them with loud talk. Or he tries to get them drunk. Or he plays in cahoots with someone else at the table. Ethical poker players frown on such tactics.

Poker's own brand of ethics is different from the ethical ideals of civilized human relationships. The game calls for distrust of the other fellow. It ignores the claim of friendship. Cunning deception and concealment of one's strength and intentions, not kindness and openheartedness, are vital in poker. No one thinks any the worse of poker on that account. And no one should think any the worse of the game of business because its standards of right and wrong differ from the prevailing traditions of morality in our society.

Discard the Golden Rule

This view of business is especially worrisome to people without much business experience. A minister of my acquaintance once protested that business cannot possibly function in our society unless it is based on the Judeo-Christian system of ethics. He told me:

"I know some businessmen have supplied call girls to customers, but there are always a few rotten apples in every barrel. That doesn't mean the rest of the fruit isn't sound. Surely the vast majority of businessmen are ethical. I myself am acquainted with many who adhere to strict codes of ethics based fundamentally on religious teachings. They contribute to good causes. They participate in community activities. They cooperate with other companies to improve working conditions in their industries. Certainly they are not indifferent to ethics."

That most businessmen are not indifferent to ethics in their private lives, everyone will agree. My point is that in their office lives they cease to be private citizens; they become game players who must be guided by a somewhat different set of ethical standards.

The point was forcefully made to me by a Midwestern executive who has given a good deal of thought to the question:

"So long as a businessman complies with the laws of the land and avoids telling malicious lies, he's ethical. If the law as written gives a man a wide-open chance to make a killing, he'd be a fool not to take advantage of it. If he doesn't, somebody else will. There's no obligation on him to stop and consider who is going to get hurt. If the law says he can do it, that's all the justification he needs. There's nothing unethical about that. It's just plain business sense."

This executive (call him Robbins) took the stand that even industrial espionage, which is frowned on by some businessmen, ought not to be considered unethical. He recalled a recent meeting of the National Industrial Conference Board where an authority on marketing made a speech in which he deplored the employment of spies by business organizations. More and more companies, he pointed out, find it cheaper to penetrate the secrets of competitors with concealed cameras and microphones or by bribing employees than to set up costly research and design departments of their own. A whole branch of the electronics industry has grown up with this trend, he continued, providing equipment to make industrial espionage easier.

Disturbing? The marketing expert found it so. But when it came to a remedy, he could only appeal to "respect for the golden rule." Robbins thought this a confession of defeat, believing that the golden rule, for all its value as an ideal for society, is simply not feasible as a guide for business. A good part of the time the businessman is trying to do unto others as he hopes others will *not* do unto him.[5] Robbins continued:

"Espionage of one kind or another has become so common in business that it's like taking a drink during Prohibition—it's not considered sinful. And we don't even have Prohibition where espionage is concerned; the law is very tolerant in this area. There's no more shame for a business that uses a secret agent than there is for a nation. Bear in mind that there already is at least one large corporation— you can buy its stock over the counter—that makes millions by providing counter-espionage service to industrial firms. Espionage in business is not an ethical problem; it's an established technique of business competition."

"We Don't Make the Laws."

Wherever we turn in business, we can perceive the sharp distinction between its ethical standards and those of the churches. Newspapers abound with sensational stories growing out of this distinction:

- We read one day that Senator Philip A. Hart of Michigan has attacked food processors for deceptive packaging of numerous products.[6]
- The next day there is a Congressional to-do over Ralph Nader's book, *Unsafe At Any Speed*, which demonstrates that automobile companies for years have neglected the safety of car-owning families.[7]
- Then another Senator, Lee Metcalf of Montana, and journalist Vic Reinemer show in their book, *Overcharge*, the methods by which utility companies elude regulating government bodies to extract unduly large payments from users of electricity.[8]

These are merely dramatic instances of a prevailing condition; there is hardly a major industry at which a similar attack could not be aimed. Critics of business regard such behavior as unethical, but the companies concerned know that they are merely playing the business game.

Among the most respected of our business institutions are the insurance companies. A group of insurance executives meeting recently in New England was started when their guest speaker, social critic Daniel Patrick Moynihan, roundly berated them for "unethical" practices. They had been guilty, Moynihan alleged, of using outdated actuarial tables to obtain unfairly high premiums. They habitually delayed the hearings of lawsuits against them in order to tire out the plaintiffs and win cheap settlements. In their employment policies they used ingenious devices to discriminate against certain minority groups.[9]

It was difficult for the audience to deny the validity of these charges. But these men were business game players. Their reaction to Moynihan's attack was much the same as that of the automobile manufacturers to Nader, of the utilities to Senator Metcalf, and of the food processors to Senator Hart. If the laws governing their businesses change, or if public opinion becomes clamorous, they will make the necessary

---

5. See Bruce D. Henderson, "Brinkmanship in Business," HBR March-April 1967, p. 49.

6. *The New York Times*, November 21, 1966.

7. New York, Grossman Publishers, Inc., 1965.

8. New York, David McKay Company, Inc., 1967.

9. *The New York Times*, January 17, 1967.

adjustments. But morally they have, in their view, done nothing wrong. As long as they comply with the letter of the law, they are within their rights to operate their businesses as they see fit.

The small business is in the same position as the great corporation in this respect. For example:

In 1967 a key manufacturer was accused of providing master keys for automobiles to mail-order customers, although it was obvious that some of the purchasers might be automobile thieves. His defense was plain and straightforward. If there was nothing in the law to prevent him from selling his keys to anyone who ordered them, it was not up to him to inquire as to his customers' motives. Why was it any worse, he insisted, for him to sell car keys by mail, than for mail-order houses to sell guns that might be used for murder? Until the law was changed, the key manufacturer could regard himself as being just as ethical as any other businessman by the rules of the business game.[10]

Violations of the ethical ideals of society are common in business, but they are not necessarily violations of business principles. Each year the Federal Trade Commission orders hundreds of companies, many of them of the first magnitude, to "cease and desist" from practices which, judged by ordinary standards, are of questionable morality but which are stoutly defended by the companies concerned.

In one case, a firm manufacturing a well-known mouth-wash was accused of using a cheap form of alcohol possibly deleterious to health. The company's chief executive, after testifying in Washington, made this comment privately:

"We broke no law. We're in a highly competitive industry. If we're going to stay in business, we have to look for profit wherever the law permits. We don't make the laws. We obey them. Then why do we have to put up with this 'holier than thou' talk about ethics? It's sheer hypocrisy. We're not in business to promote ethics. Look at the cigarette companies, for God's sake! If the ethics aren't embodied in the laws by the men who made them, you can't expect businessmen to fill the lack. Why, a sudden submission to Christian ethics by businessmen would bring about the greatest economic upheaval in history!"

It may be noted that the government failed to prove its case against him.

Cast Illusions Aside

Talk about ethics by businessmen is often a thin decorative coating over the hard realities of the game:

Once I listened to a speech by a young executive who pointed to a new industry code as proof that his company and its competitors were deeply aware of their responsibilities to society. It was a code of ethics, he said. The industry was going to police itself, to dissuade constituent companies from wrongdoing. His eyes shone with conviction and enthusiasm.

The same day there was a meeting in a hotel room where the industry's top executives met with the "czar" who was to administer the new code, a man of high repute. No one who was present could doubt their common attitude. In their eyes the code was designed primarily to forestall a move by the federal government to impose stern restrictions on the industry. They felt that the code would hamper

---

10. Cited by Ralph Nader in "Business Crime," *The New Republic*, July 1, 1967, p. 7.

them a good deal less than new federal laws would. It was, in other words, conceived as a protection for the industry, not for the public.

The young executive accepted the surface explanation of the code; these leaders, all experienced game players, did not deceive themselves for a moment about its purpose.

The illusion that business can afford to be guided by ethics as conceived in private life is often fostered by speeches and articles containing such phrases as, "It pays to be ethical," or, "Sound ethics is good business." Actually this is not an ethical position at all; it is a self-serving calculation in disguise. The speaker is really saying that in the long run a company can make more money if it does not antagonize competitors, suppliers, employees, and customers by squeezing them too hard. He is saying that oversharp policies reduce ultimate gains. That is true, but it has nothing to do with ethics. The underlying attitude is much like that in the familiar story of the shopkeeper who finds an extra twenty-dollar bill in the cash register, debates with himself the ethical problem—should he tell his partner?—and finally decides to share the money because the gesture will give him an edge over the s.o.b. the next time they quarrel.

I think it is fair to sum up the prevailing attitude of businessmen on ethics as follows:

We live in what is probably the most competitive of the world's civilized societies. Our customs encourage a high degree of aggression in the individual's striving for success. Business is our main area of competition, and it has been ritualized into a game of strategy. The basic rules of the game have been set by the government, which attempts to detect and punish business frauds. But as long as a company does not transgress the rules of the game set by law, it has the legal right to shape its strategy without reference to anything but its profits. If it takes a long-term view of its profits, it will preserve amicable relations, so far as possible, with those with whom it deals. A wise businessman will not seek advantage to the point where he generates dangerous hostility among employees, competitors, customers, government, or the public at large. But decisions in this area are, in the final test, decisions of strategy, not of ethics.

The Individual and the Game

An individual within a company often finds it difficult to adjust to the requirements of the business game. He tries to preserve his private ethical standards in situations that call for game strategy. When he is obliged to carry out company policies that challenge his conception of himself as an ethical man, he suffers.

It disturbs him when he is ordered, for instance, to deny a raise to a man who deserves it, to fire an employee of long standing, to prepare advertising that he believes to be misleading, to conceal facts that he feels customers are entitled to know, to cheapen the quality of materials used in the manufacture of an established product, to sell as new a product that he knows to be rebuilt, to exaggerate the curative powers of a medicinal preparation, or to coerce dealers.

There are some fortunate executives who, by the nature of their work and circumstances, never have to face problems of this kind. But in one form or another the ethical dilemma is felt sooner or later by most businessmen. Possibly the dilemma is most painful not when the company forces the action on the executive but when he originates it himself—that is, when he has taken or is contemplating a step which is in his own interest but which runs counter to his early moral conditioning. To illustrate:

- The manager of an export department, eager to show rising sales, is pressed by a big customer to provide invoices which, while containing no overt falsehood that would violate a U.S. law, are so worded that the customer may be able to evade certain taxes in his homeland.
- A company president finds that an aging executive, within a few years of retirement and his pension, is not as productive as formerly. Should he be kept on?
- The produce manager of a supermarket debates with himself whether to get rid of a lot of half-rotten tomatoes by including one, with its good side exposed, in every tomato six-pack.
- An accountant discovers that he has taken an improper deduction on his company's tax return and fears the consequences if he calls the matter to the president's attention, though he himself has done nothing illegal. Perhaps if he says nothing, no one will notice the error.
- A chief executive officer is asked by his directors to comment on a rumor that he owns stock in another company with which he has placed large orders. He could deny it, for the stock is in the name of his son-in-law and he has earlier formally instructed his son-in-law to sell the holding.

Temptations of this kind constantly arise in business. If an executive allows himself to be torn between a decision based on business considerations and one based on his private ethical code, he exposes himself to a grave psychological strain.

This is not to say that sound business strategy necessarily runs counter to ethical ideals. They may frequently coincide; and when they do, everyone is gratified. But the major tests of every move in business, as in all games of strategy, are legality and profit. A man who intends to be a winner in the business game must have a game player's attitude.

The business strategists's decisions must be as impersonal as those of a surgeon performing an operation—concentrating on objective and technique, and subordinating personal feelings. If the chief executive admits that his son-in-law owns the stock, it is because he stands to lose more if the fact comes out later than if he states it boldly and at once. If the supermarket manager orders the rotten tomatoes to be discarded, he does so to avoid an increase in consumer complaints and a loss of goodwill. The company president decides not to fire the elderly executive in the belief that the negative reaction of other employees would in the long run cost the company more than it would lose in keeping him and paying his pension.

All sensible businessmen prefer to be truthful, but they seldom feel inclined to tell the *whole* truth. In the business game truth-telling usually has to be kept within narrow limits if trouble is to be avoided. The point was neatly made a long time ago (in 1888) by one of John D. Rockefeller's associates, Paul Babcock, to Standard Oil Company executives who were about to testify before a government investigating committee: "Parry every question with answers which, while perfectly truthful, are evasive of *bottom* facts."[11] This was, is, and probably always will be regarded as wise and permissible business strategy.

---

11. Babock in a memorandum to Rockefeller (Rockefeller Archives).

For Office Use Only

An executive's family life can easily be dislocated if he fails to make a sharp distinction between the ethical systems of the home and the office—or if his wife does not grasp that distinction. Many a businessman who has remarked to his wife, "I had to let Jones go today" or "I had to admit to the boss that Jim has been goofing off lately," has been met with an indignant protest. "How could you do a thing like that? You know Jones is over 50 and will have a lot of trouble getting another job." Or, "You did that to Jim? With his wife ill and the all the worry she's been having with the kids?"

If the executive insists that he had no choice because the profits of the company and his own security were involved, he may see a certain cool and ominous reappraisal in his wife's eyes. Many wives are not prepared to accept the fact that business operates with a special code of ethics. An illuminating illustration of this comes from a Southern sales executive who related a conversation he had had with his wife at a time when a hotly contested political campaign was being waged in their state:

"I made the mistake of telling her that I had had lunch with Colby, who gives me about half my business. Colby mentioned that his company had a stake in the election. Then he said, 'By the way, I'm treasurer of the citizens' committee for Lang. I'm collecting contributions. Can I count on you for a hundred dollars?'

"Well, there I was. I was opposed to Lang, but I knew Colby. If he withdrew his business, I could be in a bad spot. So I just smiled and wrote out a check then and there. He thanked me, and we started to talk about his next order. Maybe he thought I shared his political views. If so, I wasn't going to lose any sleep over it.

"I should have had sense enough not to tell Mary about it. She hit the ceiling. She said she was disappointed in me. She said I hadn't acted like a man, that I should have stood up to Colby.

"I said, 'Look, it was an either-or situation. I had to do it or risk losing the business.'

"She came back at me with, 'I don't believe it. You could have been honest with him. You could have said that you didn't feel you ought to contribute to a campaign for a man you weren't going to vote for. I'm sure he would have understood.'

"I said, 'Mary, you're a wonderful woman, but you're way off the track. Do you know what would have happened if I had said that? Colby would have smiled and said, "Oh, I didn't realize. Forget it." But in his eyes from that moment I would be an oddball, maybe a bit of a radical. He would have listened to me talk about his order and would have promised to give it consideration. After that I wouldn't hear from him for a week. Then I would telephone and learn from his secretary that he wasn't yet ready to place the order. And in about a month I would hear through the grapevine that he was giving his business to another company. A month after that I'd be out of a job.'

"She was silent for a while. Then she said, 'Tom, something is wrong with business when a man is forced to choose between his family's security and his moral obligation to himself. It's easy for me to say you should have stood up to him—but if you had, you might have felt you were betraying me and the kids. I'm sorry that you did it, Tom, but I can't blame you. Something is wrong with business!'"

This wife saw the problem in terms of moral obligation as conceived in private life; her husband saw it as a matter of game strategy. As a player in a weak position, he felt that he could not afford to indulge an ethical sentiment that might have cost him his seat at the table.

Playing to Win

Some men might challenge the Colbys of business—might accept serious setbacks to their business careers rather than risk a feeling of moral cowardice. They merit our respect—but as private individuals, not businessmen. When the skillful player of the business game is compelled to submit to unfair pressure, he does not castigate himself for moral weakness. Instead, he strives to put himself into a strong position where he can defend himself against such pressures in the future without loss.

If a man plans to take a seat in the business game, he owes it to himself to master the principles by which the game is played, including its special ethical outlook. He can then hardly fail to recognize that an occasional bluff may well be justified in terms of the game's ethics and warranted in terms of economic necessity. Once he clears his mind on this point, he is in a good position to match his strategy against that of the other players. He can then determine objectively whether a bluff in a given situation has a good chance of succeeding and can decide when and how to bluff, without a feeling of ethical transgression.

To be a winner, a man must play to win. This does not mean that he must be ruthless, cruel, harsh, or treacherous. On the contrary, the better his reputation for integrity, honesty, and decency, the better his chances of victory will be in the long run. But from time to time every businessman, like every poker player, is offered a choice between certain loss or bluffing within the legal rules of the game. If he is not resigned to losing, if he wants to rise in his company and industry, then in such a crisis he will bluff—and bluff hard.

Every now and then one meets a successful businessman who has conveniently forgotten the small or large deceptions that he practiced on his way to fortune. "God gave me my money," old John D. Rockefeller once piously told a Sunday school class. It would be a rare tycoon in our time who would risk the horse laugh with which such a remark would be greeted.

In the last third of the twentieth century even children are aware that if a man has become prosperous in business, he has sometimes departed from the strict truth in order to overcome obstacles or has practiced the more subtle deceptions of the half-truth or the misleading omission. Whatever the form of the bluff, it is an integral part of the game, and the executive who does not master its techniques is not likely to accumulate much money or power.

Discussion Questions

1. Do you agree or disagree with Carr's premise?
2. Does everyone operate at the same level of bluffing?
3. How is the phrase "sound ethics is good business" characterized?

"If we don't do it, someone else will."

The rationalization of competition. Since someone will do it and make money, it might as well be us. For Halloween 1994, there were O. J. Simpson masks and plastic knives and Nicole Brown Simpson masks and costumes complete with slashes and fake blood stains. When Mrs. Simpson's family objected to this violation of the basic standard of decency, a costume shop owner commented that if he didn't sell the items, someone down the street would. While nothing about the marketing of the costumes was illegal, the ethical issues that surround earning a profit from an event as heinous as the brutal murder of a young mother abound. The manufacturer of a license plate shield that serves to prevent detection by photo radar explained, "It's not my foot to the pedal. I'm not breaking the law. I'm just filling a market void. If I don't make them and sell them, someone else will."

"That's the way it has always been done."

Corporate or business history and business practices are not always sound. The fact that for years nothing has changed in a firm may indicate the need for change and an atmosphere that invites possible ethical violations. For example, until the Securities Exchange Commission required board compensation committees to make reports and to disclose the identities of their members, the sitting members of many of these committees had conflicts of interest. For example, senior partners of law firms that represented a given corporation often sat on the client's board and on its compensation committee. The result was that a lawyer whose firm was economically dependent on the corporation as a client was making salary determinations regarding the corporation's officers, who, of course, made the decisions about which law firm would represent them and their company. A conflict of interest existed, but everybody was doing it and it was the way corporate governance had always been done. Again, unquestioning adherence to a pattern of practices or behavior often indicates an underlying ethical dilemma.

"We'll wait until the lawyers tell us it's wrong."

Lawyers are trained to provide only the parameters of the law. In many situations, they offer an opinion that is correct in that it does not violate the law. Whether the conduct they have passed upon as legal is ethical is a different question. Allowing law and lawyers to control a firm's destiny ignores the opportunity to make wise and ethical choices. For example, Orange County, California, filed for bankruptcy in 1994 because its investment strategy, involving heavy investments in financial derivative instruments, had failed and it had lost sums so large that it was rendered insolvent. Were the derivative investments legal? Absolutely. Were the derivative investments reviewed by lawyers? For both buyers and sellers. Legality is often not a sufficient standard for ethical behavior. Following the positive law does not always guarantee that a firm will avoid legal difficulties. Analyzing issues of fairness, risk, and disclosure requires input beyond just a legal opinion.

"It doesn't really hurt anyone."

When we are the sole rubberneckers on the freeway, traffic remains unaffected. But if everyone rubbernecks, we have a traffic jam. All of us making poor ethical choices would cause significant harm. A man interviewed after he was arrested for defrauding insurance companies through staged auto accidents remarked, "It didn't really hurt anyone. Insurance companies can afford it." The second part of his statement is accurate. The insurance companies can afford it—but not without cost to someone else. Such fraud harms all of us because we must pay higher premiums to allow insurers to absorb the costs of paying for and investigating fraudulent claims.

"The system is unfair."

Often touted by students as a justification for cheating on exams, this rationalization eases our conscience by telling us we are cheating only to make up for deficiencies in the system. Yet just one person cheating can send ripples through an entire system. The credibility of grades and the institution come into question as students obtain grades through means beyond the system's standards. As we see events unfold in China, Italy, and Brazil, with government employees awarding contracts and rights to do business on the basis of payments rather than on the merits of a given company or its proposal, we understand how such bribery results only in greater unfairness within and greater costs to those countries. A businessman in Brazil commented that the country's businesses and economy were not progressing because Brazil's was basically an amoral society.

The second method for spotting an ethical dilemma is to understand the categories of ethical dilemmas. All of the cases presented in this book fit into the following twelve categories, developed in *Exchange*, the magazine of the Brigham Young University school of business:

1. Taking things that don't belong to you.

Everything from making unauthorized use of the Pitney-Bowes postage meter at your office for mailing personal letters to exaggerating your travel expenses belongs in this category of ethical violations. Regardless of size, motivation, or the presence of any of the rationalizations discussed above, the unauthorized use of someone else's property or taking property under false pretenses still means taking something that does not belong to you. A chief financial officer of a large electric utility reported that after taking a cab from La Guardia International Airport to his midtown Manhattan hotel, he asked for a receipt. The cab driver handed the executive a full book of blank receipts and drove away. Apparently the problem of accurately reporting travel expenses involves more than just employees.

2. Saying things you know are not true.

Often, in the quest for promotion and advancement, fellow employees discredit their coworkers. Assigning blame or inaccurately reporting conversations is lying. While "This is the way the game is played around here" is a common justification, saying things that are untrue is an ethical violation.

3. Giving or allowing false impressions.

The salesman who permits a potential customer to believe that his cardboard boxes will hold the customer's tomatoes for long-distance shipping when he knows the boxes are not strong enough has given a false impression. A car dealer who fails to disclose that a car has been in an accident is misleading potential customers. A coworker or supervisor who takes credit for another employee's idea has allowed a false impression.

4. Buying influence or engaging in a conflict of interest.

A company awards a construction contract to a firm owned by the father of the state attorney general while the state attorney general's office is investigating that company. A county administrator responsible for awarding the construction contract for a baseball stadium accepts from contractors interested in bidding on the project paid travel around the country to other stadiums that the contractors have built. The wife of a state attorney general accepts trading advice from the corporate attorney for a highly regulated company and subsequently earns, in her first attempt at the market, over $100,000 in the commodities market in cattle futures.

All of these examples illustrate conflicts of interest. Those involved in situations such as these often protest, "But I would never allow that to influence me." The ethical violation is the conflict. Whether the conflict can or will influence those it touches is not the issue, for neither party can prove conclusively that a quid pro quo was not intended. The possibility exists, and it creates discomfort. Hence, conflicts of interest are to be avoided.

5. Hiding or divulging information.

Taking your firm's product development or trade secrets to a new place of employment constitutes an ethical violation of divulging proprietary information. Failing to disclose the results of medical studies that indicate your firm's new drug has significant side effects is the ethical violation of hiding information that the product could be harmful to purchasers.

6. Taking unfair advantage.

Many current consumer protection laws were passed because so many businesses took unfair advantage of those who were not educated or were unable to discern the nuances of complex contracts. Credit disclosure requirements, truth-in-lending provisions, and new regulations on auto leasing all resulted because businesses misled consumers who could not easily follow the jargon of long and complex agreements.

7. Committing personal decadence.

While many argue about the ethical notion of an employee's right to privacy, it has become increasingly clear that personal conduct outside the job can influence performance and company reputation. Thus, a company driver must abstain from substance abuse because of safety issues. Even the traditional company Christmas party and picnic have come under scrutiny as the behavior of employees at and following these events has brought harm to others in the form of alcohol-related accidents.

8. Perpetrating interpersonal abuse.

A manager sexually harasses an employee. Another manager is verbally abusive to another employee. Still another manager subjects employees to humiliating correction in the presence of customers. In some cases, laws protect employees. However, many situations are simply ethical violations that constitute interpersonal abuse.

9. Permitting organizational abuse.

Many U.S. firms with operations overseas, such as Levi Strauss, The Gap, and Esprit, have faced issues of organizational abuse. The unfair treatment of workers in international operations appears in the form of child labor, demeaning wages, and too-long hours. While a business cannot change the culture of another country, it can perpetuate—or alleviate—abuse through its operations there.

10. Violating rules.

Many rules, particularly those in large organizations that tend toward bureaucracy out of the need to maintain internal controls or follow lines of authority, seem burdensome to employees trying to serve customers and other employees. Stanford University experienced difficulties in this area of ethics when it used funds from federal grants for miscellaneous university purposes. Questions arose about the propriety of the expenditures (see case 8.5 "Stanford University and Government Overhead"), which quite possibly could have been approved through proper channels, but weren't. The rules for administering federal grant monies used for overhead were not followed. The results were not only an ethical violation but damage to Stanford's reputation and a new president for that university.

11. Condoning unethical actions.

In this breach of ethics, the wrong results from the failure to report the wrong. What if you witnessed a fellow employee embezzling company funds by forging her signature on a check that was to be voided? Would you report that violation? A winking tolerance of others' unethical behavior is itself unethical. Suppose that as a product designer you were aware of a fundamental flaw in your company's new product, a product predicted to catapult your firm to record earnings. Would you pursue the problem to the point of halting the distribution of the product? Would you disclose what you know to the public if you could not get your company to act?

12. Balancing ethical dilemmas.

In these types of situations, there are no right or wrong answers; rather, there are dilemmas to be resolved. For example, Levi Strauss struggled with its decision on whether to do business in mainland China because of known human rights violations perpetrated by the government. Other companies debated doing business in South Africa when that country's government followed a policy of apartheid. In some respects, the presence of these companies would help by advancing human rights and, certainly, by improving the standard of living for at least some international operations workers. On the other hand, their ability to recruit businesses could help such governments to sustain themselves by enabling them to point to economic successes despite human rights violations.

Resolving Ethical Dilemmas

Whether by language or category, an ethical dilemma can be identified. The next step is to resolve that dilemma. Fortunately, several relatively simple models can help businesspeople analyze ethical breaches and determine appropriate steps to take.

Blanchard/Peale

In evaluating an ethical dilemma, managers should ask certain questions. The Blanchard and Peale model consists of three: "Is it legal?" "Is it balanced?" "How does it make me feel?"

As I say jokingly to my students, if the answer to the first question is "no," i.e., the activity is illegal, you need not proceed with your analysis. Several cases in the book ask you to determine whether the activity is in fact legal or whether slight variations in the conduct would have made the actions illegal. Many ethical dilemmas involve no illegality. For example, the sale of tobacco is a legal activity. But, given documented tobacco-related health damage, is it an ethical activity?

The second question, regarding balance, requires you to put yourself in the position of other parties affected by your decision. For example, as an executive, you might not favor a buyout of your company because it means you will probably not have a job. However, a shareholder may stand to benefit substantially from the price to be paid for his or her shares in the buyout. But the employees of the business and their community may suffer economically if the purchaser decides to close the business or focus its efforts in a different product area.

The final question asks you to examine your comfort with a particular decision. Many people find that after reaching a decision on an issue they still experience discomfort that may manifest itself in a loss of sleep or appetite. Those feelings of conscience can serve as a guide in resolving ethical dilemmas.

In the following reading, a Wall Street executive faces the reality of conscience.

READING 1.4: THE PARABLE OF THE SADHU[12]

Bowen H. McCoy

[In 1982], as the first participant in the new six-month sabbatical program that Morgan Stanley has adopted, I enjoyed a rare opportunity to collect my thoughts as well as do some traveling. I spent the first three months in Nepal, walking 600 miles through 200 villages in the Himalayas and climbing some 120,000 vertical feet. On the trip my sole Western companion was an anthropologist who shed light on the cultural patterns of the villages we passed through.

During the Nepal hike, something occurred that has had a powerful impact on my thinking about corporate ethics. Although some might argue that the experience has no relevance to business, it was a situation in which a basic ethical dilemma suddenly intruded into the lives of a group of individuals. How the group responded I think holds a lesson for all organizations no matter how defined.

The Sadhu

The Nepal experience was more rugged and adventure-some than I had anticipated. Most commercial treks last two or three weeks and cover a quarter of the distance we traveled.

My friend Stephen, the anthropologist, and I were halfway through the 60-day Himalayan part of the trip when we reached the high point, an 18,000-foot pass over a crest that we'd have to traverse to reach to the village of Muklinath, an ancient holy place for pilgrims.

Six years earlier I had suffered pulmonary edema, an acute form of altitude sickness, at 16,500 feet in the vicinity of Everest base camp, so we were understandably

---

concerned about what would happen at 18,000 feet. Moreover, the Himalayas were having their wettest spring in 20 years; hip-deep powder and ice had already driven us off one ridge. If we failed to cross the pass, I feared that the last half of our "once in a lifetime" trip would be ruined.

The night before we would try the pass, we camped at a hut at 14,500 feet. In the photos taken at that camp, my face appears wan. The last village we'd passed through was a sturdy two-day walk below us, and I was tired.

During the late afternoon, four backpackers from New Zealand joined us, and we spent most of the night awake, anticipating the climb. Below we could see the fires of two other parties, which turned out to be two Swiss couples and a Japanese hiking club.

To get over the steep part of the climb before the sun melted the steps cut in the ice, we departed at 3:30 a.m. The New Zealanders left first, followed by Stephen and myself, our porters and Sherpas, and then the Swiss. The Japanese lingered in their camp. The sky was clear, and we were confident that no spring storm would erupt that day to close the pass.

At 15,500 feet, it looked to me as if Stephen were shuffling and staggering a bit, which are symptoms of altitude sickness. (The initial stage of altitude sickness brings a headache and nausea. As the condition worsens, a climber may encounter difficult breathing, disorientation, aphasia, and paralysis.) I felt strong, my adrenaline was flowing, but I was very concerned about my ultimate ability to get across. A couple of our porters were also suffering from the height, and Pasang, our Sherpa sirdar (leader), was worried.

Just after daybreak, while we rested at 15,500 feet, one of the New Zealanders, who had gone ahead, came staggering down toward us with a body slung across his shoulders. He dumped the almost naked, barefoot body of an Indian holy man—a sadhu—at my feet. He had found the pilgrim lying on the ice, shivering and suffering from hypothermia. I cradled the sadhu's head and laid him out on the rocks. The New Zealander was angry. He wanted to get across the pass before the bright sun melted the snow. He said, "Look, I've done what I can. You have porters and Sherpa guides. You care for him. We're going on!" He turned and went back up the mountain to join his friends.

I took a carotid pulse and found that the sadhu was still alive. We figured he had probably visited the holy shrines at Muklinath and was on his way home. It was fruitless to question why he had chosen this desperately high route instead of the safe, heavily traveled caravan route through the kali Gandaki gorge. Or why he was almost naked and with no shoes, or how long he had been lying in the pass. The answers weren't going to solve our problem.

Stephen and the four Swiss began stripping off outer clothing and opening their packs. The sadhu was soon clothed from head to foot. He was not able to walk, but he was very much alive. I looked down the mountain and spotted below the Japanese climbers marching up with a horse.

Without a great deal of thought, I told Stephen and Pasang that I was concerned about withstanding the heights to come and wanted to get over the pass. I took off after several of our porters who had gone ahead.

On the steep part of the ascent where, if the ice steps had given way, I would have slid down about 3,000 feet, I felt vertigo. I stopped for a breather, allowing the Swiss to catch up with me. I inquired about the sadhu and Stephen. They said that the sadhu was fine and that Stephen was just behind. I set off again for the summit.

Stephen arrived at the summit an hour after I did. Still exhilarated by victory, I ran down the snow slope to congratulate him. He was suffering from altitude sickness, walking fifteen steps, then stopping, walking fifteen steps, then reached them, Stephen glared at me and said: "How do you feel about contributing to the death of a fellow man?"

I did not fully comprehend what he meant.

"Is the sadhu dead?" I inquired.

"No," replied Stephen, "but he surely will be!"

After I had gone, and the Swiss had departed not long after, Stephen had remained with the sadhu. When the Japanese had arrived, Stephen had asked to use their horse to transport the sadhu down to the hut. They had refused. He had then asked Pasang to have a group of our porters carry the sadhu. Pasang had resisted the idea, saying that the porters would have to exert all their energy to get themselves over the pass. He had thought they could not carry a man down 1,000 feet to the hut, reclimb the slope, and get across safely before the snow melted. Pasang had pressed Stephen not to delay any longer.

The Sherpas had carried the sadhu down to a rock in the sun at about 15,000 feet and had pointed out the hut another 500 feet below. The Japanese had given him food and drink. When they had last seen him he was listlessly throwing rocks at the Japanese party's dog, which had frightened him.

We do not know if the sadhu lived or died.

For many of the following days and evenings Stephen and I discussed and debated our behavior toward the sadhu. Stephen is a committed Quaker with deep moral vision. He said, "I feel that what happened with the sadhu is a good example of the breakdown between the individual ethic and the corporate ethic. No one person was willing to assume ultimate responsibility for the sadhu. Each was willing to do his bit just so long as it was not too inconvenient. When it got to be a bother, everyone just passed the buck to someone else and took off. Jesus was relevant to a more individualist stage of society, and how do we interpret his teaching today in a world filled with large, impersonal organizations and groups?"

I defended the larger group, saying, "Look, we all cared. We all stopped and gave aid and comfort. Everyone did his bit. The New Zealander carried him down below the snow line. I took his pulse and suggested we treat him for hypothermia. You and the Swiss gave him clothing and got him warmed up. The Japanese gave him food and water. The Sherpas carried him down to the sun and pointed out the easy trail toward the hut. He was well enough to throw rocks at a dog. What more could we do?"

"You have just described the typical affluent Westerner's response to a problem. Throwing money—in this case food and sweaters—at it, but not solving the fundamentals!" Stephen retorted.

"What would satisfy you?" I said. "Here we are, a group of New Zealanders, Swiss, Americans, and Japanese who have never met before and who are at the apex of one of the most powerful experiences of our lives. Some years the pass is so bad no one gets over it. What right does an almost naked pilgrim who chooses the wrong trail have to disrupt our lives? Even the Sherpas had no interest in risking the trip to help him beyond a certain point."

Stephen calmly rebutted, "I wonder what the Sherpas would have done if the sadhu had been a well-dressed Nepali, or what the Japanese would have done if the sadhu had been a well-dressed Asian, or what you would have done, Buzz, if the sadhu had been a well-dressed Western woman?"

"Where, in your opinion," I asked instead, "is the limit of our responsibility in a situation like this? We had our own well-being to worry about. Our Sherpa guides were unwilling to jeopardize us or the porters for the sadhu. No one else on the mountain was willing to commit himself beyond certain self-imposed limits."

Stephen said, "As individual Christians or people with a Western ethical tradition, we can fulfill our obligations in such a situation only if (1) the sadhu dies in our care, (2) the sadhu demonstrates to us that he could undertake the two-day walk down to the village, or (3) we carry the sadhu for two days down to the village and convince someone there to care of him."

"Leaving the sadhu in the sun with food and clothing, while he demonstrated hand-eye coordination by throwing a rock at a dog, comes close to fulfilling items one and two," I answered. "And it wouldn't have made sense to take him to the village where the people appeared to be far less caring than the Sherpas, so the third condition is impractical. Are you really saying that, no matter what the implications, we should, at the drop of a hat, have changed our entire plan?"

The Individual vs. the Group Ethic

Despite my arguments, I felt and continue to feel guilt about the sadhu. I had literally walked through a classic moral dilemma without fully thinking through the consequences. My excuses for my actions include a high adrenaline flow, a superordinate goal, and a once-in-a-lifetime opportunity—factors in the usual corporate situation, especially when one is under stress.

Real moral dilemmas are ambiguous, and many of us hike right through them, unaware that they exist. When, usually after the fact, someone makes an issue of them, we tend to resent his or her bringing it up. Often, when the full import of what we have done (or not done) falls on us, we dig into a defensive position from which it is very difficult to emerge. In rare circumstances we may contemplate what we have done from inside a prison.

Had we mountaineers been free of physical and mental stress caused by the effort and the high altitude, we might have treated the sadhu differently. Yet isn't stress the real test of personal and corporate values? The instant decisions executives make under pressure reveal the most about personal and corporate character.

Among the many questions that occur to me when pondering my experience are: What are the practical limits of moral imagination and vision? Is there a collective or institutional ethic beyond the ethics of the individual? At what level of effort or commitment can one discharge one's ethical responsibilities?

Not every ethical dilemma has a right solution. Reasonable people often disagree; otherwise there would be no dilemma. In a business context, however, it is essential that managers agree on a process for dealing with dilemmas.

The sadhu experience offers an interesting parallel to business situations. An immediate response was mandatory. Failure to act was a decision in itself. Up on the mountain we could not resign and submit our résumé to a headhunter. In contrast to philosophy, business involves action and implementation—getting things done. Managers must come up with answers to problems based on what they see and what they allow to influence their decision-making processes. On the mountain, none of us but Stephen realized the true dimensions of the situation we were facing.

One of our problems was that as a group we had no process for developing a consensus. We had no sense of purpose or plan. The difficulties of dealing with the sadhu were so complex that no one person could handle it. Because it did not have a set of preconditions that could guide its action to an acceptable resolution, the group reacted instinctively as individuals. The cross-cultural nature of the group added a further layer of complexity. We had no leader with whom we could all identify and in whose purpose we believed. Only Stephen was willing to take charge, but he could not gain adequate support to care for the sadhu.

Some organizations do have a value system that transcends the personal values of the managers. Such values, which go beyond profitability, are usually revealed when the organization is under stress. People throughout the organization generally accept its values, which, because they are not presented as a rigid list of commandments, may be somewhat ambiguous. The stories people tell, rather than printed materials, transmit these conceptions of what is proper behavior.

For twenty years I have been exposed at senior levels to a variety of corporations and organizations. It is amazing how quickly an outsider can sense the tone and style of an organization and the degree of tolerated openness and freedom to challenge management.

Organizations that do not have a heritage of mutually accepted, shared values tend to become unhinged during stress, with each individual bailing out for himself. In the great takeover battles we have witnessed during past years, companies that had strong cultures drew the wagons around them and fought it out, while other companies saw executives, supported by their golden parachutes, bail out of the struggles.

Because corporations and their members are interdependent, for the corporation to be strong the members need to share a preconceived notion of what is correct behavior, a "business ethic," and think of it as a positive force, not a constraint.

As an investment banker I am continually warned by well-meaning lawyers, clients, and associates to be wary of conflicts of interest. Yet if I were to run away from every difficult situation, I wouldn't be an effective investment banker. I have to feel my way through conflicts. An effective manager can't run from risk either; he or she has to confront and deal with risk. To feel "safe" in doing this, managers need the guidelines of an agreed-on process and set of values within the organization.

After my three months in Nepal, I spent three months as an executive-in-residence at both Stanford Business School and the Center for Ethics and Social Policy at the Graduate Theological Union at Berkeley. These six months away from my job gave me time to assimilate twenty years of business experience. My thoughts turned often to the meaning of the leadership role in any large organization. Students at the seminary thought of themselves as antibusiness. But when I questioned them they agreed that they distrusted all large organizations, including the church. They perceived all large organizations as impersonal and opposed to individual values and needs. Yet we all know of organizations where people's values and beliefs are respected and their expressions encouraged. What makes the difference? Can we identify the difference and, as a result, manage more effectively?

The word "ethics" turns off many and confuses more. Yet the notions of shared values and an agreed-on process for dealing with adversity and change—what many people mean when they talk about corporate culture—seem to be at the heart of the ethical issue. People who are in touch with their own core beliefs and the beliefs of others and are sustained by them can be more comfortable living on the cutting edge. At times, taking a tough line or a decisive stand in a muddle of ambiguity is the only ethical thing to do. If a manager is indecisive and spends time trying to figure out the "good" thing to do, the enterprise may be lost.

Business ethics, then, has to do with the authenticity and integrity of the enterprise. To be ethical is to follow the business as well as the cultural goals of the corporation, its owners, its employees, and its customers. Those who cannot serve the corporate vision are not authentic business people and, therefore, are not ethical in the business sense.

At this stage of my own business experience I have a strong interest in organizational behavior. Sociologists are keenly studying what they call corporate stories, legends, and heroes as a way organizations have of transmitting the value system. Corporations such as Arco have even hired consultants to perform an audit of their corporate culture. In a company, the leader is the person who understands, interprets, and manages the corporate value system. Effective managers are then action-oriented people who resolve conflict, are tolerant of ambiguity, stress, and change, and have a strong sense of purpose for themselves and their organizations.

If all this is true, I wonder about the role of the professional manager who moves from company to company. How can he or she quickly absorb the values and culture of different organizations? Or is there, indeed, an art of management that is totally transportable? Assuming such fungible managers do exist, is it proper for them to manipulate the values of others?

What would have happened had Stephen and I carried the sadhu for two days back to the village and become involved with the villagers in his care? In four trips to Nepal my most interesting experiences occurred in 1975 when I lived in a Sherpa home in the Khumbu for five days recovering from altitude sickness. The high point of Stephen's trip was an invitation to participate in a family funeral ceremony in Manang. Neither experience had to do with climbing the high passes of the Himalayas. Why were we so reluctant to try the lower path, the ambiguous trail? Perhaps because we did not have a leader who could reveal the greater purpose of the trip to us.

Why didn't Stephen with his moral vision opt to take the sadhu under his personal care? The answer is because, in part, Stephen was hard-stressed physically himself, and because, in part, without some support system that involved our involuntary and episodic community on the mountain, it was beyond his individual capacity to do so.

I see the current interest in corporate culture and corporate value systems as a positive response to Stephen's pessimism about the decline of the role of the individual in large organizations. Individuals who operate from a thoughtful set of personal values provide the foundation of a corporate culture. A corporate tradition that encourages freedom of inquiry, supports personal values, and reinforces a focused sense of direction can fulfill the need for individuality along with the prosperity and success of the group. Without such corporate support, the individual is lost.

That is the lesson of the sadhu. In a complex corporate situation, the individual requires or deserves the support of the group. If people cannot find such support from their organization, they don't know how to act. If such support is forthcoming, a person has a stake in the success of the group, and can add much to the process of establishing and maintaining a corporate culture. It is management's challenge to be sensitive to individual needs, to shape them, and to direct and focus them for the benefit of the group as a whole.

For each of us the sadhu lives. Should we stop what we are doing and comfort him; or should we keep trudging up toward the high pass? Should I pause to help the derelict I pass on the street each night as I walk by the Yale Club en route to Grand Central Station? Am I his brother? What is the nature of our responsibility if we consider ourselves to be ethical persons? Perhaps it is to change the values of the group so that it can, with all its resources, take the other road.

Discussion Questions

Consider the closing questions Mr. McCoy poses. How do they apply to you personally and to businesses?

Front Page of the Newspaper Test

Many businesspeople utilize the so-called "front page of the newspaper test" for evaluating ethical dilemmas. The question to be asked is how a critical and objective reporter would report your decision in a front-page story in your local newspaper (or national paper, for large companies). Some managers rephrase the test for their employees: How will the headline read on this if I make this decision? This test is helpful in spotting and resolving potential conflicts of interest. When Salomon Brothers experienced difficulties with regulators, its new chairman explained to employees that before making any choice or decision they should reflect on whether they would be willing to see their decision reported in a newspaper that their family, friends, and communities would read.

Laura Nash and Questions for Our Conduct

Business ethicist and professor Laura Nash has developed a series of questions for resolving ethical dilemmas that are covered in the following article.

READING 1.5: ETHICS WITHOUT THE SERMON[13]

Laura L. Nash

As if via a network TV program on the telecommunications satellite, declarations such as these are being broadcast throughout the land:

Scene 1. Annual meeting, Anyproducts Inc.; John Q. Moneypockets, chairman and CEO, speaking: "Our responsibility to the public has always come first at our

---

13. SOURCE: Reprinted by permission of *Harvard Business Review*. "Ethics Without the Sermon," by Laura L. Nash, Vol. 59 (November/December 1981). Copyright © 1981 by the President and Fellows of Harvard College; all rights reserved.

company, and we continue to strive toward serving our public in the best way possible in the belief that good ethics is good business. . . . Despite our forecast of a continued recession in the industry through 1982, we are pleased to announce that 1981's earnings per share were up for 'he twenty-sixth year in a row."

Scene 2. Corporate headquarters, Anyproducts Inc.; Linda Diesinker, group vice president, speaking: "Of course we're concerned about minority development and the plight of the inner cities. But the best place for our new plant would be Horsepasture, Minnesota. We need a lot of space for our operations and a skilled labor force, and the demographics and tax incentives in Horsepasture are perfect."

Scene 3. Interview with a financial writer; Rafe Shortstop, president, Anyproducts Inc., speaking: "We're very concerned about the state of American business and our ability to compete with foreign companies. . . . No, I don't think we have any real ethical problems. We don't bribe people or anything like that."

Scene 4. Jud McFisticuff, taxi driver, speaking: "Anyproducts? You've got to be kidding! I wouldn't buy their stuff for anything. The last thing of theirs I bought fell apart in six months. And did you see how they were dumping wastes in the Roxburg water system?"

Scene 5. Leslie Matriculant, MBA '82, speaking: "Join Anyproducts? I don't want to risk my reputation working for a company like that. They recently acquired a business that turned out to have ten class-action discrimination suits against it. And when Anyproducts tried to settle the whole thing out of court, the president had his picture in *Business Week* with the caption, 'His secretary still serves him coffee.'"

Whether you regard it as an unchecked epidemic or as the first blast of Gabriel's horn, the trend toward focusing on the social impact of the corporation is an inescapable reality that must be factored into today's managerial decision making. But for the executive who asks, "How do we as a corporation examine our ethical concerns?" the theoretical insights currently available may be more frustrating than helpful.

As the first scene in this article implies, many executives firmly believe that corporate operations and corporate values are dynamically intertwined. For the purposes of analysis, however, the executive needs to uncoil the business-ethics helix and examine both strands closely.

Unfortunately, the ethics strand has remained largely inaccessible, for business has not yet developed a workable process by which corporate values can be articulated. If ethics and business are part of the same double helix, perhaps we can develop a microscope capable of enlarging our perception of both aspects of business administration—what we do and who we are. . . .

What is needed is a process of ethical inquiry that is immediately comprehensible to a group of executives and not predisposed to the utopian, and sometimes anticapitalistic, bias marking much of the work in applied business philosophy today. So I suggest, as a preliminary solution, a set of twelve questions that draw on traditional philosophical frameworks but that avoid the level of abstraction normally associated with formal moral reasoning.

I offer the questions as a first step in a very new discipline. As such, they form a tentative model that will certainly undergo modifications after its parts are given some exercise.

To illustrate the application of the questions, I will draw especially on a program at Lex Service Group, Ltd., whose top management prepared a statement of financial objectives and moral values as a part of its strategic planning process.[14] Lex is a British company with operations in the United Kingdom and the United States. Its sales total about $1.2 billion. In 1978 its structure was partially decentralized, and in 1979 the chairman's policy group began a strategic planning process. The intent, according to its statement of values and objectives, was "to make explicit the sort of company Lex was, or wished to be."

Neither a paralegal code nor a generalized philosophy, the statement consisted of a series of general policies regarding financial strategy as well as such aspects of the company's character as customer service, employee-shareholder responsibility, and quality of management. Its content largely reflected the personal values of Lex's chairman and CEO, Trevor Chinn, whose private philanthropy is well known and whose concern for social welfare has long been echoed in the company's personnel policies.

In the past, pressure on senior managers for high profit performance had obscured some of these ideals in practice, and the statement of strategy was a way of radically realigning various competing moral claims with the financial objectives of the company. As one senior manager remarked to me, "The values seem obvious, and if we hadn't been so gross in the past we wouldn't have needed the statement." Despite a predictable variance among Lex's top executives as to the desirability of the values outlined in the statement, it was adopted with general agreement to comply and was scheduled for reassessment at a senior managers' meeting one year after implementation.

THE TWELVE QUESTIONS

1. Have you defined the problem accurately?

How one assembles the facts weights an issue before the moral examination ever begins, and a definition is rarely accurate if it articulates one's loyalties rather than the facts. The importance of factual neutrality is readily seen, for example, in assessing the moral implications of producing a chemical agent for use in warfare. Depending on one's loyalties, the decision to make the substance can be described as serving one's country, developing products, or killing babies. All of the above may be factual statements, but none is neutral or accurate if viewed in isolation.

Similarly, the recent controversy over marketing U.S.-made cigarettes in Third World countries rarely noted that the incidence of lung cancer in underdeveloped nations is quite low (from one-tenth to one-twentieth the rate for U.S. males) due primarily to the lower life expectancies and earlier predominance of other diseases in these nations. Such a fact does not decide the ethical complexities of this marketing problem, but it does add a crucial perspective in the assignment of moral priorities by defining precisely the injury that tobacco exports may cause. . . .

Extensive fact gathering may also help defuse the emotionalism of an issue. For instance, local statistics on lung cancer incidence reveal that the U.S. tobacco industry is not now "exporting death," as has been charged. Moreover, the substantial and immediate economic benefits attached to tobacco may be providing food and health care in these countries. Nevertheless, as life expectancy and the standards of

---

14. The process is modeled after ideas in Kenneth R. Andrew's book *The Concept of Corporate Strategy* (Homewood, Ill.: Richard D. Irwin, 1980, revised edition) and in Richard F. Vancil's article "Strategy Formulation in Complex Organizations," *Sloan Management Review*, Winter 1976, p. 4.

living rise, a higher incidence of cigarette-related diseases appears likely to develop in these nations. Therefore, cultivation of the nicotine habit may be deemed detrimental to the long-term welfare of these nations.

According to one supposedly infallible truth of modernism, technology is so complex that its results will never be fully comprehensible or predictable. Part of the executive's frustration in responding to Question 1 is the real possibility that the "experts" will find no grounds for agreement about the facts.

As a first step, however, defining fully the factual implications of a decision determines to a large degree the quality of one's subsequent moral position. Pericles' definition of true courage rejected the Spartans' blind obedience in war in preference to the courage of the Athenian citizen who, he said, was able to make a decision to proceed in full knowledge of the probable danger. A truly moral decision is an informed decision. A decision that is based on blind or convenient ignorance is hardly defensible.

One simple test of the initial definition is the question:

2. How would you define the problem if you stood on the other side of the fence?

The contemplated construction of a plant for Division X is touted at the finance committee meeting as an absolute necessity for expansion at a cost saving of at least 25%. With plans drawn up for an energy-efficient building and an option already secured on a 99-year lease in a new industrial part in Chippewa County, the committee is likely to feel comfortable in approving the request for funds in a matter of minutes.

The facts of the matter are that the company will expand in an appropriate market, allocate its resources sensibly, create new jobs, increase Chippewa County's tax base, and most likely increase its returns to the shareholders. To the residents of Chippewa County, however, the plant may mean the destruction of a customary recreation spot, the onset of severe traffic jams, and the erection of an architectural eyesore. These are also facts of the situation, and certainly more immediate to the county than utilitarian justifications of profit performance and rights of ownership from an impersonal corporation whose headquarters are 1,000 miles from Chippewa County and whose executives have plenty of acreage for their own recreation.

The purpose of articulating the other side, whose needs are understandably less proximate than operational considerations, is to allow some mechanism whereby calculations of self-interest (or even of a project's ultimate general beneficence) can be interrupted by a compelling empathy for those who might suffer immediate injury or mere annoyance as a result of a corporation's decisions. Such empathy is a necessary prerequisite for shouldering voluntarily some responsibility for the social consequences of corporate operations, and it may be the only solution to today's overly litigious and anarchic world.

There is a power in self-examination: with an exploration of the likely consequences of a proposal, taken from the viewpoint of those who do not immediately benefit, comes a discomfort or an embarrassment that rises in proportion to the degree of the likely injury and its articulation. Like Socrates as gadfly, who stung his fellow citizens into a critical examination of their conduct when they became complacent, the discomfort of the alternative definition is meant to prompt a disinclination to choose the expedient over the most responsible course of action.

Abstract generalities about the benefits of the profit motive and the free market system are, for some, legitimate and ultimate justifications, but when unadorned with alternative viewpoints, such arguments also tend to promote the complacency, carelessness, and impersonality that have characterized some of the more injurious actions of corporations. The advocates of these arguments are like the reformers in Nathaniel Hawthorne's short story "Hall of Fantasy" who "had got possession of some crystal fragment of truth, the brightness of which so dazzled them that they could see nothing else in the whole universe."

In the example of Division X's new plant, it was a simple matter to define the alternate facts; the process rested largely on an assumption that certain values were commonly shared (no one likes a traffic jam, landscaping pleases more than an unadorned building, and so forth). But the alternative definition often underscores an inherent disparity in values or language. To some, the employment of illegal aliens is a criminal act (fact #1); to others, it is a solution to the 60% unemployment rate of a neighboring country (fact #2). One country's bribe is another country's redistribution of sales commissions.

When there are cultural or linguistic disparities, it is easy to get the facts wrong or to invoke a pluralistic tolerance as an excuse to act in one's own self-interest: "That's the way they do things over there. Who are we to question their beliefs?" This kind of reasoning can be both factually inaccurate (many generalizations about bribery rest on hearsay and do not represent the complexities of a culture) and philosophically inconsistent (there are plenty of beliefs, such as those of the environmentalist, which the same generalizers do not hesitate to question).

3. How did this situation occur in the first place?

Lex Motor Company, a subsidiary of Lex Service Group, Ltd., had been losing [market] share at a 20% rate in a declining market; and Depot B's performance was the worst of all. Two nearby Lex depots could easily absorb B's business, and closing it down seemed the only sound financial decision. Lex's chairman, Trevor Chinn, hesitated to approve the closure, however, on the grounds that putting 100 people out of work was not right when the corporation itself was not really jeopardized by B's existence. Moreover, seven department managers, who were all within five years of retirement and had 25 or more years of service at Lex, were scheduled to be made redundant.

The values statement provided no automatic solution, for it placed value on both employees' security and shareholders' interest. Should they close Depot B? At first Chinn thought not: Why should the little guys suffer disproportionately when the company was not performing well? Why not close a more recently acquired business where employee service was not so large a factor? Or why not wait out the short term and reduce head count through natural attrition?

As important as deciding the ethics of the situation was the inquiry into its history. Indeed, the history gave a clue to solving the dilemma: Lex's traditional emphasis on employee security *and* high financial performance had led to a precipitate series of acquisitions and subsequent divestitures when the company had failed to meet its overall objectives. After each rationalization, the people serving the longest had been retained and placed at Depot B, so that by 1980 the facility had more managers than it needed and a very high proportion of long-service employees.

So the very factors that had created the performance problems were making the closure decision difficult, and the very solution that Lex was inclined to favor again would exacerbate the situation further!

In deciding the ethics of a situation it is important to distinguish the symptoms from the disease. Great profit pressures with no sensitivity to the cycles in a particular industry, for example, may force division managers to be ruthless with employees, to short-weight customers, or even to fiddle with cash flow reports in order to meet headquarters' performance criteria.

Dealing with the immediate case of lying, quality discrepancy, or strained labor relations—when the problem is finally discovered—is only a temporary solution. A full examination of how the situation occurred and what the traditional solutions have been may reveal a more serious discrepancy of values and pressures, and this will illuminate the real significance and ethics of the problem. It will also reveal recurring patterns of events that in isolation appear trivial but that as a whole point up a serious situation.

Such a mechanism is particularly important because very few executives are outright scoundrels. Rather, violations of corporate and social values usually occur inadvertently because no one recognizes that a problem exists until it becomes a crisis. This tendency toward initial trivialization seems to be the biggest ethical problem in business today. Articulating answers to my first three questions is a way of reversing that process.

4. To whom and what do you give your loyalties as a person and as a member of the corporation?

Every executive faces conflicts of loyalty. The most familiar occasions pit private conscience and sense of duty against corporate policy, but equally frequent are the situations in which one's close colleagues demand participation (tacit or explicit) in an operation or a decision that runs counter to company policy. To whom or what is the greater loyalty—to one's corporation? superior? family? society? self? race? sex?

The good news about conflicts of loyalty is that their identification is a workable way of smoking out the ethics of a situation and of discovering the absolute values inherent in it. As one executive in a discussion of a Harvard case study put it, "My corporate brain says this action is O.K., but my noncorporate brain keeps flashing these warning lights."

The bad news about conflicts of loyalty is that there are few automatic answers to placing priorities on them. "To thine own self be true" is a murky quagmire when the self takes on a variety of roles, as it does so often in this complex modern world.

Supposedly, today's young managers are giving more weight to individual than to corporate identity, and some older executives see this tendency as being ultimately subversive. At the same time, most of them believe individual integrity is essential to a company's reputation.

The U.S. securities industry, for example, is one of the most rigorous industries in America in its requirements of honesty and disclosure. Yet in the end, all its systematic precautions prove inadequate unless the people involved also have a strong sense of integrity that puts loyalty to these principles above personal gain.

A system, however, must permit the time and foster the motivation to allow personal integrity to surface in a particular situation. An examination of loyalties is one way to bring this about. Such an examination may strengthen reputations but also may result in blowing the whistle (freedom of thought carries with it the risk of revolution). But a sorting out of loyalties can also bridge the gulf between policy and implementation or among various interest groups whose affiliations may mask a common devotion to an aspect of a problem—a devotion on which consensus can be built.

How does one probe into one's own loyalties and their implications? A useful method is simply to play various roles out loud, to call on one's loyalty to family and community (for example) by asking, "What will I say when my child asks me why I did that?" If the answer is "That's the way the world works," then your loyalties are clear and moral passivity inevitable. But if the question presents real problems, you have begun a demodulation of signals from your conscience that can only enhance corporate responsibility.

5. What is your intention in making this decision?

6. How does this intention compare with the likely results?

These two questions are asked together because their content often bears close resemblance and, by most calculations, both color the ethics of a situation.

Corporation Buglebloom decides to build a new plant in an underdeveloped minority-populated district where the city has been trying with little success to encourage industrial development. The media approve and Buglebloom adds another star to its good reputation. Is Buglebloom a civic leader and a supporter of minorities or a canny investor about to take advantage of the disadvantaged? The possibilities of Buglebloom's intentions are endless and probably unfathomable to the public; Buglebloom may be both canny investor and friend of minority groups.

I argue that despite their complexity and elusiveness, a company's intentions do matter. The "purity" of Buglebloom's motives (purely profit-seeking or purely altruistic) will have wide-reaching effects inside and outside the corporation—on attitudes toward minority employees in other parts of the company, on the wages paid at the new plant, and on the number of other investors in the same area-that will legitimize a certain ethos in the corporation and the community.

Sociologist Max Weber called this an "ethics of attitude" and contrasted it with an "ethics of absolute ends." An ethics of attitude sets a standard to ensure a certain action. A firm policy at headquarters of not cheating customers, for example, may also deter salespeople from succumbing to a tendency to lie by omission or purchasers from continuing to patronize a high-priced supplier when the costs are automatically passed on in the selling price.

What about the ethics of result? Two years later, Buglebloom wishes it had never begun Project Minority Plant. Every good intention has been lost in the realities of doing business in an unfamiliar area, and Buglebloom now has dirty hands: some of those payoffs were absolutely unavoidable if the plant was to open, operations have been plagued with vandalism-and language problems, and local resentment at the industrialization of the neighborhood has risen as charges of discrimination have surfaced. No one seems to be benefitting from the project.

The goodness of intent pales somewhat before results that perpetrate great injury or simply do little good. Common sense demands that the "responsible" corporation try to align the two more closely, to identify the probable consequences and also the limitations of knowledge that might lead to more harm than good. Two things to remember in comparing intention and results are that knowledge of the future is always inadequate and that overconfidence often precedes a disastrous mistake.

These two precepts, cribbed from ancient Greece, may help the corporation keep the disparities between intent and result a fearsome reality to consider continuously. The next two questions explore two ways of reducing the moral risks of being wrong.

7. Whom could your decision or action injure?

The question presses whether injury is intentional or not. Given the limits of knowledge about a new product or policy, who and how many will come into contact with it? Could its inadequate disposal affect an entire community? two employees? yourself? How might your product be used if it happened to be acquired by a terrorist radical group or a terrorist military police force? Has your distribution system or disposal plan ensured against such injury? Could it ever?

If not, there may be a compelling moral justification for stopping production. In an integrated society where business and government share certain values, possible injury is an even more important consideration than potential benefit. In policymaking, a much likelier ground for agreement than benefit is avoidance of injury through those "universal nos"—such as no mass death, no totalitarianism, no hunger or malnutrition, no harm to children.

To exclude *at the outset* any policy or decision that might have such results is to reshape the way modern business examines its own morality. So often business formulates questions of injury only after the fact in the form of liability suits.

8. Can you engage the affected parties in a discussion of the problem before you make your decision?

If the calculus of injury is one way of responding to limitations of knowledge about the probable results of a particular business decision, the participation of affected parties is one of the best ways of informing that consideration. Civil rights groups often complain that corporations fail to invite participation from local leaders during the planning stages of community development projects and charitable programs. The corporate foundation that builds a tennis complex for disadvantaged youth is throwing away precious resources if most children in the neighborhood suffer from chronic malnutrition.

In the Lex depot closure case I have mentioned, senior executives agonized over whether the employees would choose redundancy over job transfer and which course would ultimately be more beneficial to them. The managers, however, did not consult the employees. There were more than 200 projected job transfers to another town. But all the affected employees, held by local ties and uneasy about possibly lower housing subsidies, refused relocation offers. Had the employees been allowed to participate in the redundancy discussions, the company might have wasted less time on relocation plans or might have uncovered and resolved the fears about relocating.

The issue of participation affects everyone. (How many executives feel that someone else should decide what is in *their* best interest?) And yet it is a principle often forgotten because of the pressure of time or the inconvenience of calling people together and facing predictably hostile questions.

9. Are you confident that your position will be as valid over a long period of time as it seems now?

As anyone knows who has had to consider long-range plans and short-term budgets simultaneously, a difference in time frame can change the meaning of a problem as much as spring and autumn change the colors of a tree. The ethical coloring of a business decision is no exception to this generational aspect of decision making. Time alters circumstances, and few corporate value systems are immune to shifts in financial status, external political pressure, and personnel. (One survey now places the average U.S. CEO's tenure in office at five years.)

At Lex, for example, the humanitarianism of the statement of objectives and values depended on financial prosperity. The values did not fully anticipate the extent to which the U.K. economy would undergo a recession, and the resulting changes had to be examined, reconciled, and fought if the company's values were to have any meaning. At the Lex annual review, the managers asked themselves repeatedly whether hard times were the ultimate test of the statement or a clear indication that a corporation had to be able to "afford" ethical positions.

Ideally, a company's articulation of its values should anticipate changes of fortune. As the hearings for the passage of the Foreign Corrupt Practices Act of 1977 demonstrated, doing what you can get away with today may not be a secure moral standard, but short-term discomfort for long-term sainthood may require irrational courage or a rational reasoning system or, more likely, both. These twelve questions attempt to elicit a rational system. Courage, of course, depends on personal integrity.

Another aspect of the ethical time frame stretches beyond the boundaries of Question 9 but deserves special attention, and that is the timing of the ethical inquiry. When and where will it be made?

We do not normally invoke moral principles in our everyday conduct. Some time ago the participants in a national business ethics conference had worked late into the night preparing the final case for the meeting, and they were very anxious the next morning to get the class under way. Just before the session began, however, someone suggested that they all donate a dollar apiece as a gratuity for the dining hall help at the institute.

Then just as everyone automatically reached into his or her pocket, another person questioned the direction of the gift. Why tip the person behind the counter but not the cook in the kitchen? Should the money be given to each person in proportion to salary or divided equally among all? The participants laughed uneasily—or groaned-as they thought of the diversion of precious time from the case. A decision had to be made.

With the sure instincts of efficient managers, the group chose to forgo further discussion of distributive justice and, yes, appoint a committee. The committee doled out the money without further group consideration, and no formal feedback on the donation was asked for or given.

The questions offered here do not solve the problem of making time for the inquiry.

10. Could you disclose without qualm your decision or action to your boss, your CEO, the board of directors, your family, or society as a whole?

The old question, "Would you want your decision to appear on the front page of *The New York Times?*, still holds. A corporation may maintain that there's really no problem, but a survey of how many "trivial" actions it is reluctant to disclose might be interesting. Disclosure is a way of sounding those submarine depths of conscience and of searching out loyalties.

It is also a way of keeping a corporate character cohesive. The Lex Group, for example, was once faced with a very sticky problem concerning a small but profitable site with unpleasant (though in no way illegal) working conditions, where two men with 30 years' service worked. I wrote up the case for a Lex senior managers' meeting on the promise to disguise it heavily because the executive who supervised the plant was convinced that, if the chairman and the personnel director knew the plant's true location, they would close it down immediately.

At the meeting, however, as everyone became involved in the discussion and the chairman himself showed sensitivity to the dilemma, the executive disclosed the location and spoke of his own feelings about the situation. The level of mutual confidence was apparent to all, and by other reports it was the most open discussion the group had ever had.

The meeting also fostered understanding of the company's values and their implementation. When the discussion finally flagged, the chairman spoke up. Basing his views on a full knowledge of the group's understanding of the problem, he set the company's priorities. "Jobs over fancy conditions, health over jobs," Chinn said, "but we always *must disclose.*" The group decided to keep the plant open, at least for the time being.

Disclosure does not, however, automatically bring universal sympathy. In the early 1970s, a large food store chain that repeatedly found itself embroiled in the United Farm Workers (UFW) disputes with the Teamsters over California grape and lettuce contracts took very seriously the moral implications of a decision whether to stop selling these products. The company endlessly researched the issues, talked to all sides, and made itself available to public representatives of various interest groups to explain its position and to hear out everyone else.

When the controversy started, the company decided to support the UFW boycott, but three years later top management reversed its position. Most of the people who wrote to the company or asked it to send representatives to their local UFW support meetings, however, continued to condemn the chain even after hearing its views, and the general public apparently never became aware of the company's side of the story.

11. What is the symbolic potential of your action if understood? if misunderstood?

Jones Inc., a diversified multinational corporation with assets of $5 billion, has a paper manufacturing operation that happens to be the only major industry in Stirville, and the factory has been polluting the river on which it is located. Local and national conservation groups have filed suit against Jones Inc. for past damages, and the company is defending itself. Meanwhile, the corporation has adopted plans for a new waste-efficient plant. The legal battle is extended and local resentment against Jones Inc. gets bitter.

As a settlement is being reached, Jones Inc. announces that, as a civic-minded gesture, it will make 400 acres of Stirville woodland it owns available to the residents for conservation and recreation purposes. Jones's intention is to offer a peace pipe to the people of Stirville, and the company sees the gift as a symbol of its own belief in conservation and a way of signaling that value to Stirville residents and national conservation groups. Should Jones Inc. give the land away? Is the symbolism significant?

If the symbolic value of the land is understood as Jones Inc. intends, the gift may patch up the company's relations with Stirville and stave off further disaffection with potential employees as the new plant is being built. It may also signal to employees throughout the corporation that Jones Inc. places a premium on conservation efforts and community relations.

If the symbolic value is misunderstood, however, or if completion of the plant is delayed and the old one has to be put back in use—or if another Jones operation is discovered to be polluting another community and becomes a target of the press— the gift could be interpreted as nothing more than a cheap effort to pay off the people of Stirville and hasten settlement of the lawsuit.

The Greek root of our word *symbol* means both signal and contract. A business decision—whether it is the use of an expense account or a corporate donation— has a symbolic value in signaling what is acceptable behavior within the corporate culture and in making a tacit contract with employees and the community about the rules of the game. How the symbol is actually perceived (or misperceived) is as important as how you intend it to be perceived.

12. Under what conditions would you allow exceptions to your stand?

If we accept the idea that every business decision has an—important symbolic value and a contractual nature, then the need for consistency is obvious. At the same time, it is also important to ask under what conditions the rules of the game may be changed. What conflicting principles, circumstances, or time constraints would provide a morally acceptable basis for making an exception to one's non-normal institutional ethos? For instance, how does the cost of the strategy to develop managers from minority groups over the long term fit in with short-term hurdle rates? Also to be considered is what would mitigate a clear case of employee dishonesty.

Questions of consistency—if you would do X, would you also do Y?—are yet another way of eliciting the ethics of the company and of oneself, and can be a final test of the strength, idealism, or practicality of those values. A last example from the experience of Lex illustrates this point and gives temporary credence to the platitude that good ethics is good business. An article in the Sunday paper about a company that had run a series of racy ads, with pictures of half-dressed women and promises of free merchandise to promote the sale of a very mundane product, sparked an extended examination at Lex of its policies on corporate inducements.

One area of concern was holiday giving. What was the acceptable limit for a gift—a bottle of whiskey? a case? Did it matter only that the company did not *intend* the gift to be an inducement, or did the mere possibility of inducement taint the gift? Was the cut-off point absolute? The group could agree on no halfway point for allowing some gifts and not others, so a new value was added to the formal statement that prohibited the offering or receiving of inducements.

The next holiday season Chinn sent a letter to friends and colleagues who had received gifts of appreciation in the past. In it he explained that, as a result of Lex's concern with "the very complex area of business ethics," management had decided that the company would no longer send any gifts, nor would it be appropriate for its employees to receive any. Although the letter did not explain Lex's reasoning behind the decision, apparently there was a large untapped consensus about such gift giving: by return mail Chinn received at least twenty letters from directors, general managers, and chairmen of companies with which Lex had done business congratulating him for his decision, agreeing with the new policy, and thanking him for his holiday wishes. . . .

The situations for testing business morality remain complex. But by avoiding theoretical inquiry and limiting the expectations of corporate goodness to a few rules for social behavior that are based on common sense, we can develop an ethic that is appropriate to the language, ideology, and institutional dynamics of business decision making and consensus. This ethic can also offer managers a practical way of exploring those occasions when their corporate brains are getting warning flashes from their noncorporate brains.

Discussion Questions

1. What questions help resolve the issue of whether to accept gifts from suppliers at Christmas?
2. What is "ethics of attitude"? What is "ethics of absolute ends"?
3. Why are history and future important in the Laura Nash model?

Of course, there are much simpler models for making ethical business decisions. One stems from Immanuel Kant's categorical imperative: "Do unto others as you would have them do unto you." For example, William Aramony, the former head of the United Way, was paid like the CEO of a national firm and enjoyed CEO-style perks, such as first-class flights and homes throughout the country. From the perspective of a successful CEO, his benefits were average. But from the perspective of a wage earner who might pledge 5 percent of his or her wages to the United Way, the expenses were extravagant. How would you feel if your donations were spent this way? Treating others or others' money as we would want to be treated is a powerful evaluation technique in ethical dilemmas.

Each case in this book requires you to examine different perspectives and analyze the impact that the resolution of a dilemma has on the parties involved. Return to these models to question the propriety of the actions taken in each case. Examine the origins of the ethical dilemmas and explore possible solutions. As you work through the cases, you will find yourself developing a new awareness of values and their importance in making business decisions.

READING 1.6: WHAT'S THE MATTER WITH BUSINESS ETHICS?[15]

Andrew Stark

Why Should Managers Be Ethical?

To understand the gap between business ethics and the concerns of most managers, it pays to recall how managers and management academics thought about business ethics before it became a formal discipline. Indeed, much of the research

15. SOURCE: Reprinted by permission of *Harvard Business Review.* "What's the Matter with Business Ethics?" by Andrew Stark, Vol. 71 (May/June 1993). Copyright © 1993 by the President and Fellows of Harvard College; all rights reserved.

and writing in contemporary business ethics can be understood as a disgruntled reaction to the way ethical issues usually were addressed at business schools—in particular, to the traditional answers to the fundamental question: Why should managers be ethical?

Starting well before World War II and culminating in the 1960s and 1970s, the dominant approach to the moral dimension of business was a perspective that came to be known *as corporate social responsibility.* Largely reacting to neoclassical economics, which holds that the sole responsibility of business is to maximize its immediate bottom line subject to only the most minimal constraints of the law, advocates of corporate social responsibility argued that ethical management requires more than merely following the dictates of the law or signals of the market, the two institutions that otherwise guide business behavior. Rather, ethical management is a process of *anticipating* both the law and the market—and for sound business reasons.

For example, when managers voluntarily undertake socially responsible actions beyond the bare legal minimum required (in environmental protection, say, or antidiscrimination policy), they tend to forestall punitive social regulation. As corporate scholar E. Merrick Dodd, Jr. stated in a 1932 *Harvard Law Re*view article, the purpose of ethical management is "to catch any new spirit" and embody it in voluntary standards "without waiting for legal compulsion." Or as Berkeley professor Edwin Epstein more recently and succinctly put it, "being ethical heads off the law."

The social responsibility approach not only took an expansive view of the law but also urged managers to take an expansive view of the market. In the short term, ethical behavior may prove costly to a company's bottom line. But according to the advocates of corporate social responsibility, ultimately the market will reward such behavior. "In general, socially responsible deliberation will not lead management to decisions different from those indicated by long-range profit considerations," the management scholar Wilbur Katz wrote in 1950. Or in the by now famous words of former SEC Chairman John Shad: "Ethics pays."

Most managers were able to assimilate this response to the question "Why be ethical?" fairly easily under the heading *enlightened self-interest.* Indeed, by now the tenets of corporate social responsibility have become conventional wisdom in managerial circles. Organizations like the Business Roundtable publish studies with titles like "Corporate Ethics: A Prime Business Asset." And top corporate executives regularly use the logic of enlightened self-interest, reflected in the statement by former Dow Chairman Robert W Lundeen: "We found that if we were not running our business in the public interest, the public [would] get back at us with restrictive regulations and laws."

It was one thing, however, for social responsibility advocates to provide a broad and appealing answer to the question: Why should managers be ethical? It was quite another to answer the obvious follow-up: How can managers determine the ethical course in any particular situation and stick to it in the face of competing pressures?

To address this question, social responsibility advocates set out in the 1970s to create a brand-new managerial discipline: *business ethics.* One idea was to bring experts in moral philosophy into the business schools. Training in moral philosophy would give business ethicists the analytical frameworks and conceptual tools necessary for making fine-grained ethical distinctions and discerning the appropriate course in difficult ethical situations. Once "retooled" in management, the moral philosophers could apply their sophisticated frameworks to the day-to-day moral problems that managers face.

↘ However, things have not worked out quite the way traditional advocates of corporate social responsibility had hoped. Largely because of their background in moral philosophy, a discipline that tends to place a high value on precisely those kinds of experiences and activities where self-interest does not rule, many business ethicists found the precepts of corporate social responsibility profoundly dissatisfying. As a result, they have spent a great deal of scholarly time and energy tearing down the social responsibility position in order to erect their own. Indeed, far from taking a step closer to the real world moral problems of management, several prominent business ethicists have chosen to reopen the fundamental question: Why should managers be ethical?

The Myopia of Moral Philosophy

Business ethicists have two basic problems with the enlightened self-interest answer to the question of why managers should be ethical. First, they disagree that ethical behavior is always in a company's best interest, however enlightened. "There are no vanilla solutions," writes Bentley College ethicist W. Michael Hoffman in his article, "The Cost of a Corporate Conscience." "To behave ethically can cost dearly." In other words, ethics and interests can and do conflict.

Second, they object that even when "doing good" is in the company's best interest, acts motivated by such self-interest really can't be ethical. Moral philosophy tends to value *altruism*, the idea that an individual should do good because it is right or will benefit others, not because the individual will benefit from it. For many business ethicists, motivation can be either altruistic or self-interested, but not both. A participant in a symposium called "Do Good Ethics Ensure Good Profits?" (recently sponsored by *Business and Society Review*) put it as follows: "To be ethical as a business because it may increase your profits is to do so for entirely the wrong reason. The ethical business must be ethical because it wants to be ethical." In other words, business ethics means acting within business for nonbusiness reasons.

Each of these criticisms has its kernel of truth. Clearly, ethics and interests can conflict. Take the example of a racially segregated company in the South during the 1930s. Remaining racially segregated was ethically wrong. Yet active desegregation would have flown in the face of then-prevailing public norms and most likely would have been penalized severely by market forces over both the short and long terms.

When ethics and interest do *not* conflict, business ethicists have a point too. Certainly, there is ethical value in doing the right thing because it is right, not just because it serves one's interest. And in the real world of business, altruism is one of the many motivations that do shape managers' behavior.

However, the problem is that many business ethicists have pushed both these lines of reasoning to extremes. In the case of the potential conflict between ethics and interests, the fundamental issue for a manager is not whether such conflicts sometimes (or even frequently) occur, but rather how he or she handles them when they occur. Business ethicists have offered too little help with this problem so far. Often, they advance a kind of ethical absolutism that avoids many of the difficult (and most interesting) questions.

For example, in *Business Ethics: The State of the Art,* a recent volume of essays by leading business ethicists, edited by R. Edward Freeman, University of Kansas ethicist Richard T. DeGeorge states, "If in some instance it turns out that what is ethical leads to a company's demise," then "so be it." A participant in the *Business and Society Review* symposium echoes this sentiment by arguing that if ethical actions mean that a company's profits are reduced, then "it must accept such a trade-off without regret." Managers would be hard-pressed not to view such prescriptions as restatements of the problem, rather than as workable solutions.

In some cases, absolutism leads business ethicists to devalue such traditional business interests as making a profit or succeeding in the marketplace in favor of supposedly more important ethical demands. Take the example of one of the major works in the field, published in 1988: *Corporate Strategy and the Search for Ethics,* by R. Edward Freeman and Daniel R. Gilbert, Jr. According to the authors, no corporation is truly ethical unless it has banished all forms of *external motivation* for employees. What do Freeman and Gilbert mean by external motivation? Nothing less than traditional managerial tools such as authority, power, incentives, and leadership. Relying on such motivational tools, they argue, is just a sophisticated form of coercion and therefore "morally wrong." In order to be ethical, companies have to make sure that employees' work tasks are compatible with their own personal "projects," thus making external motivation unnecessary. While acknowledging that their view is not "practical," Freeman and Gilbert insist that it is not "optional." If corporations "cannot be run along the lines we propose," they argue, then "we would prefer to give up the idea of the corporation."

Such views may resonate with some moral philosophers but are of little help to managers. Like it or not, corporations do exist, and most managers work in them. These managers still lack solutions for the basic problem of how to balance ethical demands and economic realities when they do in fact conflict.

Surely, business ethicists are not pure moral theorists who needn't worry about the practicality of their prescriptions. Any business ethics worthy of the name should be an ethics of practice. But this means that business ethicists must get their hands dirty and seriously consider the costs that sometimes attend "doing the right thing." They must help managers do the arduous, conceptual balancing required in difficult cases where every alternative has both moral and financial costs.

Similarly, in situations where there is no conflict between ethics and interest, business ethicists must address what Robbin Derry has termed "the paradox of motivation" in her contribution to *Business Ethics.* The fact is, most people's motives are a confusing mix of self-interest, altruism, and other influences. Instead of grappling with this complexity, however, many business ethicists have tied themselves in knots over the notion that a managerial act cannot be ethical unless it in no way serves the manager's self-interest. This kind of sterile parsing of complex human motivation leads to the untenable position that managers are being genuinely ethical only when it costs them. Put simply, ethics has to hurt.

To grasp how strained such a position can become, consider the following argument made by Norman Bowie, an ethicist at the University of Minnesota's Carlson School of Management, in his article "New Directions in Corporate Social Responsibility." Bowie argues that a company adopting an inner-city elementary school is acting ethically only if other companies don't do the same thing. Bowie's curious logic: When only one company pours resources into a school, it's likely that the company won't recoup its investment. Indeed, it is other companies that almost certainly will benefit by hiring the school's better educated graduates. The fact that "some firms will ride free" on the expenditures of the sponsoring company guarantees that those "firms who [do] give money to solve social problems are altruistic."

If, of course, enough other companies were to start sponsoring schools, it would be possible for them all to recoup their investment by hiring from a much larger pool of better educated students. But then the spectre of self-interest would raise its head, and the purity of the sponsoring companies' motivation would become muddied. If there were no free riders, there would be no moral companies. An odd argument, to say the least. Some business ethicists used to caution that doing wrong is profitable only when most others are doing right. Now, apparently, they are arguing that doing right is demonstrably moral only when most others are doing wrong.

A few business ethicists have used a similar kind of reasoning to criticize companies that try to create incentives to encourage ethical behavior on the part of their employees. If a manager works in a corporate culture that rewards her for doing good, how can her behavior be considered ethical? In his contribution to *Business Ethics: The State of the Art,* Daniel Gilbert suggests that when ethical behavior is encouraged by "external stimuli," such as senior executives who "model proper behavior" or "provide others with incentives designed to induce proper behavior, " then the behavior isn't really ethical. The strong implication is that a manager can be truly *good* only in a *bad* corporation.

If a hint of self-interest is present, in other words, then altruism—and hence ethical motivation—can no longer be assumed. Ironically, neoclassical economists, who believe that all human behavior is essentially self-interested, share this view. There is, of course, an essential difference that underlies this similarity: neoclassical economists hold that self-interested motivation is not immoral; but, for many business ethicists, mixed motives deserve and receive no moral credit.

Mistakes and Missed Opportunities

Of course, many business ethicists have tried to go beyond the question "Why be moral?" to shed light on the hard ethical questions managers face. Even when they do so, their work has tended to suffer from one or more of three typical tendencies. First, it is too general—consumed with offering fundamental proposals for overhauling the capitalist system rather than ethics strategies to assist managers who must work within that system. Second, it is too theoretical—preoccupied with philosophical abstractions and anything but "user-friendly." And third, it is too impractical—concerned with prescriptions that, however morally respectable, run so contrary to existing managerial roles and responsibilities that they become untenable. As a result, such work in business ethics simply hasn't "taken" in the world of practice, especially when compared with the work of ethicists in other professions such as government, medicine, or law. These professions are, of course, monopolies and hence can more easily impose ethical strictures on their practitioners. But that's just part of the problem.

Too general. Business, like government, is not just a profession. It is also a system in which everyone, managers and nonmanagers alike, must live. As a result, the classic moral analysts of business and government have tended to be grand philosophers like Karl Marx or Friedrich von Hayek. Rather than focusing on professional norms and behavioral modes, such thinkers have advanced systemic critiques that often question the very premises of economic and political systems such as capitalism or socialism.

Medicine and law provide an instructive contrast. Because these fields are more traditional professions, their greatest moral analysts have tended to be practitioners like Hippocrates or Oliver Wendell Holmes. Such thinkers accepted and worked within the basic premises and norms of their professions. And that context has allowed them and others to come up with ethical precepts of practical value to actual doctors and lawyers.

Although management increasingly has come to be viewed as a profession in this century, a heritage of systemic moral criticism tempts business ethicists to be grand philosophers. In his contribution to *Business Ethics,* for example, Richard DeGeorge calls for the field to address questions such as "Is capitalism ethically justifiable? If so, how? If not, why not? Is socialism ethically . . . preferable?"

These are important questions. But to the considerable extent that business ethicists dwell on them, what they generate is more often high-flown social philosophy than ethics advice useful to professionals. To cite one example, in a recent *Business Horizons* piece entitled "Corporate Social Responsibility: A Critical Approach," R. Edward Freeman and Jeanne Liedtka urge managers to "see corporations . . . as places in which we can be fully unrestrained human beings, places of 'jouissance' rather than grey flannel, places of liberation and achievement rather than oppression and denial."

Too theoretical. Both medicine and management are referred to as "sciences." Business ethicists share with medical ethicists the challenge of having to bridge a gulf between their own preoccupations with morals and the harder, more "scientific" nature of the professions they study. In contrast, because government and law address the normative values of a particular political community, they are more receptive to the language of values found in moral philosophy. Medical ethicists have gained credibility within their more scientific field by displaying an understanding of the relevant hard medical-science issues. Business ethicists, by contrast, have attempted to gain credibility within their professional field primarily by girding their work with abstract moral theory.

Norman Bowie's contribution to *Business Ethics* addresses this "crisis of legitimacy" that business ethicists face in the "scientific" world of the business school. Many mainstream management scholars, he writes, see ethics as "subjective," "soft," and "normative," while regarding their own fields—finance, say, or marketing or accounting—as "objective," "hard," and "scientific." Bowie defends his field in part by pointing out that business ethics possesses the "complex body of knowledge" that defines a "true discipline." And by way of offering evidence, he notes that business ethics has "at least two major theories, utilitarianism and deontology" as well as a number of "peer-refereed journals."

To peruse recent issues of the *Journal of Business Ethics* is to get a strong sense of the kind of research that has resulted from this need to establish theoretical or scholarly bona fides. The point of one recent article, for example, is to argue that "utilitarian and situation ethics, not deontological or Kantian ethics . . . should be used in a regional code of conduct for multinational companies operating" in sub-Saharan Africa. The point of another is to "defend the view that from a purely rule-utilitarian perspective there is no sound argument favoring the immorality of hostile liquidating takeovers."

Ethical theory can help illuminate the moral problems managers face. But no other field of professional ethics has felt the need to couch its analyses so in the language of pure moral philosophy. In his new book *Ethics and Excellence: Cooperation and Integrity in Business,* University of Texas philosopher Robert C. Solomon writes that "such theorizing is . . . utterly inaccessible to the people for whom business ethics is not merely a subject of study but is (or will be) a way of life—students, executives, and corporations." Unfortunately, academic insecurity is causing business ethicists to direct their work away from addressing the real needs of managers and toward satisfying the perceived rigors of academic science in their field.

Too impractical. Even when business ethicists try to be practical, however, much of what they recommend is not particularly useful to managers. To understand why, a comparison with law is helpful. In business, as in law, ethicists are increasingly asking individual practitioners to modify their commitments to their traditional principals in order to satisfy the competing interests of nonprincipals. Managers, for example, are urged to weigh the consumer's interest in healthier products against their obligation to provide shareholders with the healthiest possible dividend. And lawyers are now being encouraged to weigh an opposing party's right not to be viciously cross-examined against their own client's right to the most vigorous possible defense.

Such questions are less characteristic of either government or clinical medicine. Rarely do we ask our government officials to put the claims of foreign citizens on a par with our own when they come into fundamental conflict. Nor have we felt comfortable asking a doctor to weigh the claims of another doctor's patient against his or her own; if helping one patient comes at the cost of helping another, we expect policymakers, not individual doctors, to make the necessary tradeoffs. At present, the most central ethical issues in clinical medicine and government arise when the diverse interests of the same principals come into conflict—for example, when a patient's interest in being told the truth conflicts with her interest in having peace of mind, or when the interest some citizens have in liberty competes with the interest others have in equality.

In one important respect, then, business ethicists and legal ethicists have an especially difficult row to hoe. Many of their current recommendations simply go against the grain of the traditional professional-principal relationship. This added difficulty doesn't necessarily mean that business ethicists should abandon their views of right and wrong. If they seek to influence the practice of management, however, they must advance their proposals with a heightened sensitivity to practitioners' understanding of their professional-principal responsibilities. As Kenneth Goodpaster argues in his thoughtful contribution to the premiere issue of *Business Ethics Quarterly,* "the challenge . . . is to develop an account of the moral responsibilities of management" that posits a "moral relationship between management and stakeholders" even as it protects "the uniqueness of the principal-agent relationship between management and stockholder."

Few business ethicists have risen to this challenge. In the same issue *of Business Ethics Quarterly,* for example, Norman Bowie uses the uncontroversial proposition that the manager "has obligations to all corporate stakeholders," as a starting point for a radical redefinition of the managerial mission. His conclusion: the "primary obligation" of the manager is "to provide meaningful work for . . . employees." Even if one believes this assertion to be true, such a claim is so alien to the institutional world inhabited by most managers that it becomes impossible for them to act on it.

Towards a New Business Ethics?

There are signs, however, that at least some business ethicists are beginning to grapple with these shortcomings. They are questioning the direction their field has taken and urging their colleagues to move beyond their current preoccupations. Although a number of their ideas have been simmering for years, the critics' discontent signals the beginning of what might be a more productive direction. Think of it as the *new business ethics*.

While differing in their specific approaches, advocates of the new business ethics can be identified by their acceptance of two fundamental principles. While they agree with their colleagues that ethics and interests can conflict, they take that observation as the starting point, not the ending point, of an ethicist's analytical task. In the fittingly final essay of *Business Ethics*, Joanne B. Ciulla provides a breath of fresh air when she writes, "the really creative part of business ethics is discovering ways to do what is morally right and socially responsible without ruining your career and company."

Second, the new perspective reflects an awareness and acceptance of the messy world of mixed motives. Accordingly, the key task for business ethicists is not to make abstract distinctions between altruism and self-interest but to participate with managers in designing new corporate structures, incentive systems, and decision-making processes that are more accommodating of the whole employee, recognizing his or her altruistic and self-interested motivations. Such structures, systems, and processes should not "be construed as the personal yielding to the corporate or the corporate giving in to the personal," suggests Fairfield University business ethicist Lisa Newton in her article "Virtue and Role: Reflections on the Social Nature of Morality." Instead, they should integrate the two roles. And the "name of that integration," writes Newton, "is *ethics.*"

Within this broad area of agreement, practitioners of the new business ethics pursue a variety of interesting and useful approaches. In *Ethics and Excellence*, for example, Robert Solomon goes back to Aristotle's conception of "virtue" to devise an ethics of practical value to managers. For Solomon, being virtuous does not "involve radical demands on our behavior." Indeed, such demands are "completely foreign to Aristotle's insistence on 'moderation.'" According to Solomon, Aristotle used the word "moral" simply to mean "practical."

In Aristotelian fashion, Solomon proceeds to establish a set of workable virtues for managers: for instance, "toughness." Neither callously self-interested nor purely altruistic, virtuous toughness involves both a "willingness to do what [is] necessary" and an "insistence on doing it as humanely as possible." Throughout his book, Solomon discusses toughness (and other morally complex managerial virtues such as courage, fairness, sensitivity, persistence, honesty, and gracefulness) in the context of real-world situations such as plant closings and contract negotiations.

In an article in *Business Ethics Quarterly* entitled "Shrewd Bargaining on the Moral Frontier: Toward a Theory of Morality in Practice," J. Gregory Dees and Peter C. Cramton develop another useful approach around the idea of "mutual trust." Dees and Cramton rightly emphasize that ethical actions don't take place in splendid isolation; in practice, for example, ethics seems to rest on reciprocity. "It is unfair to require an individual to take a significant risk or incur a significant cost out of respect for the interests or moral rights of others," they write, "if that individual has no reasonable grounds for trusting that the relevant others will . . . take the same risk or make the same sacrifice."

This is an important departure from the absolutist perspective of much contemporary business ethics, particularly from the notion that only when others are *not* making comparable sacrifices can we gain moral luster from doing so. Their "mutual trust" principle allows the authors to find a moral justification for deception in certain kinds of difficult business situations, even as they urge business ethicists to help managers "find strategies for bringing practice closer to moral ideals." And in what could well be a manifesto for the new business ethics, Dees and Cramton argue that "the most important work in business ethics" is not "the construction of arguments to appeal to moral idealists, but the creation of actionable strategies for the pragmatists."

In a similar vein, Thomas Donaldson of Georgetown and Thomas Dunfee of Wharton have emphasized the central role of "social contracts" in devising what Donaldson calls a "minimalist" as opposed to "perfectionist" view of the moral expectations that can be placed legitimately on companies. Social contracts are the implicit moral agreements that, having evolved over time, govern actual business practice. The task of the business ethicist, Dunfee writes in *Business Ethics Quarterly*, is first to identify and make explicit these diverse ethical norms and then to evaluate them against certain universal, but minimalist, moral principles.

Some existing social contracts would fail such a test—racial discrimination in real-estate sales, say. But many would not. For example, the fact that using insider information is considered more acceptable in real estate than in securities transactions does not necessarily mean that real estate agents somehow don't have their moral act together. Absent a fundamental moral principle against using nonpublic information, the ethics of doing so in any given case will depend on the "goals, beliefs, and attitudes" of the relevant business community.

This emphasis on social context finds an intriguing echo in Norman Bowie's work. In "New Directions in Corporate Social Responsibility," Bowie, in effect, turns around the ethical telescope. "If managers and stockholders have a duty to customers, suppliers, employees, and the local community," he argues, then it follows that these social actors also have duties to managers and stockholders. For example, environmentalists who want companies to produce more environmentally friendly products also must work to convince consumers to pay the added cost often necessary for manufacturing such products. In other words, business ethics is not a matter of concern for managers alone. It is everyone's responsibility.

Finally, in *Good Intentions Aside: A Manager's Guide to Resolving Ethical Problems*, Boston University School of Management Professor Laura L. Nash attempts to deliver on Joanne Ciulla's recommendation. Assuming that managers already have good intentions, the task for business ethics is to go beyond "sermonizing" in at least two ways. First, all managers face "hard issues whose solutions are not obvious," where the "reconciliation of profit motives and ethical imperatives is an uncertain and highly tricky matter. " It is precisely the need to find those solutions and reconciliations that business ethics should address.

Second, Nash contends that business ethics should concern itself with designing and developing organizations for managers who, like all human beings, display the "normal range of ethical instincts [and] have a desire to see that these instincts are not compromised at work." *Good Intentions Aside* thus zeros in on what Nash calls "the acute dilemma"—"situations where you do not know what is the right or wrong thing to do"—and the "acute rationalization"—"situations where you know what is right, but fail to do it" because of competitive or organizational pressures.

Nash develops a set of commonsense approaches to help managers deal with these two types of situations. She calls it the "covenantal ethic" defined as "a manager's primary obligation . . . to see that all parties in a commercial endeavor . . . prosper on the basis of created value." As an example, Nash cites The Stride Rite Corporation, the $500 million manufacturer of children's shoes. Unlike the products sold by many discount retailers, Stride Rite shoes are designed with a "long-standing, quasi-medical dedication to foot care." The company is also a shrewd marketer, using appealing shoe designs and aesthetically pleasing boutiques. The result: a socially responsible company that is more profitable than traditional "bottomline" manufacturers. Nash reports that former Stride Rite Chairman Arnold L. Hiatt "refused to be sucked into the ethics versus bottom line" conundrum. "'We're unashamedly out to make a profit,'" she quotes Hiatt, "'*and* we're very concerned about [children's] health. . . . We run the business on both concerns.'"

Moderation, pragmatism, minimalism: these are new words for business ethicists. In each of these new approaches, what is important is not so much the practical analyses offered (as the authors acknowledge, much remains to be worked out) but the commitment to converse with real managers in a language relevant to the world they inhabit and the problems they face. That is an understanding of business ethics worthy of managers' attention.

Unit Two
Individual Values and the Business Organization

At times, an individual who has become part of a larger organization feels that his personal values are in conflict with those of the organization. The types of ethical dilemmas that arise between an individual and his or her company include conflicts of interests and issues of honesty, fairness, and loyalty. One who negotiates contracts for an organization may find that those bidding on the contracts are willing to offer personally beneficial incidental benefits that would tend to cloud his or her judgment with respect to which vendor is best for the company. Elsewhere, an employee may find information indicating that his company is not addressing the correctable dangers of one of its products. The individual must confront such issues, pitting concerns about continuing employment and livelihood against moral standards and safety concerns.

These concerns represent the most common and difficult dilemmas businesspeople face. Studying them, reviewing alternatives, and carefully establishing values will prepare you for the dilemmas that we all must ultimately confront.

Section A
Employee Conflicts
of Interest

Do you know when your personal gain is interfering with your objectivity or your loyalty? Can you avoid or resolve conflicts of interest?

> The conscience that is dark
>   with shame for his own deeds or for another's,
>   may well, indeed, feel harshness in your words;
>
> Nevertheless, do not resort to lies,
>   let what you write reveal all you have seen,
>   and let those men who itch scratch where it hurts.
>
> Though when your words are taken in at first
>   they may taste bitter, but once well-digested
>   they will become a vital nutrient.

Dante, *Paradisio* XVII.124–132)

Case 2.1: Commodities, Conflicts, and Clintons

In October 1978, Hillary Rodham Clinton, wife of then-attorney general of Arkansas and gubernatorial candidate William Jefferson Clinton, opened a margin account with a $1,000 investment at Refco, a commodities brokerage firm. Commodities market regulators had disciplined Robert L. "Red" Bone, Mrs. Clinton's chief broker at Refco, for his practice of allocating trades among his customers only after learning whether the actual trades made were positive or negative.

Mrs. Clinton was given advice on her trades by James B. Blair, corporate counsel for Tyson Foods, Inc. Tyson Foods, Inc., is the nation's largest producer of frozen chicken patties and pieces for grocery market sales and fast food franchises. Like any poultry processor, Tyson is subject to strict federal and state regulation. Don Tyson, then-CEO of Tyson Foods, contributed to Mr. Clinton's campaigns for public office. Mr. Blair has stated that Mrs. Clinton alone decided the size of her commodities trades but that they discussed whether her trades should be short or long.

Between October 1978 and October 1979, Mrs. Clinton's $1,000 investment grew as follows:

Day 1—First Trade—profit of $5,300
October 1978—December 31, 1978— $49,069—profits
$22,548—losses
$26,541—net profit
January 1979—July 1979— $109,600—profits
$36,600—losses
$72,996—net profit

After Mr. Clinton was elected governor of Arkansas in November 1978, he appointed several Tyson executives to state government positions, and Tyson received favorable regulatory decisions on several actions pending in state agencies. Tyson awarded its outside legal work to the Rose Law Firm in Little Rock, where Mrs. Clinton was a partner. A Tyson spokesman has stated, "There is absolutely no evidence that Jim Blair's relationship with Bill or Hillary Clinton had any impact on our treatment."

Commented a commodities trader: "The idea that Mrs. Clinton could turn $1,000 into $100,000 trading a cross-section of markets such as cattle, soybeans, sugar, hogs, copper and lumber just isn't believable. To make 100 times your money is possible, but it's difficult to understand how a newcomer could do it. I don't care who is advising her. It just isn't very likely."

In 1992, Mr. Clinton was elected president of the United States. For more information on the role of Tyson at the federal government level following Mr. Clinton's election, see Case 2.6.

Discussion Questions

1. Did Mr. Blair have a conflict of interest in providing Mrs. Clinton with assistance on her trades?
2. Did Mrs. Clinton have a conflict of interest in accepting Mr. Blair's assistance on the trades?
3. Is there evidence of a quid pro quo?
4. Did Mr. Clinton have a conflict of interest?
5. Did Tyson's employment of the Rose Law Firm as outside counsel constitute a conflict of interest?
6. Evaluate all these decisions using the front-page-of-the-newspaper test.
7. What questions from Laura Nash's analysis provide insight into the ethical issues here?
8. Is the Tyson spokesperson's statement about there being no evidence of Mr. Blair's conduct having any influence relevant in determining whether a conflict of interest existed?

CASE 2.2: THE CITY COUNCIL EMPLOYEE

Bimini Outdoors is an outdoor advertising firm that is experiencing the crunch of environmental controls on the number and type of billboards the city of Wikieup will permit it to erect. The mayor of Wikieup has discussed the signs, which she calls "gigantic litter," with James Houston, Bimini's CEO. The mayor has told Houston that one of her goals for her four-year term is to eliminate completely billboard advertising.

Houston recognizes that Bimini has not diversified and that a ban on outdoor advertising in Wikieup would render Bimini defunct. Houston is a member of the city's public relations trade group, which often has debated the billboard issue at its luncheons. Some members see the billboards as eyesores and environmental disasters. Others offer figures to support their notion that the signs are safety hazards for drivers. Still another faction in the group calls the billboards effective and "environmentally sound" because they don't produce the waste that flyers or newspaper ads do.

A city council election will take place in three months. Three of the five seats on the council are open. Houston has noticed that Jake Gilbert, a candidate for one of the seats, is very vocal about the need to retain billboard advertising. Gilbert has referred to the billboards as a "clean, efficient, and effective" means of advertising.

Gilbert is a graphic artist and a well-respected member of the community who has served on the school board. He is a board officer for Wikieup's symphony and a key fund raiser for the city's Child Crisis Center.

One month before the election, Houston learns from Ralph Dewey, one of his managers, that Jake Gilbert was the victim of downsizing at his firm. Because of his loss of employment and resultant financial constraints, Gilbert is considering withdrawing from the race. Coincidentally, Bimini has just sent several graphic artists requests for proposals for upcoming projects. Houston tells Ralph Dewey, "Why don't we get an RFP [request for proposal] to Gilbert and tell him to freelance until he gets another job? I'd even be willing to take graphics in-house if Gilbert would take the job."

Dewey tells Houston that he is concerned about how Bimini would appear, having a potential city council member with a pro-billboard position as an employee. Houston responds, "We need a graphic artist. He's a graphic artist. Get the RFP to him and let him know we've got a job if he's interested."

Discussion Questions

1. Why would Dewey be worried, if Houston needs graphic art work?
2. If Gilbert were hired, how would the Wikieup newspaper report the story?
3. Would you feel differently if Houston helped Gilbert get a job with one of the members of his public relations group?
4. What if Gilbert submits a bid that is the best in terms of cost, proposal, and quality? Should he be hired?
5. Should Gilbert run for office on a platform that advocates keeping billboards if he accepts the position with the company?
6. Does Gilbert have a conflict of interest in accepting employment or work from Bimini?

CASE 2.3: CONFLICTS OF INTEREST IN REFERRALS

Tina Reese is the administrator of a large metropolitan hospital that is private and nonprofit. Tina has discovered that many of the physicians with privileges at the hospital are post-release care providers or are shareholders in the corporations that provide the hospital with the following services:

- radiology center,
- MRI facility (MRI = magnetic resonance imaging, a diagnostic tool),
- home health care and nurse services,
- medical equipment leasing and sales,
- physical rehabilitation centers,
- nursing homes, and
- radiation therapy facilities.

In most instances, the facilities have no outside investors, and annual returns for the physician shareholders are significant. Indeed, in many cases, the providers court physician investment and ownership in these supplemental service and diagnostic areas because of the referrals investing physicians will bring to the providers. Tina, researching the issue of physician ownership of referral facilities and programs, has discovered the following:

A Blue Cross study (1983) has shown that physician ownership leads to increased referrals for testing and post-release care and increased prices.

Tina has also found a 1991 study by Public Citizen Health Research Group that reveals that physicians in Florida who engaged in self-referral are twice as likely to order tests.

Further, some testing facilities owned by physicians with privileges at Tina's hospital are competing successfully with hospital-based services and testing centers. Because the physicians are referring patients to physician-owned facilities that are, as a bonus, easily accessible, the hospital's testing facilities are now being used less and less.

In researching the law as it relates to medical practice, Tina has found that physician-owned services and testing facilities and physician self-referrals have become controversial areas in the past few years, attracting the attention of both the public and regulators. The Department of Health and Human Services (HHS) promulgated regulations prohibiting self-referral if a doctor owns more than 40 percent of an x-ray or other diagnostic lab. HHS covers Medicare and Medicaid insurance programs. Some states currently have disclosure requirements for physicians who refer patients to their own facilities. Those disclosure statutes require physicians to reveal to patients any ownership interests they may have in referred facilities and services before the patient commits for the services. California, for instance, requires physicians to disclose any ownership they have in facilities or programs to which they refer their patients. Florida bans self-referral, and bills to curb self-referral are pending in two dozen state legislatures.

However, the American Medical Association, in its 1992 annual meeting, endorsed physician referrals of patients to labs and other facilities in which those physicians have a financial interest. Given the AMA position, Tina feels uncomfortable proposing a different policy for her hospital. Then again, Tina realizes she would want to know if her physician owned a referral facility.

Discussion Questions

1. Should Tina implement a disclosure requirement for the physicians at her hospital? Why or why not?
2. If you were a patient, would you want to have the ownership interest of your physician disclosed?
3. Is there a conflict of interest between physician ownership and self-serving referrals?
4. In what light would physician-ownership of facilities and services be depicted in a newspaper story?

CASE 2.4: BARBARA WALTERS AND HER ANDREW LLOYD WEBBER CONFLICT

Barbara Walters is a network correspondent for ABC News as well as a co-host of the ABC prime-time news show *20/20*. In December, 1996, Ms. Walters interviewed British composer Andrew Lloyd Webber and the interview aired that same month as a segment on *20/20*.

Two months after the interview aired, a report in the *New York Post* revealed that Ms. Walters had invested $100,000 in Webber's Broadway production of his musical, *Sunset Boulevard*. ABC News responded that had it known of the investment, it would have disclosed it before the interview aired. ABC does have a policy on conflicts that permits correspondents to cover "businesses in which they have a minority interest."

Webber's *Sunset* cost $10 million to produce and investors received back 85% of their initial investment. Ms. Walters' interest in *Sunset* was one percent.

Ms. Walters acknowledged a mistake, "In retrospect, I should have discussed it. I didn't even think about it."[1]

Discussion Questions

1. What interests are in conflict on the part of Ms. Walters?
2. When should she have disclosed her investment? When it was made, or before she did the interview or before the show aired?
3. In a recent *20/20* show, Ms. Walters, in announcing a segment on the *Jerry Springer* show said that her day-time program, *The View*, is seen opposite *Jerry Springer* and that she had no part in the idea for or production of the *20/20* segment. Why did Ms. Walters make this disclosure?

---

1. Peter Johnson, "Walters Missed Her Cue to Disclose 'Sunset' Backing," *USA Today*, Feb. 20, 1997, 3D.

CASE 2.5: THE LOAN OFFICER AND THE DEBTORS

Ben Garrison is a senior loan officer with First National Federal Bank, the second-largest financial institution in Wyoming. Ben, who has been with First National Federal for ten years, handles loan applications from all over the state.

Following the savings and loan debacle of the late 1980s, First National Federal implemented many institutional changes. Some of the changes were operational; others involved the bank's lending policy. A change that Ben found frustrating was an increasing emphasis on ethics. Ben complained to one of his loan officers, "I don't get this ethics stuff. If it's legal, I'm ethical." One of the loan officers, Shelby Grant, a recent graduate of the University of Wyoming School of Business, replied, "Well, sometimes doing what's ethical helps you avoid legal problems." Ben replied, "Sometimes doing what's ethical just costs you more money!"

Later that morning, following their discussion, Ben appeared in Shelby's office with a loan application from Doug Whitton, a rancher in the northwestern part of the state. He told Shelby that they needed to take a trip to evaluate the proposed collateral for the loan. An on-site evaluation of collateral is a required procedure for loan processing at First National Federal. Ben added, "Whitton's paying our way up there for the evaluation." Shelby asked, "Shouldn't the bank pay our way, since we may not make the loan and we wouldn't want to be obligated to Whitton?" Ben responded, "Now why in the hell would I want to pay our way up there and increase my costs when he's offering to pay?" Shelby was uncertain about the propriety of the proposal.

Ben added that First National Federal's annual fundraiser picnic was coming up and that they were planning to have the usual prize drawing. "So," he told Shelby, "just get on the phone to all the customers whose loans you handle and see what prizes they're willing to donate for this year's drawings." Shelby asked, "Isn't it wrong for us to pressure our customers into donating prizes?" Ben replied angrily, "These prizes are not for us! The money is not for us! This is charity! What could be unethical about that?"

Shelby went home that evening to prepare for the trip to the ranch. She hadn't called any of her customers for donations, and she didn't want to go on the trip unless the bank paid. She was also $20,000 in debt from school, and it had taken her four months after graduation to find this job. "I guess this is just the way business is done," she concluded.

Discussion Questions

1. Is Shelby correct? Are both these issues "just the way business is done"?
2. Is the appearance of impropriety an important ethical constraint?
3. What problems arise in having the potential borrower pay for the collateral evaluation trip?
4. What problems arise in soliciting donations from loan customers?
5. How would it be different if a merchant offered to donate items without being asked?
6. If you were Shelby, would you pursue the donations issue or just follow the process the bank has always used?

Section B
Inappropriate Gifts

Taking gifts from vendors or compensation from outside interests can cloud your perspective, no matter how objective you profess to be. As you review these cases, think of how a code of ethics might help employees who are presented with inappropriate gifts and the resulting conflicts of interest.

Case 2.6: The Secretary of Agriculture, Chicken Processors, and Football Skybox Seats

President Bill Clinton appointed Mike Espy as Secretary of Agriculture in 1993. Mr. Espy accepted from Tyson Foods, Inc., the world's largest producer of fresh and processed poultry products, a ride on a Tyson corporate jet, free lodging at a lakeside cabin owned by Tyson, and seats in Tyson's skybox at a Dallas Cowboys game. Mr. Espy went to the 1994 Super Bowl at government expense, saying he made the trip because Smokey the Bear was being honored in public service announcements at the game. Additionally, Mr. Espy's girlfriend received a $1,200 college scholarship from Tyson Foods. At the time, Tyson and other regulators were fighting proposed Department of Agriculture guidelines (ultimately not implemented for poultry processors and withdrawn for other meat processors) that would have imposed a "zero tolerance" on the presence of fecal matter during processing.

Mr. Espy reimbursed Tyson for the cost of the airfare, the Cowboys tickets, and the cabin rental. As a former member of Congress, Mr. Espy felt the benefits he had accepted were so small in terms of monetary value that his accepting them was not an issue. Don Tyson, the CEO of Tyson Foods, contributed $25,000 to the Clinton presidential campaign.

Public reaction to Mr. Espy's relationship with Tyson resulted in his resignation as Secretary of Agriculture as of December 31, 1994. Donald Smaltz was appointed as a special prosecutor to investigate the legality of Mr. Epsy's acceptance of the things Tyson had offered and whether he had granted any favors to Tyson in exchange. The prosecutor examined the following issues:

Influence and an Aide, 1990s
Ronald Blackley, who became Mr. Espy's chief of staff at the Agriculture Department, has acknowledged that while a congressional aide to Mr. Espy, he was also on the payroll of farmers seeking support payments from the government. Mr. Blackley has said he closed his consulting business before joining the Agriculture Department. The department's inspector general is examining these actions.

Poultry Inspections, March 1993
Mr. Blackley ordered aides to stop work on proposals for tougher standards for poultry inspections, the aides have said.

Arkansas Trip, May 1993
Tyson Foods provided lodging at its management center in Russellville, Arkansas, to Mr. Espy and a friend, Pat Dempsey, while Mr. Espy was in the state to speak before the Arkansas Poultry Federation. A Tyson plane flew them back to Washington on May 16. Mr. Espy reimbursed the company the price of a first-class ticket.

Chicago Basketball Game, June 1993
The chief executive of Quaker Oats, William D. Smithburg, gave Mr. Espy a ticket to a June 18, 1993 Chicago Bulls playoff game after the Chicago-based company received a request from the secretary of agriculture's office.

Tyson Scholarship, Fall 1993
A senior White House official said that a Tyson company foundation awarded Ms. Dempsey, Mr. Espy's girlfriend, a $1,200 scholarship in fall 1993 to allow her to continue her education.

Henry Espy, Fall 1993
Henry Espy, brother of Mike Espy, ran unsuccessfully to fill his brother's congressional seat. Issues of campaign contributions from agribusinesses arose.

Birthday Gifts, November 1993
Richard Douglas, a longtime friend of Mr. Espy who is also the chief lobbyist for Sun-Diamond Growers of California, an almond and raisin cooperative based in California, and others held a lavish birthday party for Mr. Espy. The inspector general of the Department of Agriculture investigated whether any of the 150 employees who attended were pressed for contributions to cover the party's cost.

Dallas Football Game, January 1994
Mr. Espy and Ms. Dempsey sat in the Tyson company skybox when the Dallas Cowboys met the New York Giants in a playoff game. Later, a car paid for by the company took them shopping, then to the airport for the return trip to Washington. Mr. Espy said he reimbursed Tyson $60 for his ticket. Total cost of the trip was $2,271.

As a result of the special prosecutor's investigation, the following charges, verdicts and pleas occurred:

Party	Charge	Result
Sun-Diamond	Charged with making illegal gifts to Mr. Espy and illegal campaign contributions to Henry Espy ($4,000)	Convicted; fine of $1.5 million
Richard Douglas (lobbyist for Sun-Diamond Growers of California)	Charged with making illegal gifts (luggage plus a trip to the U.S. Open tennis tournament that cost $4,590)	Convicted
	Charged with furnishing Mr. Espy's girlfriend with a $3,100 plane ticket so that she could accompany him to Greece	Jury deadlocked
James Lake (Washington lobbyist for Sun-Diamond)	Wire fraud, violations of Federal Election Campaign Act (a $4,000 gift to Henry Espy)	Convicted
Sun-Diamond Growers	Illegal gratuities	Convicted
Crop Growers Corp.	Concealment of corporate campaign contributions to Henry Espy ($46,000)	Convicted
American Family Life Assurance Co.	Illegal corporate conduit for campaign contributions to Henry Espy	Civil penalty of $80,000
John Hemmingson (Chairman of Crop Growers Corporation)	Fraud/money laundering; illegal campaign contributions to Henry Espy	Convicted
Tyson Food, Inc.	Charged with making illegal gifts ($12,000 in tickets, travel, and lodging)	Guilty plea; $4 million in fines plus costs of the investigation ($2 million)
Jack Williams (lobbyist for Tyson Foods)	Four-count indictment for bribery and illegal gifts involving Mr. Espy; two-counts for making false statements to regulators	Conviction; reversed on appeal; new trial ordered
Don Tyson (CEO of Tyson Foods)		Granted immunity for everything except perjury in exchange for his testimony
Henry Espy (Mike Espy's brother)	Defrauding election authorities; false statements in loan applications	Charges dismissed for lack of evidence
Ron Blackley (Mike Espy's chief of staff at Agriculture)	Lying to government authorities	Convicted/ sentenced to 27 months in prison
Mike Espy	39-count indictment; accepting and soliciting gifts and favors from agribusinesses; witness tampering; procuring illegal campaign contributions	4 counts dismissed; pleaded innocent; trial pending

Discussion Questions

1. Is the value of these items an issue in determining whether Mr. Espy acted ethically? In a statement released by Tyson Foods upon its indictment was the following sentence, "The company deplores the independent counsel's apparent view that acts of hospitality—consisting of a couple of meals and a football game—can rise to the level of criminal conduct." Is this a sound view for government relations?

2. Does Mr. Espy's reimbursement change the ethical issues?

3. What tests could Mr. Espy have used prior to accepting these items that would have required him to refuse them on ethical grounds?

4. Did Mr. Espy create a conflict of interest?

5. Evaluate each of the matters the special prosecutor investigated. Are there ethical breaches regardless of any illegality?

6. Mr. Smaltz spent $9 million on his investigation. Is this amount justified for the size of the gifts? Mr. Smaltz stated when Tyson Foods entered its guilty plea, "Such conduct must continue to invite outrage, never passivity, from those who are regulated, the public, and our lawmakers." Is Mr. Smaltz correct?

CASE 2.7: THE PURCHASING AGENTS' WONDER WORLD TRIP

Paul Backman is the head of the purchasing department for LA East, one of the so-called "baby bells" or regional phone companies that came into existence in 1984 after the divestiture of AT&T. Backman's department is responsible for purchasing everything from wire for equipment lines to napkins for the headquarter's cafeteria.

S.C. Rydman, an electronics firm and a major LA East supplier, is a cosponsor of an exhibit at Wonder World in Florida. LA East, which has used Rydman as its major supplier since 1984, makes contract decisions on the basis of bids that Rydman and others submit in response to its requests for proposals. Paul Backman has final say on the electronics contracts because of the significant amounts of money involved.

S.C. Rydman's vice president and chief financial officer, Gunther Fromme, visited Backman in his office on April 3, 1998. Rydman had no bids pending and had been awarded a six-month contract by LA East on March 1, 1998. Fromme explained to Backman, "Look, I'm just here for goodwill. But Rydman does have a block of rooms with room service at one of the hotels in Wonder World. If you like, you and your staff could go down there and use them. We also get free passes to the park. You could go to the park and see the good work we've done on our exhibit there. You and your families would just have to pay airfare. If you're interested, just let me know when and how many."

Paul Backman relayed the offer at the next staff meeting, where it was warmly received by everyone except Sheila Tate, who asked, "Should we accept free rooms and passes from a supplier?" Backman responded, "I could understand your concern if Rydman had a bid pending, but there won't be anything for Rydman to even bid on for at least three months. If we go now, it's just a friend's favor."

All the purchasing agents except Sheila Tate signed up for the trip. Backman and the agents and their families planned a five-day excursion to Wonder World. As her coworkers discussed their plans, Sheila wondered whether someone should be told about the trip.

Discussion Questions

1. Should Sheila Tate talk with someone outside her department about the planned trip?
2. Is it enough for Sheila simply to forego the trip?
3. Suppose that after the trip, the CEO of LA East learns of it and takes disciplinary action. Should Sheila be disciplined for not reporting the others' conduct?
4. If found to violate company policy, what sanctions would best address the ethical breach? Suspension without pay? Firing? Reimbursement of expenses? Would firing the agents be too harsh a sanction?

Section C
Security of
Company Records

Information is a powerful business tool and often a competitor's edge. Inside information released too early to the press can harm both a company and its personnel. Employees must recognize the value and ownership of company information.

Case 2.8: The Sale of Sand to the Saudis

Joe Raymond's position as sales manager for Granite Rock and Sand was in jeopardy. His unit had been low performer in terms of sales for the last seven quarters. Joe's supervisor, vice president Tom Haws, told Joe that he had through the next quarter to pull his unit out of last place. Haws also told Joe that Joe would have to be replaced if the improvement did not occur.

Joe and his wife had just purchased their first home. With their mortgage payments totaling $1,100 per month, the loss of Joe's salary would mean the loss of their home.

Following Tom's warning, Joe began interviewing candidates for a vacant sales position in his unit. Joe had conducted three interviews when the final candidate, Jessica Morris, arrived. During the interview with Morris, Joe learned that she was the victim of a layoff by a competitor, Silt, Sand and Such. Joe was not terribly impressed with Morris, but just before she left, she opened her briefcase and offered Joe a sheet of paper bearing the name of an official in the Saudi Arabian government. Morris explained:

> When I was with Silt, Sand and Such, we started a program for finding innovative markets for our products. You know, we wanted to tap markets no one had ever thought of. After a lot of research, we discovered that Saudi desalinization plants need a particular type of sand they don't have over there, but we have here. We're the only firm that knows about this. If you hire me, I can see the sale through for Granite.

Morris added:

> Look, I need this job. You need your sales up. Think about it and call me.

After Morris left, Joe sat in his office and felt his problems were solved. Or were they?

Discussion Questions

1. If you were Joe, would you hire Morris?
2. Would anyone be harmed if you hired Morris?
3. What long-term problems could you foresee if Morris were hired?
4. Would using the information from Morris be illegal? Would Morris be committing a crime?
5. Would you be able to trust Morris if you hired her?

CASE 2.9: THE COMPLIANCE OFFICER WHO STRAYED

Marisa Baridis, 29, was the legal compliance officer at Morgan Stanley, Dean Witter, Discover and Company. Ms. Baridis was in charge of what is commonly referred to as the "Chinese wall" in brokerage houses. Her job was to be certain that sensitive information did not cross from the side of the house putting together deals to that side of the house that buys stock. Her responsibilities included making certain that confidential information about Morgan Stanley clients did not leak to the brokerage side of the business so that Morgan Stanley brokers would not use inside information for trading.

Ms. Baridis met Jeffrey Streich, 31, in the summer of 1997. Mr. Streich was a broker who specialized in speculative stocks. Over a six-month period, Ms. Baridis allegedly provided Mr. Streich with information in exchange for $2,500 in cash for each tip. However, late in October, 1997, Mr. Streich and Ms. Baridis would have their last meeting because Mr. Streich went to their meeting wearing a hidden recorder and there was a camera across the street that videotaped them both sitting in the window of a restaurant. The tape shows Mr. Streich handing Ms. Baridis $2,500 in one-hundred dollar bills.

Ms. Baridis, who was charged with trading on inside information to make a profit, was fired from her $70,000 a year job. Her father posted her $250,000 bail.

Ms. Baridis entered a guilty plea in exchange for a lighter sentence contingent upon her cooperation. A college friend of Ms. Baridis also entered a guilty plea in federal court to charges of insider trading. Mr. Mitchell Sher, 32, admitted that he made cash payments to Ms. Baridis in exchange for her furnishing confidential information about pending events such as mergers for Morgan Stanley clients.

Mr. Sher admitted that he used information provided to him by Ms. Baridis to trade in shares of Georgia-Pacific Corp., Burlington Resources and two other companies. Unlike the other 10 individuals charged in the case, Mr. Sher was not a broker but rather a vice president for a book distributor and also admitted in his plea that Ms. Baridis had fed him confidential information in exchange for cash when she worked for Smith Barney earlier in her career.

Ms. Baridis had an upscale Manhattan apartment with rent of $2,400 per month. The extra money from the sale of information afforded her a comfortable New York lifestyle. Her assets have been frozen and prosecutors are seeking $100,000 in a seizure of those assets.

Discussion Questions

1. What is troublesome about insiders using information in advance of public disclosure to make money?
2. Why do regulators police such exchanges of information?
3. What does this case say about compliance programs and officers?

CASE 2.10: ESPIONAGE AND JOB-HOPPING

Employees throughout a company have access to proprietary information, including customer lists, management techniques, and future plans.

What happens when those employees want to leave their current employer and go to work for a competitor? Or what happens when employees use or sell proprietary information?

Consider the following examples:

a. Steven L. Davis, a lead process control engineer with Wright Industries, Inc., was part of a team working on the development and fabrication of equipment for Gillette Co's secret new shaving system. The new Gillette shaving system, predicted to be revolutionary, had been kept a very closely held secret. Wright Industries had been hired by Gillette. Mr. Davis was indicted by a federal grand jury on ten counts of wire fraud and theft of trade secrets. The indictment alleged Mr. Davis sent five faxes and electronic mail messages to Gillette's competitors with language intended to solicit interest in the purchase of Gillette's new technology. The messages included Mr. Davis's complaint that he had been passed over for a promotion.

One of the competitors that received the fax alerted Gillette. Gillette contacted federal authorities and after an undercover investigation, Mr. Davis was charged. Mr. Davis then sent follow-up messages to the companies he had originally contacted complaining that someone "had betrayed him."

Discussion Questions

1. Is Mr. Davis's situation different because he did not work directly for Gillette?
2. If you had been one of the competitors Mr. Davis allegedly contacted, would you have notified Gillette?
3. Is there any irony in Mr. Davis's comment about betrayal?

b. J. Ignacio Lopez left his position at General Motors (GM) in 1993 just as he was about to be named head of GM's North American Operations. Mr. Lopez left to work in Germany as Volkswagen's production chief. In litigation that is still pending, GM has alleged that Mr. Lopez took with him proprietary information about GM including fairly complete information about GM's supply chain management system and trade secrets.

Discussion Questions

1. Will an executive always have access to trade secrets?
2. Is it impossible for an executive to go to work for a competitor?
3. What are the pros and cons of covenants in employee contracts that prohibit them (for a period of time) from working for a competitor? Some examples of recently enforced covenants:

   - Daniel O'Neill, the former head of Campbell Soup Co.'s soup division, could go to work for H.J. Heinz Co., but not in its soup division until August 1998 (a one-year ban).
   - Kevin R. Donohue, a former executive vice president with Kodak, was prohibited from working for a competitor (Fuji had hired him and Kodak sued for breach of contact) for one year.
   - William Redmond, a soft-drink marketing executive with PepsiCo, was prohibited from going to work for the beverage division of Quaker Oats for six months.

4. Are these employees capable of working for a competitor without divulging information? Consider the perspective of one executive, "It's difficult to have a competitive advantage over other companies unless there's something that you can call sacred to your company."

Section D
Personal Honesty

Is your resume accurate, or does it cross the line of demarcation in exaggeration? How far would you go to win a prestigious office in a college club? Is it acceptable to "puff" when you are a reference? Personal standards of behavior often come into play as we confront dilemmas of qualifications and landing that important job or title.

Case 2.11: The Rigged Election

The Finance Club at Harvard University is a prestigious organization for Harvard MBA students. The student members have the opportunity to interact with public officials like Senator William Proxmire and business executives such as Bruce Wasserstein. The Finance Club also serves as a network for job hunting.

Each spring, the club holds elections for its officers, including two co-presidents. In the spring of 1992, after initial balloting, there was a tie between two teams of two co-presidents. Murry Gunty was one member of one of the teams and busily recruited students to vote in a run-off election. Two of the students he recruited voted under names of absentee members of the Finance Club. The new votes gave Mr. Gunty his victory. However, two of the votes were from students who were not members of the club, but used someone else's name to vote.

After an anonymous tip, the elections were set aside and the runners-up installed as co-presidents. Mr. Gunty was required to write a paper on ethics.

Discussion Questions

1. In the words of the school newspaper publisher, "Why would anyone do this? It's just a club."
2. Was anyone really hurt by the conduct?
3. Would you have reported the conduct anonymously or disclosed it publicly?
4. What are the long-term implications for Mr. Gunty?

CASE 2.12: PUFFING IN THE RESUME

The resume is a door opener for a job seeker. What's on them can get you in the door or cause the door to be slammed in your face. With that type of pressure, it is not surprising to learn that one 1997 study by a group of executive search firms showed that 25 percent of all resumes contain misstatements. A 1988 Equifax study (Equifax is a credit-reporting agency often used by employers for background checks) also found the following:

Eleven percent of all applicants lied about their reasons for leaving a previous job;

Four percent fudged job titles on their resumes;

Three percent listed fake employers;

Three percent fabricated jobs; and

Three percent pretended to have a college degree.

Ed Andler, an expert in credential verification, says that one-third of all resumes contain some level of "creative writing." Mr. Andler notes that assembly-line workers don't mention misdemeanor convictions and middle-managers embellish their educational background. One reference-checking firm looked into the background of an applicant for security guard and found he was wanted for manslaughter in another state.

Vericon Resources, Inc., a background check firm, has found that two percent of the applicants they investigate are hiding a criminal past. Vericon also notes, however, that potential employers can easily discover whether job candidates are lying about previous employment by requesting W-2s from previous employers.

In one resume "puffing" case, according to Michael Oliver, a former executive recruiter who is presently director of staffing for Dial Corporation, a strong candidate for a senior marketing management position said he had an MBA from Harvard and four years' experience at a previous company, where he had been a vice president of marketing. Actually, Harvard had never heard of him, he had worked for the firm for only two years, and he had been a senior product manager, not a vice president.

In a wrongful firing case brought against Honeywell by a former employee, a federal court permitted Honeywell to use the defense that the employee had lied on her resume (over eight years before the litigation) by stating that she had a college degree when she had taken only six courses (two as audits) and that she had managed property during a time when she owned no property and was unemployed. Her discharge had nothing to do with the puffing on her resume, but the court ruled that "an employer may defend a wrongful discharge claim on the basis of facts unknown at the time of discharge." A subsequent court decision has held that a previously unknown fact is not a defense to discrimination, but it can always be used as grounds for termination.

In 1997, Dianna Green, a senior vice president at Duquesne Light, left her position at that utility. The memo from the CEO described her departure as one that would allow Ms. Green to pursue "other career interests she has had for many years." While the memo expressed sadness at her departure, Ms. Green had been fired for lying on her resume by stating that she had a master's degree in business administration when, in fact, she had no master's degree.[2]

Ms. Green had worked her way up through the company and had been responsible for handling the human resources issues in Duquesne's nine years of downsizing. At the time of her termination, she was a director at Pennsylvania's largest bank and known widely for her community service.

On the day following her termination, Ms. Green was found dead of a self-inflicted gunshot wound.[3]

Discussion Questions

1. Would it be wrong to engage in resume puffing and then disclose the actual facts in an interview?
2. Suppose that you had earned but, due to a hold on your academic record because of unpaid debts, had never been formally awarded a college degree. Would you state on your resume that you had a college degree?
3. Suppose that, in an otherwise good career track, you were laid off because of an economic downturn and remained unemployed for thirteen months. Would you attempt to conceal the thirteen-month lapse in your resume?
4. Won't complete candor prevent you from ever getting a job?
5. Is puffing a short-term solution in a tight job market?
6. Was the tragedy of Ms. Green avoidable? Was Duquesne Light justified in terminating her?
7. What dangers arise if applicants are not honest?

CASE 2.13: THE GLOWING RECOMMENDATION

Jake Spacek is a credit manager for a medium-sized electrical supply business. He has a full staff of analysts, collectors, and clerical employees who report to him. One of Jake's analysts, Bob Guthrie, has just come to Jake and said, "I've got a great job offer from Edison Electric Supply in Cleveland. But it's contingent on a background check and a good reference from you, Jake."

Jake would classify Bob as an average and conscientious employee who reports to work on time and puts in a full day. Over the years, however, Jake has caught a number of errors Bob has made. Though at times he has barely managed to save the firm from great expense and embarrassment, Jake has not objected to the errors because Bob is a pleasant fellow and a good friend. Jake has thought often of replacing Bob but has been hesitant because of their friendship.

---

2. The information was revealed after Ms. Green was deposed in a suit by a former subordinate for termination. Because Ms. Green hesitated in giving a year for her degree, the plaintiff's lawyer checked and found no degree and notified Duquesne officials. Duquesne officials then negotiated a severance package.

3. It should be noted that Ms. Green was suffering from diabetes to such an extent that she could no longer see well enough to drive. Also, during the year before her termination, her mother had died of a stroke and her youngest brother also had died. Carol Hymowitz and Raju Narisetti. "A Promising Career Comes to a Tragic End, And a City Asks Why." *Wall Street Journal*, 9 May 1997, A1, A8.

If Jake gives him a good recommendation, Bob will get the job and Jake can bring in a new hire to ease his own workload.

Discussion Questions

1. If you were Jake, what kind of recommendation would you give?
2. Should Jake have done something about Bob's work prior to being placed in this dilemma?
3. Has Jake been more loyal to his friend than he was to his employer?
4. Is this type of recommendation commonly given to get rid of employees?
5. Should friendship have a higher value than honesty?

CASE 2.14: THE UNOFFICIAL GOVERNMENT CONTRACT AND THE ACCOUNT SALE

You are a credit manager for a large, interstate equipment supplier. You have had difficulties collecting on an account worth approximately $50,000. The customer/ debtor no longer has a line of credit with your firm, and you have simply been trying to collect the balance due. Currently, you are negotiating the sale of the account. Given the account's history and the customer's assets and existing debt structure, sale of the account should bring about $10,000. Your cousin's firm, in which you are a stockholder, is interested in buying the account. You have disclosed your relationship to the buyer to your company, which would be happy just to get the cash and be rid of the account. Just before the sale takes place, you learn, unofficially, that the customer/debtor has won a substantial government contract that will run for five years.

Discussion Questions

1. Will you go through with the sale? (Assume no binding contract as yet.)
2. Will you make additional disclosures?
3. Should you have had someone else handle the sale from the outset?

CASE 2.15: RADAR DETECTORS AND THE LAW

Just recently the state of Connecticut legalized the use of radar detectors, reversing a previous statute that permitted state police to fine motorists for using the devices. Representative Alex Knopp, one of the legislators who objected to the legalization of the devices, stated, "The bottom line is that speeding kills and that radar detectors will cause more speeding in the state of Connecticut." In 1993, Congress passed a law banning the use of radar detectors by tractor-trailer drivers. Senator Frank R. Lautenberg of New Jersey stated, "It's unacceptable to have devices designed to thwart the law. I want to get rid of these things."

Discussion Questions

1. Are radar detectors a means of breaking the law and avoiding getting caught?
2. Is it morally wrong to speed?
3. Is it morally wrong to use a radar detector?
4. Is it possible that speeding laws constitute positive law but do not reflect any ethical or moral standard?
5. New technology has allowed the development of photo radar along with license plate shields so that the automatic cameras cannot photograph the offending driver's license plate. Do these license plate covers facilitate breaking the law?

CASE 2.16: THE ETHICS OF LOOKING BUSY

"Some bosses just like you to be there, whether you need to be there or not. So I've come up with ways to look like a workaholic," Jane Nugent said. "I can be off shopping or on a two-hour lunch, and everyone back at the office thinks I'm still there," she noted, smiling. Jane then listed her strategies:

- Before leaving, place a fresh, steaming cup of coffee on your desk; people will assume you'll be right back;
- Always leave the lights on and the computer running;[4]
- Hang around at the office until the last supervisor leaves—then go;
- Arrive early and let them see you, your car, and your office up and running, and then leave for the morning;
- Go in on Saturday and stay for a few hours—you don't need do work, just make sure someone sees you;
- If you leave early, call back in and ask someone to look something up in your office—they'll assume you're at an out-of-office meeting;
- If you must make personal calls, always have a pad in front of you, write on it frequently and speak firmly (the rest of the office will think you're negotiating); and
- Leave personal belongings (coat, jacket) in your office to give the impression that you're returning.[5]

Discussion Questions

1. Evaluate Jane's strategies from an ethical perspective.
2. Should Jane consider flexible hours?

---

4. Note: Some offices have motion-detector energy savers. When activity in the office ceases, the lights go off. Therefore, Jane notes, instruct your secretary to go into your office periodically and jump around while you're gone.

5. Jane notes that she has dumped the contents of her purse into a paper bag so that she can leave her purse behind while she disappears for a few hours.

3. Does Jane have enough to keep her busy at her job? Is it dishonest for her to continue her facade?
4. How should Jane's secretary respond to being asked to go in and jump around in Jane's office so that Jane can be gone?
5. Are Jane's actions just a response to management's basis of evaluation that time spent in the office equals performance?

CASE 2.17: THE EMPLOYMENT APPLICATION LIE THAT HAUNTS THE APPLICANT

Susan Weissman was hired by Crawford and worked for the company for approximately 18 months. Weissman had several ongoing disputes with her supervisor including one between Weissman, her supervisor and the Department of Labor over the number of breaks she was entitled to take. Weissman wanted, lunch, restroom, drink and rest breaks with the rest breaks not involving any of the other activities. With the break issue yet to be resolved, Weissman requested a personal leave day. Weissman's supervisor denied her request because Weissman had failed to follow Crawford's policy of asking for personal leave days at least two weeks in advance.

Weissman did not show up for work anyway on the day she had requested and she was terminated for insubordination. Weissman then filed suit against Crawford for breach of contract, promissory estoppel, outrageous conduct, and wrongful discharge. During the course of discovery in the case, Crawford discovered that Weissman had omitted one place of employment from her application for employment at Crawford. Weissman had failed to list a former employer who had also terminated her and against whom she had filed suit. Weissman had signed the application to Crawford below the following declaration:

> The information I am presenting in this application is true and correct to the best of my knowledge, and I understand that any falsification or misrepresentation herein could result in my discharge and in the event I am hired by Crawford & Company.

Discussion Questions

1. Should Weissman be terminated?
2. Was her warning adequate?
3. Was her conduct ethical?

CASE 2.18: TRAVEL EXPENSES: A CHANCE FOR EXTRA INCOME

The *New York Times Magazine* (Sunday, March 8, 1998, p. 100), profiled the problems with employees' submissions for travel and entertainment expenses reimbursement. American Express reports that employees spend $156 billion annually on travel and entertainment related to business. Internal auditors at companies listed types of expenses for which employees have sought reimbursement: hairdresser, traffic tickets and kennel fees.

While the IRS has raised the amount allowable for undocumented expenses to $75, most companies will keep their limit for employees at $25. One company auditor commented that all taxi cab rides now cost $24.97 and if the company went with the IRS limit, the cab fares would climb to $74.65.

Some of the horror stories submitted by auditors on travel and entertainment expenses submitted by employees:

> One employee submitted a bill for $12 for a tin of cookies. When questioned, he could not explain how it had been used but asked for reimbursement anyway because all he would have to do is "make up" a couple of taxi rides to get it back anyway;

> $225 for three hockey tickets except that the names on the tickets were the employee's family members;

> $625 for wallpapering. The employee had included it with her other travel expenses and even had the wallpaper receipt written in a different language in order to throw off any questions; and

> $275 sports jacket submitted as a restaurant bill. The travel office called the number listed on the receipt and asked if food was sold there. The response was, "No, we're a men's clothing store."

Discussion Questions

1. The auditors noted that employees who are confronted often respond with similar justifications:

   "The company owes it to me."
   "It doesn't really hurt anyone."
   "Everybody does this."

   Are these justifications or rationalizations?
2. Why do employees risk questionable expenses?
3. Who is harmed by dishonest expense submissions?

Case 2.19: Do Cheaters Prosper?

In a new book entitled, *Cheaters Always Prosper: 50 Ways to Beat the System Without Being Caught*, James Brazil, (a pen name) a college student from the University of California at Santa Barbara has provided 50 ways to obtain a "free lunch." One suggestion is to place shards of glass in your dessert at a fancy restaurant and then "raise hell." The manager or owner will then come running with certificates for free meals and probably waive your bill.

Another suggestion is, rather than spend $400 on new tires for your car, rent a car for a day for $35 and switch the rental car tires with your tires. So long as your car tires are not bald, the rental car company employees will not notice, and you will have your new tires for a mere $35.

Discussion Questions

1. Are these suggestions ethical?
2. Was publishing the book with the suggestions ethical?
3. Do any of these suggestions cost anyone any money?

Unit Three
Individual Rights and the Business Organization

"Good intentions are not a substitute for good actions."

Marianne Jennings

In this section, the focus moves from how the individual treats the organization to how the organization treats the individual. How much privacy should employees have? What pre-employment tests and screening are appropriate? What obligations does an employer have with respect to the workplace atmosphere? Should employees have job security? The conflicts between employers and their employees' rights take many forms.

Section A
Corporate
Due Process

Should fairness be a criterion in employer decisions? Must employers provide a forum for employee grievances?

Case 3.1: Ann Hopkins, Price Waterhouse, and the Partnership

Ann Hopkins was a senior manager in the Price Waterhouse Office of Government Services in Washington, D.C. She began her work there in 1977 and by 1982 had been proposed as a candidate for partnership along with eighty-eight other Price Waterhouse employees.

At that time, Price Waterhouse was a nationwide professional accounting partnership. A senior manager became a candidate for partnership when the partners in her office submitted her name for partnership status.

In 1982, Price Waterhouse had 662 partners, 7 of whom were women. Hopkins was responsible for bringing to Price Waterhouse a two-year, $25 million contract with the Department of State.

All of the firm's partners were invited to submit written comments regarding each candidate on either "long" or "short" evaluation forms. Partners chose a form according to their exposure to the candidate. All partners were invited to submit comments, but not every partner did so. Of the thirty-two partners who submitted comments on Hopkins, one stated that "none of the other partnership candidates at Price Waterhouse that year [has] a comparable record in terms of successfully procuring major contracts for the partnership."

After reviewing the comments, the firm's Admissions Committee made recommendations about the partnership candidates to the Price Waterhouse Policy Board. The recommendations consisted of accepting the candidate, denying the promotion, or putting the application on hold. The Policy Board then decided whether to submit the candidate to a vote, reject the candidate, or hold the candidacy.

There were no limits on the number of persons to whom partnership could be awarded and no guidelines for evaluating positive and negative comments about candidates.

Of the eighty-eight candidates for partnership in 1982, Hopkins was the only woman. Thirteen of the thirty-two partners who submitted comments on Hopkins supported her; three recommended putting her "on hold"; eight said they did not have enough information; and eight recommended denial.

The partners in Hopkins' office praised her character as well as her accomplishments, describing her in their joint statement as "an outstanding professional" who had a "deft touch," a "strong character, independence and integrity." Clients appear to have agreed with these assessments. One official from the State Department described her as "extremely competent, intelligent," "strong and forthright, very productive, energetic and creative." Another high-ranking official praised Hopkins' decisiveness, broadmindedness, and "intellectual clarity"; she was, in his words, "a stimulating conversationalist." Hopkins "had no difficulty dealing with clients and her clients appear to have been very pleased with her work." She "was generally viewed as a highly competent project leader who worked long hours, pushed vigorously to meet deadlines and demanded much from the multidisciplinary staffs with which she worked."

On too many occasions, however, Hopkins' aggressiveness apparently spilled over into abrasiveness. Staff members seem to have borne the brunt of Hopkins' brusqueness. Long before her bid for partnership, partners evaluating her work had counseled her to improve her relations with staff members. Although later evaluations indicate an improvement, Hopkins' perceived shortcomings in this important area eventually doomed her bid for partnership. Virtually all of the partners' negative remarks about Hopkins—even those of partners who supported her—concerned her "interpersonal skills." Both "[s]upporters and opponents of her candidacy [ ] indicated that she was sometimes overly aggressive, unduly harsh, difficult to work with and impatient with staff."

Clear signs indicated, though, that some of the partners reacted negatively to Hopkins' personality because she was a woman. One partner described her as "macho," while another suggested that she "overcompensated for being a woman"; a third advised her to take "a course at charm school." Several partners criticized her use of profanity. In response, one partner suggested that those partners objected to her swearing only "because it[']s a lady using foul language." Another supporter explained that Hopkins "ha[d] matured from a tough-talking somewhat masculine hardnosed manager to an authoritative, formidable, but much more appealing lady partner candidate." In order for Hopkins to improve her chances for partnership, Thomas Beyer, a partner, suggested that she "walk more femininely, talk more femininely, dress more femininely, wear make-up, have her hair styled, and wear jewelry."

Dr. Susan Fiske, a social psychologist and associate professor of psychology at Carnegie-Mellon University, reviewed the Price Waterhouse selection process and concluded that it was likely influenced by sex stereotyping. Dr. Fiske indicated that some of the partners' comments were gender-biased, while others that were gender-neutral were intensely critical and made by partners who barely knew

Hopkins. Dr. Fiske concluded that the subjectivity of the evaluations and their sharply critical nature were probably the result of sex-stereotyping.

Of the eighty-eight candidates, forty-seven were admitted to partnership; twenty-one were rejected; and Hopkins and nineteen others were put on hold for the following year. Later, two partners withdrew their support for Hopkins, and she was informed that she would not be reconsidered the following year. Hopkins then resigned.

Ms. Hopkins, who litigated the Price Waterhouse denial of her partnership as a violation of Title VII of the Civil Rights Act of 1964 (which prohibits discrimination in employment practices), has stated she filed the suit to find out why Price Waterhouse made "such a bad business decision." She did not learn of the partners' comments until discovery during the case. The Supreme Court found for Ms. Hopkins. In 1990, on remand, Ms. Hopkins was awarded her partnership[1] and $350,000 in damages.

Today at Price Waterhouse offices in Washington, D.C., 44 percent of the professional staff are women and 22 percent are minorities. In accounting firms generally, the number of female principals has grown from 1 percent in 1983 to 18 percent today.

Discussion Questions

1. What ethical problems do you see with the Price Waterhouse partnership evaluation system?
2. Suppose that you were a partner and a member of either the Admissions Committee or the Policy Board. What objections, if any, would you have made to any of the comments by the partners? What would have made it difficult for you to object? How might your being a female partner in that position have made objection more difficult?
3. In what ways, if any, do you find the subjectivity of the evaluation troublesome? What aspects of the evaluation would you change?
4. To what extent did the partners' comments reflect mixed motives (i.e., to what extent did their points express legal factors while others expressed illegal ones)?
5. Ms. Hopkins listed three factors to help companies avoid what happened to her: a) clear direction from the top of the enterprise; b) diversity in management; and c) specificity in evaluation criteria. Give examples for implementing these factors.

---

1. Technically, Ms. Hopkins was made a principal, a title reserved for those reaching partner status who do not hold CPA licenses. Ms. Hopkins has a master's degree in mathematics.

Section B
Employee Screening

What can an employer do to check an employee's background, personality, and potential? How do we know such tests are accurate? Could they destroy opportunities?

Case 3.2: Handwriting Analysis and Employment

Thomas Interior Systems, Inc., employs analysts to examine candidates' handwriting. President Thomas Klobucher says, "At first I thought [handwriting analysis] was hocus-pocus. But I've learned to depend on it."[2] "It has been said handwriting is civilization's casual encephalogram."[3]

Though much more prevalent in Europe and Israel, graphology is used in two to three thousand U.S. organizations. Companies that have used graphology in personnel selection include Ford, General Electric, Mutual of Omaha, H & R Block, Firestone, USX Corp., and Northwest Mutual Life Insurance Company. In 1980, the Library of Congress changed the classification of graphology from "occult" to "psychology" under the Dewey Decimal System.

Views on the accuracy of handwriting analysis vary. Psychologist John Jones says, "No body of research shows that handwriting consistently predicts job behavior."[4] James Crumbaugh, a retired clinical psychologist, notes that although traditional personality tests, such as the inkblot test, are hard to validate, their use continues.

---

2. Michael J. McCarthy, "Handwriting Analysis as Personnel Tool," *Wall Street Journal*, 25 August 1988, 19.

3. David L. Kurtz, et al., "CEOs: A Handwriting Analysis," *Business Horizons* (January-February 1989): 41–43.

4. Ibid.

Handwriting analysis is growing in popularity as a means of screening potential employees. A Honeywell manager explains, "I'm looking for any means that I think is credible to avoid a hiring mistake."[5]

The same manager adds, "I don't know if [prospective employees are] mass murderers or not; I simply learn if they'll operate well as sales representatives."[6]

Among other handwriting factors, a graphologist will analyze

[t]he height of the signature. Those people with signatures above 1/4" in height, particularly when placed on the far right, are enterprising and motivated by prestige. They are good salespeople. Those with small signatures (less than 1/8" in height) are objective, cool, good listeners and negotiators. Those with medium signatures are team players. The dots on "i's", the bars on "t's", loops and hooks are all linked by graphologists to various personality traits. The absence of "i" dots, for example, can be indications of wandering attention and disregard for detail. Variances in pen pressure can demonstrate those same personality traits. A light pen pressure means the person is not aggressive. Rounded letters and variations in letter forms suggest listener more than persuader. Inconsistent legibility is linked with a lack of patience.[7]

Graphologists charge between $150 and $500 for an analysis. Traditional areas of examination, apart from handwriting size, include slant, regularity, margins, pressure, lines, connection between letters, and word and line spacing.

Problems have accompanied the use of handwriting samples. One applicant for a truck driving position had his wife write his sample. Some applicants change their handwriting when providing a sample for analysis, and experts have raised the issue of discrimination in the use of graphology. A test by the *Wall Street Journal* in which the same writing sample was submitted to three graphology firms yielded often conflicting results among the firms. Richard Klimoski, professor of psychology at Ohio State University, says, "The better the studies [of handwriting analysis] have been, the less support they offer to proponents. My reading of the evidence is that there is nothing there that's worth your time and money."[8]

Discussion Questions

1. What concerns would you have about the relevancy of handwriting analysis?
2. Would you impose handwriting analysis as a requirement for employment?
3. Are you comfortable with the accuracy of handwriting analysis?
4. One employer states that graphology has revealed so much to him that he feels as if such analysis constitutes an invasion of privacy. How might this employer balance his concerns regarding this "invasion" with his concerns regarding the accuracy of graphology?
5. If handwriting analysis produced disparate statistics in terms of male/female hires, would you still continue to use it?
6. An employer that had conducted a national search for a key executive had Phoenix graphologist Mark Hopper perform handwriting analysis on the top

5. Kurtz, 41–43.
6. McCarthy, 19.
7. Guy Webster, "Job Applicants' Fate Written in the Script," *Arizona Republic*, 1 September 1991, F2.
8. *Ibid.*

candidate. Mr. Hopper's analysis confirmed what the company's top officers believed about the candidate based on their interviews: bright, talented and motivated. However, Hopper also cautioned that there was a high risk of substance abuse in the candidate. The company raised the issue with the candidate and he confessed to being a recovering alcoholic. He was hired but the bar in the executive suite was removed. What issues do you see in this use of handwriting analysis?[9]

CASE 3.3: HEALTH AND GENETIC SCREENING

During the past decade, biologists have made significant strides in the field of genetics. Media attention has focused on gene splicing, the creation of new forms of life, and the increase in the quality, size, and disease resistance of agricultural products.

However, this new technology is also enabling biologists to delve into complex genetic information. Soon DNA tests will be able to provide full physical and mental profiles of human beings. Apart from the issues that such testing will present for parents-to-be, complexities could develop in the workplace as well.

The Office of Technology Assessment of the House Committee on Science and Technology surveyed the five hundred largest U.S. industrial companies, fifty private utilities, and eleven unions and found that seventeen had used genetic testing to screen employees for the sickle-cell trait or enzyme deficiencies.

Genetic screening also could reveal an individual's tolerance for or susceptibility to chemicals used in the workplace. With health insurance costs increasing exponentially, employers are trying to improve employee health with routine medical screening, creation of smoke-free environments, and drug testing. Genetic profile tests could be used to hire only those individuals who meet certain minimum health requirements and are thus likely to keep health insurance costs down.

Insurers have used AIDS screening as a prerequisite for medical insurance coverage; similarly, genetic tests could predict susceptibility to heart disease and cancer. Genetic tests allow insurers to screen applicants and either deny coverage or create higher-risk pools for those in high risk groups.

Scientist Robert Weinberg has stated:

> A belief that each of us is ultimately responsible for our own behavior has woven our social fabric. Yet in the coming years, we will hear more and more from those who write off bad behavior to the inexorable forces of biology and who embrace a new astrology in which alleles rather than stars determine individuals' lives. It is hard to imagine how far this growing abdication of responsibility will carry us.
>
> As a biologist, I find this prospect a bitter pill. The biological revolution of the past decades has proven extraordinarily exciting and endlessly fascinating, and it will, without doubt, spawn enormous benefit. But as with most new technologies, we will pay a price unless we anticipate the human genome project's dark side. We need to craft an ethic that cherishes our human ability to transcend biology, that enshrines our spontaneity, unpredictability, and individual uniqueness. At the moment, I find myself and those around me ill equipped to respond to the challenge.[10]

9. Ken Western, "Firms Turning to Graphology in Screening," *Arizona Republic*, 8 December 1996, D1, D4.

10. Robert Weinberg, "Genetic Screening," *Technology Review* (April 1991), 51.

Starting in 1972, DuPont screened its black employees for sickle-cell anemia, which affects one in every four to six hundred black Americans. Requested by the Black DuPont Employees Association to perform the genetic screening, DuPont administered the voluntary test not to deny jobs, but to offer employees relocation to chemical-free areas where the disease would not be triggered.

Critics of DuPont said the testing allowed the company to transfer workers rather than clean up its work environment. DuPont's medical director responded,

> This is a very naive view. No one can operate at zero emissions, exposures—zero anything. There has to be an agreed-upon practical, safe limit. But there are some employees who are more susceptible to certain diseases than others. It's only common sense to offer them the opportunity to relocate.[11]

In the 1960s, certain workers at an Israeli dynamite factory became ill with acute hemolytic anemia, which causes the walls of the red blood cells to dissolve, thus decreasing the cells' ability to circulate oxygen throughout the body. The workers were transferred to other parts of the plant, but genetic screening revealed that all of them had a G-6-PD deficiency, which causes hemolytic anemia upon exposure to chemicals. The information allowed the factory to place workers properly and led it to reduce chemical levels in the plant.[12]

Discussion Questions

1. What impact does genetic screening have on an employee's privacy?
2. In what ways should employers regard genetic screening as necessary?
3. Is DuPont's sickle-cell anemia screening program justifiable? Explain.
4. Discuss how genetic screening might lead to discrimination.
5. Will genetic screening help employers increase safety in the workplace?
6. What impact might the Americans with Disabilities Act have on genetic screening?

---

11. William P. Patterson, "Genetic Screening." *Industry Week* 1 June 1987, 48.

12. Thomas H. Murray, "Genetic Testing at Work: How Should It Be Used?" *Personnel Administrator* (September 1985), 90–92.

Section C
Employee Privacy

Does a line separate my private life from my employment? How much can I be watched at work? Are mandatory drug tests a violation of my privacy or necessary for safety in my field?

Case 3.4: The Smoking Prohibition

Janice Bone was a payroll clerk for Ford Meter Box, a small manufacturer in Wabash, Indiana. Ford Meter Box prohibited its employees from smoking and conducted urine tests to verify compliance.

Nicotine traces showed up in Bone's urinalysis, and she was fired. Bone filed suit; consequently, the Indiana legislature passed a statute protecting from termination workers who smoke outside the workplace.

Ford Meter is one of many companies that assess the impact of their employees' health on their performance and the cost of insurance benefits. Twenty states now have laws that address employee activity off the job. Six of those states protect employees from being discriminated against for any legal off-the-job activity. The remaining states afford protection for off-the-job smoking only. Senator Carl Franklin, a supporter of Oklahoma's Off-the-Job Smoking Protection Statute, says, "When they start telling you you can't smoke on your own time, the next thing you know they'll tell you you can't have sex but once a week, and if you have sex twice a week, you're fired."[13]

Some companies impose health insurance surcharges for smokers. Baker Hughes, an oil field equipment manufacturer, and Texas Instruments impose a $10 per month charge, and U-Haul International imposes a biweekly charge of $5 on the health insurance premiums of employees who smoke, chew tobacco, or exceed weight guidelines. Turner Broadcasting will not hire smokers.

---

13. Z. Schiller, "If You Light Up On Sunday, Don't Come In On Monday." *Business Week*, 26 August 1991, 68.

The American Civil Liberties Union is sympathetic to firms' positions on smokers because of the direct link between smoking, health hazards, and resultant health costs. However, the ACLU fears that the list of prohibitions will expand, as it did at U-Haul, to include weight and alcohol consumption or—as it did in Athens, Georgia—to mandate cholesterol-level tests for all applicants for city jobs.

Discussion Questions

1. What would be a more positive approach to creating a healthier workforce? Discuss how, for example, an employer might utilize a reward system for employee health.
2. Are smoking prohibitions a justified invasion of privacy? Explain.
3. Discuss the difficulties employers will face in balancing employee privacy interests against employer risk as types of prohibited conduct grow.
4. Are hiring prohibitions on smokers discriminatory?
5. Would it be an invasion of privacy for an employer to refuse to hire employees who engage in hazardous activities (defined to include activities such as skydiving, motorcycle riding, piloting private aircraft, mountain climbing, and motor vehicle racing)? What if a company were unable to afford health coverage for its workers without this exclusion?

CASE 3.5: DUI AND DELIVERIES

John Lawn, the former director of the Drug Enforcement Administration (DEA), supported mandatory drug testing, calling it "critical [i]n those occupations where either the public trust or public safety is involved." He listed doctors, lawyers, airline pilots, truck drivers, and teachers as examples and urged the professions to develop their own rules and regulations for drug testing.

The federal government has Supreme Court approval for 113 drug testing programs, but state law regulates private employers in the administration of their tests. Some states limit testing to safety-sensitive jobs; other states require probable cause as a prerequisite for testing employees. Courts continue to address issues of employer need and employee privacy, along with questions involving drug test reliability.

> A Seattle equipment company worker complains: I am so tired of hearing that I have a right to privacy. What about our right to safety?[14]

J. F. Spencer, a production manager for Pennwalt Pharmaceutical of Rochester, New York, expresses his feelings as follows:

> People at work who are illegally using drugs are infringing on the rights of law-abiding individuals. It is an invasion of privacy, but until someone comes up with a better way to keep people on drugs out of high-risk jobs, I will put up with it.[15]

---

14. "Test Workers for Drugs?" *Industry Week*, 14 December 1987, 17.

15. *Industry Week*, 17.

But a Boston executive maintains, "Individual rights are too precious to be compromised by this route. Other ways must be found to combat drug problems in the workplace."[16] New Jersey Superior Court Judge Donald A. Smith, Jr., wrote in a decision striking down the discharge of an employee who tested positive for marijuana and Valium, "Whether it be a private or public employer, a free-for-all approach to drug testing cannot be tolerated."[17]

Kim Haggart, a quality-assurance manager at Dragon Valves, Inc., adopts the following position: "If the job is high-risk or safety-sensitive, testing should be required because impairment can affect the health and safety of others."[18]

You are the manager of a pizzeria that operates solely as a pizza delivery business. As you contemplate drug testing for your drivers, consider the following questions.

Discussion Questions

1. What safety issues are involved with your drivers?
2. Will your testing be random or scheduled? Explain your choice.
3. Will you test all employees or just your drivers? Explain.
4. Will you test employees who are in an accident? Why? Why not?
5. Why do you think you should—or should not—test your employees?
6. Will you test only suspicious drivers?
7. What penalties will you impose on employees who test positive?
8. What opportunities for rehabilitation will you offer for employees who test positive?
9. How will you ensure the accuracy of the tests?
10. Will you inform drivers of your testing policy before hiring them? Why? Why not?

CASE 3.6: CORPORATE ANTHROPOLOGY: IS THE BOSS SPYING VIA TECHNOLOGY?

Surveillance by Employers

Internal theft, liability for harm to customers, the need to ensure good driving records, and customer service are a few of the reasons businesses give for keeping a secret eye on employees. From the well-known secret shoppers of the retail industry to phone company monitoring of operator performance, employers are gathering data on employee performance and wrongdoing.

Safeway Stores, Inc., a large multistore grocery chain, has dashboard computers in its 782 delivery trucks. The computers monitor speed, oil pressure, engine RPMs and idling, and the length of stops. Safeway touts the program for its efficacy with regard to driver safety and truck maintenance.

---

16. Ibid., 17.

17. Wayne A. Green, "Drug Testing Becomes Corporate Mine Field." *Wall Street Journal*, 21 November 1989, B1.

18. *Industry Week*, 18.

In other businesses, high-tech developments enable employers to eavesdrop on employees' telephone and office conversations, while small cameras monitor employee work habits and behavior through pinholes in office walls.

The electronic surveillance of phone conversations has increased as employers seek to monitor productivity, accuracy, and courtesy. Such monitoring is permissible if the monitored party (the employee) consents. Legislation proposed at the state level would require employers to sound a beeping tone when monitoring begins to alert the employee under observation. But an AT&T official notes that employers need the ability to monitor without notice: "Factory supervisors don't blow whistles to warn assembly-line workers they're coming."[19]

In contrast, Barbara Otto, the director of *9 to 5*, a national association of working women, maintains that monitoring affects personal calls: "Employers start catching non-work-related information. They discover that employees are spending weekends with a person of the same sex or talking about forming a union."[20]

The American Civil Liberties Union objects to monitoring because of the current lack of required notice and also because employees lack access to the information employers gather about them via electronic means.

E-Mail and Privacy

Other issues of employee privacy center around electronic mail systems. Electronic mail (e-mail) systems enable employees to communicate and interact by typing messages on their personal computers. E-mail is often described as a cross between a telephone conversation and a memo. The result is a means of communication, more casual than a memo, that allows users to relax and say more. On the other hand, unlike a telephone conversation, e-mail produces a written record of often casual conversations.

Employers have access to employee files and e-mail messages; moreover, employers can retain backup files of such messages even when users have deleted them. Courts have ruled that e-mail messages belong not to the employee but to the employer and are discoverable in litigation, whereupon they must be turned over to the opposing party. In one case an e-mail message from a corporate president to an employee's manager, deleted from the president's and manager's files but saved on the company's hard drive, read, "I don't care what it takes. Fire the _____ bitch." After the message was produced during discovery in the employee's suit, the result was an immediate $250,000 settlement.

In addition to the litigation issues of e-mail, there are the employee usage issues. For example, Michelle Murphy, a former customer-service representative at The Principal Financial Group, was fired after she used company e-mail to send jokes such as "A Few Good Reasons Cookie Dough is Better Than Men" and "Top 10 Reasons Why Trick-or-Treating Is Better Than Sex." Principal Financial's employee handbook included the following:

> The corporation's electronic mail system is business property and is to be used for business purposes. The corporation reserves the right to monitor all electronic messages.

---

19. Richard Lacayo, "Nowhere to Hide," *Time*, 11 November 1991, 34.
20. Ibid., 39.

Murphy has appealed her termination.

Michael Smyth, a manager for Pillsbury in Pennsylvania sent an e-mail to his supervisor complaining about company executives and threatening to "kill the backstabbing bastards." Shortly after, he was fired. He sued for wrongful discharge.

E-Mail and Theft

Yet another problem with e-mail comes from unauthorized access by hackers. Employees should exercise caution about the type of information sent via e-mail because hackers use information for corporate espionage, insider trading and even just mischief. For a 1997 article in *Fortune*, and with the company's permission, hackers hired by the magazine were able to access the company's system within a 16-hour period. With access, the hackers obtained a $5,000 bonus authorization from the CEO for an employee. Their access allowed them to read, modify and destroy files or plant a destructive virus.

Voice Mail and Privacy

Voice mail or telephone messaging is a technological convenience used by nearly 100 percent of all companies with five or more employees. In many situations, such companies do business and enter into contracts using only voice mail. However, voice mail carries with it the same privacy issues as e-mail. Employers can review the voice mail of employees and the messages and their content is discoverable in litigation.

The Fax

Faxed documents reduce mailing costs and facilitate rapid negotiations and deal refinements. However, fax technology can also facilitate dishonesty. It would be difficult, for example, to determine the lack of authenticity of a signature transferred from another document to a fax. Facsimile machine technology has not evolved to the point where we can tell whether a fax has been sent, received, or sent or received in its entirety. Finally, centrally located fax machines present privacy problems as faxed materials are pulled off the machines by others and then delivered to the intended recipient.

Discussion Questions

1. Is corporate spying necessary?
2. How does secret or electronic monitoring differ from a manager's decision to, without notice, walk around an office to observe behavior and work?
3. To what extent does an employee have a right to privacy in the workplace?
4. How would disclosure of monitoring activities lessen their invasion of employee privacy?
5. How does electronic surveillance differ from going through an employee's desk?
6. How would the nature of a given business affect your decision regarding surveillance?

7. What ethical standards should businesses adopt with respect to these three forms of technology?

8. What procedures might eliminate some of the ethical dilemmas noted here?

9. Should employers disclose to potential and current employees their ability to access e-mail and voice mail?

10. Is it fair that all e-mail and voice mail generated in the workplace belongs to the employer? Why or why not?

11. What policies would you adopt with regard to subject matter in your employees' voice and e-mail?

12. How do voice mail and e-mail provide opportunities for dishonesty in contracts? How might companies guarantee the authenticity of messages that utilize these devices?

CASE 3.7: THE ATHLETE ROLE MODEL

On August 20, 1996, the North Texas Toyota Dealers Association filed suit against Michael Irvin, the Dallas Cowboys player who entered a no contest plea to charges of cocaine possession earlier in the month. The Toyota dealers' suit alleges Mr. Irvin represented himself as a moral person when he signed an endorsement contract with the Association and, that with the drug plea, he can no longer be used as a spokesperson. The suit also asks for the return of the Toyota Land Cruiser (valued at $50,000) that Mr. Irvin was given as part of the endorsement contract.

Mr. Irvin returned the car voluntarily and has received a sentence of four years, deferred adjudication, $10,000 and 800 hours of community service. He was also suspended by the NFL for the first five games of the 96–97 season for his involvement with drugs.

The lawsuit also asks for the costs of the aborted campaign and $1.2 million in lost sales. The total damages requested are $1.4 million.

Discussion Question

1. Do you think Mr. Irvin breached his endorsement contract?
2. Is morality a condition for being a spokesperson?
3. Is it implied in the contract?
4. Is illegal conduct a grounds for termination of an endorsement contract?

Section D
Sexual Harassment

Sexual harassment, the topic of the '90s, captured the nation's attention with the 1991 Senate confirmation hearings of Supreme Court Justice Clarence Thomas. While the Anita Hill accusations against Justice Thomas brought the issue to the forefront, the 1998 allegations by Paula Jones and Kathleen Willey against President Clinton caused a re-examination of what constitutes sexual harassment. In the two following pieces, Ms. Anita Hill and Ms. Gloria Steinem offer their thoughts on what constitutes sexual harassment. What is it? Can it be controlled? Are employer and governmental inaction problems?

Reading 3.8: A Matter of Definition[21]

Anita Hill

Several months ago when President Clinton called for a national conversation on race, he became the first President since the passage of the civil rights acts of the 1960's to try to focus our attention on race relations and the problems of discrimination in this country.

But almost as soon as the conversation on race began, it was eclipsed by a national conversation on sex, sparked by allegations about the President's own behavior. At the core of this discussion is "sexual harassment," a phrase that has legal meaning but in popular culture has become such a catchall that we are in danger of turning it into an irrelevance.

Though the statute does not include the term sexual harassment, Title VII of the Civil Rights Act of 1964 prohibits employment discrimination that results from such behavior. In 1976 a Federal trial court, in Williams v. Saxbe, first granted a right of action for sexual harassment.

---

21. Source: *The New York Times*, March 19, 1998, A23. Copyright © 1998 by the New York Times Company. Reprinted with permission.

In 1986 the Supreme Court declared, in Meritor Savings Bank v. Vinson, that sexual harassment violated a victim's civil rights. With the Clarence Thomas confirmation hearing in 1991 the term became part of the popular culture.

But in our new national conversation on sex, including our discussions of the Paula Jones lawsuit and the resulting revelations from Monica Lewinsky and Kathleen Willey, the references to sexual harassment have expanded far beyond the legal prescriptions. The term has become cliche, and the perception of sexual harassment as a civil rights violation is now diminished.

The trend of popular discourse on the serious legal and social issue of sexual harassment has had some positive results. The problem, once thought to be rare and perhaps even a fabrication, is now exposed. Last year more than 17,000 sexual harassment claims, more than ever before, were filed with the Equal Employment Opportunity Commission, the Federal agency charged with enforcing antidiscrimination law. And overt acts of sexual harassment appear to be declining.

However, the cases that are a part of the national conversation often bear little relationship to those that occur in the everyday work world. In fact, these high-profile cases can misinform the public about what to expect in a sexual harassment complaint, as well as how to defend against one.

The public does not see these high-profile cases as being driven by the law as it has developed over the years in cases filed by ordinary citizens. Instead, it sees the cases in the news as setting the standards and the stakes for claims by average Americans. That is not how our legal system works.

In addition, the use of the term sexual harassment to describe any and every kind of sexually related transgression trivializes the protections offered by Title VII. Among the recent high-profile cases, the court-martial of Sgt. Maj. Gene McKinney most resembles a Title VII sexual harassment claim. Yet this case is still not a sexual harassment lawsuit—Sergeant Major McKinney was tried in a military criminal court that has entirely different procedures and a different burden of proof.

The Paula Jones case—brought as a job discrimination sexual harassment claim, but not under Title VII—further confuses the public. The information that has become public so far suggests that the case relies heavily on the allegation that Mr. Clinton made a crude sexual overture to Ms. Jones while he was Governor of Arkansas. But the revelations so far provide little evidence that Ms. Jones suffered employment-related repercussions as a result of the incident.

Newscasters are describing Kathleen Willey's encounter with the President as sexual harassment. As was true in my situation with Clarence Thomas, Ms. Willey has not brought a sexual harassment claim against Mr. Clinton. Moreover, Ms. Willey has not alleged that the one incident she described was so severe and pervasive as to become a condition of her employment, which is what the law on sexual harassment requires.

Some commentators also have suggested that Monica Lewinsky may have suffered sexual harassment, even though if a sexual relationship existed with the President, it was consensual.

Finally, the inordinate amount of attention to incidents of overzealous enforcement of sexual harassment rules, like those cases where a young child is suspended from school for kissing a classmate, further expands the reach of the term and misinforms the public discussion.

In short, with the broad definition being given the term sexual harassment, it is no wonder that the public appears confused.

Ambiguous and inaccurate use of the term sexual harassment may make for interesting conversation, but it threatens to dull the concept's effectiveness as a weapon against sexism in the workplace. Bringing a genuine sexual harassment claim was difficult enough before the current charges made headlines, but if public confusion turns to skepticism, bringing a claim could prove to be even harder in the future.

Admittedly, sex sells all sorts of products, from perfume to beer to news broadcasts. The opportunity in popular culture to have a polite or not-so-polite conversation on sex is irresistible. Yet we are in danger of forgetting that laws forbidding sexual harassment in the workplace are not about sex. They are about employment discrimination.

READING 3.9: FEMINISTS AND THE CLINTON QUESTION[22]

Gloria Steinem

If all the sexual allegations now swirling around the White House turn out to be true, President Clinton may be a candidate for sex addiction therapy. But feminists will still have been right to resist pressure by the right wing and the media to call for his resignation or impeachment. The pressure came from another case of the double standard.

For one thing, if the President had behaved with comparable insensitivity toward environmentalists, and at the same time remained their most crucial champion and bulwark against an anti-environmental Congress, would they be expected to desert him? I don't think so. If President Clinton were as vital to preserving freedom of speech as he is to preserving reproductive freedom, would journalists be condemned as "inconsistent" for refusing to suggest he resign? Forget it.

For another, there was and is a difference between the accusations against Mr. Clinton and those against Bob Packwood and Clarence Thomas, between the experiences reported by Kathleen Willey and Anita Hill. Commentators might stop puzzling over the President's favorable poll ratings, especially among women, if they understood the common sense guideline to sexual behavior that came out of the women's movement 30 years ago: no means no, yes means yes.

It's the basis of sexual harassment law. It also explains why the media's obsession with sex is offensive to some, titillating to many and beside the point to almost everybody. Like most feminists, most Americans become concerned about sexual behavior when someone's will has been violated; that is, when "no" hasn't been accepted as an answer.

Let's look at what seem to be the most damaging allegations, those made by Kathleen Willey. Not only was she Mr. Clinton's political supporter, but she is also old enough to be Monica Lewinsky's mother, a better media spokeswoman for

---

22. SOURCE: *Gloria Steinem. "Feminists and the Clinton Question." The New York Times,* March 22, 1998, WK15. Reprinted with permission.

herself than Paula Jones, and a survivor of family tragedy, struggling to pay her dead husband's debts.

If any of the other women had tried to sell their stories to a celebrity tell-all book publisher, as Ms. Willey did, you might be even more skeptical about their motives. But with her, you think, "Well, she needs the money."

For the sake of argument here, I'm also believing all the women, at least until we know more. I noticed that CNN polls taken right after Ms. Willey's interview on "60 Minutes" showed that more Americans believed her than President Clinton.

Nonetheless, the President's approval ratings have remained high. Why? The truth is that even if the allegations are true, the President is not guilty of sexual harassment. He is accused of having made a gross, dumb and reckless pass at a supporter during a low point in her life. She pushed him away, she said, and it never happened again. In other words, President Clinton took "no" for an answer.

In her original story, Paula Jones essentially said the same thing. She went to then-Governor Clinton's hotel room, where she said he asked her to perform oral sex and even dropped his trousers. She refused, and even she claims that he said something like, "Well, I don't want to make you do anything you don't want to do."

Her lawyers now allege that as a result of the incident Ms. Jones described, she was slighted in her job as a state clerical employee and even suffered long-lasting psychological damage. But there appears to be little evidence to support those accusations. As with the allegations in Ms. Willey's case, Mr. Clinton seems to have made a clumsy sexual pass, then accepted rejection.

This is very different from the cases of Clarence Thomas and Bob Packwood. According to Anita Hill and a number of Mr. Packwood's former employees, the offensive behavior was repeated for years, despite constant "no's." It also occurred in the regular workplace of these women, where it could not be avoided.

The women who worked for Mr. Packwood described a man who groped and lunged at them. Ms. Hill accused Clarence Thomas of regularly and graphically describing sexual practices and pornography. In both cases, the women said they had to go to work every day, never knowing what sexual humiliation would await them—just the kind of "hostile environment" that sexual harassment law was intended to reduce.

As reported, Monica Lewinsky's case illustrates the rest of the equation: "Yes means yes." Whatever it was, her relationship with President Clinton has never been called unwelcome, coerced or other than something she sought. The power imbalance between them increased the index of suspicion, but there is no evidence to suggest that Ms. Lewinsky's will was violated; quite the contrary. In fact, her subpoena in the Paula Jones case should have been quashed. Welcome sexual behavior is about as relevant to sexual harassment as borrowing a car is to stealing one.

The real violators of Ms. Lewinsky's will were Linda Tripp, who taped their talks, the F.B.I. agents who questioned her without a lawyer and Kenneth Starr, the independent prosecutor who seems intent on tailoring the former intern's testimony.

What if President Clinton lied under oath about some or all of the above? According to polls, many Americans assume he did. There seems to be sympathy for keeping private sexual behavior private. Perhaps we have a responsibility to make it O.K. for politicians to tell the truth—providing they are respectful of "no means no; yes means yes"—and still be able to enter high office, including the Presidency.

Until then, we will disqualify energy and talent the country needs—as we are doing right now.

Discussion Questions

1. What is the significance of a refusal in sexual harassment?
2. Can one offensive contact constitute sexual harassment?
3. What ethical tests could serve as a guideline on sexual harassment?

CASE 3.10: *SEINFELD* IN THE WORKPLACE

Jerold Mackenzie, an executive with Miller Brewing Company, discussed a *Seinfeld* television episode in March 1993 with co-worker Patricia Best. The *Seinfeld* episode is one in which Jerry forgets the first name of a woman he is dating but does recall that her name rhymes with a part of the female anatomy (Dolores was the woman's name). Ms. Best said she didn't "get it," and Mackenzie made a photocopy of the word clitoris from the dictionary. Best reported the incident to her supervisor and Miller fired Mackenzie for "unacceptable managerial performance."

Mackenzie filed suit for wrongful discharge and a jury awarded him $26.6 million. The jurors in the case (10 women and 2 men) said the *Seinfeld* story did not offend them and they wanted to send a message with the size of the award that "sexual harassment has to be more important" than a story from a TV show.

Discussion Questions

1. Do you think Mackenzie's conduct was sexual harassment?
2. Do you think Mackenzie's conduct was professional?
3. Is the award excessive?

CASE 3.11: HOOTERS: MORE THAN A WAITRESS?

Hooters is a successful chain of restaurants and bars that features waitresses in tight shirts and very short shorts. Hooters also markets T-shirts that bear its name as well as its slogan, "More Than a Mouthful."

Former Hooters waitresses have filed a class action lawsuit, alleging that the atmosphere Hooters created in its restaurants allowed them to be sexually harassed. One waitress noted on a talk show: "We thought it was a family restaurant. [The uniforms] made us look stupid." The former waitresses have noted that Hooters hired no male wait staff; and that all of the waitresses at its restaurants are very young and mostly blonde. Customers, cooks, and managers, according to the women, made lewd comments and, on occasion, touched them. The women contend that Hooters' atmosphere, their mandatory uniforms, and all-male management caused them to be sexually harassed.

Discussion Questions

1. Should the women have known of the problems when they agreed to work at Hooters? What bearing should such knowledge have on their right to allege harassment?

2. What ethical obligations does an employer such as Hooters owe its employees in the creation of its atmosphere?

3. What role should managers play in minimizing customer harassment?

4. Would you work for and/or patronize Hooters?

5. Every Wednesday, the Chicago-area Hooters restaurants donate half of what they earn selling spicy chicken wings to the Holy Family Lutheran church. Between 1993 and 1995, the Hooters restaurant gave $15,000 to the church. On one Wednesday, Hooters brought in calendar girls and a Playboy Playmate for autographs in order to increase business. When asked about the combination of Hooters and religion, Pastor Charles Infelt responded, "We're not asking people to go there. I live in a larger Lutheran world. We try not to get into that side of life. We just accept their money. We don't evaluate. Our role is to be gracious and thankful. I don't want to get into negative thoughts." Evaluate this relationship.

SECTION E
AFFIRMATIVE ACTION/
EQUAL EMPLOYMENT
OPPORTUNITY

Diversity in the workplace continues to be a stated goal, yet we still face difficult dilemmas, such as fetal endangerment when a prospective mother takes a higher-paying but higher-risk job. When has an employer done enough in terms of employee diversity and safety? Are current goals sufficient?

CASE 3.12: ON-THE-JOB FETAL INJURIES

Johnson Controls, Inc., is a battery manufacturer. In the battery manufacturing process, the primary ingredient is lead. Exposure to lead endangers health and can harm a fetus carried by a female who is exposed to lead.

Before Congress passed the Civil Rights Act of 1964, Johnson Controls did not employ any women in the battery manufacturing process. In June 1977, Johnson Controls announced its first official policy with regard to women who desired to work in battery manufacturing, which would expose them to lead:

> Protection of the health of the unborn child is the immediate and direct responsibility of the prospective parents. While the medical professional and the company can support them in the exercise of this responsibility, it cannot assume it for them without simultaneously infringing their rights as persons.
>
> Since not all women who can become mothers wish to become mothers (or will become mothers), it would appear to be illegal discrimination to treat all who are capable of pregnancy as though they will become pregnant.

The policy stopped short of excluding women capable of bearing children from jobs involving lead exposure but emphasized that a woman who expected to have a child should not choose a job that involved such exposure.

Johnson Controls required women who wished to be considered for employment in the lead exposure jobs to sign statements indicating that they had been told of the risks lead exposure posed to an unborn child: ". . . that women exposed to lead have a higher rate of abortion . . . not as clear as the relationship between cigarette smoking and cancer . . . but medically speaking, just good sense not to run that risk if you want children and do not want to expose the unborn child to risk, however small."

By 1982, however, the policy of warning had been changed to a policy of exclusion. Johnson Controls was responding to the fact that between 1979 and 1982, eight employees became pregnant while maintaining blood lead levels in excess of thirty micrograms per deciliter, an exposure level that OSHA categorizes as critical. The company's new policy was as follows:

> It is Johnson Controls' policy that women who are pregnant or who are capable of bearing children will not be placed into jobs involving lead exposure or which would expose them to lead through the exercise of job bidding, bumping, transfer or promotion rights.

The policy defined women capable of bearing children as "all women except those whose inability to bear children is medically documented." The policy defined unacceptable lead exposure as the OSHA standard of thirty micrograms per deciliter in the blood or thirty micrograms per cubic centimeter in the air.

In 1984, three Johnson Controls employees filed suit against the company on the grounds that the fetal-protection policy was a form of sex discrimination that violated Title VII of the Civil Rights Act. The three employees included Mary Craig, who had chosen to be sterilized to avoid losing a job that involved lead exposure; Elsie Nason, a fifty-year-old divorcee who experienced a wage decrease when she transferred out of a job in which she was exposed to lead; and Donald Penney, a man who was denied a leave of absence so that he could lower his lead level because he intended to become a father. The trial court certified a class action that included all past, present, and future Johnson Controls' employees who had been or would continue to be affected by the fetal-protection policy Johnson Controls implemented in 1982.

At the trial, uncontroverted evidence showed that lead exposure affects the reproductive abilities of men and women and that the effects of exposure on adults are as great as those on a fetus, although the fetus appears to be more vulnerable to exposure. Johnson Controls maintained that its policy was a product of business necessity.

The employees argued in turn that the company allowed fertile men, but not fertile women, to choose whether they wished to risk their reproductive health for a particular job. Johnson Controls responded that it had based its policy not on any intent to discriminate, but rather on its concern for the health of unborn children. Johnson Controls also pointed out that inasmuch as more than forty states recognize a parent's right to recover for a prenatal injury based on negligence or wrongful death, its policy was designed to prevent its liability for such fetal injury or death. The company maintained that simple compliance with Title VII would not shelter it from state tort liability for injury to a parent or child.

Johnson Controls also maintained that its policy represented a bona fide occupational qualification and that it was requiring medical certification of non-child-bearing status to avoid substantial liability for injuries.

Discussion Questions

1. As the director of human resources for Johnson Controls, would you support or change the policy on women performing lead-exposure tasks? Why?
2. Why should women be given—or not given—the choice to accept the risk of exposure?
3. To what extent should a woman have the right to make decisions that will affect not only her health but the health of her unborn child? To what extent should a woman's consent to or acknowledgment of danger mitigate an employer's liability? What if a child born with lead-induced birth defects sues? Should the mother's consent apply as a defense?
4. The U.S. Supreme Court eventually decided Johnson Controls' policy was discriminatory and a violation of Title VII (*International Union v. Johnson Controls, Inc.*). What steps would you take as director of human resources to create a "policy-free" work setting?
5. At what times, if any, should discrimination issues be subordinate to other issues, such as the risk of danger to unborn children?

CASE 3.13: DENNY'S: DISCRIMINATORY SERVICE WITH A SMILE

On March 24, 1993, a group of minority customers filed a lawsuit in San Jose, California, against the Denny's restaurant chain. Denny's was requiring its minority customers to pay cover charges and to prepay for meals. In April, Denny's settled the charges with the Justice Department.

On May 24, 1993, six African-American secret service agents filed suit against Denny's, claiming the wait staff at the Annapolis, Maryland, Denny's had been deliberately slow in serving them (the agents had waited 55 minutes), thereby effectively denying them service. Their white colleagues had been served in a timely fashion.

Other Denny's customers who are black complained that they were told they would have to pay first if they wanted to eat at Denny's.

In July 1993, Denny's signed a $1 billion pact to settle the secret service case and all other claims. In the pact, Denny's agreed to:

- Buy nearly $700 million in food, paper, and supplies from black-owned businesses.
- Launch a training and recruitment program to increase black representation in Flagstar's[23] management ranks from 4.4 percent to 12 percent.
- Add 53 black-run franchises. Denny's had 1,485 restaurants, only one of which was operated by a black franchisee.
- Funnel Flagstar business to black accountants, lawyers, ad agencies, and banks.

Denny's also agreed to pay $46 million to black patrons and $8.7 million for legal fees. An additional $28 million was paid to California customers to settle civil

---

23. Flagstar is the parent company for Denny's.

rights cases there. The six agents in the Annapolis restaurant will split $17.7 million. The customers in the class action suit each received about $180 each as their part of the settlement.

Denny's now buys $50 million in supplies from minority contractors and one in four of it's store managers is black. At the time of the settlement, Denny's had only two minority contractors. In 1997, Denny's began a $5 million ad campaign that features black families entering Denny's restaurants. Denny's CEO now tells employees, "I will fire you if you discriminate."

Discussion Questions

1. In what ways could you say that Denny's is an example of a firm failing to monitor its practices?
2. How costly was Denny's discrimination?
3. How effective would encouraging employees to report discrimination be as a step in changing the corporate culture at Denny's and other service organizations?

CASE 3.14: TEXACO: THE JELLY BEAN DIVERSITY FIASCO

In November, 1996, Texaco, Inc., was rocked by the disclosure of tape-recorded conversations among three executives about a racial discrimination suit pending against the company. The suit, seeking $71 million, had been brought by 6 employees, on behalf of 1500 other employees, who alleged the following forms of discrimination:

> I have had KKK printed on my car. I have had my tires slashed and racial slurs written about me on bathroom walls. One co-worker blatantly called me a racial epithet to my face.

> Throughout my employment, three supervisors in my department openly discussed their view that African-Americans are ignorant and incompetent, and, specifically, that Thurgood Marshall was the most incompetent person they had ever seen.

> Sheryl Joseph, formerly a Texaco secretary in Harvey, Louisiana, was given a cake for her birthday which occurred shortly after she announced that she was pregnant. The cake depicted a black pregnant woman and read, "Happy Birthday, Sheryl. It must have been those watermelon seeds."

The suit also included data on Texaco's workforce:

1989	Minorities as a percentage of Texaco's workforce	15.2%
1994	Minorities as a percentage of Texaco's workforce	19.4%

# of Years to Promotion by Job Classification		
Minority Employees	Job	Other Employees
6.1	Accountant	4.6
6.4	Senior Accountant	5.4
12.5	Analyst	6.3
14.2	Financial Analyst	13.9
15.0	Assistant Accounting Supervisor	9.8

Senior Managers

	White	Black
1991	1,887	19
1992	2,001	21
1993	2,000	23
1994	2,029	23

Racial Composition (% of Blacks) by Pay Range

Salary	Texaco	Other Oil Companies
$51,100	5.9%	7.2%
$56,900	4.7%	6.5%
$63,000	4.1%	4.7%
$69,900	2.3%	5.1%
$77,600	1.8%	3.2%
$88,100	1.9%	2.3%
$95,600	1.4%	2.6%
$106,100	1.2%	2.3%
$117,600	0.8%	2.3%
$128,800	0.4%	1.8%

(African-Americans make up 12% of the U.S. population)

The acting head of the EEOC wrote in 1995, "Deficiencies in the affirmative-action programs suggest that Texaco is not committed to insuring comprehensive, facility by facility, compliance with the company's affirmative-action responsibilities."

Faced with the lawsuit, Texaco's former treasurer, Robert Ulrich, senior assistant treasurer, J. David Keough, and senior coordinator for personnel services, Richard A. Lundwall, met and discussed the suit. A tape transcript follows:

They look through evidence, deciding what to turn over to the plaintiffs.

Lundwall   Here, look at this chart. You know, I'm not really quite sure what it means. This chart is not mentioned in the agency, so it's not important that we even have it in there . . . . They would never know it was here.

Keough   They'll find it when they look through it.

Lundwall   Not if I take it out they won't.

The executives decide to leave out certain pages of a document; they worry that another version will turn up.

Ulrich   We're gonna purge the [expletive deleted] out of these books, though. We're not going to have any damn thing that we don't need to be in them—

Lundwall   As a matter of fact, I just want to be reminded of what we discussed. You take your data and . . .

Keough   You look and make sure it's consistent to what we've given them already for minutes. Two versions with the restricted and that's marked clearly on top—

Ulrich   But I don't want to be caught up in a cover-up. I don't want to be my own Watergate.

Lundwall   We've been doing pretty much two versions, too. This one here, this is strictly my book, your book . . .

Ulrich   Boy, I'll tell you, that one, you would put that and you would have the only copy. Nobody else ought to have copies of that.

Lundwall   O.K.?

Ulrich   You have that someplace and it doesn't exist.

Lundwall   Yeah, O.K.

Ulrich   I just don't want anybody to have a copy of that.

Lundwall,   Good. No problem.

Ulrich   You know, there is no point in even keeping the restricted version anymore. All it could do is get us in trouble. That's the way I feel. I would not keep anything.

Lundwall   Let me shred this thing and any other restricted version like it.

Ulrich   Why do we have to keep the minutes of the meeting anymore?

Lundwall   You don't, you don't.

Ulrich   We don't?

Lundwall   Because we don't, no, we don't because it comes back to haunt us like right now—

Ulrich   I mean, the pendulum is swinging the other way, guys.

The executives discuss the minority employees who brought the suit.

Lundwall   They are perpetuating an us/them atmosphere. Last week or last Friday I told . . .

Ulrich   [Inaudible.]

Lundwall   Yeah, that's what I said to you, you want to frag grenade? You know, duck, I'm going to throw one. Well, that's what I was alluding to. But the point is not, that's not bad in itself but it does perpetuate us/them. And if you're trying to get away and get to the we . . . you can't do that kind of stuff.

Ulrich   [Inaudible.] I agree. This diversity thing. You know how black jelly beans agree . . . .

Lundwall   That's funny. All the black jelly beans seem to be glued to the bottom of the bag.

Ulrich   You can't have just we and them. You can't just have black jelly beans and other jelly beans. It doesn't work.

Lundwall   Yeah. But they're perpetuating the black jelly beans.

Ulrich   I'm still having trouble with Hanukkah. Now, we have Kwanza (laughter).

The release of the tape prompted the Reverend Jesse Jackson to call for a nation-wide boycott of Texaco. Sales fell 8%, Texaco's stock fell 2%, and several institutional investors were preparing to sell their stock.

Texaco did have a minority recruiting effort in place and the "jelly bean" remark was tied to a diversity trainer the company had hired. The following are excerpts from Texaco's statement of vision and values:

Respect for the Individual

Our employees are our most important resource. Each person deserves to be treated with respect and dignity in appropriate work environments, without regard to race, religion, sex, age, national origin, disability or position in the company. Each employee has the responsibility to demonstrate respect for others.

The company believes that a work environment that reflects a diverse workforce, values diversity, and is free of all forms of discrimination, intimidation, and harassment is essential for a productive and efficient workforce. Accordingly, conduct directed toward any employee that is unwelcome, hostile, offensive, degrading, or abusive is unacceptable and will not be tolerated.

A federal grand jury began an investigation at Texaco to determine whether there had been obstruction of justice in the withholding of documents.

Within days of the release of the tape, Texaco settled its bias suit for $176.1 million, the largest sum ever allowed in a discrimination case. The money will allow a 11% pay raise for blacks and other minorities who joined in the law suit.

Texaco's chairman and CEO, Peter I. Bijur, issued the following statement after agreeing to a settlement:

Texaco is facing a difficult but vital challenge. It's broader than any specific words and larger than any lawsuit. It is one we must and are attacking head-on.

We are a company of 27,000 people worldwide. In any organization of that size, unfortunately, there are bound to be people with unacceptable, biased attitudes toward race, gender and religion.

Our goal, and our responsibility, is to eradicate this kind of thinking wherever and however it is found in our company. And our challenge is to make Texaco a company of limitless opportunity for all men and women.

We are committed to begin meeting this challenge immediately through programs with concrete goals and measurable timetables.

I've already announced certain specific steps, including a redoubling of efforts within Texaco to focus on the paramount value of respect for the individual and a comprehensive review of our diversity programs at every level of our company.

We also want to broaden economic access to Texaco for minority firms and increase the positive impact our investments can have in the minority community. This includes areas such as hiring and promotion; professional services such as advertising, banking, investment management and legal services; and wholesale and retail station ownership.

To assist us, we are reaching out to leaders of minority and religious organizations and others for ideas and perspectives that will help Texaco succeed in our mission of becoming a model of diversity and workplace equality.

It is essential to this urgent mission that Texaco and African-Americans and other minority community leaders work together to help solve the programs we face as a company—which, after all, echo the problems faced in society as a whole.

Discrimination will be extinguished only if we tackle it together, only if we join in a unified, common effort.

Working together, I believe we can take Texaco into the 21st century as a model of diversity. We can make Texaco a company of limitless opportunity.. We can make Texaco a leader in according respect to every man and woman.

Even after the announcement, Texaco stock was down $3 per share, a loss of $800 million total, and the boycott was continued. Texaco's proposed merger with Shell Oil began to unravel as Shell's CEO expressed concern about Texaco's integrity. However, after the settlement, additional information about the case began to emerge.

Holman W. Jenkins, Jr. wrote the following piece for the *Wall Street Journal*:

Quietly, corporate America is debating whether Texaco's Peter Bijur did the right thing.

Mr. Bijur gets paid to make the hard calls, and with the airwaves aflame over "nigger" and "black jelly beans," Texaco took a battering in the stock and political markets. He had every reason for wanting to put a stop-loss on the media frenzy. "Once the taped conversations were revealed," he says, settling was "reasonable and honorable." So now Texaco is betting $176 million that paying off minority employees and their lawyers is the quickest way out of the news.

But as the company's own investigation showed, the truly inflammatory comments reported in the media never took place. They were purely a fabrication by opposing lawyers, and trumpeted by a credulous New York Times. And some digging would have shown this problem cropping up before in the career of Mike Hausfeld, lead attorney for the plaintiffs.

In an antitrust case years ago, he presented a secret recording that he claimed showed oil executives conspiring to threaten gasoline dealers. But a check by the same expert who handled the Nixon Watergate tapes showed no such thing. Says Larry Sharp, the Washington antitrust lawyer who opposed Mr. Hausfeld: "To put it generously, he gave himself the benefit of the doubt in making the transcript."

But this time the lie has been rewarded, and the broader public, unschooled in legal cynicism, heads home believing Texaco an admitted racist.

The catechism of corporate crisis management says you can't fight the media. Mr. Bijur had to consider that Jesse Jackson was threatening a boycott if Texaco failed to "regret, repent and seek renewal." Mr. Jackson pointedly added that "any attempt to shift to denial would add insult to injury"—a warning against trying to spread some egg to the faces of those who were fooled by the fake transcript.

There may have been wisdom, if not valor, in Mr. Bijur's decision to run up the white flag. But he also evinced symptoms of Stockholm Syndrome, telling CNN that Texaco was just the "tip of the iceberg" of corporate racism. Ducking this fight so ignominiously may yet prove a penny-wise, pound-foolish strategy. The City of Philadelphia has decided to dump its Texaco holdings anyway, partly out of fear of more litigation.

What else could Texaco have done? It could have apologized for any offense, but stuck up for its former treasurer Bob Ulrich, who was wronged by the phony transcript and stripped of his medical benefits by Texaco. And the company could have vowed to fight the lawsuit like the dickens, arguing that Texaco is not the cause of society's racial troubles but has tried to be part of the solution.

Start with the tapes: A fair listening does not necessarily reveal a "racist" conversation by executives at Texaco, but certainly a candid conversation about the problems of race at Texaco. They spoke of "jelly beans" dividing into camps of "us" and "them," an honest representation of life at many companies, not just in the oil patch.

Mr. Bijur could have made this point, starting with the New York Times, which has been embroiled in its own discrimination lawsuit with Angela Dodson, once its top-ranking black female. In a complaint filed with New York City's Human Rights Commission, she claims the paper was "engaged in gender-based harassment and disability-based discrimination . . . because The Times no longer wanted me, as a black person, to occupy a position as Senior editor."

Her deepest ire is reserved for Times veteran Carolyn Lee, who is white and more accustomed to being lauded as a champion of women and minorities. Ms. Dodson told the Village Voice: "It got to the point that whenever I was in her presence or earshot she made remarks [about other black people] that could only be taken as negative."

This sounds remarkably like the anecdotes filed in the Texaco complaint. All an outsider can safely conclude is that race makes everything more complicated, as sensitivity begets sensitivity. Mr. Bijur would have done more for racial understanding had he used his platform to open up this subject.

Yes, the cartoonist racists are out there, he might have said, but the Times coverage of Texaco only found cartoonist racists. The paper could have looked to its own experience for another story—a story about how garden-variety interpersonal conflict can land even decent people in the snares of racial mistrust.

This is what affirmative action, by throwing people together, was supposed to get us past. And it may be no accident that our most quota-ridden newspaper, USA Today, jumped off the bandwagon on the Texaco tapes, noting the ambiguity of whether the "jelly bean" remarks were meant to be hostile or friendly to blacks.

And McPaper kept on asking intelligent questions, like whether the New York Times had been "used by plaintiffs in the case to promote a faulty but more inflammatory transcript?" ("Not unless the court was used," answered Times Business Editor John Geddes, sounding like a lawyer himself).

So Mr. Bijur was not facing a uniformly hopeless media torrent. The truth, even a complicated truth, catches up with the headlines eventually.

In time, he might have found surprising allies drifting to his side. The New Republic and the New Yorker have run thoughtful articles arguing that businesses should be allowed to use quotas but shouldn't be subject to harassment litigation if they don't. Right now, we do the opposite: Forbid companies to promote by quota, then sue them under federal "adverse impact" rules when they don't.

In effect, liberal voices are arguing that business could do more for minorities with less conflict if freedom of contract were restored. The world is changing, and companies have their own reasons nowadays for wanting minorities around. They need input from different kinds of people on how to deal with different kinds of people. No doubt this is why McPaper feels free to thumb its nose at the conformity crowd on stories like Texaco and church-burnings. (See September's Harvard Business Review for what business is thinking about diversity now.)

If companies were set free to assemble the work forces most useful to them, they could sweep away a heap of excuses for recrimination. Whites couldn't feel cheated out of jobs. Blacks wouldn't end up at companies that want them only for window-dressing. And the world could go back to feeling OK about being an interesting place. We might even allow that cultural patterns other than racism may explain why so many rednecks, and so few blacks, become petroleum engineers.

Mr. Bijur may have made the best of a bad deal for his shareholders. Whether it was best for America is a different judgment.[24]

Richard Lundwall, the executive who taped the sessions with the other executives was charged with one count of obstruction of justice. Lundwall had turned over the tapes of the conversations to lawyers for the plaintiffs in the discrimination suit on October 25, 1996. Lundwall had been terminated.

Texaco hired attorney Michael Armstrong to investigate the underlying allegations. Mr. Armstrong found the tapes had not been transcribed correctly.

As part of its settlement, Texaco agreed to, at a cost of $55 million, assign a task force to police hiring and promotion as well as requiring mentors for black employees and sensitivity training for white employees.

The following interview with CEO Bijur appeared in *Business Week*:

Q: *How did your legal strategy change once the news of the tapes was printed?*
A: When I saw [the story], I knew that this lawsuit was pending and moving forward. I made the judgment that we needed to accelerate the settlement process. And those discussions on settlement commenced almost immediately.

Q: *It has been reported that you didn't get the board of directors involved with the settlement talks and other issues. Why not?*
A: You're drawing conclusions that are erroneous. The board was fully involved throughout the entire process. I talked to numerous directors personally. We had several board and executive committee meetings. The board was fully supportive of our actions.

Q: *Have you met with shareholders?*
A: Yes, of course. I went down to [New York] and met with the Interfaith Center on Corporate Responsibility, which is a group of religious shareholders. I expressed our position on this and listened carefully to their position and got some good counsel and guidance. But I wanted to provide our side of the issue as well. I have met with [New York State Comptroller] Carl McCall and [New York City Comptroller] Alan Hevesi about concerns that they had, and I will continue to meet with other shareholders as I normally do.

Q: *Why do you think the oil industry has such a poor reputation on issues of racial diversity and gender equality? How does Texaco stack up against the others?*
A: The percentage of minorities within Texaco is just about average for the petroleum industry. We have made really significant progress in the last several years in improving the percentage. But there are some very interesting points that need to be examined to place in context what may be going on in this industry. I just read a study that showed that in 1995, there were only nine petroleum engineering minority graduates that came out of all engineering schools in the United States— only nine. That's not an excuse. But it is indicative of why it is difficult for this industry to have a lot of people in the pipeline. Now, of course, that does not apply

---

24. Reprinted with permission of *The Wall Street Journal* © 1996 Dow Jones & Company, Inc. All rights reserved.

to accountants, finance people, and anybody else. But we are a very technically oriented industry.

Q: *Have you personally witnessed discrimination at Texaco?*
A: In the nearly 31 years I have been with Texaco, I have never witnessed an incident of racial bias or prejudice. And had I seen it, I would have taken disciplinary action. I've never seen it.

Q: *Is there a widespread culture of insensitivity at Texaco?*
A: I do not think there is a culture of institutional bias within Texaco. I think we've got a great many very good and decent human beings, but that unfortunately we mirror society. There is bigotry in society. There is prejudice and injustice in society. I am sorry to say that, and I am sorry to say that probably does exist within Texaco. I can't do much about society, but I certainly can do something about Texaco.

Q: *What are your views on affirmative action?*
A: Texaco's views on affirmative action have not changed a bit. We have supported affirmative action, and we will continue to support affirmative action.

Q: *This is your first big trial since taking over. What have you learned?*
A: I've learned that as good as our programs are in the company—and they really are quite good, even in this area—there's always more we can do. We've got to really drill down into the programs. We've got to make certain that they're meeting the objectives and goals we've set for them.

Q: *Are there other lessons in terms of your style of management?*
A: I don't think I would do anything different the next time than what I did this time.

Q: *How will you make sure the spirit as well as the letter of the policy is followed at Texaco?*
A: We're going to put more and more and more emphasis on it until we get it through everybody's head: Bigotry is not going to be tolerated here.[25]

Robert W. Ulrich was indicted in 1997. Mr. Lundwall entered a "not guilty" plea on July 8, 1997, and J. David Keough has sued Texaco for libel. Texaco named Mary Bush, a financial consultant, as its first black female board member.

As Lundwall's prosecution has proceeded, new discoveries have been made. For example, "purposeful erasures" have been found on the tapes.

In an interim report on its progress toward the settlement goals, Texaco revealed the following:

Polishing the Star
As part of its settlement of a discrimination lawsuit brought by black employees, Texaco has moved on a half-dozen fronts to alter its business practices.

Hiring Asked search firms to identify wider arrays of candidates. Expanded recruiting at historically minority colleges. Gave 50 scholarships and paid internships to minority students seeking engineering or technical degrees.

---

25. Smart, Tim. "Texaco: Lessons From A Crisis-in-Progress." Reprinted from December 2, 1996, issue of *Business Week* by special permission, © 1997 by McGraw Hill, Inc.

Career Advancement Wrote objective standards for promotions. Developing training program for new managers. Developing a mentoring program.

Diversity Initiatives Conducted two-day diversity training for more than 8,000 of 20,000 U.S. employees. Tied management bonuses to diversity goals. Developing alternative dispute resolution and ombudsman programs.

Purchasing Nearly doubled purchases from minority- or women-owned businesses. Asking suppliers to report their purchases from such companies.

Financial Services Substantially increased banking, investment management and insurance business with minority- and women-owned firms. A group of such firms underwrote a $150 million public financing.

Retailing Added three black independent retailers, 18 black managers of company-owned service stations, 12 minority or female wholesalers, 13 minority- or women-owned Xpress Lube outlets and 6 minority- or women-owned lubricant distributors.

In May 1998, the Texaco executives were acquitted of all criminal charges.

Discussion Questions

1. Provide a summary of the players and their concerns.
2. Discuss the ethics of the recording.
3. Why do you think the executives discussed document destruction?
4. What ethical issues surround diversity training and affirmative action?
5. Read the following and discuss whether Mr. Bijur acted in the shareholders' interests.

READING 3.15: A TEXACO CHAIRMAN WHO BELIEVED THE N.Y. TIMES[26]

Paul Craig Roberts

Texaco and its shareholders are the first victims of the 1991 Civil Rights act. This legislation permits plaintiffs in job-discrimination cases to be awarded compensatory and punitive damages in addition to back pay.

Before the 1991 act, class-action suits threatened companies that lacked race and gender proportion in their work force with having to fork over years of back pay to preferred minorities who had not been hired. Since there was seldom any evidence that the companies had actually discriminated against any of the individuals, the companies would sometimes fight these suits rather than settle them.

This rankled the sharp lawyers who make tens of millions of dollars off such lawsuits and civil rights groups that need voluntary settlements of discrimination

---

26. Paul Craig Roberts. "A Texaco Chairman Who Believed The N.Y. Times." *The Washington Times*, 15 December 1996, 32. Reprinted with permission of *The Washington Times*.

suits as proof of institutionalized racism. They wanted a bigger club over the companies to force faster and easier settlements, and the Bush administration gave it to them by adding compensatory and punitive damages.

This tripled the cost to a company of losing a discrimination suit in court, thereby making settlement instead of trial a near certainty. Since the accused company just wants to settle, the accuser does not need evidence that would have to stand up in court.

The Texaco case illustrates this perfectly. Michael Hausfeld, the lawyer for the black employees, claimed to have an audio tape of Texaco executives using racial slurs while conspiring to hide evidence of Texaco's discrimination. He gave what he said was a transcript of the incriminating tape to Kurt Eichenwald of the New York Times. Mr. Eichenwald was not sufficiently professional to recognize Mr. Hausfeld's vested interest ($38.3 million is his and co-counsel Dan Berger's share of the settlement), and he did not ask to listen to the tape and to check the transcript against it. He quoted on trust from the inflammatory transcript that was handed to him.

The next mistake in the farce was made by Texaco Chairman Peter I. Bijur. He believed the New York Times still had reportorial integrity and was horrified by what he read about his executives. He quickly announced a generous settlement and placed financial sanctions on the presumed guilty executives. All of this happened before anyone listened to the tapes. When the tapes were finally transcribed by disinterested professionals, it turned out that Mr. Eichenwald's report, the catalyst for the record settlement, was inaccurate. No one had used a racial epithet, and the reference to black employees as jelly beans was an innocent multicultural metaphor that diversity trainers had taught the company to use. All Texaco employees are jelly beans, and the different colors are supposed to be appropriately mixed in the jar. What the company executives are actually protesting in the taped conversation is the "us-them" attitude of black employees: "You can't have just we and them. You can't just have black jelly beans and other jelly beans. It doesn't work," said Texaco treasurer Robert Ulrich.

The outcome is that the New York Times reporter's predisposition to believe in a racist corporate America made it easy for a sharp lawyer to use him to win a big case and establish a precedent: Companies that established quotas for hiring now will have to establish them for promotions. If they do not, every one of the preferred minorities on their payrolls can use the club of compensatory and punitive damages to extort large settlements.

But this is the least of it. Texaco's abject surrender to a lie has cemented into the belief system the image of racist America that civil rights plaintiffs have labored to establish. Corporate America is in a dither. Quotas are not more important to success than marketing, finance, or manufacturing. There is talk of providing boards of directors with full-time staffs to implement and monitor "diversity goals."

The ultimate casualty may be California's Civil Rights Initiative (already, a federal judge temporarily has blocked its implementation). The initiative, which passed comfortably in the November elections, seeks to reestablish equality before the law in California state and local government employment and university admissions. But it will prove difficult to admit students and to hire and promote government employees by individual merit alone when group rights are the rule in corporate America.

CASE 3.16: HUNTER TYLO: PREGNANCY IS NOT A BFOQ

Hunter Tylo was hired by Spelling Entertainment Group to play a character who would "strut in a bikini to steal actress Heather Locklear's husband" on the show, *Melrose Place*. Ms. Tylo never began work on the contract because she was fired after she disclosed to the show's executives that she was pregnant.

Mr. Spelling, the owner of the Spelling Entertainment Group, explained that Ms. Tylo was fired because he did not think it was fair to have scripts rewritten around a character and actress who had not yet appeared on the show. Mr. Spelling noted that he had worked with Ms. Locklear during her pregnancy, using various camera angles to avoid revealing Ms. Locklear's pregnancy.

In a letter to Mr. Spelling from actress Gabrielle Carteris, who plays a character on Mr. Spelling's other show, *Beverly Hills 90210*, Ms. Carteris expressed support for Mr. Spelling, "I just had to let you know how sorry I am with regards to the trial. It was particularly upsetting, when for me you were so very supportive of my getting pregnant."

Mr. Spelling also said that following Ms. Tylo's termination, he offered her a contract for the following season that would have paid more than her fee of $13,500 per episode that was provided on the terminated contract and that the new contract would have run for more episodes. Ms. Tylo refused the offer and filed suit. She was awarded $4 million by a jury for emotional distress and $894,601 for economic loss.

Discussion Questions

1. Is there a distinction between Ms. Tylo's circumstances and Ms. Locklear's?
2. Is not being pregnant a BFOQ for playing a "vixen" on a television series?
3. Did Mr. Spelling give sufficient justification for Ms. Tylo's termination?

SECTION F
EMPLOYMENT AT WILL

Does an employer have the right, for any reason, to terminate an employee? Do employees have any guarantees of employment?

CASE 3.17: RUDY GRANSER: FROM CHIEF CHEF TO BOTTLEWASHER

Rudolph Granser was employed at the Box Tree restaurant and hotel as chef and general manager from 1974–85 and again from 1991–92. Granser talked with the CEO of Box Tree, Augustin Paege, and threatened to report various health and safety violations in the hotel and restaurant to the Department of Buildings.

The alleged violations included that the hotel portion of the business was unlicensed; fireplaces were installed in hotel rooms without obtaining a permit; construction work was performed without appropriate permits; the restaurant regularly violated its certificate of occupancy by serving 60 patrons instead of 26; and the premises had inadequate safety exits.

Following Granser's threats to "blow the whistle," Paege demoted Granser. Excerpts from their depositions follow:

Paege's deposition:

Q: Let me bring you back to the conversation you had when he left the employment of the Box Tree. You asked him to go and become the chef?

A: Yes. I said, go take over the kitchen. Get in the whites.

He said, he did not want to do that. Then he said, okay, I will do that, but I want to be paid the same.

I said, I cannot pay you the same because I am taking a bigger part of it, at which point I was expected to negotiate with him a pay somewhat lower, not necessarily much, much lower, but somewhat lower. Since the other responsibilities will be taken away from him, there was no room for that. He ran out of room, and today is first time I have seen him since.

113

The relevant pages of Granser's testimony are as follows:

Q: Can you tell me the circumstances under which you left the Box Tree?
A: The date when I was told to leave?
Q: Did you have a conversation with Mr. Paege regarding your leaving the Box Tree?
A: That day, yes.
Q: On December 14th?
A: Yes.
Q: Tell me abut [sic] that conversation.
A: We had a meeting, he wanted to restructure the Box Tree, things are not working. He thought that the food is not adequate. He offered me the position as a chef. I asked him, "Are they the same terms?"
And he said, "No," and I said, "I consider myself fired," and I left.
Q: Did he ever say to you that you were fired?
A: I do not recall.
Q: Did you discuss what conditions, what salary, he would offer you to stay on as chef?
A: No, but he refused when I asked him if the terms are the same.
Q: You didn't take that discussion any further though; is that correct?
A: No.
Q: You left on the spot?
A: Yes.

New York's Labor Law 740 prohibits retaliatory personnel action by an employer against an employee who discloses or threatens to disclose an activity of the employer that is in violation of a law, rule or regulation when the violation creates and presents a substantial and specific danger to public health or safety.

Discussion Questions

1. Should an employer have the right to dismiss an employee, with or without good cause, for a loss of confidence? Why? Why not?
2. Should employees be entitled to some form of due process requiring warnings and justification before dismissal occurs? Explain.
3. Do protections for employees inhibit an employer's ability to make rapid, needed changes for flexibility in operations?
4. Do whistle-blower statutes protect dysfunctional employees?

CASE 3.18: THE DILEMMAS IN JOB HOPPING

The problems with executive "job-hopping," as the *Wall Street Journal* calls it continue. Executives leave their positions at one company and then take positions at competitors, often being responsible for the same product line at their new jobs. The following is a list of examples and what the courts and parties have done in order to protect the former employer from the former employee's potential disclosure of proprietary information.

In 1995, a federal appeals court issued an injunction prohibiting William Redmond, formerly a marketing officer with PepsiCo, from working in the beverage unit of Quaker Oats, his new employer, for six months. The injunction also prohibited Mr. Redmond from disclosing any of PepsiCo's trade secrets or other proprietary information.

In 1997, GE hired 14 of Dow Chemical's employees from its plastics unit. The fourteen former Dow employees were hired to work in GE's plastic division. Following Dow's suit against GE, the parties reached a settlement that both sides agreed to have remain confidential.

In 1997, Daniel O'Neill, the head of Campbell Soup Company's soup division, left to work for the H.J. Heinz Co. A nasty series of lawsuits resulted with the parties settling the matter by Campbell permitting Mr. O'Neill to work for Heinz, but not in the Heinz soup division until August 1998.

Kevin R. Donohue was an executive vice president with the Qualex Inc. subsidiary of Eastman Kodak Co. with a noncompete clause in his employment contract that provided he would not go to work for a competitor for one year following his termination at Qualex. Mr. Donohue took a job at Fuji Photo Film Co., and Kodak filed suit alleging breach of contract by Mr. Donohue. The parties reached a settlement in 1997 that all three parties agreed not to disclose.

Most recently, Bayer has filed suit against GE because GE hired Vishal Wanchoo, a former vice president of Bayer in charge of marketing for Bayer's electronic-imaging-systems. These systems permit hospitals to use a simple and efficient means for storing patients' x-rays in digital form. Bayer is asking that Mr. Wanchoo not be permitted to take the job because he possesses significant trade secrets at a critical time in the industry when the marketing and sales of this product are just beginning. One of the allegations in the suit is that in the final days before he left Bayer, Mr. Wanchoo requested and received briefings on the product line and in the course of those briefings was privy to highly confidential information.

Discussion Questions

1. Discuss the ethical issues involved in these cases of job-hopping.
2. What weight should be given to the right-to-work?
3. What is the importance of proprietary information?
4. Would you hire someone from another company in order to gain information about a competitor?

Section G
Whistle-Blowing

In a true confrontation between personal values and company policy, employees are often faced with the knowledge that their employer is acting unethically in a way that does or could hurt someone else. How should they react? What should they do? Why do employers often ignore employees' concerns?

Case 3.19: Beech-Nut and the No-Apple-Juice Apple Juice

Jerome J. LiCari was the director of research and development for Beech-Nut Nutrition Corporation. Beech-Nut, at the time of LiCari's employment (in the late 1970s and early 1980s), was the second-largest baby food manufacturer in the United States. Beech-Nut is a subsidiary of Nestlé, the international food producer based in Switzerland.

In 1977, Beech-Nut entered into an agreement with Interjuice Trading Corporation for apple juice concentrate. The deal was a lifesaver for Beech-Nut because Interjuice's prices were 20 percent below market and Beech-Nut was heavily in debt, had only 15 percent of the baby food market, and was operating out of a badly maintained eighty-year-old plant in Canajoharie, New York.

Beech-Nut had once had a profitable product line with its chewing gum, but its parent, Squibb Corp., sold the chewing gum segment and the Beech-Nut name in 1973. The baby food division had never been a profitable part of Squibb's business, and by 1978, creditors and debts were mounting.

With apple concentrate in 30 percent of Beech-Nut's baby food products, the 1977 Interjuice contract marked the company's turnaround point. Nestlé was attracted and bought Beech-Nut in 1979. But, because of its substantially increased marketing costs, Beech-Nut's money pressures remained.

Rumors of adulteration (or the addition or substituted use of inferior substances in a product) were flying in the apple juice industry at the time of the Beech-Nut/Interjuice contract. Chemists in LiCari's department were suspicious. At that

116

time, accurate tests for adulteration did not exist, but LiCari and his chemists devised tests that revealed added ingredients, such as corn sugar, in the concentrate.

LiCari sent two Beech-Nut employees to Interjuice in Queens, New York, in 1978. Interjuice executives told the Beech-Nut employees the juice was imported from Israel. The Beech-Nut employees were not permitted to see plant processing operations; they were shown only storage tanks.

By 1981, LiCari was convinced the Interjuice concentrate was adulterated and worked to develop new tests for the juice. LiCari felt that "fake" apple juice would greatly harm Beech-Nut's nutritional image. While he developed the tests, LiCari took the circumstantial evidence he had collected on costs, the corn sugar, and the Interjuice plant tour and went to Beeech-Nut's head of operations, John F. Lavery, with his concerns. LiCari suggested that Beech-Nut do what Gerber does: require its suppliers to prove their concentrate is genuine or lose their supply contracts. Lavery, calling LiCari "Chicken Little," told him personally to produce proof that Interjuice's apple juice wasn't real juice.

By August 1981, LiCari and his chemists felt that their tests had established that the concentrate contained no apple juice. LiCari sent a memo to Lavery suggesting that Beech-Nut switch suppliers. Lavery did not respond to the memo, and when LiCari went to see him, Lavery said LiCari wasn't a team player and could be fired.

LiCari then took his evidence to Neils Hoyvald, the president and CEO of Beech-Nut. Hoyvald told LiCari he would take up the issue. Several months later, after no action had been taken, LiCari resigned. In his evaluation of LiCari's performance for 1981, John Lavery said that LiCari had great technical ability but that his judgment was "colored by naivete and impractical ideals."[27]

After leaving Beech-Nut, LiCari wrote an anonymous letter to the Food and Drug Administration (FDA) disclosing the juice adulteration at Beech-Nut. He signed the letter, "Johnny Appleseed."

After LiCari left, the pressure at Beech-Nut to continue using the adulterated apple juice increased because of operating losses. In 1982, a private investigator for the Processed Apples Institute, Inc., showed Canajoharie plant operators documents from the Interjuice dumpster and new tests indicating that the juice was adulterated. The institute invited Beech-Nut to join its lawsuit against Interjuice.

Beech-Nut did not join the suit (which eventually closed Interjuice) but did cancel its contracts. However, Beech-Nut continued to sell the juice and juice products it had on hand until the FDA ordered it to issue a juice recall. Beech-Nut had $3.5 million in apple-juice-product inventory. An FDA investigator observed:

> They played a cat-and-mouse game with us. When FDA would identify a specific apple juice lot as tainted, Beech-Nut would quickly destroy it before the FDA could seize it, an act that would have created negative publicity.[28]

When New York state government tests revealed that a batch contained little or no apple juice, Beech-Nut had the juice moved during the night using nine tanker trucks.

The company shipped some of its inventory to the Caribbean. Bogus juice was sold until March 1983.

---

27. Chris Welles, "What Led Beech-Nut Down the Road to Disgrace." *Business Week*, 22 February 1988, 128.

28. Ibid.

Both Neils Hoyvald and John Lavery were indicted for consumer fraud. Hoyvald was indicted for 358 violations of the Food, Drug and Cosmetic Act. Lavery was indicted for conspiracy, eighteen counts of mail fraud, and 429 violations of federal food and drug laws. Both Hoyvald and Lavery were convicted, but the convictions were overturned because the trial had been held in the wrong jurisdiction. State officials vowed to bring other charges against them. Beech-Nut pleaded guilty to 215 felony counts for violations of federal food and drug laws and agreed to pay a $2 million fine.

LiCari testified at the trials, "I thought apple juice should be made from apples."[29]

Discussion Questions

1. No one was ever made ill or harmed by the "fake" apple juice. Was LiCari justified in his concern?
2. Did LiCari follow the lines of authority in his efforts? Is this important for a "whistle-blower"? Why?
3. LiCari had only circumstantial evidence at one point. Is this type of evidence sufficient?
4. What pressures contributed to Beech-Nut's unwillingness to switch suppliers?
5. When no change was made in the supply contract, could LiCari have stayed with Beech-Nut?
6. Why did LiCari write anonymously to the FDA?
7. Is it troublesome that Hoyvald and Lavery escaped criminal conviction on a technicality? Does this "break" demonstrate that unethical behavior pays?

CASE 3.20: NEW ERA—IF IT SOUNDS TOO GOOD TO BE TRUE, IT IS TOO GOOD TO BE TRUE

The Foundation for New Era Philanthropy was founded in 1989 by Mr. John G. Bennett, Jr. New Era took in over $200 million between 1989 and May, 1995, when the SEC brought suit against New Era and the foundation went into bankruptcy.

Mr. Bennett is a charismatic individual who was able to bring in many individual and institutional investors (most of them nonprofit organizations which included many colleges and universities) with the promise of a double-your-money return. Mr. Bennett often met personally with investors or their representatives and opened and closed his sessions with them with prayer. Among the individual investors in New Era were Laurance Rockefeller, Pat Boone, President of Procter & Gamble, John Pepper, and former Treasury Secretary William Simon. The institutional investors included the University of Pennsylvania, the Nature Conservancy and the National Museum of American Jewish History. In 1991, Melenie and Albert Meyer moved from their native south Africa to Michigan where Mr. Meyer took a tenure-track position as an accounting Professor at Spring Arbor College in Michigan. Because there were only three accounting majors at the time he was hired, Mr. Meyer was also required to work part-time in the business office at the Christian college in the small Michigan community.

---

29. Welles, 128.

During his first month in the business office, Mr. Meyer found that the college had transferred $294,000 to Heritage of Values Foundation, Inc. He connected the term "Heritage" with Reverend Jim Bakker and went to the library to research Heritage of Values Foundation, Inc. While he found no connection to Jim Bakker, he could find no other information on the foundation. Mr. Meyer asked his supervisor, the vice president for business affairs, Ms. Janet M. Tjepkema, about Heritage of Values and the nature of the transfer. She explained that Heritage was the consultant that had found the New Era Foundation and had advised the college to invest in this "double your investment" fund.

Mr. Meyer attempted to research New Era but could find no registration for it in Pennsylvania, its headquarters location (there was no registration in Pennsylvania ever filed and no tax returns were filed until 1993). He could not obtain information directly from New Era. Mr. Meyer continued to approach administrators of the college, but they seemed annoyed. He still continued for the next two years to collect information about New Era. He gathered income tax returns and even spoke directly with Mr. Bennett. Mr. Meyer remained silent during the time that he gathered information because he was untenured and on a temporary work visa.

After he had collected files of information on New Era, which he labeled "Ponzi File," Mr. Meyer wrote a letter to the president of Spring Arbor as well as the chairman of the board of trustees for the college warning them about his concerns regarding New Era. Mr. Meyer had also tried to talk with his colleagues about the information he had uncovered. He felt shunned by administrators and his colleagues and by April 1994, he and his wife were no longer attending any social functions held by the college. He was told by administrators that raising funds was tough enough without his meddling. He repeatedly tried to convince administrators not to place any additional funds with New Era. His advice was ignored and Spring Arbor invested an additional $1.5 million in New Era in 1994. At that time, Spring Arbor College's total endowment was $6 million.

In March 1995, Mr. Meyer received tenure and began to try to help others by warning them about his concerns about New Era. He wrote to the SEC and detailed his information and concerns. The SEC then notified Prudential Securities which was holding $73 million in New Era stock. Prudential began its own investigation and found resistance from New Era officers in releasing information. New Era began to unravel and by June 1995, it was in bankruptcy. The $1.5 million invested by Spring Arbor will be lost as part of the New Era Bankruptcy. There were 300 creditors named and net losses were $107 million. A settlement netted the charities about 60 to 65 percent of their original investment. Prudential agreed to pay in $18 million as part of its settlement.

Mr. Bennett was sentenced in October, 1997. The judge, in particularly harsh language, lectured Mr. Bennett on the egregious nature of his conduct and sentenced Mr. Bennett to 12 years with no possibility of parole. Judge Ludwig called the damage Mr. Bennett had done to charities "incalculable."

Discussion Questions

1. Why did Mr. Meyer have so much difficulty convincing his college administrators that there was a problem with New Era?

2. Did Mr. Meyer follow the right steps in trying to bring New Era the attention of the college officials?

3. What impact did Mr. Meyer's personal situation (visa and tenure issues) have on his desire to carry through with his concerns?

4. Why were administrators so reluctant to hear Mr. Meyer out? Mr. Bennett notified Spring Arbor College officials when Mr. Meyer called him and asked administrators to keep Mr. Meyer quiet. How would you read this kind of request? What would you do if you were an administrator?

5. About forty of the nonprofit organizations that had invested in New Era and withdrawn their funds and earnings prior to its collapse voluntarily agreed to return their money to the bankruptcy pool. An administrator from Lancaster Bible College, in explaining the return of his college's funds to the trustee, quoted St. Paul's letter to the Philippians, "Let each of you look not only to his own interest, but also to the interests of others," Hans Finzel, head of CB International, a missionary fund, said his organization would not be returning the money, "It's true that it's tainted money, but it's also true that we received it in good faith." Compare and contrast the positions of the parties. Would you return the money?

CASE 3.21: DOW CORNING AND THE SILICONE IMPLANTS: QUESTIONS OF SAFETY AND DISCLOSURE

A. The Development of the Silicone-Filled Breast Implant

In the early 1960s, Dow Corning and other manufacturers began marketing silicone-filled implants for use in breast enlargement procedures. The silicone implants are breast-shaped bags filled with silicone gel. The bag itself is made of another form of silicone that is like a heavy plastic; this latter material is the same substance used in sealant and the children's toy, Silly Putty.

The other companies that manufactured the implants included Heyer-Schulte Corporation, to which several Dow Corning scientists and salesmen had migrated along with their silicone gel implant knowledge, and McGhan Medical Corporation, an offspring corporation resulting from the subsequent departure of the Dow migrants from Heyer-Schulte. Much of the attention regarding the implants has focused on Dow Corning because the Heyer-Schulte and McGhan implants simply duplicated the Dow Corning product, and these other manufacturers relied upon Dow's implant tests.

Transfers of the ownership of implant firms have exacerbated the complexity of implant liability. That complexity is somewhat simplified in Figure 2–1.

In the mid-seventies, Dow Corning conducted animal studies regarding problems with leakage from the implants. Though Dow furnished the studies to the FDA, it did so under a confidentiality procedure that prevented their disclosure under the Freedom of Information Act.

In the course of conducting its research, Dow Corning found that laboratory animals exposed to silicone gels developed tumors. A panel of research experts examined the Dow Corning studies and concluded that 80 percent of the exposed animals had developed tumors. The figure was so high that the panel deemed the

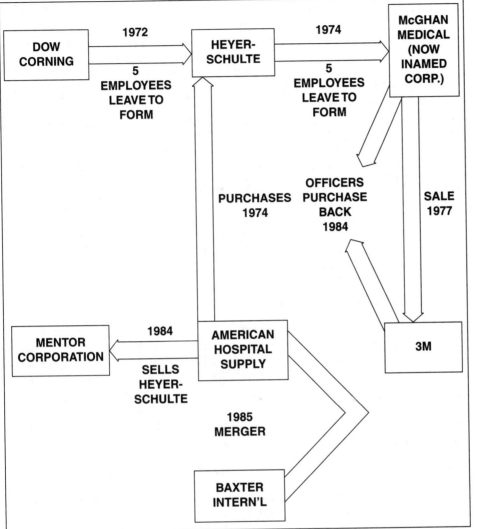

FIGURE 2–1
History and Ownership
of Silicone Implant
Manufacturers

research suspect and labeled the study "inconclusive." A 1975 study eventually discovered during litigation in 1994 explained that silicone implants harmed the immune systems of mice. A lawyer representing women in a class action suit against Dow found the study among Dow documents.

B. Internal Studies and Safety Questions

Thomas D. Talcott, a Dow materials engineer, disputed the panel's conclusions and resigned from the firm in 1976 after a dispute with his supervisors over the safety of the implants. Internal documents from Dow Corning, revealed later in ongoing litigation, indicate that Mr. Talcott was not a lone dissenter on the safety issue. Also in 1976, the chairman of the Dow Corning task force working on the new implants wrote, "We are engulfed in unqualified speculation. Nothing to date is truly quantitative. Is there something that migrates out or off the mammary prosthesis? Yes or no? Does it continue for the life of the implant or is it limited or controlled for a period of time? What is it?"[30] According to a Dow Corning salesman's 1980 characterization, "[the Dow Corning decision to sell a] questionable lot of mammaries on the market has to rank right up there with the Pinto gas tank."[31] Other internal documents revealed in litigation verified that early on, the company had known that the silicone gel could "bleed" and "migrate" into women's bodies.

In a deposition in an implant case against 3M, a Heyer-Schulte chemist disclosed that "[t]his phenomenon [gel bleeding] started to become of interest in the mid '70s."[32] He indicated that a breast implant placed on a blotter would leave a mark, especially if you applied pressure to the implant and allowed time to pass.

In 1983, a Dow Corning scientist, Bill Boley, wrote in an internal memo, "I want to emphasize that, to my knowledge, we have no valid long-term implant data to substantiate the safety of gel for long-term implant use."[33]

Mr. Jan Varner, a former Dow Corning employee who currently is president of McGhan Medical (Inamed), maintains that very few implants leaked and any leakage was "very, very small."[34]

C. Other Companies' Concerns

Outside Dow Corning, other companies expressed their own concerns about silicone implants. James Rudy, then-president of Heyer-Schulte Corporation, wrote a "Dear Doctor" letter in 1976 to inform physicians about the risk of the implants rupturing. Between 1976 and 1978, Congress gave the FDA its first authority to regulate medical "devices" such as implants. Nevertheless, despite the studies and warnings, the implants continued to be sold to approximately 150,000 women per year. It was also at this time that a two-year Dow Corning study found malignant tumors in 80 percent of the laboratory animals exposed to silicone gels.

The study concluded:

> As you will see, the conclusion of this report is that silicone can cause cancers in rats; there is no direct proof that silicone causes cancer in humans; however, there is considerable reason to suspect that silicone can do so.

In response, the FDA noted:

> The sponsor [of the study], Dow Corning, does not dispute the results of the current bioaesay, i.e., Dow Corning agrees that silicone gel is sarcomagenic. However, this sponsor contends that induction of sarcoma in rats is due to solid-state carcinogenesis (Oppenheimer effect). This is uniquely a rodent phenomenon. Therefore, that it is of no human health consequence as a solid-state cancer in man has not been documented. In support of these contentions, an epidemiological study by Delpco, et. al. [sic], has been cited and shows no increased incidence of cancer in breast implant recipients.[35]

---

30. "Records Show Firm Delayed Breast Implant Safety Study," *Mesa Tribune*, 13 January 1992, A1.

31. "Silicone Blues," *Time*, 24 February 1992, 65.

32. Thomas Burton, "Several Firms Face Breast-Implant Woes," *Wall Street Journal*, 23 January 1992, B1.

33. Judy Foreman, "Choice on Breast Implants Divides Women," *Arizona Republic*, 21 January 1992, C1.

34. Thomas Burton, "Several Firms Face Breast-Implant Woes," *Wall Street Journal*, 23 January 1992, B1.

35. Tim Smart, "Breast Implants: What Did the Industry Know, and When?" *Business Week*, 10 June 1991, 94; and Smart, "This Man Sounded the Silicone Alarm in 1976," *Business Week*, 27 January 1992, 34.

FDA staff members added the following comment in their report on the studies:

> Solid-state tumor has been reported in rats, mice, chickens, rabbits and dogs. It is biologically unconvincing that man is a uniquely resistant species.[36]

At the time of the report, the FDA proposed reclassification of the gel implants as medical devices required to be proven safe before they could be sold. The agency imposed the stricter classification over the objections of both surgeons and sellers of the implants. Data regarding the safety of the implants was not required, however, until April 1991.

D. Problems with the Implants Begin

As the regulatory arena for the implants changed, product liability suits by women experiencing implant-related side effects began. Their problems included rupturing of the silicone sacs, which then spilled the silicone gel into their bodies, causing painful inflammations as their bodies' autoimmune systems tried to combat the invading foreign substance. Other autoimmune disorders appeared in women who experienced leakage or ruptures:

- scleroderma: a disorder which thickens and stiffens the skin and results in the build-up of fibrous tissue in the body's organs;
- lupus erythematosus: a disease characterized by chronic joint pain and rashes; and
- rheumatoid arthritis: a disease of stiffening of the joints.[37]

In a 1984 landmark case, a federal district court, in awarding Maria Stern of Nevada $1.5 million in punitive damages, held that Dow Corning had committed fraud in marketing the implants as safe. In ruling on a post-trial motion, U.S. District Judge Marilyn Hall Patel wrote that although Dow Corning's own studies "cast considerable doubt on the safety of the product, the company had not disclosed those studies to patients, including Stern, an act that she labeled "highly reprehensible."[38]

Following the Stern case, in 1985 Dow began to place in its implant packages inserts that mentioned the possibility of "immune system sensitivity and possible silicone migration following rupture."[39]

In a 1987 position statement, Dow Corning did not dispute the possibility of implant leakage but did discount the linkage between those leaks and immune-system problems. A 1982 medical study that the company cited in the statement supported Dow Corning's assertion that there was no connection between implants and breast cancer. Also, the statement indicated that any leaked silicone would be picked up by the lymph system and excreted or stored. The position statement discounted the immune-system problems, maintaining that only silicone of lesser purity would cause such problems.

Following Dow Corning's position statement, litigation activity increased as the FDA received twenty-five hundred reports of illnesses or injuries associated with

36. Ibid.

37. Andrew Purvis, "A Strike Against Silicone," *Time*, 20 January 1992, 40–41.

38. Tim Smart, at 98.

39. Ibid.

the implants.[40] By the end of 1991, nearly one thousand implant lawsuits were pending against manufacturers.[41]

Early in the year, a New York jury awarded $4.5 million, nearly three times the Stern award, to a woman who alleged that her 1983 silicone implant with a polyurethane-foam covering had caused her breast cancer.

E. Regulatory Action

While Dow Corning appealed the New York case, Bristol-Myers withdrew its implant following the FDA's confirmation of a study that linked the foam used to coat the implant with a cancer-causing agent known as 2-toluene diamine (TDA). In the 1970s, the FDA banned the foam, used primarily in air and auto filters, from use in hair dyes because of the risk of birth defects. The FDA's order requiring manufacturers to prove the safety of their implant products or withdraw them from the market became effective in May 1991 and mandated that the proof from the manufacturers be forthcoming within a decade.

At the same time, Ralph Nader's group, the Public Citizen Health Research Group, met in Washington, D.C., with trial lawyers, women who had had the implants, and others. The group called for the full release of all implant-related safety data to date.

Sybil Goldrich, one of the women leading the movement against implants, had received implants in 1983, following her bilateral mastectomy for breast cancer. Nearly a decade of medical problems, including the removal of her ovaries and uterus, resulted; her doctors attributed those problems to the implants. Ms. Goldrich has commented, "There is no way to detoxify from this chemical." Her suit is pending in Los Angeles.[42]

In September of 1991, the FDA required implant manufacturers to provide risk information to women considering implant surgery. The agency, which specified the information required to be disclosed, issued the rule as an interim measure while it reviewed data on implant safety. These were the risks required to be disclosed:

- hardening of tissue around the implant,
- interference with mammography and tumor detection, and
- the possibility of leakage, autoimmune diseases, and cancer.

The FDA began its hearings on the silicone implants in October 1991. Speakers on both sides of the issue offered impassioned testimony. Manufacturers had boxes of data to support their claims that their products were harmless. Nearly four hundred women from thirty-seven states traveled to Washington to testify in favor of the implants. Recruited by plastic surgeons, the women testified about the importance of the implants to their physical and mental well-being and their freedom of choice. The women spoke of how the implants had helped them to recapture their self-esteem and gain psychological boosts in their battles with breast cancer.[43]

---

40. Hal Mattern, "New Concerns About Breast Implants," *Arizona Republic*, 7 January 1992, C1, C4.

41. Michele Galen, John Byrne, Tim Smart and David Woodruff, "Debacle at Dow Corning: How Bad Will It Get?" *Business Week*, 2 March 1992, 36.

42. Tim Smart, at 98.

43. "Women State Case for Breast Implants," *Mesa Tribune*, 21 October 1991, A3.

Physicians and professors of pharmacology and toxicology offered testimony to the contrary. Sybil Goldrich, by now the founder of Command Trust Network, a group advocating further study, asked of the women who testified:

"Do they know that silicone is bleeding into their bodies steadily? Do they know that implants are only good for a limited time and they will have to have surgery again and again?"

Speaking from a different perspective, Sharon Green, the executive director of the Y-ME National Organization for Breast Cancer Information, supported implant sales:

"Who are these women and why have so many of them rebuilt their bodies? As can be expected, many of our callers are breast cancer survivors. They have faced breast loss, a year or two of chemotherapy, and some have had their chests radiated. They face each day hoping that they have overcome cancer. Many no longer want to be reminded every morning and night of the cancer that played havoc with their bodies.

"It is estimated that one-third of current breast cancer patients are having reconstruction, most often with silicone implants. Saline implants can be an alternative, but they are not as aesthetically pleasing. An estimated 20% of implants are performed to reconstruct the breast; the rest, for augmentation. Y-ME's most recent survey (October 1991) of its own Hotline counselors—all breast cancer survivors—showed that among the respondents who had implants, the overwhelming majority were satisfied with their implants and 87% believed the devices helped their emotional recovery.

"Y-ME's position is clear and simple. If silicone breast implants can be scientifically proved dangerous, then this information should be made available to women. If the data are inconclusive, we demand full disclosure of all information so women can make decisions based on fact and not on unscientific claims and anecdotes. We also understand that no medical device can be guaranteed 100% safe and that some people are willing to take greater risks to improve the quality of their lives. However, it should be a personal choice based on all the medically verified evidence as it is known today.

"To ban or severely limit silicone breast implants based on inconclusive data would be one more insult to women by taking away their right to make informed decisions regarding their own bodies. For others to deny the right of a woman to implants because they fundamentally believe implants are unnecessary is arrogance in its ugliest form."[44]

After the hearings, the panel recommended unanimously that implants stay on the market but also called for continuing safety tests, concluding that the tests conducted by the four largest manufacturers had been inadequate. The panel cited the following hazards, offered during the hearings, for specific testing:

Scarring and hardening of breast tissue,

Implant leakage,

Reduced effectiveness of mammograms,

Autoimmune reactions,

Infections, and

Cancer.

---

44. Testimony of Sharon Green, Food and Drug Administration hearings on Silicone Breast Implants, Fall 1991.

F. Impact on Corning

In December 1991, another plaintiff, Mariann Hopkins, was awarded $7.3 million by a San Francisco jury that found Dow Corning had knowingly sold her a defective implant. The court of appeals for the ninth circuit affirmed the decision in 1994.

On December 30, 1991, the FDA sent Dow Corning a warning letter regarding the information Dow Corning was providing via a toll-free telephone number carried in ads about the safety of the implants. The FDA stated in the letter that the hotline information was used in a "confusing or misleading context."

On January 6, 1992, the FDA asked the medical device industry to halt the sale of silicone-gel implants until the agency could review new safety studies. FDA commissioner David Kessler asked all plastic surgeons to discontinue their use of the implants until the FDA could review information from Dow Corning that came to light in two product liability suits against a Dow Corning subsidiary.

Following the disclosure of the information in the product liability suits, by mid-January 1992, Corning's stock had sunk $10 in price to $68.375 per share, while Dow Chemical's stock had fallen 87.5 cents per share. The two companies are joint venturers in manufacture and sale of breast implants. Within days of the stock price slip, investors had filed suits against the company. Ten suits were pending by March.

In February of 1992, the General and Plastic Surgery Devices Panel of the FDA recommended that the use of implants for cosmetic enlargement be restricted but that implants be made available to women with breast cancer and "anatomical defects."[45]

By March, Dow Corning had announced its intent to withdraw from the implant market. Class-action suits by women with immune-system disorders are pending against the company, and Ira Reiner, the Los Angeles County district attorney, began a criminal probe into whether Dow Corning concealed health risks associated with the implants. Reiner proceeded under California's new so-called "be-a-manager-go-to-jail" law, which holds executives criminally liable for product defects that cause harm to either a company's employees or its customers. Reiner has observed, "There's no deterrent like a clank of a jail cell closing behind you."[46]

In early 1992, two women were hospitalized after using razors to remove their implants because they could not afford surgery for removal. Both were suffering from autoimmune diseases. Both had complications from the attempted self-removals and had to undergo surgery to complete the implant removals.[47] By the summer of 1992, Dow Corning reported that its second-quarter earnings had dropped 84.4 percent because of a $45 million pretax charge for eliminating its silicone gel breast-implant business. Even without the one-time charge, Dow Corning's earnings were down 19 percent.[48]

---

45. Jeff Nesmith, "Scientific Panel Suggests Breast Implant Restrictions," *Mesa Tribune*, 21 February 1992, A1, A12.

46. Ronald Grover, "The L.A. Lawman Gunning for Dow Corning," *Business Week*, 2 March 1992, 38.

47. "Woman Cuts Breast to Get Implant Aid," *Mesa Tribune*, 15 May 1992, A1; and "Woman Claims She Removed Her Own Implants," *Phoenix Gazette*, 17 April 1992, A2.

48. "Dow Corning's Profits Down 84.4% in Quarter," *New York Times*, 28 July 1992, C2.

G. Ongoing Warnings

In mid-1992, the Department of Health and Human Services established a Breast Implant Information Service that offered information and study enrollment for women with implants. The following is an excerpt:

UPDATE ON SILICONE GEL-FILLED BREAST IMPLANTS[49]

On April 16, 1992, FDA announced that, in keeping with the recommendations of its outside advisory panel, it would allow silicone gel-filled breast implants to be available, but only under special conditions.

Since FDA continues to be concerned about the safety of these devices, all patients to receive breast implants must be enrolled in clinical studies. FDA recognizes that there is a public health need for the implants among patients who have lost a breast because of cancer or trauma, or who have a serious malformation of the breast requiring reconstruction. Thus any woman who needs the implant to reconstruct the breast will be permitted access to such studies. Implants for the purpose of augmentation (breast enlargement) will be available only to a very limited number of women who are enrolled in controlled clinical studies approved by FDA and designed to study specific safety questions relevant to the device.

The following should help to answer questions about how FDA's decision will affect women, and what they should know about the implants.

Under what circumstances will the implants be available?

Silicone gel-filled implants will be available for clinical studies in three stages.

Stage 1:
Since FDA's April 16 decision, women with an urgent need for reconstruction with the implants have been allowed access to them. This category includes:

- women with temporary tissue expanders in place for breast reconstruction following mastectomy, who need to complete their reconstruction with gel-filled implants;
- women with silicone gel-filled implants who need replacement for medical reasons, such as rupture, gel leakage or severe contracture; and
- women having mastectomies before the studies are in place and for whom immediate reconstruction at the time of mastectomy is medically and surgically more appropriate than implantation at a later time. For women in this category, physicians must document that saline-filled implants are not a satisfactory alternative.

In order for a woman to get the implants in Stage 1, her doctor must first certify that she falls into one of the above three categories. She will have to sign a special form certifying that she has been told about the risks of the implants, and agree to enroll in a registry so that she can be notified in the future, if necessary, about new information on the implants.

Stage 2:
In this stage, breast implant manufacturers will set up studies which will enroll any woman who needs the gel-filled implants for breast reconstruction. FDA must approve these studies before they can begin.

Eligible women will include those who have had breast cancer surgery, severe injury to the breast, or a medical condition causing a severe breast abnormality. Women who must have an existing implant replaced for medical reasons will also be eligible.

---

49. FDA's Breast Implant Information Service. Issued May 25, 1992.

As in Stage 1, all women will have to be told about the risks, provide informed consent, and be enrolled in a registry. It will probably take until mid-summer until plans are in place for these studies.

Stage 3:

In addition to the Stage 2 studies, FDA will require carefully controlled research studies for each model of silicone implant that manufacturers wish to continue marketing. These Stage 3 studies will include both reconstruction and augmentation patients and will be focused on specific safety questions about the implants, such as how often rupture and hardening of the scar tissue around the implants occur. They will also evaluate the psychological benefits of the implants. The studies will be limited to the number of patients required to answer the safety questions.

As in Stages 1 and 2, women will have to be told about the risks, provide informed consent, and be enrolled in a registry. In addition, women in the Stage 3 studies will be followed more extensively to check for problems related to the implants.

Designing these Stage 3 studies will take time, and so they cannot begin as quickly as the Stage 2 studies.

How can a woman get enrolled in these studies?

She should contact the doctor who would be performing the implant surgery. The doctor can then contact the manufacturer of the implants to find out which hospitals or doctors' offices are taking part in the studies in that particular area.

H. The Settlement

In April 1994, Dow (along with Bristol-Myers Squibb and Baxter Healthcare Corp.) reached a \$4.2 billion[50] settlement with women who claimed to have health problems resulting from the implants. 3M, Union Carbide, Inamed, Wilshire Foam, and Applied Silicone, all suppliers of silicone to implant manufacturers, settled with the women for approximately \$500 million.

In February 1995, a jury in a case in Houston, Texas, held Dow Chemical Company liable in a breast implant litigation case. Dow Chemical has appealed the case which awarded \$5.2 million to two women plaintiffs.

By October 1995, the global \$4.2 billion settlement had fallen apart and Bristol-Myers Squib, Baxter and 3M joined together to make their own settlement proposal. Since then, Bristol, Baxter and 3M have settled with two-thirds of the women who have brought claims, paying between \$10,000 and \$250,000 each. Bristol also won two jury verdicts in August 1997.

In February 1996, a Harvard medical school study of 10,830 women with silicone implants concluded that there was a "small but statistically significant increased risk" of contracting immune-system illnesses once a woman has the implants.

In 1997, a Mayo Clinic study found that 25% of women with implants required reoperations to fix problems such as abnormal tissue growth or chronic pain. The rate for reoperation was higher (34%) among post-cancer patients with implants.

By this point, Dow was faced with 19,000 product liability lawsuits and proposed a reorganization plan for emerging from Chapter 11 bankruptcy. Under the plan \$600 million would be set aside for women to settle their lawsuits and

---

50. Burton, Thomas M, "Frequency of Reoperations for Woman with Breast Implants Put at Nearly 25%." *Wall Street Journal*, 6 March 1997, B6.

another $1.4 billion would go to women with implants if a jury trial found causation between the presence of the implants and immune-system illnesses. About 1,000,000 women have implants. Creditors, under the proposal, would receive $1 billion.

Also during this time, it was revealed that John E. Swanson, an executive at Dow Corning for 27 years, who had helped shape its ethics program, concluded that his wife Colleen's devastating illnesses were caused by her Dow Corning implants. Colleen Swanson had sued Dow Corning in 1992.

Colleen settled her suit in 1993, and 3 months later Swanson left Dow Corning. Swanson then cooperated with senior writer for *Business Week*, John A. Byrne for Byrne's book, *Informed Consent: A Story of Personal Tragedy and Corporate Betrayal . . . Inside the Silicone Breast Implant Crisis.*

In August, 1997, Dow Chemical lost its first class action suit, involving 1,800 women in federal district court in New Orleans. The case held the parent responsible. Two other verdicts were rendered previously against Dow Chemical, but they were not class action suits. The first verdict was overturned by the trial judge and the second is on appeal. Dow appealed the New Orleans case.

Also in 1997, a federal district judge appointed a panel of scientists to review articles and studies to assist him with evidentiary rulings. The issue the parties disputed at length was whether the cases could be consolidated for trial. The federal court of appeals consolidated 10,000 cases into one trial in federal district court in Detroit. Baxter, Bristol-Myers Squibb and 3M were unsuccessful in getting their cases consolidated with Dow Corning's in Detroit.

In 1998, the tort committee representing the women in the Dow Corning bankruptcy proposed a $3.8 billion settlement to be paid over two to three years. The parties still disagree over the requirement of a single causation issue trial. Nearly 200,000 women have now filed claims.

Discussion Questions

1. Who is morally responsible for the harms alleged from the implants? Should the information from the 1975 study have been disclosed?
2. Did Thomas Talcott act ethically in resigning in 1976?
3. If you had been Talcott, what would you have done?
4. Is the freedom of choice issue a moral standard?
5. Did members of the FDA staff have moral responsibilities with respect to the women with implants?
6. Did James Rudy relieve himself of any responsibility through his "Dear Doctor" letter?
7. What would you have done if you were Swanson?

CASE 3.22: THE CHANGING TIME CARDS

John Michael Gravitt was hired in 1980 at the General Electric jet engine plant as a machinist for $9.69 per hour. A Vietnam veteran, Gravitt was pleased to be among the eighteen thousand people working at GE's mile-long plant in Cincinnati, Ohio.

The plant, which produced engines for both military and commercial aircraft, manufactured the engine for the U.S. military's B-1 bomber.

Gravitt had an excellent performance record. After eleven weeks as a machinist, he was promoted to the supervisory position of foreman. As a foreman, he was in a position to see workers' time cards. Gravitt discovered that workers' training and idle time were being charged to defense jobs. He also noticed that time cards were being altered so that work on projects that had overrun their budgets was being charged to other projects. To facilitate making the changes, the foremen received, in their mailboxes, "hot sheets" listing the projects that were in cost overruns.

Gravitt himself was encouraged to alter his workers' time cards, and during his first year as foreman, he did as he was told, charging his machinists' time to specified contracts. (For example, he was told to charge the workers' nonproductive time to expensive contracts.) After the first year, however, he began to question the practice. Sometimes overruns were charged to projects that weren't even in the plant yet. Gravitt first complained to his unit manager, who sent him to a plant supervisor, who gave Gravitt a "this-happens-everywhere-in-the-real-world" speech. Concerned because GE was dealing with the federal government, Gravitt went to a private attorney. The attorney also gave him the "real world" speech. Gravitt went on with his work but ignored the "hot sheets" and refused to alter time cards. His supervisor did it for him.

John F. Tepe Jr., a foreman who worked with Gravitt, followed orders and altered 50 to 60 percent of his workers' daily time cards. When Gravitt confronted Tepe and told him he could go to jail for altering the cards, Tepe replied that he was "just carrying out orders and there wasn't any chance of getting caught."[51]

By early 1983, Gravitt had decided to gather proof of the time card alterations. For two months, on weekend shifts, he went into the office of his supervisor's secretary, Karen Kerr, who had prepared the "hot sheets," and photocopied both "hot sheets" and time cards. Gravitt also wrote an eight-page letter, which he delivered, along with his documentation, to Brian H. Rowe, a senior vice president at the Cincinnati plant, on June 29, 1983. Gravitt was fired that day.

An internal audit by GE showed that 80 percent of Gravitt's allegations were true and 20 percent could not be disproved.

Gravitt testified before the Senate Subcommittee on Administrative Practice and Procedure and filed suit against GE under the 1863 False Claims Act, which allows private citizens to bring suit against profiteers and recover part of the bounty collected. Fines under the False Claims Act are $5,000 to $10,000 per violation, with 30 percent going to those who successfully bring the case. Gravitt felt that the fines would have an impact on future conduct at GE and at other businesses: "It's the only way people will know they can do something to correct what isn't right."[52] Others argued that the False Claims Act encourages employees not to talk first with employers about problems they spot.[53] Mr. Gravitt settled his suit with GE in 1989 for an undisclosed amount.

---

51. Gregory Stricharchuk, "Ex-Foreman May Win Millions for His Tale About Cheating at GE," *Wall Street Journal*, 23 June 1988, 16.

52. Ibid.

53. Amal Kumar Naj, "GE's Drive to Purge Fraud Is Hampered by Workers' Mistrust," *Wall Street Journal*, 22 July 1992, A1.

Discussion Questions

1. Did altering the cards harm anyone?
2. Did Mr. Gravitt make an ethical choice in reporting the time card alterations?
3. Did Mr. Gravitt have to violate Ms. Kerr's privacy to collect documentation?
4. Was Mr. Tepe correct in saying that he was not responsible because he was just following orders?
5. Mr. Gravitt commented that a GE executive who spoke at his foreman's training session explained "how to succeed at GE." The executive's advice was that if a superior asks what 2 + 2 is, your answer should be "whatever you want it to be." What effect would such a philosophy have on a firm's ethical climate?
6. Mr. Gravitt noted that foremen's bonuses at GE were tied to time cards and vouchers. Does such an incentive send the wrong signal to employees?
7. Mr. Gravitt has been unable to find work with any GE contractor in Cincinnati, but he remains proud of his actions, his suit, and the money the federal government recovered. His advice for companies: "Listen to the honest people. Protect them. Transfer them or promote them and clean up the problem." What would GE need to change to implement Mr. Gravitt's ideas?[54]

---

54. Since the time of Mr. Gravitt's testimony GE has implemented a program the *Wall Street Journal* describes as a "remarkable effort" to encourage employees to act ethically and report any wrongdoing. For example, managers can spring pop quizzes on employees by asking questions such as "What are the three ways to report wrongdoing?" Employees who respond correctly get a gift such as a coffee mug.

Section H
Employee Rights

Compliance with labor laws. Employment benefits programs. These issues affect employees' attitudes at work and the reputation of a business.

Case 3.23: The Extension of Benefits to Partners of Homosexual Employees

In 1987, Margie Bleichman, an employee of Lotus Development Corporation, requested the personnel department to provide health insurance benefits for her female companion. Other employees made similar requests, and in 1991, Lotus Corporation announced that it would extend to the partners of homosexual employees the same benefits it offered to the spouses of heterosexual employees.

In spite of the offer, only twelve of an estimated three hundred and ten employees applied for the coverage because, as one Lotus employee observed, "most people don't want to come out." Some firms, such as Ben & Jerry's Homemade, Inc. provide coverage for both homosexual and heterosexual partners. A summary of the coverage provided by selected private and public sector employers to homosexual and unmarried heterosexual couples appears on page 133.[55]

Upon Lotus's announcement of its new benefits program, employees sent so many messages on the company's electronic bulletin board that the system crashed. A heterosexual employee commented, "Unless the world follows Lotus, it will almost certainly, over time, make Lotus increasingly gay." Another employee wrote, "I'm insulted that Lotus is going to replace the term spouse with spousal equivalent in all policies. Lotus is taking it upon itself to recognize same-sex couples as married. I find it to be profoundly immoral."

Homosexual employees felt that the availability of the policy was, in itself, a way to force them to disclose their sexual orientation. Whereas disclosing a hetero-

---

55. William M. Bulkeley, "Lotus Creates Controversy by Extending Benefits to Partners of Gay Employees," *Wall Street Journal*, 25 October 1991, B1, B6.

sexual marriage would have no impact on a career, disclosing a homosexual partnership to obtain benefits could create a career ceiling for some employees.

Since the time of the Lotus controversy, the extension of benefits to life partners has increased. In 1996, 230 firms offered domestic/life partner benefits. In 1997, there were 505 companies offering such benefits, and 25 of those companies are Fortune 500 firms. A recent survey by the Society for Human Resource Management (SHRM) of 3,000 firms found that one in ten firms now make benefits available to domestic partners. Of those firms, 43 percent make benefits available to same-sex and opposite-sex life partners. Twenty-one percent of the firms extend the benefit only to same-sex partners.

Employer	Date Instituted	Number of Employees	Homosexual Couples	Unmarried Heterosexual Couples
Village Voice	1982	231	Yes	Yes
American Psychological Association	1983	1,500	Yes	Yes
Ben & Jerry's	1989	350	Yes	Yes
Montefiore Medical Center (New York)	1991	9,000	Yes	No
Lotus Development	1991	4,000	Yes	No
Berkeley, CA	1985	1,625	Yes	Yes
Santa Cruz, CA	1987	650	Yes	Yes
Seattle	1990	10,000	Yes	Yes
San Francisco	1991	30,000	Yes	Yes

Discussion Questions

1. Is it fair for a policy to cover homosexual couples but not unmarried heterosexual couples?
2. Is the disclosure issue a privacy problem for the employees who could benefit?
3. Evaluate the reactions of Lotus employees to the new policy.
4. Would companies be better served by redefining the term "dependents" as opposed to redefining covered relationships?
5. How would managers, whose religious beliefs run contra to recognition of homosexual relationships, manage benefit programs for their companies?

CASE 3.24: CHEAP LABOR: CHILDREN, SWEAT SHOPS AND THE FIFTY-HOUR WORK WEEK

With the passage of GATT and NAFTA, a world-wide market has been emerging. In addition to the international market for goods, there is also an international market for labor. Many U.S. firms have subcontracted out the production of their products to factories in China, Southeast Asia, Central and South America.

The National Labor Committee (NLC), an activist group, periodically releases information on conditions in foreign factories and the companies utilizing those factories. In 1998, the NLC issued a report that Liz Claiborne, Wal-Mart, Ann Taylor, Esprit, Ralph Lauren, J.C. Penney, and K-Mart were using subcontractors in China that use Chinese women (between the ages of 17 and 25) to work 60–90 hours per week for as little as 13–23 cents per hour. The Chinese subcontractors do not pay overtime, house the workers in crowded dormitories, feed them a poor diet, and operate unsafe factories.

Levi Strauss pulled its manufacturing and sales operations out of China in 1993 because of human rights violations, but announced in 1998 that it would expand its manufacturing there and begin selling clothing there. Peter Jacobi, the president of Levi Strauss, indicated that it had the assurance of local contractors that they would adhere to Levi's guides on labor conditions. Jacobi stated, "Levi Strauss is not in the human rights business. But to the degree that human rights affect our business, we care about it."

The Mariana Islands is currently a site of investigation by the Department of Interior for alleged indentured servitude of children as young as 14 in factories there. Wendy Doromal, a human rights activist, issued a report that workers there have tuberculosis and oozing sores. Approximately $820 million worth of clothing items are manufactured each year on the islands, which are a U.S. territory. Labels manufactured there include The Gap, Liz Claiborne, Banana Republic, J.C. Penney, Ralph Lauren, and Brooks Brothers.

U.S. companies' investments in foreign manufacturing in major developing nations like China, Indonesia, and Mexico have tripled in 15 years to $56 billion, a figure that does not include the subcontracting work. In Hong Kong, Singapore, South Korea and Taiwan, where plants make apparel, toys, shoes and wigs, national incomes have risen from 10 percent to 40 percent of American incomes over the past 10 years. In Indonesia, since the introduction of U.S. plants and subcontractors, the portion of malnourished children in the country has gone from one-half to one-third.

In a practice that is widely accepted in other countries, children, ages ten to fourteen, labor in factories for fifty or more hours per week. Their wages enable their families to survive. School is a luxury, and a child attends only until he or she is able to work in a factory. The Gap, Levi Strauss, Esprit, and Leslie Fay have all been listed in social responsibility literature as exploiting their workers. In 1994, the following appeared in a quarter-page ad in the *New York Times*:

The Price of Corporate Greed at Leslie Fay

Marie Whitt is fighting to keep the job she has held for 17 years at a Leslie Fay plant in Wilkes-Barre. Marie earns $7.80 an hour—hardly a fortune. On June 1st, she and 1,800 co-workers were forced to strike because Leslie Fay plans to dump them. Ninety percent are women whose average age is 50. They have given their whole working lives to the company and losing their jobs would be a disaster. Marie knows she will never find a comparable job in today's economy. Without her union benefits, she and her husband won't be able to pay for his anti-cancer medication. "What Leslie Fay wants to do is so rotten," she says. "You've got to draw the line somewhere and fight."

Dorka Diaz worked for Leslie Fay in Honduras, alongside 12- and 13-year-old girls locked inside a factory where the temperature often hits 100° and where there is no clean drinking water. For a 54-hour week, including forced overtime, Dorka was paid a little over $20. With food prices high—a quart of milk costs 44 cents—Dorka and her three-year-old son live at the edge of starvation. In April, Dorka was fired for trying to organize a union. "We need jobs desperate," she says, "but not under such terrible conditions."[56]

Leslie Fay executives claim they can only "compete" by producing in factories like Dorka's. But identical skirts—one made by Dorka, the other by Marie—were recently purchased at a big retail chain here. Both cost $40. Searching the world for ever-cheaper sources of labor is not the kind of competition America needs. Leslie Fay already does 75% of its production overseas. If it really wants to compete successfully in the global economy, it would modernize its facilities here in the U.S. as many of its competitors have done. But Leslie Fay wants to make a fast buck by squeezing every last drop of sweat and blood out of its workers. Marie Whitt and Dorka Diaz don't think that's right. And they know it's a formula for disaster—for all of us.

You can help by not buying Leslie Fay products—until Leslie Fay lives up to its corporate responsibilities at home and overseas.

Don't buy Leslie Fay! Boycott all clothing made by Leslie Fay and sold under these labels: Leslie Fay, Joan Leslie, Albert Nipon, Theo Miles, Kasper, Le Suit, Nolan Miller, Castleberry, Castlebrook.[57]

In the United States, the issue of sweatshops came to the public's attention when it was revealed that talk-show host Kathie Lee Gifford's line of clothing at Wal-Mart had been manufactured in sweatshops in Guatemala and CBS ran a report on conditions in Nike subcontractor factories in Vietnam and Indonesia. The reports on Nike's factories issued by Vietnam Labor Watch included the following: women required to run laps around the factory for wearing non-regulation shoes to work; payment of subminimum wages; physical beatings, including with shoes, by factory supervisors; and most employees are women between the ages of 15 and 28. Philip Knight, CEO of Nike, included the following in a letter to shareholders:

Q: Why on earth did NIKE pick such a terrible place as Indonesia to have shoes made?
A: Effectively the US State Department asked us to. In 1976, when zero percent of Nike's production was in Taiwan and Korea, Secretary of State Cyrus Vance asked Charles Robinson . . . to start the US-ASEAN Business Council to fill the vacuum left by the withdrawal of the American military from that part of the world . . . Chuck Robinson accepted the challenge, put together the council and served as Chairman of the US side for three years. Mr. Robinson was a Nike Board member at that time as he is today . . . "Nike's presence in that part of the world", according to a senior state department official at that time, "is American foreign policy in action".

Nike sent former U.N. Ambassador Andrew Young to its overseas factories in order to issue a report to Knight, the board, and the shareholders. Young did tour factories but only with Nike staff and only for a few hours. Young issued the following findings:

- Factories that produce Nike goods are "clean, organized, adequately ventilated, and well-lit"
- No evidence of a "pattern of widespread or systematic abuse or mistreatment of workers"

---

56. From Ms. Diaz's testimony before a hearing of the Subcommittee on Labor-Management Relations, Committee on Education and Labor, U.S. House of Representatives, Wilkes-Barre, Pennsylvania, 7 June 1994.

57. From a statement published by the International Ladies Garment Workers Union in the *New York Times*, 9 June 1994, A16.

- Workers don't know enough about their rights or about Nike's own code of conduct
- Few factory managers speak the local language, which inhibits workers from lodging complaints or grievances
- Independent monitoring is needed because factories are controlled by absentee owners and Nike has too few supervisors on site

On October 18, 1997, there were international protests against Nike in 13 countries and 70 cities. On October 13, 1997, 6,000 Nike workers went on strike in Indonesia followed by a strike of 1,300 in Vietnam.

On November 8, 1997, an Ernst & Young audit about unsafe conditions in a Nike factory in Vietnam was leaked to the *New York Times* and made front-page news.

Michael Jordan, NBA and Nike's superstar endorser, agreed to tour Nike's factories in July 1998, stating, "the best thing I can do is go to Asia and see for myself. The last thing I want to do is pursue a business with a negative over my head that I don't have an understanding of. If there are issues . . . if it's an issue of slavery or sweatshops, [Nike executives] have to revise the situation."

From June 1997 to January 1998, Nike distributed 100,000 plastic "code of conduct" cards to plant workers. The cards list workers' rights. Nike's performance has dropped. Its stock price has dropped from a 1996 high of $75.75 per share to a March 1998 low of $43 per share.

Retailers have been canceling orders so that sales are decreased 3% for 1997. Nike will reduce its labor force by 10–15% or 2100–3100 positions.

Press for Change and Global Exchange, an activist group made the following demands of Nike in 1998:

1. **Accept independent monitoring by local human rights groups to ensure that Nike's Code of Conduct is respected by its subcontractors.** The GAP has already accepted independent monitoring for its factories in El Salvador, setting an important precedent in the garment industry. If Nike were to accept such monitoring in Indonesia, it would set a similar positive precedent in the shoe industry, making Nike a true leader in its field.
2. **Settle disputes with workers who have been unfairly dismissed for seeking decent wages and work conditions.** There are dozens of Indonesian workers who have been fired for their organizing efforts, and thousands who have been cheated out of legally-promised wages. Nike must take responsibility for the practices of its subcontractors, and should offer to reinstate fired workers and repay unpaid wages.
3. **Improve the wages paid to Indonesian workers.** The minimum wages in Indonesia is $2.26 a day. Subsistence needs are estimated to cost at least $4 a day. While Nike claims to pay double the minimum wage, this claim includes endless hours of overtime. We call on Nike to pay a minimum of $4 a day for an eight-hour day, and to end all forced overtime.

The American Apparel Manufacturers Association (AAMA) which counts 70 percent of all U.S. garment makers in its membership as well, has a database for its members to check labor compliance by contractors. The National Retail Federation has established the following statement of Principles on Supplier Legal Compliance (now signed by 250 retailers):

1. We are committed to legal compliance and ethical business practices in all of our operations.
2. We choose suppliers that we believe share that commitment.

3. In our purchase contracts, we require our suppliers to comply with all applicable laws and regulations.

4. If it is found that a factory used by a supplier for the production of our merchandise has committed legal violations, we will take appropriate action, which may include canceling the affected purchase contracts, terminating our relationship with the supplier, commencing legal actions against the supplier, or other actions as warranted.

5. We support law enforcement and cooperate with law enforcement authorities in the proper execution of their responsibilities.

6. We support educational efforts designed to enhance legal compliance on the part of the U.S. apparel manufacturing industry.

The U.S. Department of Labor has recommended the following to improve the current situation:

1. All sectors of the apparel industry, including manufacturers, retailers, buying agents and merchandisers, should consider the adoption of a code of conduct.

2. All parties should consider whether there would be any additional benefits to adopting more standardized codes of conduct [to eliminate confusion resulting from a proliferation of different codes with varying definitions of child labor.]

3. U.S. apparel importers should do more to monitor subcontractors and homeworkers [the areas where child labor violations occur].

4. U.S. garment importers-particularly retailers-should consider taking a more active and direct role in the monitoring and implementation of their codes of conduct.

5. All parties, particularly workers, should be adequately informed about codes of conduct so that the codes can fully serve their purpose.

Discussion Questions

1. One executive noted, "We're damned if we do because we exploit. We're damned if we don't because these foreign economies don't develop. Who's to know what's right?"

   Levi Strauss & Company, discovering that youngsters under the age of fourteen were routinely employed in its Bangladesh factories, could either fire forty underage youngsters and impoverish their families or allow them to continue working. Levi compromised and provided the children both access to education and full adult wages.

   Nike has shoe factories in Indonesia, and the women who work in those factories net $37.46 per month. However, as Nike points out, their wages far exceed that of other factory workers. Nike's Dusty Kidd notes, "Americans focus on wages paid, not what standard of living those wages relate to."

   Economist Jeffrey D. Sachs of Harvard has served as a consultant to developing nations such as Bolivia, Russia, Poland and Malawi. He observes that the conditions in sweatshops are horrible, but they are an essential first step toward modern prosperity. "My concern is not that there are too many sweatshops, but that there are too few. These are precisely the jobs that were the stepping stone for Singapore and Hong Kong, and those are the jobs that have to come to Africa to get them out of their backbreaking rural poverty."

   Business executives respond as follows:

   "If someone is willing to work for 31 cents an hour, so be it—that's capitalism. But throw in long hours, abusive working conditions, poor safety conditions, and no benefits, and that's slavery. It was exactly those same conditions that spawned the union movement here in the U.S." John Waldron

"If the wages of 31 cents per hour were actually fair wages, adults would gladly do the work instead of children." Wesley M. John

"Just when you think the vile remnants of those who would build empires on the blood and bones of those less fortunate than ourselves have slithered off into the history books, you come across this kind of tripe. For shame for rationalizing throwing crumbs to your fellow human beings so that you and your ilk can benefit at their expense." Jose Guardiola

Discuss the economic, social and ethical issues of plants and wages in developing countries. Consider the following excerpt from *The Economist*:

If a Chinese manufacturing worker can be hired for only 25 cents an hour, compared with $17 in America or $32 in Germany, surely it makes sense for western firms to shift all their production to China? International comparisons of labour costs often provoke such a question. They also provoke protests by trade unions and others in the rich world, who fear that unless governments do something, workers there will either see their wages driven down to third-world levels too, or face a jobless future. That "something" could mean blocking cheap imports or subsidizing exports.

Some jobs are inevitably being sucked out of the rich world and into the poorer one as western firms seek to cut their costs. Yet the threat that low-wage countries pose to employment in the rich countries is greatly exaggerated. After all, if cheap labour guaranteed economic success, nations such as Bangladesh or Mozambique would dominate global output.

So why don't they? One reason is that wages largely reflect international differences in productivity: cheap labour in emerging economies goes hand in hand with lower productivity. Cassandras draw little comfort from this. As poor countries get hold of the latest production techniques, they argue, richer ones will lose their traditional advantage. Third-world producers will be able to combine low wages with first-world technology—and hence productivity levels—making themselves super-competitive. This is nonsense. In the long run, increases in productivity will be offset by higher wages or a stronger exchange rate. Witness the experience of South Korea, where wages have risen from less than one-tenth to more than two-fifths of American levels over the past ten years.[58]

2. Would you employ a twelve-year-old in one of your factories if it were legal to do so?
3. Would you limit hours and require a minimum wage even if it were not legally mandated?
4. Would you work to provide educational opportunities for these child laborers?
5. Why do you think the public seized on the Kathie Lee Gifford and Nike issues?

---

58. From "Invasion of the job snatchers," *The Economist*, November 2, 1996, p. 18. © 1996 The Economist Group Inc. Reprinted with permission. Further reproduction prohibited.

Unit Four
Business Operations

"If we were making that decision now in light of the press scrutiny we have been receiving, we probably would not have taken that risk."

Robert C. Winters
Chairman, Prudential Insurance

"Cookies." "Raisins."

The code words at Phar-Mor for a second set of books and false entries, respectively.

From cash and internal controls to "grease" payments in foreign operations, businesses face continuing dilemmas about the propriety of the use and flow of funds.

From production to shutdown, everything a business does affects its workers, their well-being, the environment, and the community. Decisions in these areas require a careful balancing of many interests.

Section A

Financial and Cash Management Procedures

Control of funds offers opportunities for misuse of funds. A lack of careful supervision can present tempting opportunities for personal and business gain that later could serve to destroy the firm. Who's in charge? How much information do they have? Can misuse be controlled? As you review these cases, think of how better management and ethical codes could have helped these firms.

Case 4.1: BCCI and the Role of Internal Auditors

The Bank of Credit & Commercial International (BCCI) was a $20 billion banking empire that operated in seventy countries. Incorporated in Luxembourg and headquartered in London, BCCI owned First American Bankshare in Washington, D.C. (with Clark Clifford, former U.S. secretary of defense, as chairman), and the National Bank of Georgia.

With First American, Clifford had complex roles beyond that of chairman. He was also the managing partner of Clifford & Warnke, the law firm that represented First American. Clifford & Warnke also defended BCCI during its money-laundering charges in 1988. In addition, Clifford and his law partner, Robert A. Altman, had borrowed $12 million from BCCI to buy shares in First American Bankshare. BCCI found a buyer for Clifford's shares eighteen months later, and Clifford realized an $11 million pretax profit.

BCCI had what regulators referred to as a "black network," consisting of fifteen hundred employees who used spy equipment, arms deals, bribery, espionage, extortion, and drug trafficking to advance the bank's presence worldwide.[1] BCCI was the bank used for the exchange of money in the Iran-Contra deals. The CIA also had BCCI accounts. Customers of BCCI included Manuel Noriega, Saddam Hussein, and Ferdinand Marcos.

Regulators shut down BCCI in sixty-two countries on July 5, 1991. A source for *Time's* story on BCCI told the magazine's reporter, Jonathan Beaty, of the complexity of BCCI's operations. Beaty reported, "First, he said that as long as I thought of BCCI as just a bank, I wouldn't understand it. It is a nation with its own intelligence service, army, and national bank. It deals in commodities (oil, drugs, grain-even cement, some of which is laced with bricks of heroin) and is one of the largest arms dealers in the world. Banking was important to this nation's success, but it was far from its only field of operations. Second, this was the first time we heard of the 'black network,' the covert-operations arm of BCCI, which was for hire and very capable. This is the first global scandal, made possible by the information revolution with its instant transfers of money and real time, worldwide operations."[2]

After the July 5th shutdown, mysteries about BCCI's operations unfolded. When Manhattan District Attorney Robert Morgenthau announced that BCCI had been indicted on charges of defrauding investors and stealing more than $30 million, he explained that BCCI's structure was nothing more than a global Ponzi scheme in which money was shifted to maintain a healthy appearance for auditors and regulators while the masterminds kept funds for themselves.[3]

An independent audit undertaken by Price Waterhouse for British authorities, completed and fully released in 1992, concluded that BCCI's board was "taken in" by "dominant and deceitful management."[4] Price Waterhouse also concluded that accounts existed "for the purposes of fraudulently routing funds."[5]

Still facing ongoing investigations by various agencies, BCCI, a hollow shell, pleaded guilty to federal and state charges of racketeering, fraud, and money laundering in December 1991. A New York grand jury indicted Sheik Khalid bin Mahfouz, a top officer of Saudi Arabia's National Commercial Bank, a BCCI subsidiary, to recover a $170 million fine.

At the end of July 1992, both Clark Clifford and his law partner, Robert Altman, were indicted for conspiracy and concealing material facts in the BCCI downfall.[6] In August 1993, Robert Altman was acquitted following a five-month trial. Mr. Clifford, eighty-seven years old, never stood trial on the charges because he was deemed too ill. Altman, Clifford, and fourteen other lawyers in their firm have been named in civil suits requesting $200 million in damages and alleging breaches of fiduciary duty.

The losses of depositors at BCCI were estimated at $10 billion. The civil suit has produced settlements so far of $626 million. Assets were sold to recover slightly

---

1. Jonathan Beaty and Sam C. Gwynne, "The Dirtiest Bank of All," *Time*, July 1991, 42–45.

2. BCCI: Uncovering A Rogue Empire," *Time Insider*, 29 July 1991, 1–3.

3. Elizabeth Kurylo, "Indictment of BCCI Charges 'Largest Bank Fraud in History,'" *Mesa Tribune*, 30 July 1991, A3.

4. Thomas Petzinger Jr., and Peter Truell, "Biggest Saudi Bank Took Part in Effort to Hide Fraud at BCCI, Auditors Say," *Wall Street Journal*, 9 February 1992, A18.

5. Ibid.

6. Steve Lohr, "Indictment Charges Clifford Took Bribes," *New York Times*, 30 July 1992, A1, C5; "An Icon Falls in the BCCI Scandal," *Time*, 10 August 1992, 12–13.

less than $1 billion. In 1993, Mr. Clifford stepped in and served temporarily as White House Counsel for the Clinton administration.

Discussion Questions

1. Would it be possible to sit on the board of BCCI or one of its subsidiary banks and not realize the extent of its activities?
2. Would it be possible for an auditor to issue financial statements that were clean for BCCI?
3. At what point are internal investigations warranted?
4. Suppose you were a member of the BCCI internal audit department and you unraveled the black network. What would you do with the information?
5. Can directors or internal auditors ever detect fraud?
6. Did Clifford and Altman have any conflicts of interest in their various roles?
7. Was BCCI's large, multinational structure a key in avoiding regulatory oversight? Did the principals in BCCI find a legal loophole? Were they justified in their conduct because there was no direct supervision?
8. The Department of Justice received 700 tips on BCCI between 1979 and 1991 and set up a group to investigate, but took no action until 1992. Does this indicate that whistle-blowing is ignored?

CASE 4.2: MEDICAL BILLING ERRORS AND PRACTICES

Billie Jean Young is the administrator for Los Lomas, a private hospital located in Palm Springs, California. Los Lomas serves patients who carry insurance in 95 percent of the procedures the hospital performs. Los Lomas' noninsurance procedures tend to be plastic surgery; all plastic surgery patients pay in advance. The nature of the medical business at Los Lomas is largely the result of the hospital's location in an upper-middle class retirement/resort area.

Young has just read a recent study that shows that 98 percent of all hospital bills contain errors. Internal data for Los Lomas shows that the hospital receives complaints of errors on approximately 20 percent of the bills it issues.

The study indicates that doctors are "fudging" on insurance claims. For example, coding the removal of a mole as a larger procedure (known as "upcoding") will bring additional funds from an insurer. Breaking down surgeries (or "unbundling" them) into segments such as exploration, removal, and repair of scar tissue will substantially increase claims. Itemizing each test in a battery of tests ("exploding" the battery) can triple the cost of a single blood sample. Doctors accomplish all these billing strategies by savvy use of the coding process.

Insurers do have computer programs to check for "code creeps" (increased billing by coding), but often they reject such claims in a report to the patient that explains how the charges exceed "usual and customary limits." The patient must then pay personally the amounts considered excessive.

In many cases, miscoding is done to help provide patients with insurance coverage when coverage might not otherwise be available. For example, a patient's insurance might not cover routine tests as part of a physical but would cover those same tests if they were coded "to rule out cancer." Infertility procedures would not be covered, but diagnostic surgery to determine the presence of endometriosis would.

Many of these practices result from the inability to collect bills from uninsured patients who are simply unable to pay. Hospitals often use billings for insured patients to cover the costs they must absorb in providing care for uninsured patients. For example, one Florida hospital charged an insured patient $15 for one ounce of petroleum jelly. However, the five-digit CPT coding system is complex, confusing, and fraught with ambiguities. Some errors are the result of these factors.

Medicare recently announced a "bundling" payment policy for heart surgeries, under which it will pay a package price for coronary bypass procedures. The price will include all charges for both hospitals and doctors. Medicare officials maintain that "unbundled" bills encourage doctors to perform more procedures. Doctors maintain that the policy will sacrifice quality of care and their autonomy in making treatment decisions.

Discussion Questions

1. Should Ms. Young commission a study of the billing practices at Los Lomas and implement any changes that would correct the overbilling described?
2. Will Ms. Young be able to affect physicians' conduct in coding?
3. Do fudging, upcoding, exploding, and unbundling really harm anyone? Aren't many patients helped by these practices?
4. If patients are not complaining, is it a wise use of resources to audit bills?
5. In many cases, hospitals and physicians maintain these billing practices in order to shift costs. That is, they receive payment from insured patients to make up for the lack of payment from the uninsured who are unable to pay. Is this fair? Is it honest? Should it be disclosed?

Case 4.3: Creative Billing

Columbia/HCA Healthcare Corporation, Inc., the nation's largest hospital chain (342 hospitals), is under investigation for the common industry practice of "upcoding." Medical care providers and insurers, including the federal government, speak in "code." All these parties follow a billing system based on 500 groups of 3,500 medical procedures and 12,574 diagnostic codes. How an illness is coded can make a substantial difference in the amount of reimbursement the medical provider receives for the care of the patient. For example, a Columbia newsletter noted that the difference between coding a hip or femur procedure is $4,493.

Most medical care providers hire consultants to help them with "upcoding." One consultant noted, "Every hospital does it or they die." Still another consultant noted, "Why shouldn't they go for the higher one?" But another consultant noted, "Oh, I grant you, there are shades of gray, but when hospitals cross the line, they know it." He also labeled the art of upcoding a "pathetic commentary on our times. These guys should be figuring out how to better treat patients in their hospitals."

Columbia began conducting an internal probe as the FBI investigated. Three executives were indicted in July 1997 on charges of defrauding the government by overbilling. In September 1997 Columbia warned its profits would decline with earnings per share dropping from 46 cents per share to 20 or 25 cents per share.

By October 1997, the FBI filed an affidavit in its investigation describing the fraud at Columbia/HCA as "systemic."

Shareholder lawsuits against Columbia are pending around the country. Between March 1997 and August 1997, the value of Columbia's stock dropped by one-third.

Several whistle-blowers are assisting the FBI. U.S. Attorney James Sheehan said, "The whistle-blowers get you inside, share the company's intent and knowledge and provide a road map for routines and systems."

Discussion Questions

1. If everyone is doing it, why is there a concern about ethics or possible illegality?
2. If there are shades of gray in diagnosing, is there any problem with always taking the higher code?
3. Do hospitals exist to make money or treat the ill?
4. How did shades of gray turn into allegations of systemic fraud and criminal indictments?
5. Why are there whistle-blowers in this case?

CASE 4.4: MINISCRIBE AND THE AUDITORS

MiniScribe, founded in 1980 and based in Longmont, Colorado, was a disk drive manufacturer. When MiniScribe hit a slump in the mid-1980s because it had lost its largest customer, IBM, the board of directors brought in Q.T. Wiles. Called the "Mr. Fix-It" of high technology industries, Wiles had turned around Adobe Systems, Granger Associates, and Silicon General, Inc.

When Wiles took over at MiniScribe, he engaged the venture-capital and investment banking firm of Hambrecht & Quist to raise the capital needed for the firm's turnaround. Hambrecht & Quist raised $20 million in 1987 through the sale of debentures. Wiles was, at that time, the chairman of Hambrecht & Quist. Hambrecht & Quist purchased $7.5 million of the debentures and also purchased a 17 percent interest in MiniScribe.

With new capital and simultaneous cost cuts, MiniScribe's sales went from $113.9 million in 1985 to a projected $603 million in 1988. In 1987, MiniScribe's board asked Wiles to stay on for another three years. That year, MiniScribe's stock climbed to $14 per share.

During 1988, the computer industry underwent another slump, and by May, Wiles and other officers were selling stock. Wiles sold 150,000 shares for between $11 and $12 per share, and seven other officers sold 200,000 shares.

By the time the shares were sold, MiniScribe held the unenviable position of having high inventory and high receivables. Industry sales were down, and MiniScribe customers were not paying their bills. In early 1989, MiniScribe announced a $14.6 million loss for the final quarter of 1988. MiniScribe's ratio of inventory to sales was 33 percent (the industry average was 24 percent), and its receivables were ninety-four days behind (the industry average was seventy days). The amount of receivables went from $109 million to $173 million in the last quarter of 1988.

MiniScribe's release of the new financial information resulted in an in-house audit, shareholder lawsuits, and an investigation of stock trading by the Securities and Exchange Commission (SEC). Scrutiny by regulators, outside directors, and the SEC revealed that Wiles, through his unrealistic sales goals, had created a high-pressure environment for managers. In interviews, managers described "dash meetings" in which Wiles spouted his management philosophies. In one such meeting, Wiles had two controllers stand as he fired them, saying, "That's just to show everyone I'm in control of the company."[7] Wiles' attorney described him as "fairly autocratic and very demanding of the people who work for him."[8]

The in-house audit uncovered that by late 1986, financial results had become the sole criterion for performance evaluations and bonuses at MiniScribe. To be sure that they hit their quotas, MiniScribe sales personnel had used creative accounting maneuvers. For example, in one case a customer was shipped two times as many disk drives as had been ordered-at a value of $9 million. Although the extra drives were returned, the sale for all the drives had already been booked.

The investigation also revealed that, in some orders, sales were booked at the time of shipment even though title would not pass to the customer until completion of shipment. An examination of MiniScribe's financial records showed that the company had manipulated its reserves to offset its losses. MiniScribe posted only 1 percent as reserves, whereas the industry range was 4 to 10 percent. In some of the transactions the audit uncovered, shipments sent to MiniScribe warehouses were booked as sales when, in fact, customers were not even invoiced until the drives were shipped from the warehouse.

Through these creative manipulations and others, MiniScribe officers kept up a rosy fiscal appearance for the firm's auditors, Coopers & Lybrand. For example, for the 1987 audited financials, company officials packaged and shipped construction bricks (pretend inventory valued at $3.66 million) so that these products would count as retail sales. When bricks were returned, the sales were reversed but inventory increased. Obsolete parts and scraps were rewrapped as products and shipped to warehouses to be counted in inventory.

It was discovered that during the 1986 audit by Coopers & Lybrand, company officials broke into trunks containing the auditors' work papers and increased year-end inventory figures.

With the disclosure of the internal audit and the discovery of these creative accounting practices and inventory deceptions, MiniScribe's stock continued to drop, selling for $1.31 per share by September 1989. By 1990, MiniScribe had filed for bankruptcy and was purchased by Maxtor Corporation.

Lawsuits against Hambrecht & Quist, Wiles, and Coopers & Lybrand were brought by Kempner Capital Management, the U.S. National Bank of Galveston, and eleven other investors in the debentures sold by Hambrecht & Quist. In February

---

7. Andy Zipser, "Recipe for Sales Led to Cooked Books," *Denver Post*, 14 August 1989, 2B–3B.

8. Ibid.

1992, a jury awarded the investors $28.7 million in compensatory damages and $530 million in punitive damages. Coopers & Lybrand was held responsible for $200 million, Wiles for $250 million, Hambrecht & Quist for $45 million, and Mr. Hambrecht for $35 million.

Discussion Questions

1. What types of pressures led managers to "cook the books" at MiniScribe?
2. Were the auditors, Coopers & Lybrand, morally responsible for the investors' losses?
3. Suppose you were a manager who was asked to wrap construction bricks in disk drive packaging. Would you ask, "Why?" Would you be able to continue your employment? Would you be morally responsible for investors' losses by wrapping the bricks?
4. Were the internal control people (internal auditors) at MiniScribe morally responsible for the investors' losses?
5. Were the auditors just duped? Should deceived auditors be held responsible for investors' losses?

CASE 4.5: PHAR-MOR EARNINGS

Founded in 1982, Phar-Mor, the discount drug store chain, enjoyed a decade of phenomenal financial success. From 1982 to 1992, its sales grew to $3 billion. In that same period, Phar-Mor expanded from a single store to 305 stores in 33 states. It employed 23,000 workers in 1992. Phar-Mor's concept was to use warehouse-size-and-style stores that offered prescription drugs as well as items ranging from spaghetti sauce to videotapes.

Founders Michael I. Monus and David S. Shapira utilized the concept of low margins to infiltrate even those markets where discount pharmacies were already operating. Opening nearly sixty stores each year, Phar-Mor was ranked as the forty-ninth largest privately held company in the United States in 1991.

Monus, a sports fan, started the World Basketball League (WBL) for short players (those six feet, seven inches or less in height) and also was a part owner and promoter of the Colorado Rockies. The WBL had only ten teams in midsize towns like Erie, Pennsylvania, but Mr. Monus spared no expense in running the league. League officials enjoyed limousine service, and the perks for the WBL commissioner included a Cadillac.

On July 20, 1992, Phar-Mor officers were told (anonymously) of a transfer of Phar-Mor funds to the WBL in the amount of $100,000. An internal audit examination didn't find the $100,000 but did uncover several questionable transactions.

By July 28, 1992, Mr. Monus, who was Phar-Mor's president, had been demoted to vice chairman. On July 31, 1992, Mr. Monus was fired, and the remaining Phar-Mor officers alerted federal authorities. Additionally, Phar-Mor's chief financial officer, Patrick Finn, and its outside auditor (Coopers & Lybrand) were dismissed.

David S. Shapira was appointed as Phar-Mor's chief executive officer. In a statement, Mr. Shapira said that about $10 million in Phar-Mor funds had been funneled to the WBL. Mr. Shapira also stated that Mr. Finn and Mr. Monus had engaged in a "fraudulent scheme to cover up failures in the company and operating losses." As a result, Phar-Mor had had, in reality, no profits for the last three years: the company had overstated its profits by $350 million. Mr. Shapira referred to the work of Mr. Monus and Mr. Finn as "intricate criminal activity to defraud the company and its investors." Phar-Mor took a one-time reduction in earnings of $350 million in fiscal year 1993.

Mr. Monus was tried for fraud and embezzlement. In an earlier trial, there was a hung jury and investigations for jury tampering. Mr. Monus was convicted of 109 felony counts of fraud and embezzlement in 1995 and was sentenced to 235 months in prison. Mr. Monus said at his sentencing,

> "In the 10 years I was at Phar-Mor, Phar-More grew to 300 stores in some 35 states and 20,000 employees. The important thing is not the numbers to me . . . , but the employees—all those dedicated, loyal and highly motivated people.
>
> "I want them to know the sorrow and regret that I have. The sorrow and regret will live with me for the rest of my life."

In response to the news of the company's problems and earnings reductions, many suppliers stopped shipping goods to Phar-Mor, except on a C.O.D. basis. Banks began filing liens on Phar-Mor properties, and the company contemplated a proposal to close 100 stores. By August 17, 1992, Phar-Mor had filed for Chapter 11 bankruptcy. The general counsel for Coopers & Lybrand issued a statement saying that Phar-Mor had showed "no remorse for the hiring, retaining and promoting of this senior management the board now claims are 'crooks.' Responsible boards have oversight of their management and knowledge of their company's operations. Phar-Mor is a closely held non-public company in which the owners, managers and the board are closely allied. Collusion and fraud at the senior management level did not occur in a vacuum."

A lawyer of the American Institute of Certified Public Accountants (AICPA) stated that "if the fraud involves collusion among a number of people, the ordinary auditing procedures wouldn't necessarily uncover it."

The final independent examiner's report on the Phar-Mor losses, completed in January 1994, revealed that those involved had kept two sets of books: the official books, which contained false entries, and a second set of records (called "cookies"), where the false entries (called "raisins") were monitored. The final loss figure due to insider fraud was $1 billion: Phar-Mor had had no earnings during the five-year period preceding the 1992 Chapter 11 filing.

The court-appointed auditor discovered the following:

- a memo from general counsel warning Mr. Shapira of a lack of financial controls and conflicts of interest involving top executives;
- the back-dating of promissory notes by officers to exercise expired stock options;
- executives hiring (with company funds) cheerleaders in hot pants to escort them around Las Vegas;
- an internal memo questioning the expenditure of $30,000 for Nicole Miller neckties;
- the purchase by Phar-Mor of costume jewelry for sale in its stores from a firm in which Monus's brother was a part owner. Phar-Mor would have saved $2.1 million by purchasing the jewelry from another vendor; and

- the fact that in 1989, Phar-Mor had adopted an essentially invisible code of ethics: officers questioned by the examiner were unaware of its existence.

Phar-Mor emerged from Chapter 11 bankruptcy in 1995 with a new CEO, David Schwartz, and board. Its annual revenues were at that time $1.1 billion, down from its 1992 high of $3.1 billion. The number of employees was reduced by two-thirds and the company was closely held with Robert Haft holding a 31% share. Phar-Mor was to have merged with Shopko Stores in 1996, but it was acquired by Avatex in 1997.

Discussion Questions

1. List the ethical violations by the various parties at Phar-Mor.
2. What elements in the company allowed such a large fraud to occur?
3. Was the company treated as a personal asset of the officers? What problems resulted from this attitude?
4. Suppose you had drafted the internal memo that expressed concerns about internal controls and conflicts of interest. What would you have done if the company took no action in response? What would you do next?
5. If you, as a Phar-Mor employee, had discovered the two sets of books, whom would you tell?
6. List those who have been harmed by the collusion at Phar-Mor.

CASE 4.6: THE ETHICS OF DERIVATIVES

Generically called "derivatives," financial instruments from secondary lease obligation bonds (SLOBS) to swaps and hedging have captured financial news headlines since February 1994. Derivatives are securities that derive value from something else investors buy, such as stocks, bonds, foreign currencies, or commodities contracts. Derivatives have allowed corporations, financial firms, and government entities to hedge their exposure to interest rates-and to speculate on market changes. At one end are options, which allow a purchaser to buy or sell a fixed amount of an asset within a given period. They are traded on major exchanges and have been around for nearly a decade.

Other forms of derivatives, such as swaps, are traded over the counter. Interest-rate swaps, for example, allow one party to make payments on a fixed rate of interest in exchange for another party's payments based on a variable rate. Swaps may also derive their value from being tied to several indexes or financial assets.

Mortgage derivatives are securities created by pooling government-backed mortgages and then separating them into either just the interest portion or the principal; they are not contracts between two parties. Because these instruments are essentially bets on the pace at which homeowners will refinance their mortgages (thus influencing cash flow), they are tied directly to changes in interest rates. When the Federal Reserve raised rates in 1994, the market for mortgage derivatives disappeared, and they could be sold only at a loss.

From the risky and leveraged investment of a gamble on stock market prices going up or down to secondary mortgage pool investments, the range of derivative instruments is broad and complex. With these instruments, investors could substantially leverage their portfolios and, if correct in their judgment, reap huge returns. If they were wrong and substantially leveraged, however, the losses could bankrupt them.

The first forms of derivative investments appeared in 1986. Six years later, the total derivatives market was $12.1 trillion. European firms were among the earliest and heaviest investors in derivative instruments. Metallgesellschift, a large German industrial conglomerate, was heavily invested in 1992 and eventually took a $1 billion write-off. U.S. government agencies and several large U.S. corporations, including Procter & Gamble, Gibson Greetings, Mellon Bank, and Bankers Trust New York, made significant investments in derivatives in 1992. In Canada, the Bank of Montreal was heavily invested in mortgage derivatives.

A variety of government entities and other organizations invested in derivatives via leveraged funds. Among these were Orange County, California; Charles County, Maryland; Cuyahoga County, Ohio; West Virginia; Florida; and the Shoshone Tribe. Odessa College in Texas was one of several colleges that invested in collaterized mortgage obligations.

The market estimate of total derivatives investments rose to $35 trillion in 1993. At the end of that year, however, losses from derivatives began to surface. Procter & Gamble announced that it would take a $157 million charge to cover its losses. As a result of the Procter & Gamble losses, the Financial Accounting Standards Board (FASB) promulgated and eventually adopted stricter standards regarding the reporting of derivative investments and disclosure of such investments, their risks, and potential exposure in the management discussion and analysis. FASB, along with the Securities and Exchange Commission (SEC), sets financial reporting requirements for publicly traded companies.

The most commonly asked question by shareholders at annual meetings during the spring of 1994 was, "What derivative exposure does this company have?" During 1994, losses due to derivative investments continued to mount. The following table illustrates losses by various investors.

Entity	Loss
Charles County	$ 8.3 million (98 percent of its assets in collateralized mortgage obligations)
Cuyahoga County	$137 million (leveraged its $1.8 billion fund)
West Virginia	$279 million
Florida	$175 million
Metallgesellschift	$1 billion
Askin Capital Management	$2 billion (firm is liquidated)
Procter & Gamble	$102 million
Gibson Greetings	$23 million
Bankers Trust	$130 million

By mid-1994, derivatives were referred to as the "D word," and the SEC demanded accelerated FASB action. Several class action lawsuits were filed against entities that had losses as well as their brokers, including:

Paine Webber	(Settled for $33 million)
Piper Jaffray	(Settled for $70 million)
Bankers Trust	(Pending)
Gibson Greetings	(Settled for $23 million)

In November 1994, the SEC brought a fraud action against Bankers Trust. The commission focused on Bankers Trust because of its involvement with Gibson Greetings. The case was settled for $10 million in fines.

In December 1994, Orange County, facing a $1.5 billion loss, filed for bankruptcy—possibly the largest bankruptcy ever. School projects were put on hold, and the funds of 185 school districts, towns, and local agencies, including their employee pension funds, were put on hold. As a result, the Commodity Futures Trading Commission launched a probe into the Orange County derivative portfolio and the actions of its treasurer, Robert Citron. Mr. Citron was sentenced to one year in prison in 1996 and fined $100,000 following a guilty plea to several counts of fraud.

On February 25, 1995, losses from derivatives also led to the downfall of Barings, a 233-year-old British bank that financed the Napoleonic Wars and the Louisiana Purchase. Barings announced its collapse on February 25, 1995, due to the staggering loss of $1.2 billion in derivatives trading by Nick Leeson, a 28-year-old employee in its Singapore offices. Leeson had traded futures contracts pegged to the Nikkei Number 225, one of Japan's major indexes. He had been arbitraging and had bet that the Nikkei exchange would go up. Instead, Japan's economy (and the January 1995 earthquake) caused the index to plummet.

Following the Barings debacle, the SEC held a panel discussion on March 3–4, 1995, for securities lawyers that raised several key questions:

- Should brokers be held liable for failing to disclose derivative risk?
- Should brokers be required to explain investment vehicles to clients?
- Should companies be required to highlight their total derivative portfolio in their financial statements?
- Should boards of directors be held liable for setting inappropriate risk levels for investments?
- Should the SEC, in light of the FASB's failure to act, set standards for financial reporting?

In a March 1995 report, an advisory group of six securities firms offered to voluntarily tighten their oversizing on customers' derivatives exposure. However, the report concluded that "derivatives transactions are predominantly arms length transactions" for which customers ultimately have the obligation to review for potential risks and should seek independent advice.

Currently, proposals on derivatives and financial reporting are in limbo. But firms continue to rely on derivative financial investments with 49% of companies using them to manage cash flow volatility and 42% using them to manage the volatility of "accounting earnings". Fifty-nine percent of all firms with assets of $250 million or more use derivatives.

Discussion Questions

1. Suppose that you were the treasurer and chief financial officer for Gibson Greetings in 1986. You learn of several derivative vehicles with a 15 percent rate of return through Bankers Trust. The risk on these investments is substantially greater than any Gibson has had before. However, the pension fund requires contributions this year, competition is very threatening from Hall-

mark's success with its Shoebox Greeting division, and Bankers Trust indicates Procter & Gamble and several municipalities are already heavily invested. In making your decision:

    a. Determine who will be affected by your decision.

    b. Apply at least two appropriate ethical models to your investment dilemma and reach a conclusion about the ethics of this derivative investment by Gibson.

2. What drove Procter & Gamble, Orange County, and others to make risky derivative investments?

3. What motivated Leeson's decisions and the resulting exposure of Barings?

4. Before his last "bet," Leeson had served Barings well, earning high returns on his investment decisions in the derivatives market. Why didn't anyone at Barings question his highly leveraged portfolio?

5. In the business section of the *New York Times* for September 1, 1996, there is the story of two sisters, Olga Monetti and Fannie Monetti, who became victims of the derivative investment craze.

    The Monetti sisters had saved for 40 years all that they were able to set aside from their jobs as a technician at a blood bank (Olga) and file clerk at Borden (Fannie). The sisters shopped for their clothing at thrift stores and refinished used furniture for their East Harlem apartment that they shared with their ill mother and until she died in 1993.

    By 1991, the sisters had saved $1.2 million, noting that in one year they had earned $57,000 in interest. They had employed a conservative investment strategy, relying on certificates of deposit and Treasure bonds.

    In 1991, the Monetti sisters responded to an ad for high C.D. yields. At first, the company placing the ad, High Yield Management Securities, placed the sisters' funds in conservative bond investments because of their ages then of 57 and 64. Slowly, however, their funds were moved over into derivatives, particularly the high-yield but high-risk collateralized mortgage obligations (CMOs).

    The Monettis not only lost their $1.2 million, they lost an additional $1.3 million. A securities arbitration panel ruled that the Monettis did not have to pay the $1.3 million because the risk of the CMOs was not explained to them. The same panel also ordered the owner of High Yield, Philip Eitman, to pay the Monettis $1 million for his failure to disclose to them the risk associated with CMOs. The Monettis have not been able to collect the $1 million. High Yield has filed for bankruptcy, and Mr. Eitman, who says he also faces problems with the IRS, is struggling to avoid personal bankruptcy.

    The Monettis now struggle from month to month trying to meet expenses. Fannie has a social security check of $550 per month and a $45 per month pension from her clerk job at Borden. Olga's take-home pay from her job is $520 per week. Olga, who is a polio survivor, requires special shoes that cost over $200. The sisters own the brownstone building in which their apartment is located and they rent the other two apartments, but maintenance expenses eat up their profits. A sale of the brownstone, because it is located in such a bad neighborhood, would bring only $100,000. Olga asks, "How can we live? I didn't think things like this could happen in America."

    How does personalizing harms help avoid poor ethical choices? Would you have made more disclosures to the Monetti sisters? Would you have placed their money in the CMO derivative? Are the Monetti sisters at the same level of sophistication as Procter & Gamble and Gibson Greetings who also lost money in derivative investments?

  Why is this story relevant in the evaluation of the ethics of derivatives? Is high finance limited to high finance or are others affected?

CASE 4.7: OVERSTATED EARNINGS: BAUSCH & LOMB

The Hong Kong division of Bausch & Lomb enjoyed double-digit growth during the 1980s and 1990s. In some years earnings increased 25% and by 1993, the Hong Kong operation had total revenues of $100 million.

  Earnings on contact lenses sales seemed to be absolutely unbeatable with sales increasing at double-digit pace.

  It was in 1994, that Bausch & Lomb's 12 continuous years of double-digit growth in both sales and earnings (excluding one-time events) came to a halt with a company announcement that excessive distributor inventories would result in a significant reduction in 1994 earnings. The final result was a decline of 54% in earnings to $88.5 million. Sales were down only slightly to $1.9 billion. The following table reflects the shortfalls:

Division	1993	1994 Planned MILLIONS OF DOLLARS	1994 Actual
TOTAL BAUSCH & LOMB			
Sales	1872.2	2051.9	1850.6
Operating Earnings	300.9	344.7	168.8
US EYEWEAR			
Sales	190.1	200.0	153.5
Operating Earnings	42.3	48.6	19.7
US CONTACT LENS			
Sales	151.0	176.0	85.8
Operating Earnings	16.8	20.5	-61.7
ASIA-PACIFIC			
Sales	148.9	169.7	107.8
Operating Earnings	34.6	46.8	4.0
ORAL CARE			
Sales	68.8	73.0	50.8
Operating Earnings	2.6	4.2	-10.3
MIRACLE EAR**			
Sales	-	57.9	37.3
Operating Earnings	-	2.3	-12.9
CANADA AND LATIN AMERICA			
Sales	126.1	154.0	113.4
Operating Earnings	17.8	27.3	6.4
EUROPE, MIDDLE EAST, AFRICA			
Sales	246.5	249.0	240.6
Operating Earnings	60.7	60.3	53.0

**Acquired during 1993.

An SEC investigation, as well as one by *Business Week,* revealed some underlying problems in operations of Ray-Ban Sunglasses. For example, the Hong Kong unit was faking sales to real customers but then dumping the glasses at discount prices to gray markets. The contact lens division shipped products that were never ordered to doctors in order to boost sales. Some distributors had up to two years of unordered inventories. The U.S., Latin and Asian contact lens divisions also dumped lenses on the gray market forcing Bausch & Lomb to compete with itself.

The SEC charged Bausch & Lomb with violation of federal securities law for overstatement of earnings. Bausch & Lomb settled the charges with the SEC in 1997. Without admitting or denying the allegations, Bausch & Lomb agreed to a cease and desist order and John Logan, a regional sales director for the contact lens division, agreed to pay a $10,000 fine. The cease and desist order also named the former president of Bausch & Lomb's contact lens division, the former controller, the vice president of finance, and the former director of distributor sales.

Bausch & Lomb emphasized that the SEC found no evidence that top management knew of the overstatement of profits at the time it was made. However, the SEC's associate director of enforcement said, "That's precisely the point. Here is a company where there was tremendous pressure down the line to make the numbers. The commission's view is that senior management has to be especially vigilant where the pressure to make the numbers creates the risk of improper revenue recognition."

Former employees testified they were given a target number each year by operating unit and no excuses were accepted. One division manager, expecting a shortfall, said he was told to make the numbers but "don't do anything stupid." The manager said, "I'd walk away saying, 'I'd be stupid not to make the numbers.'" Another manager said that in order to meet targets they did 70% of their shipments in the last three days of the month.

Bausch & Lomb also settled a shareholder lawsuit over the overstatement of earnings for $42 million.

Discussion Questions

1. What went wrong with the Bausch & Lomb culture?
2. How was the company affected? Financially? Competitively?
3. Why are all those named in the consent decree "former" employees?
4. What changes would you make to prevent these types of issues?

CASE 4.8: THE INSIDE SCOOP—TRADING STOCK ON INSIDE INFORMATION

- Arjun Sekhri, a junior member of Salomon Smith Barney's "deal team," was charged in April with passing inside information to friends and relatives on six pending deals, including the WorldCom/MCI bid. Mr. Sekhri, 32 and an NYU business school graduate, was also named in a suit filed by the SEC requesting that he be ordered to disgorge himself of the alleged $1.7 million earned from the use of information he obtained from his work at Salomon.

The suit also alleges that after Mr. Sekhri's friends and relatives netted $375,000 on the MCI information, they wired $80,545 to Mr. Sekhri's father-in-law who used the money to purchase a 1998 Lexus which was then driven by Mr. Sekhri. Mr. Sekhri returned to India shortly after one of his friends, a former college roommate, who had profited from the use of the information was served with a subpoena from the SEC.

- Dr. Milton Mutchnick and his assistant, Dr. Rangarao Panguluri, conducted research on the prescription drug, Thymosin, a treatment for hepatitis B, for its manufacturer Alpha 1 Biomedicals at the gastroenterology department at Wayne State University Medical School. Both had exuded confidence about the drug and Dr. Mutchnick had even urged friends to purchase Alpha 1 Biomedicals stock. However, on April 25, 1994, during the course of the final phase of their lab work on the drug, it became clear to both men that Thymosin was ineffective. Dr. Mutchnick got on the phone and told his friends to sell their Alpha 1 stock. Dr. Panguluri phoned the two California doctors with whom he had interviewed and offered previous insights on Thymosin and told them to unload their stock. The tippees of the researchers avoided $300,000 in losses that would have resulted had they waited until after the public announcement of the failure of the tests which drove the price of Alpha 1 stock down to $2 per share, a drop of 68%. Dr. Mutchnick and his wife agreed to pay a $163,000 fine and Dr. Panguluri settled for an undisclosed amount.

- Dale J. Lange, a clinical investigator and associate professor of neurology at Columbia's College of Physicians and Surgeons, performed research work on Myotrophin, a drug developed by Cephalon, Inc. for treatment of Lou Gehrig's disease. Based on its promising performance in tests, Professor Lange purchased 3,000 shares and netted a profit of $26,496. A member of Cephalon's scientific advisory board also learned of Myotrophin's potential and told his sons. The sons purchased 615 and 200 shares, respectively. The graphic artist hired by Cephalon to enhance the look of the slides depicting the research results on Myotrophin and his son purchased call options based on their reading of the slides. Their profits totaled $40,821.

- Roger D. Wyatt, a consultant to Chantal Pharmaceutical, learned in 1993 that the company's acne drug had not performed well in its clinical tests. Upjohn canceled its contract with Chantal and Wyatt sold his shares, thus avoiding a loss of $21,963 that would have occurred had he sold after the public announcement of the clinical test results. Mr. Wyatt used a broker in the Cayman Islands for his sales and denied under oath to the SEC that he had made the sales. He entered a guilty plea to perjury in 1998, and will repay his profits plus $159,000 in fines and interest.

- In August, 1994, Mervyn Cooper, a psychotherapist, was providing marriage counseling to a Lockheed executive. The executive had been assigned to conduct the due diligence of Martin Marietta for the proposed merger between the two. At a session on August 22, 1994, the executive revealed to Dr. Cooper the pending, but nonpublic merger. Following the session, Dr. Cooper contacted Kenneth Rottenberg, a friend, and they both agreed Rottenberg would purchase call options on behalf of the both of them. When the broker expressed concern to Rottenberg about the riskiness of the call options, Rottenberg assured him that "Lockheed will be announcing a major business combination shortly." Dr. Cooper and Rottenberg repaid their profits of $176,000.

- The U.S. Attorney in Manhattan filed charges against eight brokers who work the floor of the NYSE charging that the brokers used a complex scheme when large buy orders were rumored on the floor in order to personally profit from the upcoming surge in purchases by buying the shares themselves through an off-exchange brokerage and using pre-stamped purchase orders that made it look as if their buy orders came in before they actually did.

  The scheme worked as follows:

  1. The floor brokers would learn that a large buy order was about to hit the floor, which would boost the price of the stock, for example, a large buy order for Microsoft shares.
  2. The floor brokers would then buy shares of Microsoft before the large buy order drove the price up. They would buy at 10:30 AM.
  3. The floor brokers then call an off-the-exchange broker where they hold personal accounts and ask the broker to issue a buy order with a pre-stamped time of 10:25 AM filled out as a buy order for Microsoft. This buy order would then throw off investigators because it would look like their buy order came in before they actually made the Microsoft purchase at 10:30 AM. This set-up was a precaution that would derail investigators and confuse them as to where the buy order actually originated.
  4. The rumored big buy order for Microsoft then hits the exchange at 10:35 AM, and the brokers are able to cash in on the increase in price of Microsoft shares because they bought shares before the price increase resulting from the large purchase took hold.

Discussion Questions

1. Why is there concern about trading stock on information that is not available to the public?
2. Do you think the people who engaged in these trades understood the law? Why?
3. Is it a defense that trading on inside information is so common?
4. Why do you think these individuals engaged in selling information?

CASE 4.9: THE INSIDE TRACT: DAN DORFMAN

Late in 1995, and early in 1996, reports about Dan Dorfman, a markets expert who commentates for CNBC, emerged in the business press regarding Mr. Dorfman's relationship with a stock trader and the possibility of insider trading. The reports included statements that Mr. Dorfman was under investigation by the SEC, a statement the SEC and Justice Department officials neither confirmed nor denied.

The reports alleged that Mr. Dorfman moved particular stocks for friends and then profited by trading in those stocks. After the business press reported the allegations, *Money* magazine terminated Mr. Dorfman but noted that the termination was because Mr. Dorfman was hired to increase subscriptions and those numbers had, in fact, not improved. CNBC's parent company hired a law firm to conduct an investigation into the allegations.

Mr. Dorfman was famous for his saying, "I own three stocks-AT&T, Boeing and Gannett-and I never write about them."

On May 7, 1996, Mr. Dorfman suffered a mild stroke and his reports could not be aired on CNBC. On August 30, 1996, CNBC announced that its internal investigation was complete, that Mr. Dorfman had cooperated fully and that the law firm could find no evidence of illegal activity. The law firm did note, however, that it did not have the power of subpoena available to the U.S. government and that it had not examined records beyond what was publicly available and what Mr. Dorfman could furnish. According to the law firm's analysis, Mr. Dorfman's relationship with the stock promoter did not include any illegal activity.

Discussion Questions

1. What are the ethical issues in this scenario?
2. Are there any ethical breaches that you can see?
3. CNBC and *Money* were placed in difficult situations that many employers must confront. What happens when allegations are made against an employee or a contractor who works for your company? What steps should the employer take? The mere suspension of an employee, even with pay, can harm the employee's reputation. However, an employer, particularly one whose own reputation is tied to the work of the employee, is at issue and it is often not possible to simply wait for the government to take action, if such action is planned. In Mr. Dorfman's case, the dilemma of the employer was compounded because Mr. Dorfman's health prevented his continuing appearances. Did CNBC act responsibly? Could they have done anything differently? What can an employer do to protect both its reputation and that of its employee?

CASE 4.10: THE ETHICS OF BANKRUPTCY

In 1980, there were 287,570 personal bankruptcies filed in the United States. In 1996, the number of personal bankruptcies topped one million for the first time in history. In 1997, the number of bankruptcies reached 1.2 million. That number translates to a bankruptcy for 1 of every 100 households in the United States. The rate of bankruptcy filing in the United States for 1996 was eight times higher than the bankruptcy rate during the Great Depression.

The number one reason for bankruptcy declaration for the past three years was not loss of job or health problems or divorce. Nearly 30 percent of all bankruptcy filings were attributed by the petitioner to simply being "overextended." Over 70 percent of those filing for personal bankruptcy chose Chapter 7, or full bankruptcy, as opposed to Chapter 13 for a consumer debt adjustment plan.

Most consumer debt is owed by those who earn between $50,000 and $100,000 a year. As one lender remarked, "These are people who could afford to save and buy later." (Consumer installment debt is at 85% of disposable income-an increase of 23% in the past decade.)

Current laws are perhaps too permissive and make the declaration of bankruptcy very easy and very tempting. Changing the laws and requiring different standards could hamper investment, yet the average loss of $11,000 in debt write-off per bankruptcy costs each family in the United States $100 in higher prices as creditors try to cover the losses of bankruptcy.

Some experts have noted that the bankruptcy process is being used for strategic planning and a way to avoid contracts. The following examples illustrate:

TLC was an Atlanta rhythm, blues, and hip-hop band that performed at clubs in 1991. The three-woman group signed a recording contract with LaFace Records. The group's first album that LaFace produced—"Oooooohhh . . . on the TLC Tip" in 1992-sold almost three million albums. The group's second album, "Crazysexycool," also produced by LaFace, sold five million albums through June 1996. The two albums together had six top-of-the-chart singles.

LaFace had the right to renew TLC's contract in 1996 following renegotiation of the contract terms. Royalty rates in the industry for unknown groups, as TLC was in 1991, are generally 7 percent of the revenues for the first 500,000 albums, and 8 percent for sales on platinum albums (albums that sell over one million copies). The royalty rate increases to 9.5 percent for all sales on an eighth album.

Established artists in the industry who renegotiate often have royalty rates of 13 percent, and artists with two platinum albums can command an even higher royalty.

The three women in TLC, Tionne Watkins (T-Boz), Lisa Lopes (Left-Eye), and Romanda Thomas (Chili), declared bankruptcy in July 1995. All three listed debts that exceeded their assets, which included sums owed to creditors for their cars and to Zale's and The Limited for credit purchases. Lopes is being sued by Lloyd's of London, which claims Lopes owes it $1.3 million it paid on a policy held by her boyfriend on his home. Lopes has pleaded guilty to one count of arson in the destruction of the home but denies that she intended to destroy the house.

Lopes has asked that the Lloyd's claim be discharged in her bankruptcy. All three members of TLC have asked that their contract with LaFace be discharged in bankruptcy because being bound to their old contract could impede their fresh financial starts.

During 1996 the members of three music groups declared bankruptcy just before their contracts were due for renegotiation. One record company executive has noted that record company owners are frightened by the trend: "You invest all the money and time in making them stars. Then they leave for the bigger companies and a higher take on sales. It has all of us scared."

Pop singer Billy Joel also had a record contract with a small company during the initial stages of his career. When the company refused, during renegotiations, to increase his royalty rate, Joel did not produce another album during the period of the contract renewal option. Instead, he used a clause in the contract that limited him to night club and "piano bar" appearances in the event another album was not produced. For three years, Joel played small clubs and restaurants and did not produce an album. At the end of that period when his contract had expired, he negotiated a contract with Columbia. His first album with Columbia was "Piano Man," a multi-platinum album.

Discussion Questions

1. Do the three women meet the standards for declaring bankruptcy? Evaluate whether Lopes's Lloyd's claim should be discharged. Determine whether the record contract should be discharged.

2. Is declaring bankruptcy by the members of these musical groups legal? Is it ethical? Are the musicians using bankruptcy as a way to avoid contract obligations? Are the musicians using bankruptcy as a way to maximize their income?

3. Did Joel take an ethical route? Is his solution more ethical than bankruptcy?

4. Is there a presumption of good faith built into the bankruptcy code?

Section B
Conflicts between the Corporation's Ethical Code and Business Practices in Foreign Countries

Although we have a global market, we do not have global safety laws, ethical standards, or cultural customs. Businesses face many dilemmas as they decide whether to conform to the varying standards of their host nations or to attempt to operate with universal (global) standards.

Case 4.12: Product Dumping

Once the Consumer Product Safety Commission prohibits the sale of a particular product in the United States, a manufacturer can no longer sell the product to U.S. wholesalers or retailers. However, the product can be sold in other countries that have not prohibited its sale. The same is true of other countries' sales to the United States. For example, Great Britain outlawed the sale of the prescription sleeping pill, Halcion, but sales of the drug continue in the United States. The British medical community reached conclusions regarding the pill's safety that differed from the conclusions reached by the medical community and the Food and Drug Administration here. Some researchers who conducted studies on the drug in the United States simply concluded that stronger warning labels were needed.

159

The Consumer Product Safety Commission outlawed the sale of three-wheel all-terrain cycles in the United States in 1988. While some manufacturers had already turned to four-wheel models, other manufacturers still had inventories of three-wheel cycles. Testimony on the cycles ranged from contentions that the vehicles themselves were safe but the drivers too young, too inexperienced, and more inclined to take risks (i.e., to "hot dog"). However, even after the three-wheel product was banned here, outlawed vehicles could still be sold outside the United States.

For many companies, chaos follows a product recall because inventory of the recalled product may be high. Often, firms must decide whether to "dump" the product in other countries or to take a write-off that could damage earnings, stock prices, and employment stability.

Discussion Questions

1. If you were a manufacturer holding a substantial inventory of a product that has been outlawed in the United States, would you have any ethical concerns about selling the product in countries that do not prohibit its sale?
2. Suppose the inventory write-down that you will be forced to take because of the regulatory obsolescence is material—nearly a 20 percent reduction in income will result. If you can sell the inventory in a foreign market, legally, there will be no write-down and no income reduction. A reduction of that magnitude would substantially lower share market price, which would in turn lead your large, institutional shareholders to demand explanations and possibly seek changes in your company's board of directors. In short, the write-down would set off a wave of events that would change the structure and stability of your firm. Do you now feel justified in selling the product legally in another country?
3. Is selling the product in another country simply a matter of believing one aspect of the evidence—that the product is safe?
4. Would you include any warnings with the product?

CASE 4.13: THE TABOO OF WOMEN IN MANAGEMENT

International management consulting firm Burns & McCallister is listed by *Working Mother* magazine as one of the top fifty firms in the United States for employment of working mothers and by *Working Woman* magazine as one of the top ten firms for women. The firm has earned this reputation for several reasons. First, nearly 50 percent of its partners are women. Second, it has a menu of employee benefits that includes such things as flex hours, sabbaticals, family leave, home-based work, and part-time partner-track positions.

However, Burns & McCallister recently has been the subject of a series of reports by both the *Los Angeles Times* and the *New York Times* that scrutinize its policy on female executives in certain nations. Burns & McCallister has learned, through fifty years of consulting, that certain countries in which it negotiates for contracts prohibit the use of women in the negotiation process. The cultures of many of these countries do not permit women to speak in a meeting of men. Consequently, Burns & McCallister has implemented a policy prohibiting women partners from being assigned these potential account negotiations and later the accounts themselves. Clerical help in the offices can be female, but any contact with the client must be through a male partner or account executive.

For example, Japan still has a two-track hiring system with only 3 percent of professional positions open to women. The remainder of the women in the Japanese corporate workforce become office ladies who file, wear uniforms, and serve tea. Dentsu, Inc., a large Japanese ad firm, had a picture of the typical Dentsu "Working Girl" in its recruiting brochure. Surrounding the photo are comments primarily about her physical appearance: (1) Her breasts are "pretty large." (2) Her bottom is "rather soft."

In response to criticism regarding Burns & McCallister's posture, the head of the firm's New York office has explained:

> "Look, we're about as progressive a firm as you'll find. But the reality of international business is that if we try to use women, we don't get the job. It's not a policy on all foreign accounts. We've just identified certain cultures in which women will not be able to successfully land or work on accounts. This restriction does not interfere with their career track. It does not apply in all countries."

The National Organization for Women (NOW) would like Burns & McCallister to apply to all its operations the standards that it employs in the United States. No restrictions are placed on women here, the organization argues, and other cultures should adapt to our standards; we should not change U.S. standards to adapt to their culture. NOW maintains that without such a posture, change can never come about.

Discussion Questions

1. Do you agree with Burns & McCallister's policy for certain cultures with regard to women partners?
2. Is Burns & McCallister doing anything that violates federal employment discrimination laws?
3. Given Burns & McCallister's record with regard to women, is the issue really relevant to women's advancement in the firm?
4. What if the cultures in which the prohibition of women applied traditionally bring in the highest dollar accounts? Would your opinion regarding the posture be different?
5. Do you agree with the position that change can never come about if Burns & McCallister does not take a stand?
6. Would Burns & McCallister be sacrificing revenues in changing its policies? Is this an appropriate sacrifice?

SECTION C
UNAUTHORIZED PAYMENTS TO FOREIGN OFFICIALS

What we would call a bribe and illegal activity in the United States may be culturally acceptable and necessary in another country. Could you participate in such a practice?

CASE 4.14: THE ADOPTION AGENCY AND SEÑOR JOSE'S FEES

Ninos and Ninas, Inc., is an adoption agency located in El Paso, Texas, that focuses on international adoptions. Most of the infants Ninos and Ninas places are from South American countries.

Couples, primarily from the United States, work with Ninos and Ninas to adopt children. The fee for Ninos and Ninas' work ranges from $15,000 to $20,000. Couples pay the fee willingly because of the agency's twenty-year history of excellent work and its extensive knowledge of adoption requirements in South American countries.

Joan and David Ryan have applied with Ninos and Ninas to adopt a child. Their U.S. certification is complete, and they have submitted their application along with a $10,000 deposit to Ninos and Ninas.

After their application is processed, the Ryans receive a notice from Esther Tomkin, Ninos and Ninas' director of adoption services, that a baby girl is now available. Ms. Tomkin instructs them that she will need an additional $5,000 as well as $5,000 in cash in unmarked bills in an envelope to be placed in a postal box located in El Paso. Ms. Tomkin's letter explains:

> You should bring the $5,000 with you when you come to El Paso to pick up your new daughter. Once you have paid the $5,000 to Ninos and Ninas and deposited the $5,000 in cash, you will have your little girl within 24 hours. You should be prepared to come to El Paso on April 10. The envelope with the cash should be marked for "Señor Jose."

162

Joan is concerned about the odd cash payment and phones Ms. Tomkin to discuss it. Ms. Tomkin assures Joan that "the payment is just the way adoption works in these countries. It is not a bribe; it is not a violation of the Foreign Corrupt Practices Act; it is simply a requirement t͏ get the adoption paperwork through. Your adoption just can't get through the system without it. This is the way we've been doing business for twenty years." Joan asks, "Who is Señor Jose?" Ms. Tomkin responds, "He's just an official in the social agency who handles adoptions. He isn't even the judge who approves the adoption. Without this money, your little girl ends up a street child or malnourished in an orphanage."

Discussion Questions

1. Would the payment to Señor Jose violate U.S. laws? Does the international nature of the adoption agency's operations affect its operational standards?
2. Is the payment a bribe or a facilitating "grease" payment? Is there a difference? Does the fact that the payment is legal control the determination of whether it is ethical?
3. Does the benefit to the infant girl justify the method for accomplishing that benefit?
4. Would you go forward with the adoption?
5. Would you feel comfortable working for or adopting from Ninos and Ninas?

Case 4.15: Facilitation or Bribery: Cultural and Ethical Disparities

Geletex, Inc., is a U.S. telecommunications corporation attempting to expand its operations worldwide. As Geletex begins its operations in other countries, it has discovered cultural, governmental, and ethical standards that differ significantly from country to country and from those in the United States. Geletex has had a code of ethics for its U.S. operations since 1975. The company's director of compliance, Jed Richardson, provides ongoing training for employees, runs a hotline through which employees can report problems, and is well known and respected throughout the company for his high standards and trustworthiness. As Geletex's international operations grow, Jed is becoming increasingly uncomfortable with what appear to be double standards for the company's U.S. operations and its operations in other countries. Jed, who has been traveling to each of the Geletex international offices, has found the following situations, which since have been causing him some sleepless nights:

■ In the Lima, Peru, office, Jed, in reviewing financial records, discovered that the commissions expense for the branch is unusually high. Geletex pays its salespeople commissions for each commercial customer they recruit for cellular or long-distance services. Jed knows from experience that some companies pay unusually high sales commissions to disguise the fact that salespeople are paying kickbacks in exchange for contracts. In the United States, such payments would be commercial bribery and a violation of Geletex's code of ethics. When Jed confronted the Lima, Peru, district manager and questioned him about the high commissions, he responded, "Look, things are different down here. We've got a job to do. If the company wants results, we've got to get things moving any way we can."

- In the Stockholm, Sweden, office, Jed noted a number of college age student employees who seemed to have little work to do. Again, Jed questioned the district manager, who responded, "Sure, Magnus is the son of a telecommunications regulator. Caryl is the daughter of a judge who handles regulatory appeals in utilities. Andre is a nephew of the head of the governing party. They're bright kids, and the contacts don't hurt us. In the Scandanavian culture, giving jobs to children is part of doing business."

- In the Bombay, India, office, Jed noted that many different payments had been made to both the Indian government and government officials. When Jed voiced his concern, the district manager responded, "I can explain every payment. On this one, we needed the utilities [water and electricity] for our offices turned on. We could have waited our turn and had no services for ninety days, or we could pay to get moved to the top of the list and have our utilities turned on in forty-eight hours. On the check for licensing, again, we could have waited six months to get licensed or pay to expedite it and be licensed."

Jed is an expert on the Foreign Corrupt Practices Act (FCPA). The act permits "facilitation" or "grease" payments but prohibits bribes. Facilitation opens doors or expedites processes; it does not purport to influence outcomes. Jed is unsure about Geletex's international operations and compliance with the law. He is very unsure about Geletex having an international code of ethics.

Discussion Questions

1. Do any of the offices' actions violate the FCPA?
2. Must a business adopt the ethical standards of a host culture in order to succeed?
3. Are all of the actions in the various offices ethical?
4. If you were Jed, what ethical standards would you develop for international operations?
5. Does Jed's firm create any internal problems by allowing different conduct in different countries and cultures?
6. The American Bar Association reports that there have been only 16 bribery prosecutions under the FCPA since 1977. However, thousands of others have settled voluntarily rather than go to trial. Is the FCPA necessary for international business operations? Does it impede U.S. businesses' success in other countries?

Section D
Workplace Safety

Certain safety issues continue to evolve. While given hazards await regulation, workers eventually will experience harm. How much responsibility does an employer have? Is an employer required to be proactive?

4.16 Electromagnetic Fields: Exposure for Workers and Customers

EMFs Are Discovered

Technology has brought us the phenomenon of electromagnetic fields (EMFs)—magnetic fields that result from electrical current. These fields can be found around transmission lines, home appliances, and video display terminals for computers. Wherever there is electric power, there are electric and magnetic fields that result from the charge in the electric power system. The amount of the charge produces the electric field, and the motion of the charge produces the magnetic field. Together, these two types of fields are often called an electromagnetic field (EMF).[9] Much has been written recently about the health hazards of electromagnetic fields, but the controversy has in fact been developing for over forty years.

In 1950, following its first study of electromagnetic fields, the U.S. Public Health Service reported that workers who were exposed to alternating electromagnetic fields developed cancer at a rate significantly higher than that of the population as a whole. Following this first study, public concerns about EMFs arose as utilities turned more and more to extra high voltage (EHV) transmission lines to handle increases in electrical demand. The public first noticed EHV lines as nuisances; the lines impaired TV and radio reception.

During the 1960s, Dr. Robert O. Becker found, in experiments conducted with salamanders, that the electric current associated with the animals' nervous systems

---

9. "Biological Effects of Power Frequency Electric and Magnetic Fields," Congressional Background Paper, Office of Technology Assessment, 1989.

triggered their regenerative process. Later Dr. Becker, working with Dr. Howard Friedman, discovered that exposing human volunteers to pulsed magnetic fields of similar frequency and considerably greater strength than those associated with magnetic storms significantly reduced the volunteers' ability to react to the appearance of light.

While EMF research continued, U.S. military projects spurred the first public involvement in the EMF issue. A Navy and GTE Sylvania project for an extralow-frequency (ELF) test facility in Wisconsin (called Project Sanguine) met with powerful objections in 1968 from environmental groups. Neighbors of the Navy's test facility at Clam Lake reported that they were receiving electrical shocks when they turned on water faucets.[10] Environmentalists claimed that alternating magnetic fields generated by the ELF antennas could produce dangerously high voltages in power and telephone lines.[11] The Navy responded to the objections in an environmental impact statement by demonstrating that household appliances give off stronger magnetic fields than the ELF facility.

Concerns about EMF were initially minimal for two reasons. First, no transfer of energy occurs, as in X-rays where chemical bonds are broken or microwaves where tissue is heated. Second, all cells in the body have natural electric fields that are at least one hundred times more intense than any induced by exposure to common power-frequency fields.[12]

Becker strongly urged the Institute of Electrical and Electronic Engineers at its summer 1972 meeting to begin a program to study human exposure to electromagnetic fields. In 1973, Becker was asked to serve on the Navy's Bureau of Medicine and Surgery to review the Navy's research on the biological and ecological effects of ELF radiation. Though Becker and other members of the advisory committee recommended that the Navy further study the effects of Project Sanguine on human beings and animals, the Navy proceeded with the project. The advisory committee's warnings were never made public.[13]

Power Line Placement Becomes an Issue

During the time of the initial EMF research and the military controversies, the siting of power lines became an issue as the public became more aware of EMF. In 1973, the Power Authority of the State of New York (PASNY) was considering the construction and placement of a 765-kilovolt power line in upstate New York. Becker wrote to the PASNY and urged it to delay its decision on placement until the Project Sanguine experiments were completed. The Public Service Commission of New York (PSC) began hearings on the 765-kilovolt line in 1973.

The hearings were long and complicated, with utility experts testifying that the line's placement would present no biological hazard to citizens. Andrew Marino, a colleague of Becker, testified about his work in exposing rats to sixty-hertz (ELF) electric fields. The exposed rats gained less weight, drank less water, and showed

10. Paul Brodeur, "Annals of Radiation: The Hazards of Electromagnetic Fields," *New Yorker*, 12 June 1989, 51–58, 62.

11. Ibid.

12. "Biological Effects of Power Frequency," 1.

13. Brodeur, 67.

altered levels of blood proteins and enzymes compared to control rats. After Marino testified that ELF radiation could biologically affect humans, the utilities involved requested and received a postponement of the PSC hearings for a year. The hearings resumed in late 1975, and after pressure from Governor Hugh Carey, the PSC authorized construction of the line in 1976 but left open the issue of the required right-of-way width.

Both Becker and Marino were strongly attacked following their testimony at the PSC hearing. The chair of the National Academy of Sciences Committee told the *Saturday Review*:

> The judges threw out the case with prejudice. They ruled that Marino's not a believable witness, that he's evasive and deceitful. Here we were, being attacked by people who ultimately were thrown out of a court of justice in that way. They've all been thrown out. These guys are all a bunch of quacks.[14]

At the same time, politically based environmental opposition drove Project Sanguine from Wisconsin. The Navy's advisory committee report with Becker's recommendation to study the effects of Project Sanguine on residents near Clam Lake finally was made public after Senator Gaylord Nelson of Wisconsin received a copy of it. In a press release, Nelson accused the Navy of suppressing evidence and failing to follow through on the effects of radiation.[15]

The Werthemeier Seminal Study on EMFs

In the spring of 1974, epidemiologist Nancy Werthemeier began to study children who had died from leukemia in the greater Denver area. The results suggested a connection between the proximity of the children's homes to transmission lines and the incidence of leukemia. The studies, published in the *American Journal of Epidemiology*, concluded that the cancer rate of children from homes located near high-current configurations (HCC) was two to three times the normal rate of cancer. That is, if one child in a thousand gets cancer in the general population, two to three children living near HCCs would be expected to get it.[16] The homes affected included those that were less than:

1. Forty meters from large-gauge primary wires or arrays of six or more thin primary wires;
2. Twenty meters from an array of thirty-five thin primary wires or high-tension (50,230-kilovolt) wires; and
3. Fifteen meters from 240-volt wires.[17]

Dr. David Savitz repeated a Werthemeier-type study in Denver and released his results in 1986. Savitz agreed with the Werthemeier conclusion that exposure to EMF may increase the risk of developing cancer in children. However, Savitz also suggested that simple reconfiguration of the wires on transmission lines could reduce that risk substantially.

14. Ibid., at 76.

15. Brodeur, 63.

16. Nancy Werthemier, and Ed Leeper, "Electrical Wiring Configuration and Childhood Cancer," *American Journal of Epidemiology* 109 (1979): 273.

17. Ibid., at 277.

Cape Cod's PAVE PAWS

In 1976, the Air Force proposed installing a PAVE PAWS radar facility at Cape Cod, Massachusetts. No environmental impact statement was prepared, and installation began with no public input. PAVE PAWS is an acronym for Precision Acquisition of Vehicle Entry Phased Array Warning System. PAVE PAWS differs from regular radar in that instead of a rotating antenna, it has solid-state components that are controlled by computer and steered electronically; it emits ELF radiation. PAVE PAWS was used to detect sea-launched ballistic missiles.[18] The Air Force issued a 250-page report on environmental issues surrounding ELF that mentioned PAVE PAWS might cause cardiac pacemakers to skip a beat. However, construction of the project was approved and work began.

As construction began on the PAVE PAWS facility, local residents sought help from their congressman, Gerry E. Studds, who asked the Air Force for the research supporting its conclusion that PAVE PAWS presented no long-term danger to human health. At a town meeting, an Air Force official told residents that he could not guarantee that they would be safe from the effects of PAVE PAWS radiation.[19]

Following these public meetings, the Cape Cod Environmental Coalition sued the Air Force for violating the National Environmental Policy Act by not issuing an environmental impact statement (EIS) before constructing PAVE PAWS. As a result of the suit, the Air Force agreed to study the radiation from facility towers and do an EIS.

In January 1980, Adey denounced the Air Force for its unwillingness to study PAVE PAWS and its effects on residents before building the towers. Reports of Adey's denunciation appeared in newspapers across the country.

At about the same time that the issue of ELF impact was gaining national momentum, the New York PSC issued its final decision on the 765 kilovolt line. The PSC reached the conclusion that ELF fields could have effects on humans, yet still authorized the line provided the right of way was widened to 350 feet.

Corroboration of Werthemeier's Work

Scientific studies about ELF and EMF continued. W. Ross Adey released the results of his studies that showed weak ELF fields could alter the flow of calcium from brain cells and thereby alter the chemistry of the brain. Adey had used brain tissue from chicks in his studies and had also observed the behaviors of monkeys and cats. In 1976 and 1979, Carl F. Blackman, an Environmental Protection Agency (EPA) scientist duplicated Adey's work and reached the same conclusions.[20]

In June 1982, a preliminary report of a Swedish study of childhood leukemia by Dr. Lennart Tomenius corroborated Werthemeier's results. Also in 1982, Werthemeier and Leeper published the results of their adult cancer study that indicated a correlation between transmission lines and the incidence of cancer in adults. At nearly the same time, Dr. Samuel Milham's study correlating leukemia to occupational exposure to electric and magnetic fields was published in the *New England*

---

18. Paul Brodeur, "Annals of Radiation: The Hazards of Electromagnetic Fields Part II." *New Yorker* 19 June 1989, 47.

19. Ibid., at 48.

20. Ibid., at 47.

Journal of Medicine. Later that year, studies from the University of Southern California School of Medicine confirmed Milham's findings.[21]

Late in 1982, an article in the *Cape Cod Times* about the possible health effects of PAVE PAWS revealed that Arthur Guy was conducting a study for the Air Force of the long-term effects of low-level microwave radiation. The article entitled "PAVE PAWS: Where Has the Controversy Gone?" discussed the studies to date and questioned the Air Force figures.

In 1983, Adey and Daniel B. Lyle published the results of their further studies in *Bioelectromagnetics.* They concluded that a PAVE PAWS carrier frequency could significantly suppress the ability of cultured T-lymphocyte cells in mice to kill cultured cancer cells.

At the same time, the first studies of electrical workers appeared when Michael McDowell released the results of his studies that showed an increased risk of leukemia among workers in all electrical occupations. A 1984 study of white males in Maryland who had died of brain tumors revealed that a significantly higher than expected number had been employed in electrical occupations. Leading electronics and communications firms formed the Electromagnetic Energy Policy Alliance in 1984 to downplay the hazards of radiation. That same year, the Illinois Institute of Technology Research prepared a report for the Navy that showed that the strength of magnetic fields from household appliances dropped off so quickly with distance that such devices could not be considered major sources of indoor exposure.

In 1985, Dr. Guy released the results of his study for the Air Force, which found higher incidences of cancer in rats exposed to microwave radiation. A study done by Stanislaw Szmigielski and published that same year indicated that Polish military personnel who worked with or near radiation-emitting devices were more than three times as likely to develop cancer as unexposed personnel.

Houston Lighting Case and Public Knowledge of EMF

The first court case involving power lines was brought by Houston Lighting & Power Company in 1985 against the Klein Independent School District for the district's refusal to grant right-of-way access for the construction of power lines. The jury found for the school district and awarded compensatory and punitive damages. An appellate court later reversed the punitive damages but upheld the right of the school district to refuse the right-of-way on the grounds that the electromagnetic fields of the lines presented potential health hazards.

Following the Houston case, studies on EMF and health hazards were conducted and reported in a nearly continuous stream. In 1986, Werthemeier and Leeper released another study that demonstrated a direct connection between fetal development and the use of electric blankets and water beds. Electromagnetic fields from the water bed heaters and the blankets sent pulses that resulted in a significantly higher rate of defects in exposed fetuses. Also in 1986, the utility-funded Electric Power Research Institute (EPRI) released results of a study that indicated lower birth weights and a significant increase in the number of birth defects among swine exposed to electromagnetic radiation.

---

21. Ibid.

As these study results were being released, the impact of operating projects was assessable based on epidemiological studies. In March 1986, the Massachusetts Department of Health reported that women living near the Cape Cod PAVE PAWS facility had a significantly higher rate of cancer than the general population.

By 1987, Congress and state legislatures and agencies began to conduct both generic and specific-issue hearings on the placement of power lines. With all the public attention, the issue of overhead power lines near property became a discussion topic in seminars for real estate developers and agents.

The first lawsuits alleging declines in property value because of power line location and public fear began in 1988, when New York landowners sued the New York Power Authority alleging that the 345-kilovolt line, the subject of the landmark hearings in the 1970s, created a "cancer corridor" and had destroyed the market value of their properties.

The Follow-Up Studies

Studies continued to indicate the dangers of EMF. A study of Texas utility workers showed that they had a cancer rate thirteen times greater than that of workers who were not exposed to electromagnetic fields. A later study by the University of Southern California established that electrical workers with ten years on the job had a higher risk for certain forms of brain tumors than those with five years' experience. By 1990, many counties had approved measures limiting construction of power lines. School boards, following the lead of the Houston case, closed off buildings near power lines to protect their children.[22]

A Congressional Office of Technology Assessment report on EMF concluded: "The emerging evidence no longer allows one to categorically assert that there are no risks."[23] Department of Energy researchers noted, "There is clearly cause for concern but not for alarm."[24] Dr. David Carpenter, dean of the school of public health at the State University of New York, Albany observed, "This is really harming people. In my judgment the present state of affairs is like the correlation between smoking and lung cancer 30 years ago."[25]

Utilities, through EPRI, have quadrupled spending on EMF research since 1986. But public concern continues to build. Some environmental consultants predict that EMF will become the biggest environmental challenge electric utilities face.

Cyrus Noe, editor of *Clearing Up*, a utility newsletter, says that electricity is a necessity of modern life and "no one is going to say that we have to turn off the lights. But utilities cannot simply gin up a plan, award a bunch of contracts and spend the EMF dilemma away. We just don't know the answers."[26]

A 1993 study conducted by Dr. David Savitz reported in *Epidemiology* and based on his examination of 36,221 Southern California Edison workers, concluded there was no evidence of increased levels of leukemia, brain cancer, or lymphoma from EMF exposure. Savitz commented on the study's credibility and indicated that

22. David Kirkpatrick, "Can Power Lines Give You Cancer?" *Fortune*, 31 December 1990, 80–85.

23. Ibid.

24. Ibid.

25. Ibid.

26. Keith Schneider, "Electricity and Cancer? The Mystery Increases," *New York Times*, 3 February 1991, E3.

workplace EMF exposure probably could not be linked to cancer. However, he noted that further research is needed on childhood exposure to EMF and the incidence of leukemia.

In 1995, the *American Journal of Epidemiology* reported the largest study of utility workers to date. The EPRI-funded study looked at 138,905 men who worked for power companies between 1950 and 1986, including 20,733 who had died. It was the first study to take actual measurements of exposure levels.

Overall, the workers' death risk was lower than that of the general population. However, the brain cancer risk was 50 percent higher for men who worked more than five years as a lineman or electrician. Further, those who were exposed to the highest levels of EMFs had more than double the risk of brain cancer. The study found that brain cancer is so rare that electrocution and work accidents should be the focus of safety measures. Further, it found no association between EMF exposure and leukemia.

Where EMF Stands Today

In 1996, the National Research Council (NRC) issued its report on EMF after examining 500 studies over 17 years. The NRC study was sponsored by the U.S. Department of Energy. The NRC is a private, non-profit institution that provides research and technological advice to Congress. The NRC issued the following observations about the Werthemeier and Savitz studies:

> "The weak link shown between proximity to power lines and childhood leukemia may be the result of factors other than magnetic fields that are common to houses with the types of external wiring identified with the disease. These include: a home's proximity to high traffic density, local air quality, and construction features of older homes that fall into this category."

The NRC report also concluded that only at levels between 1,000 and 100,000 times stronger than residential fields do cells show reaction to EMF exposure, and there is no evidence that such reactions produce adverse health effects.[27] Finally, the NRC review concluded that even high exposure to EMF does not affect the DNA of the cell, it does not act as a carcinogen, and also does not affect reproduction, development, or behavior in animals.

Several recommendations for future research were offered by the NRC:

1) Further research on occupational exposure because its efforts focused on low-frequency electric and magnetic fields in homes; and
2) Determining the reason(s) for the small increase in childhood leukemia (rare) among children in homes near power lines.

In 1997, the National Cancer Institute reported its findings on children living near high voltage power lines and cancer in the *New England Journal of Medicine*. The study's authors concluded "that exposure to electromagnetic fields does not increase a child's risk of leukemia" after reviewing the health records and EMF levels in the homes of 629 children with leukemia and 619 healthy children in a nine-state area. The study found that children without cancer were exposed to the

27. In fact, several studies showed that the exposure helped by speeding up the healing process after a bone is broken. *National Research Council News*, Oct. 31, 1996, p. 2 as excerpted from POSSIBLE HEALTH EFFECTS OF EXPOSURE TO RESIDENTIAL ELECTRIC AND MAGNETIC FIELDS, 1996, National Academy Press.

nine-state area. The study found that children without cancer were exposed to the same levels of EMF energy as those with cancer.

Lawsuits against utilities over EMF have begun. In one action over the leukemia death of a child whose home was near a transformer, the jury found for the utility. Still pending are economic-loss lawsuits in which homeowners are seeking recovery for property value losses due to their home's location next to transformers or wires and public fears about such proximity and EMF. The Office of Technology and Assessment estimates that the cost of EMF litigation is between $1 billion and $3 billion per year.

Discussion Questions

1. Does a clear causal connection exist between EMFs and cancer?
2. What companies should be concerned about liability for exposure to EMFs?
3. What regulations do you foresee being enacted to address the EMF issue?
4. What problems do you see for owners of land located near power lines?
5. If you were a human resources officer in an electric utility, what, if any, action would you take to protect your company's workers?
6. If you were a manufacturer or seller of electric blankets or water beds, would you warn purchasers of your products about the possible dangers of EMFs?
7. Should electric utilities make any workplace changes for safety because of EMFs?
8. Should electric utilities reconfigure wiring to minimize EMF exposure of residents near power lines?

CASE 4.17: DOMINO'S PIZZA DELIVERS

Thomas S. Monaghan invented today's pizza delivery system when, in 1960, he opened the first Domino's in Ypsilanti, Michigan. By 1993, the company had grown to 5,300 U.S. franchises. Part of Domino's success was due to its 30-minute guarantee: the pizza is delivered in 30 minutes, or it's free.

Domino's fleet of drivers across the United States ranges from 75,000 to 80,000. Because of the time pressure, some drivers were speeding and breaking the law. In 1990, 20 traffic fatalities in the United States involved Domino's drivers.

In 1985, Frank Kranack and his wife, Mary Jean, were struck by a Domino's delivery car while driving in their station wagon just outside a suburban Pittsburgh Domino's store. Frank suffered whiplash, and Mary Jean had neck and back injuries plus permanent disability in her right arm, the area of her body nearest the impact. When the accident occurred, the manager of the Domino's store rushed out to the wreckage and told the driver, "Let's get this pizza on the road." The Kranacks filed suit seeking damages and a halt to the Domino's 30-minute policy.

In 1991, Domino's changed the on-time policy to a $3 refund if delivery is late to curb fraud by college students who gave incorrect directions to slow their deliveries.

In December 1992, a St. Louis jury awarded $78 million to Jean Kinder, who had been hit by an 18-year-old Domino's delivery driver in 1989. Within one week of that award, Domino's dropped its 30-minute guarantee. Monaghan noted:

I believe we are the safest delivery company in the world. But there continues to be a perception that the guarantee is unsafe.

Some franchisees had already abandoned the 30-minute guarantee. A marketing strategist commented on the decision:

The critical issue to them is still home delivery. It's their franchise. Abandoning a time limit isn't necessarily "mortally wounding" if they can come up with another way of talking about how terrific they deliver to the home.

Discussion Questions

1. Even with monitoring, screening and training of its drivers, could Domino's guarantee that all of them would drive safely? Was the risk too great?
2. Was the public perception of safety issues hurting Domino's more than the 30-minute guarantee helped it?
3. Did the $78 million jury verdict punish Domino's for its focus on the 30-minute delivery time?
4. Would you have made the same decision as Domino's?
5. How would you characterize the ethics of the college students who purposely gave incorrect directions to get their pizzas free?

SECTION E
PLANT CLOSURES AND DOWNSIZING

Economic downturns, intense competition, and the need to cut costs often force employers to close facilities and lay off workers. What obligations do businesses have to their employees? To the communities where their facilities are located? The dilemma of employer loyalty and shareholder profit is a difficult one to resolve.

CASE 4.18: THE GENERICS OF DOWNSIZING

According to a *New York Times* analysis of Labor Department figures, 43 million jobs have been eliminated in the United States since 1979. The distinction between this period of layoffs and others in U.S. history is that those workers earning at least $50,000 per year account for two times as many of the lost jobs. Of those who experienced a layoff in this same period, 56% had only held one job in their adult lives. Seventy-two percent of all adult Americans say they have been laid off or had someone in their household, a relative, or a close friend laid off.

A sample list of layoffs follows:

Year	Company	# of Employees
1998	AT&T	15,000
1998	Seagate Technology	10,000
1998	Intel	1,100
1998	J.C. Crew	100
1997	Kodak	2,000 (middle managers); 10,000
1997	General Motors	42,000
1997	Fruit of the Loom	2,900
1997	Waste Management	1,200
1997	Polaroid	5,000
1997	Kemet Corp.	1,000
1997	RJR Nabisco	2,800
1997	Apple Computer	4,100

1997	H.J. Heinz	2,500
1997	Hasbro	2,500
1997	Boeing	12,000
1997	Levi Strauss	6,395
1996	Best Products	10,000
1996	Aetna	8,200
1996	Sunbeam	6,000
1996	Wells Fargo	3,800

The following chart shows the largest downsizings since 1991:

COMPANY	STAFF CUTBACKS
IBM	85,000
AT&T	83,500
General Motors	74,000
U.S. Postal Service	55,000
Sears	50,000
Boeing	30,000
Nynex	22,000
Hughes Aircraft	21,000
GTE	17,000
Martin-Marietta	15,000
Dupont	14,800
Eastman Kodak	14,000
Philip Morris	14,000
Procter & Gamble	13,000
Phar Mor	13,000
Bank of America	12,000
Aetna	11,800
GE Aircraft Engines	10,250
McDonnell Douglas	10,200
Bellsouth	10,200
Ford Motor	10,000
Xerox	10,000
Pacific Telesis	10,000
Honeywell	9,000
US West	9,000

Data Source: People Trends

Consider the following piece on the impact of downsizing:

The Fallout From Dumping Workers[28]

The best description of the U.S. economy could be the age-old insight of the philosopher Heraclitus: "All is flux." But that's cold comfort to millions of Americans who have been the targets of the latest wave of corporate downsizing. In the wake of announced job cuts totaling 40,000 at AT&T, CEO Robert Allen and other corporate downsizers are being demonized as executioners. Politicians on both the left and right are proposing dubious measures to stem the layoffs, such as special tax breaks for companies that don't shed workers in order "to maximize profits," as Massachusetts Democratic Senator Edward Kennedy puts it. Corporate executives, many of whom had the bad timing to reap huge pay hikes even as they handed out pink slips, are

---

28. Susan Dentzer, "The Fallout From Dumping Workers," *U.S. News & World Report*, March 11, 1996, 58.

understandably nervous about the growing public backlash. It's a good time to revisit what's behind the downsizing and examine how it really affects everyone involved.

For starters, it's important to dispel the notion that the current downsizing constitutes something new for the U.S. economy. Thanks to recent research, we know that our economy has long been a churning ocean where as many as one fifth of all the tens of millions of jobs have been either newly created or destroyed each year. Moreover, throughout the 1970s, '80s and apparently into the '90s, notes University of Maryland economist John Haltiwanger, two thirds of the jobs killed in any given year were in establishments that cut employment by 25 percent or more. The good news is that over time, our economy has always created far more jobs than it has destroyed. In fact, to end up with the 8 million net new jobs that have been created since 1992, as many as 40 million new positions probably sprang up to offset around 32 million that were restructured out of existence, Haltiwanger estimates.

Upsizers. If big job cuts are business as usual, why are they now in the spotlight? That may be related to the types of workers being let go. From the 1990–91 recession on, older and better-educated workers who might have expected to escape job cuts have become more popular targets of downsizing. This is partly because firms, after cutting production workers in the '80s, downsized middle management in the '90s. Princeton economist Henry Farber writes that these new victims "may have more influence on the public mood" than the blue-collar workers who long bore the brunt of job cuts. At any rate, the lower-paid workers were probably less likely than their better-placed peers to gain journalists' attention.

Another reason job cuts seem so jarring is that they are often followed by a jump in a company's share price in an already booming stock market. But Wall Street's euphoria doesn't last long. Research by the Greensboro, N.C.-based Center for Creative Leadership shows that stock prices rise for a very short period immediately after corporate layoffs but then fall back quickly to previous levels.

Why should that be—especially given the widespread belief that getting rid of workers represents firms' sure-fire route to greater profitability? Probably because research shows that it takes a couple of years for a firm or plant to reorganize itself and improve productivity, or output per worker, after it downsizes. Small wonder: In the human ant colonies called corporations, morale plummets and confusion reigns when lots of workers are let go. Indeed, it isn't downsizers that demonstrate big productivity gains, it's upsizers that do. Here again, research has shown that productivity growth occurs fastest not in firm or plants that are downsizing but in establishments that are growing like gangbusters.

So, are big job cuts good news or bad news for the economy? In the long run, probably good news. One of our economy's strengths is that it shuffles labor from less productive places to more productive ones—away from firms that no longer have a competitive edge to those that do. If we tried to stop the process, "economic growth would stagnate," Haltiwanger says. The shuffling seems likely to accelerate as U.S. firms encounter heightened domestic and global competition. "I don't think we're anywhere near finished with downsizing, and the pressure on companies that don't grow will only get worse," says Dwight Gertz of Mercer Management Consulting.

None of the economic benefits negate the fact that downsizing is painful for people. A recent Bureau of Labor Statistics study showed that just three quarters of adult workers who lost full-time jobs in 1991–92 had found new full-time jobs by February 1994. Moreover, only about half of those re-employed full timers had found jobs that paid at least as much as, or more than, their old positions did. More broadly, there's little doubt that while today's economy may thrive on turbulence, not many humans do. As management expert Peter Drucker writes in *Managing in a Time of Great Change*, "society, community and family are all conserving institutions . . . but the modern organization is a destabilizer."

Discussion Questions

1. What does downsizing do to stock price?
2. Do you think that management downsizes to please shareholders? Does it help shareholders in the long run?
3. A survey by Deloitte Touche found that employee morale and the impact of downsizing are the top two human resource issues for companies. How does downsizing affect employees?
4. Does the reason for downsizing make a difference to employees? What if technology permits fewer employees? What is the difference between past blue-collar downsizings and the downsizings of the 1990s?

CASE 4.19: THE CLOSURE OF THE STROH'S PLANT UPON MERGER

When Stroh's Brewery of Detroit acquired Schlitz Brewing Company in 1982, it got five breweries more modern than its own Detroit plant that had been operating for over seventy years Three years later, Stroh's decided to close the Detroit brewery with its 1,100 jobs, sixty of which were managerial. Eighty-five percent of the hourly employees and 22 percent of the salaried employees had worked at the plant for more than twenty years.

The president of Stroh's, Peter Stroh, was keenly aware of the impact the closure would have. Unemployment in Detroit was a staggering 9 percent. To lessen the impact on employees and the sagging Detroit economy, Stroh's announced the closure four months before the actual shutdown.[30]

Peter Stroh worked with other CEOs in the Detroit area to find jobs for the displaced workers. Stroh's and the brewery workers' union established an outplacement program, Stroh's spent $1.5 million on it, while state and local governments contributed $600,000. Ron Cupp, manager of corporate personnel at Stroh's, stated:

> The people who had come to work here came to stay. It was very tough to have to let them go. We wanted to develop an aggressive program that would assist these people in a new beginning—be that a new career, their own business, retirement, or whatever their goal might be. In short, we wanted every employee to feel that Stroh's was a good place to work while it was open and a good company to have been associated with after it closed.[31]

The outplacement program offered:

> Orientation sessions to explain the overall concept and give employees ample opportunity to ask questions;
>
> Individual skills testing and assessment;
>
> Development of an individualized job-search strategy;

---

30. Under the 1988 federal Worker Adjustment and Retraining Notification Act (WARN), Stroh's would have been required to give 180 days' notice of closure. The law applies to employers of 100 or more employees.

31. Joseph Jannotta, "Stroh's Outplacement Success," *Management Review*, January 1987, 52–53.

A job-development effort and a computerized job bank;

Individual job-search counseling;

Job-search skills workshops;

Counseling sessions on financial planning, retirement planning, relocation, and starting a new business;

Psychological counseling;

A research library, free phones, and secretarial facilities; and

Extended health and severance benefits.[32]

In just slightly over a year, all of Stroh's 125 salaried employees and 98 percent of the 655 hourly (unionized) employees had found other employment. The layoff and outplacement costs, including Stroh's and government contributions, were $2,000 per employee.

Discussion Questions

1. Was the outplacement program an appropriate expenditure for Stroh's?
2. Would the announcement of the closure four months early have an impact on morale at the plant?
3. Would the announcement of the closure four months early affect Stroh's cost of capital in the marketplace? Its share value?
4. Suppose Detroit represented a significant sales market for Stroh's. Could the outplacement program be viewed as a means of building goodwill?

CASE 4.20: GM PLANT CLOSINGS AND EFFORTS AT OUTPLACEMENT

Bleeding from losses of $4.45 billion for 1991, General Motors (GM) announced on February 24, 1992, that it would close twenty-one plants over the next few years, with twelve to be shutdown in 1992 affecting over 16,300 workers.

GM is the nation's largest manufacturer, and the $4.45 billion loss was the largest ever in American corporate history. Robert C. Stempel, then-GM chairman, said the United States was in an unusually deep automotive slump: "The rate of change during the past year was unprecedented. And no one was immune to the extraordinary events which affected our lives and the way in which we do business."[33]

More than 3,400 workers at GM's North Tarrytown, New York, plant were to be laid off by 1995. The plant manufactured GM mini-vans: the Chevrolet Lumina, the Pontiac Trans Sports, and the Oldsmobile Silhouette. The mini-van, originally designed in the United States, was executed by GM with a wide stance and a sloping, futuristic nose. From 150,000 to 200,000 of the vans were expected to be sold annually, but sales reached only 100,000 per year—one-half of the Tarrytown plant's

32. Jannotta, 52–53.

33. Doran P. Levin, "GM Picks 21 Plants to Be Shut as It Reports a Record U.S. Loss," *New York Times*, 25 February 1992, A1.

capacity. Dealers maintained the shape of the van was too avant-garde for significant sales. "It looks like a Dustbuster," noted a GM manager anonymously.[34]

GM executives acknowledged that building one model per plant was a sloppy and expensive way to do business.

The Tarrytown UAW local had negotiated with GM in 1987 to bring the mini-van production to the plant. The union members voted to accept innovative and cooperative work rules to replace expensive practices under the old contract. Also, state and local governments contributed job training funds, gave tax breaks, and began reconstructing railroad bridges to win the mini-van production plant.

Dan Luria, automotive analyst for the Industrial Technology Institute, a non-profit institute in Ann Arbor, Michigan, said "The workers did all the right things to get the mini-van but GM was just too optimistic about how many it could sell."[35]

In his speech announcing the closures, Stempel said, "We are asking you to help remake the world's largest automobile company. We can't wait."[36]

Tarrytown was only the beginning of the GM closures. In February 1993, GM announced the closure of 21 plants with resulting layoffs of 16,300 workers. Another closure was the Willow Run plant in Ypsilanti Township, Michigan, a loss of 2,200 jobs. However, Ypsilanti Township and Washtenaw County filed suit challenging the closure because GM had promised to build cars at Willow Run through the late 1990s in exchange for tax abatements. The suit alleged $13.5 million was owed in back taxes by GM for reneging on its promise to operate the plant. The suit was settled in 1994 with GM agreeing to pay half the abated taxes.

Discussion Questions

1. When unions and governments provide financial assistance in exchange for promises from a manufacturer to locate a plant in a particular area, should the plant owner have an obligation to continue operations?
2. Did GM just make a business decision to stop losses?
3. Should workers and governments absorb the cost of business risks, such as a poor-selling mini-van?
4. Did GM renege on its promise to Ypsilanti Township and Washtenaw County? Should business setbacks excuse plant closures? Should tax abatements be repaid?

CASE 4.21: AARON FEUERSTEIN AND MALDEN MILLS

Aaron Feuerstein is the chief executive officer and chairman of the board of Malden Mills, a 93-year-old privately-held company that manufactures Polartec and is located in Mathuen, Massachusetts. Polartec is a fabric made from recycled

---

34. Doran P. Levin, "Vehicle's Design Dooms Van Plant," *New York Times*, 26 February 1992, C4.

35. Ibid.

36. William McWhirter, "Major Overhaul," *Time*, 30 December 1991, 56.

plastic that stays dry and provides warmth. It is used in everything from ski parkas to blankets by companies such as L.L. Bean, Patagonia, Land's End and Eddie Bauer. Malden employs 2,400 locals and Mr. Feuerstein and his family have steadfastly refused to move production overseas. Their labor costs are the highest in the industry—an average of $12.50 per hour.

On December 11, 1995, a boiler explosion at Malden Mills resulted in a fire that injured 27 people and destroyed three of the buildings at Malden Mills' factory site. With only one building left in functioning order, many employees assumed they would be laid off temporarily. Other employees worried that Mr. Feuerstein, then 70-years-old, would simply take the insurance money and retire.

Instead, Mr. Feuerstein announced on December 14, 1995, that he would pay the employees their salaries for at least 30 days. He continued that promise for six months, when 90% of the employees were back to work. During that time, Malden ran its Polartec through its one working facility as it began and completed the reconstruction of the plant. Interestingly, production output during this time was nine times what it had been before the fire. One worker noted, "I owe him everything. I'm paying him back."

After the fire and Feuerstein's announcement, customers pledged their support with one customer, Dakotah, sending in $30,000 to help. Within the first month, following the fire, $1,000,000 in donations were received.

Malden Mills was rededicated in September 1997 with new buildings and technology. About 10% of the 2400 employees were displaced by the upgraded facilities and equipment, but Feuerstein created a job training and placement center on site in order to ease these employees' transition.

Discussion Questions

1. Mr. Feuerstein has stated, "I don't deserve credit. Corporate America has made it so that when you behave the way I did, it's abnormal." Is he right? Was he right in continuing the salaries?
2. What impact would a closure of Malden Mills have had on Mathuen?
3. Does the fact that Malden Mills is privately held make a difference in Feuerstein's flexibility?

Section F
Environmental Issues

The quality of the environment has become a personal issue. Many consumers base their buying decisions on the commitment of manufacturers and other businesses to protect the environment. The environment has become a stakeholder in business operations.

Case 4.22: Herman Miller and Its Rain Forest Chairs

In March 1990, Bill Foley, research manager for Herman Miller, Inc., began a routine evaluation of new woods to use in the firm's signature piece—the $2,277 Eames chair. The Eames chair is a distinctive office chair with a rosewood exterior finish and a leather seat.

At that time, the chair was made of two species of trees: rosewood and Honduran mahogany. Foley realized that Miller's use of the tropical hardwoods was helping destroy rain forests. Foley banned the use of the woods in the chairs once existing supplies were exhausted. The Eames chair would no longer have its traditional rosewood finish.

Foley's decision prompted former CEO Richard H. Ruch to react: "That's going to kill that [chair]."[37] Effects on sales could not be quantified.

Herman Miller, based in Zeeland, Michigan, and founded in 1923 by D. J. DePree, a devout Baptist, manufactures office furniture and partitions. The corporation follows a participatory-management tradition and takes environmentally friendly actions. The vice president of the Michigan Audubon Society noted that Miller has cut the trash it hauls to landfills by 90 percent since 1982. "Herman Miller has been doing a super job," he said.[38]

---

37. David Woodruff, "Herman Miller: How Green Is My Factory?" *Business Week*, 16 September 1991, 54–55.

38. Ibid.

Herman Miller built an $11 million waste-to-energy heating and cooling plant. The plant saves $750,000 per year in fuel and landfill costs. In 1991, the company found a buyer for the 800,000 pounds of scrap fabric it had been dumping in landfills. A North Carolina firm shreds it for insulation in car-roof linings and dashboards. Selling the scrap fabric saves Miller $50,000 per year in dumping fees.

Herman Miller employees once used 800,000 Styrofoam cups a year. But in 1991, the company passed out 5,000 mugs to its employees and banished styrofoam. The mugs carry the following admonition: "On spaceship earth there are no passengers . . . only crew." Styrofoam in packaging was also reduced 70 percent for a cost savings of $1.4 million.

Herman Miller also spent $800,000 for two incinerators that burn 98 percent of the toxic solvents that escape from booths where wood is stained and varnished. These furnaces exceeded the 1990 Clean Air Act requirements. It was likely that the incinerators would be obsolete within three years, when nontoxic products became available for staining and finishing wood, but having the furnaces was "ethically correct," former CEO Ruch said in response to questions from the board of directors.[39]

Herman Miller keeps pursuing environmentally safe processes, including finding a use for its sawdust by-product. However, for the fiscal year ended May 31, 1991, its net profit had fallen 70 percent from 1990 to $14 million on total sales of $878 million.

In 1992, Herman Miller's board hired J. Kermit Campbell as CEO. Mr. Campbell continued in the Ruch tradition and wrote essays for employees on risk-taking and for managers on "staying out of the way." From 1992–1995, sales growth at Herman Miller was explosive, but as one analyst described it, "expenses exploded." Despite sales growth during this time, profits dropped 89% to a mere $4.3 million.

Miller's board, concerned about Campbell's lack of expedience, announced Campbell's resignation, and began an aggressive program of downsizing. Between May and July, 1995, 130 jobs were eliminated. Also in 1995, sales dropped from $879 million to $804 million. The board promoted Michael Volkema, then 39, and head of Miller's file cabinet division to CEO.

Volkema refocused Herman Miller's name with a line of well-made, lower-priced office furniture using a strategy and division called SQA (Simple, Quick and Affordable). The dealers for SQA work with customers to configure office furniture plans and Miller ships in less than two weeks all the pieces ordered.

Revenues in 1997 were $200 million with record earnings of $78 million. In 1998, Miller will be acquiring dealerships around the country and downsizing from its current 1,500 employees.

Volkema notes that staying too long with an "outdated strategy and marketing" nearly cost the company.

Discussion Questions

1. Evaluate Foley's decision on changing the Eames chair woods. Consider the moral standards at issue for various stakeholders.
2. Is it troublesome that Miller's profits were off when Foley made the decision?
3. Is Herman Miller bluffing with "green marketing"? Would Albert Carr support Herman Miller's actions for different reasons?

---

39. Ibid.

4. Why would Herman Miller decide to buy equipment that exceeded the 1990 Clean Air Act standards when it would not be needed in three years?

5. Would you be less comfortable with Herman Miller's environmental decisions if it advertised them?

6. Has Herman Miller changed its focus? Why?

CASE 4.23: GREEN MARKETING AS A BUSINESS BLUFF

British statesman Henry Taylor said, "Falsehood ceases to be falsehood when it is understood on all sides that the truth is not expected to be spoken." Examples would include human interaction in situations that involve diplomacy or poker. Albert Carr maintains that Taylor's idea also applies to business. All action business takes would be with the understanding that it is done to help the business and not necessarily for some noble cause. Thus, even though a business may tout a decision as ethical or socially responsible, its decision is still based on the bottom line of profit, either for the short term or over the long run.

A common example of business bluffing is the attention given to environmental concerns. Some critics maintain that businesses are not really interested in the environment but only take environmentally sound positions to get an edge in the market because of consumers' commitments to the environment. In other words, businesses may be doing the right things but not for a noble reason.

Star-Kist offers its tuna as "dolphin free." No nets are used that would also catch and kill dolphins. The manufacturers of detergents, prewash stain removers, and other soap products focus on their products' biodegradable qualities. Known as "green marketing," a company's targeting of environmental issues in its ads often raises doubts about its sincerity. In many cases, the "environmental qualities" of the product do increase sales.

The Federal Trade Commission (FTC) is examining the issue of "green advertising" to determine whether standards should be set that a company would have to reach before it could claim that its product is good for the environment.

Discussion Questions

1. Is it unethical to do the right thing for the wrong reason?
2. Is it unethical to increase sales and profits by focusing on a social cause?
3. Are companies being dishonest when they profess their commitment to the environment?
4. Does the motive behind introducing environmentally sound qualities in a product or service matter?

CASE 4.24: EXXON AND ALASKA

On March 24, 1989, the Exxon *Valdez* ran aground on Bligh Reef, south of Valdez, Alaska, and spilled nearly 11 million gallons of oil into Prince William Sound. The captain of the tanker was Joseph Hazelwood.

Hazelwood had a history of drinking problems and had lost his New York driver's license after two drunken-driving convictions. In 1985, with the knowledge of Exxon officials, Hazelwood joined a twenty-eight-day alcohol rehabilitation program. Almost a week after the Prince William Sound accident, Exxon revealed that Hazelwood's blood-alcohol reading was 0.061 in a test taken ten and one-half hours after the spill occurred—a level that would indicate intoxication. Exxon also announced it had fired Hazelwood.

The magnitude of the spill seemed almost incomprehensible. U.S. Interior Secretary Manual Lujan called the spill the oil industry's "Three Mile Island." After ten days, the spill covered 1,000 square miles and leaked out of Prince William Sound onto beaches along the Gulf of Alaska and Cook Inlet. A clean-up army of 12,000 was sent in with hot water and oil-eating microbes. The workers found more than 1,000 dead otters, 34,400 dead sea birds, and 151 bald eagles that had died from eating the oil-contaminated remains of sea birds.

By September 15, Exxon pulled out of the cleanup efforts after having spent $2 billion but recovering only 5 to 9 percent of the oil spilled. Alaskan officials said about 20 to 40 percent of the oil evaporated. This meant that 50 to 75 percent of the oil was either on the ocean floor or the beaches.

Hazelwood was indicted by the state of Alaska on several charges, including criminal mischief, operating a watercraft while intoxicated, reckless endangerment, and negligent discharge of oil. He was found innocent of all charges except the negligent discharge of oil, fined $50,000, and required to spend 1,000 hours helping with the cleanup of the beaches. Exxon paid Hazelwood's legal fees. Hazelwood now works as a maritime consultant for a New York City law firm and still holds a valid sea license.

When the *Valdez* was being repaired, shipworkers observed that Hazelwood and his crew had kept the tanker from sinking by quickly sealing off the hatches to the ship's tank, thus making a bubble that helped stabilize the ship. Citing incredible seamanship, the workers noted that an 11-million-gallon spill was preferable to a 60 million one—the tanker's load.

Following the spill, critics of Exxon maintained that the company's huge personnel cutbacks during the 1980s affected the safety and maintenance levels aboard its tankers. Later hearings revealed that the crew of the *Valdez* was overburdened with demands for speed and efficiency. The crew worked ten- to twelve-hour days and often had their sleep interrupted. Lookouts frequently were not properly posted, and junior officers were permitted to control the bridge without the required supervision. Robert LeResche, oil-spill coordinator for Alaska said, "It wasn't Captain Ahab on the bridge. It was Larry and Curly in the Exxon boardroom."[40] In response to critics, Exxon's CEO Lawrence Rawl stated:

> And we say, 'We're sorry, and we're doing all we can.' There were 30 million birds that went through the sound last summer, and only 30,000 carcasses have been recovered. Just look at how many ducks were killed in the Mississippi Delta in one hunting day in December! People have come up to me and said, 'This is worse than Bhopal.' I say, 'Hell, Bhopal killed more than 3,000 people and injured 200,000 others!' Then they say, 'Well, if you leave the people out, it was worse than Bhopal.'

---

40. Jay Mathews, "Problems Preceded Oil Spill," *Washington Post*, 18 May 1989, A1, A18.

On January 1, 1990, a second Exxon oil spill occurred when a pipeline under the Arthur Kill waterway between Staten Island and New Jersey burst and spilled 567,000 gallons of heating oil. New York and New Jersey officials criticized Exxon, citing shoddy equipment and poor maintenance. It was six hours after an alarm from the pipeline safety system went off before Exxon workers shut down the pipeline. Albert Appleton, New York City commissioner on the environment, said, "Exxon has a corporate philosophy that the environment is some kind of nuisance problem and a distraction from the real business of moving oil around."[41]

Late in February 1990, Exxon was indicted on federal felony charges of violating maritime safety and antipollution laws in the *Valdez* spill. The charges were brought after Exxon and the Justice Department failed to reach a settlement. The oil company also faced state criminal charges. Alaska and the Justice Department also brought civil suits against Exxon for the costs of cleaning up the spill. Approximately 150 other civil suits were filed by fishing and tour boat operators whose incomes were eliminated by the spill. At the time of the federal indictment, Exxon had paid out $180 million to 13,000 fishermen and other claimants.

By May 1990, Exxon had renewed its cleanup efforts at targeted sites with 110 employees. Twice during 1991, Exxon reached a plea agreement with the federal government and the state on the criminal charges. After Alaska disagreed with the terms of the first, a second agreement was reached in which Exxon consented to plead guilty to three misdemeanors and pay a $1.15 billion fine. The civil litigation was settled when Exxon agreed to pay $900 million to both Alaska and the federal government over ten years.

The plea agreement with the governments did not address the civil suits pending against Exxon. At the end of 1991, an Alaska jury awarded sixteen fishers more than $2.5 million in damages and established a payout formula for similar plaintiffs in future litigation against Exxon. As of September 1994, Exxon had spent $2 billion to clean up shores in Alaska.

Exxon has had a stream of payouts since 1991—a total of $3.4 billion of its $5.7 billion in profits for that period. Payouts included:

- $20 million to 3,500 native Alaskans for damages to their villages;
- $287 million to 10,000 fishers;
- $1.5 billion for damages to wildlife; and
- $9.7 million for damages to Native American land.

In September 1994, a federal jury awarded an additional $5 billion in punitive damages against Exxon for the suits filed since 1991. Exxon appealed the verdict to the Ninth Circuit. Exxon's stock fell two and five-eighths points following the verdict. However, in 1996, during a court review of the distribution of an award, in an Alaskan case, a *Wall Street Journal* article revealed that Exxon had reached secret agreements with fish processors that would require them to refund the punitive damages awarded by juries. Apparently, some type of high/low settlement was reached with the plaintiffs prior to trial, but the jury trial proceeded without disclosure of the settlement and potential refund by the plaintiffs.

U.S. District Judge H. Russel Holland learned of the refund requirements and called the agreements an "astonishing ruse" to "mislead" the jury. Judge Holland set aside the agreements and allowed punitive damages to stand.

---

41. Barbara Rudolph, "Exxon's Attitude Problem," *Time*, 22 January 1990, 51.

By November 1, 1996, Exxon had settled all of the Valdez cases and settled with its insurers for its claims. Exxon recovered $780 million of its $2.5 billion in costs, including attorney fees. Exxon had been in litigation with its insurers over coverage. Eugene Anderson, a lawyer who represents corporations in insurance actions noted that insurance companies virtually always deny all large claims because "they pay lawyers much less each year in these cases than they earn in interest."

Discussion Questions

1. Evaluate Exxon's "attitude" with regard to the spill.
2. Why did the company cut back on staff and maintenance expenditures?
3. Was Hazelwood morally responsible for the spill?
4. Was Exxon management morally responsible for the spill?
5. What changes in Exxon's ethical environment would you make?
6. Would Exxon make the same decisions about Hazelwood and cost-cutting given the costs of the spill?
7. Evaluate the ethics in Exxon's secret deal on punitive damages.
8. Evaluate the ethics of the insurers in denying large claims in order to earn the interest while litigation over the claim is pending.

CASE 4.25: THE DEATH OF THE GREAT DISPOSABLE DIAPER DEBATE

In the late 1980s, environmentalists raised concerns about the disposal of diapers in municipal landfills, space for which is scarce and becoming more so. The average child uses 7,800 diapers in the first 130 weeks of life.

The debate over disposable diapers was complex. Disposable diapers account for just 2 percent of municipal solid waste. The time required for plastic to break down is 200 to 500 years. Eighteen billion disposable diapers go into landfills each year. An Arthur D. Little study comparing the environmental impact of cloth and disposable diapers over the products' lifetimes found cloth diapers consume more energy and water than disposables. Cloth diapers also cost more (not counting diaper-service fees) and create more air and water pollution through washing. Critics point out that the study was commissioned by Procter & Gamble, the largest maker of disposable diapers, with 50 percent of the market. However, the study was a sophisticated "life-cycle analysis" that used elaborate computer models, and Arthur D. Little is considered an eminent research firm.

In surveys in the early 1990s, four of five American parents preferred disposables. Most hospital staffs and day care centers favor using disposables even though many personally use cloth diapers. Switching from disposable to cloth diapers costs about 2.5 percent more. The disposability of the diapers was also improving with companies devoting significant R & D dollars to reducing the time for biodegradation. Procter & Gamble created advanced techniques for industrial composting of solid waste and spent $20 million to develop diapers that break down into humus.

Environmentalists, however, were quite successful in obtaining regulation of disposables. Twenty states considered taxes or complete bans on disposables. Nebraska banned nondegradable disposables, with a law that took effect in October 1993. Maine required day-care centers to accept children who wear cloth diapers. New York considered requiring that new mothers be given information explaining the environmental threat of disposables. In 1990, the Wisconsin legislature barely defeated a measure to tax disposables.

Alternatives to disposables were being developed. Currently, R Med International distributes Tender Care, a disposable diaper that degrades in two to five years because its outer lining is made of cornstarch. However, the price of these diapers was substantially higher than that of other disposables and made mass market appeal impossible.

The great disposable diaper debate peaked on Earth Day in 1990. After the Little study appeared, parents' guilt about rain forests and land fills was relieved and by 1997, 80% of all babies were wearing disposables. Many attribute the change in attitude as well as the halt in legislative and regulatory action to Procter & Gamble's effective public relations using the Little study results. Also, Allen Hershkowitz, a senior scientist at the Natural Resources Defense Council said, "The pediatric dermatology clearly seemed to favor disposables, while the environmental issues were murky." Environmentalists referred to Mr. Hershkowitz as "the skipper of the Exxon Valdez."

Also by 1997, the National Association of Diaper Services (NADS) reported its membership at an all-time low with closings of cloth diaper services even in ecologically conscious Boston. There are no diaper services, located in any of New York City's five boroughs. Their current marketing campaign emphasizes a 2½ year guarantee for potty-training with diapers free after that. Babies, the NADS says, can't feel the wetness in disposables.

Discussion Questions

1. Did Arthur D. Little have a conflict of interest with Procter & Gamble's sponsorship of its work?
2. Would it be a breach of duty to the hospital's patients and shareholders to adopt a position (that is, using cloth diapers) that increases costs?
3. Do people ignore environmental issues for the sake of convenience? Do your arguments depend on whether you must change diapers?
4. What lessons are learned from this case for applicability in other industries?
5. Did environmentalists exaggerate?

SECTION G
PURCHASING:
CONFLICTS AND BRIBERY

Purchasing agents hold powerful positions. They make the choices to award business to other companies. Often, contractors employ tools of influence to gain favor. When are such tools unethical? Can an agent accept gifts for the award of business?

CASE 4.26: J. C. PENNEY AND ITS WEALTHY BUYER

Purchasing agent Jim G. Locklear began his career as a retail buyer with Federated Department Stores in Dallas, where he became known for his eye for fashion and ability to negotiate low prices. After ten years with Federated, he went to work for Jordan Marsh in Boston in 1987 with an annual salary of $96,000. But three months later, Locklear quit that job to take a position as a housewares buyer with J. C. Penney so he could return to Dallas. His salary was $56,000 per year, he was 38 years old, he owed support payments totaling $900 per month for four children from four marriages, and the bank was threatening to foreclose on his $500,000 mortgage.

Locklear was a good performer for Penney. His products sold well, and he was responsible for the very successful J. C. Penney Home Collection, a color-coordinated line of dinnerware, flatware, and glasses that was eventually copied by most other tabletop retailers. Locklear took sales of Penney's tabletop line from $25 million to $45 million per year and was named the company's "Buyer of the Year" several times.

However, Locklear was taking payments from Penney's vendors directly and through front companies. Some paid him for information about bids or to obtain contracts, while others paid what they believed to be advertising fees to various companies that were fronts owned by Locklear. Between 1987 and 1992, Locklear took in $1.5 million in "fees" from Penney's vendors.

Penney hired an investigator in 1989 to look into Locklear's activities, but the investigator uncovered only Mr. Locklear's personal financial difficulties.

During his time as a buyer, Locklear was able to afford a country club membership, resort vacations, luxury vehicles, and large securities accounts. While his life-style was known to those who worked with him, no questions were asked again until 1992, when Penney received an anonymous letter about Locklear and his relationship with a Dallas manufacturer's representative. Penney investigated and uncovered sufficient evidence of payments to file a civil suit to recover those payments and referred the case to the U.S. attorney in Dallas for criminal prosecution.

Mr. Locklear was charged by the U.S. attorney with mail and wire fraud. Mr. Locklear entered a guilty plea and provided information to the U.S. attorney on suppliers, agents, and manufacturers' reps who had paid him "fees." Mr. Locklear was sentenced to 18 months in prison and fined $50,000. Penney won a $789,000 judgment against him and Mr. Locklear's assets have been attached for collection purposes.

Discussion Questions

1. What ethical violations did Locklear commit?
2. Was anyone really harmed by Locklear's conduct? List the stakeholders who were affected.
3. Given Locklear's life-style, why did it take so long for Penney to take action? Do you see any red flags in the facts given?
4. A vendor who paid Locklear $25,000 in exchange for a Penney order stated, "It was either pay it or go out of business." Evaluate the ethics of this seller.
5. Do you agree that both the buyer and the seller are guilty in commercial bribery cases? Is the purchasing agent "more" wrong?
6. Many companies provide guidelines for their purchasing agents on accepting gifts, samples, and favors. For example, under Wal-Mart's "no coffee" policy, its buyers cannot accept even a cup of coffee from a vendor. Any samples or models must be returned to vendors once a sales demonstration is complete. Other companies allow buyers to accept items of minimal value. Still others place a specific dollar limit on the value, such as $25. What problems do you see with any of these policies? What advantages do you see?
7. Describe the problems that can result when buyers accept gifts from vendors and manufacturer's representatives.
8. Mr. Locklear said at his sentencing, "I became captive to greed. Once it was discovered, I felt tremendous relief." Mr. Locklear's pastor said Locklear coached little league and added, "Our country needs more role models like Jim Locklear." Evaluate these two quotes from an ethical perspective.

CASE 4.27: CARS FOR CARS: HONDA EXECUTIVES' ALLOCATION SYSTEM

From 1978 through early 1992, the amazing popularity of Honda cars, including its luxury car Acura, created excessive demand for both the cars and the franchises (dealerships). Dealers were able to sell the vehicles at thousands of dollars above the sticker price, virtually guaranteeing high profits. This intense demand and resulting guaranteed success led to Honda America executives getting cash and gifts from dealers and potential dealers in exchange for auto delivery allocations and the award of franchises. One man who was eventually awarded a dealership presented a Honda executive with a Mercedes-Benz. Some Honda executives accepted cash payments of up to $1 million in exchange for a franchise. Others received such gifts as swimming pools, paintings (one worth $50,000), Rolex watches, and laser karaoke machines.

Honda officials in Japan were unaware of this activity by Honda America executives. Meanwhile, one person, Joseph R. Hendrick, was awarded 28 dealerships during this time. An assistant U.S. attorney in New Hampshire, Michael J. Conolly, presented evidence in court that Hendrick sent payments to Stanley James Cardiges, senior vice president of sales for Honda America. Cardiges and sixteen other Honda executives have pleaded guilty to federal charges of racketeering, mail fraud, and conspiracy to commit mail fraud and have forfeited $10 million to the U. S. government. Two other Honda executives were found guilty of accepting more than $15 million in kickbacks from auto dealers that were the basis of federal fraud charges in a scheme that involved dealers in thirty states. In the trial of these two executives, Cardiges has testified that the practice of accepting gifts was widespread in the executive suite.

The total of former Honda executives and employees to plead guilty or be convicted reached 20 in 1995. Cardiges was sentenced to five years and fined $364,000.

In 1996, a federal judge ruled that Honda dealers who claim injury from the company-wide bribery scheme can file suit against Honda for racketeering and antitrust violations. The judge also ruled that high-ranking Honda Japanese executives could be named in the suit.

The dealers who have brought suit claim that they lost millions in business because they refused to pay bribes and were not given car allocations at a time when Hondas could be sold at thousands above the sticker price.

Throughout the country, indictments of dealers who paid bribes to the Honda USA executives have continued. The dealers have been charged with conspiracy, money laundering, and mail fraud. Mr. Hendrick was indicted on 13 counts of money laundering, one count of conspiracy, and one count of mail fraud. Mr. Hendrick's brother, John, was also indicted. Mr. Hendrick stated that he gave Mr. Cardiges gifts, but called them gifts to a friend, not for influence.

Discussion Questions

1. What type of atmosphere did Honda America have to have for this scheme to go on for so long?
2. To whom did the money and goods paid to the executives actually belong? Were the Honda executives collecting economic rents that belonged to Honda because of the high demand for its cars?
3. Why does it matter that these executives enjoyed some extra money from Honda's success? Are these economic rents that belong to Honda?
4. If you were an executive, how would you confront your fellow officers about such payments and your unwillingness to accept them? Could you lose your job for taking such a position?
5. A defense lawyer in the trial of two executives said that Honda's top management "turned a blind eye to the kick backs and that bribe-taking was implicit, though unofficial, company policy, and therefore did not constitute a crime." Evaluate his statement.

UNIT FIVE
BUSINESS AND
ITS COMPETITION

A business's relations with its competitors are evidenced in its advertising, product similarity, and pricing. The heat of competition often creates dilemmas on what to say in ads or how similar to make a product.

SECTION A
ADVERTISING CONTENT

Ads sell products. But how much can the truth be stretched? Are ads ever irresponsible by encouraging harmful behavior?

CASE 5.1: JOE CAMEL:
THE CARTOON CHARACTER WHO SOLD CIGARETTES
AND NEARLY FELLED AN INDUSTRY

Old Joe Camel, originally a member of a circus that passed through Winston-Salem, North Carolina, each year, was adopted by R. J. Reynolds (RJR) marketers in 1913 as the symbol for a brand being changed from "Red Kamel" to "Camel." In the late 1980s, RJR revived Old Joe with a new look in the form of a cartoon. He became the camel with a "Top Gun" flier jacket, sunglasses, a smirk, and a lot of appeal to young people.

In December 1991, the *Journal of the American Medical Association (JAMA)* published three surveys that found that the cartoon character Joe Camel reached children very effectively. Of children between the ages of three and six who were surveyed, 51.1 percent recognized Joe Camel as being associated with Camel cigarettes.[1] The six-year-olds were as familiar with Joe Camel as they were with the Mickey Mouse logo for the Disney Channel. The surveys also established that 97.7 percent of students between the ages of twelve and nineteen have seen Old Joe and 58 percent thought the ads he was used in were cool. Camel was identified by 33 percent of the students who smoke as their favorite brand.[2]

Before the survey results appeared in *JAMA*, the American Cancer Society, the American Heart Association, and the American Lung Association had petitioned

---

1. Kathleen Deveny, "Joe Camel Ads Reach Children, Research Finds," *Wall Street Journal*, 11 December 1991, B1.

2. Walecia Konrad, "I'd Toddle a Mile for a Camel," *Business Week*, 23 December 1991, 34. While the studies and their methodology have been questioned, their impact was made before the challenges and questions were raised.

192

the FTC to ban the ads as "one of the most egregious examples in recent history of tobacco advertising that targets children."[3]

In 1990, Camel shipments rose 11.3 percent. Joe Camel helped RJR take its Camel cigarettes from 2.7 percent to 3.1 percent of the market.[4]

Michael Pertschuk, former FTC head co-director of the Advocacy Institute, an antismoking group, said, "These are the first studies to give us hard evidence, proving what everybody already knows is true: These ads target kids. I think this will add impetus to the movement to further limit tobacco advertising.[5] Joe Tye, founder of Stop Teenage Addictions to Tobacco, stated, "There is a growing body of evidence that teen smoking is increasing. And it's 100 percent related to Camel."[6]

A researcher who worked on the December 1991 *JAMA* study, Dr. Joseph R. DiFranza, stated, "We're hoping this information leads to a complete ban of cigarette advertising."[7] Dr. John Richards summarized the study as follows, "The fact is that the ad is reaching kids, and it is changing their behavior."[8]

RJR spokesman David Fishel responded to the allegations with sales evidence: "We can track 98 percent of Camel sales; and they're not going to youngsters. It's simply not in our best interest for young people to smoke, because that opens the door for the government to interfere with our product."[9] At the time the survey results were published, RJR, along with other manufacturers and the Tobacco Institute, began a multimillion-dollar campaign with billboards and bumper stickers to discourage children from smoking but announced it had no intention of abandoning Joe Camel. The Tobacco Institute publishes a free popular pamphlet called "Tobacco: Helping Youth Say No."

Former U.S. Surgeon General Antonia Novello was very vocal in her desire to change alcohol and cigarette advertising. In March 1992, she called for the withdrawal of the Joe Camel ad campaign: "In years past, R. J. Reynolds would have us walk a mile for a Camel. Today it's time that we invite old Joe Camel himself to take a hike."[10] The AMA's executive vice president, Dr. James S. Todd, concurred:

> This is an industry that kills 400,000 per year, and they have got to pick up new customers. We believe the company is directing its ads to the children who are 3, 6 and 9 years old.[11]

Cigarette sales are, in fact, declining 3 percent per year in the United States.

The average Camel smoker is thirty-five years old, responded an RJR spokeswoman: "Just because children can identify our logo doesn't mean they will use our product."[12] Since the introduction of Joe Camel, however, Camel's share of the under-eighteen market has climbed to 33 percent from 5 percent. Among

3 Deveny, B1.

4. Konrad, 34.

5. Deveny, B6.

6. Laura Bird, "Joe Smooth for President," *Adweek's Marketing Week*, 20 May 1991, 21.

7. Konrad, 34.

8. "Camels for Kids," *Time*, 23 December 1991, 52.

9. Ibid.

10. William Chesire, "Don't Shoot: It's Only Joe Camel," *Arizona Republic*, 15 March 1992, C1.

11. Ibid.

12. Konrad, 34.

eighteen- to twenty-five-year-olds, Camel's market share has climbed to 7.9 percent from 4.4 percent.

The Centers for Disease Control reported in March 1992 that smokers between the ages of twelve and eighteen prefer Marlboro, Newport, or Camel cigarettes, the three brands with the most extensive advertising.[13]

Teenagers throughout the country were wearing Joe Camel T-shirts. Brown & Williamson, the producer of Kool cigarettes, began testing a cartoon character for its ads, a penguin wearing sunglasses and Day-Glo sneakers. Company spokesman Joseph Helewicz stated that the ads are geared to smokers between twenty-one and thirty-five years old. Helewicz added that cartoon advertisements for adults are not new and cited the Pillsbury Doughboy and the Pink Panther as effective advertising images.

In mid-1992, then-Surgeon General Novello, along with the American Medical Association, began a campaign called "Dump the Hump" to pressure the tobacco industry to stop ad campaigns that teach kids to smoke. In 1993, the FTC staff recommended a ban on the Joe Camel ads. In 1994, then-Surgeon General Joycelyn Elders blamed the tobacco industry's $4 billion in ads for increased smoking rates among teens. RJR's tobacco division chief, James W. Johnston, responded, "I'll be damned if I'll pull the ads." RJR put together a team of lawyers and others it referred to as in-house censors to control Joe's influence. A campaign to have Joe wear a bandana was nixed, as was one for a punker Joe with pink hair.

In 1994, RJR CEO James Johnston testified before a Congressional panel on the Joe Camel controversy and stated, "We do not market to children and will not," and added, "We do not survey anyone under the age of 18."

As health issues related to smokers continued to expand, along with product liability litigation and state attorneys' general pursuit of compensation for their states' health system costs of smokers, more information about the Joe Camel campaign was discovered. Lawyers in a California suit against RJR discovered charts from a presentation at a September 30, 1974 Hilton Head, South Carolina retreat of RJR top executives and board. The charts offered the following information:

Company	Brand	Share of 14-24-year-old market
Philip Morris	Marlboro	33%
Brown & Williamson	Kool	17%
Reynolds	Winston	14%
Reynolds	Salem	9%

RJR's then-vice president of marketing, C.A. Tucker said, "As this 14-24 age group matures, they will account for a key share of total cigarette volume for at least the next 25 years." The meeting then produced a plan for increasing RJR's presence among the under-35 age group which included sponsoring NASCAR auto racing. Another memo described plans to study "the demographics and smoking behavior of 14-to-17 year olds."

Internal documents about targeting young people were damaging. A 1981 RJR internal memo on marketing surveys cautioned research personnel to tally underage smokers as "age 18". A 1981 Philip Morris internal document indicated information about smoking habits in children as young as 15 was important because

---

13. "Selling Death," *Mesa Tribune*, 16 March 1992, A8.

"today's teen-ager is tomorrow's potential regular customer." Other Philip Morris documents from the 1980s expressed concerns that Marlboro sales would soon decline because teen-age smoking rates were falling.

A 1987 marketing survey in France and Canada by RJR before it launched the Joe Camel campaign showed that the cartoon image with its fun and humor attracted attention. One 1987 internal document uses the phrase "young adult smokers" and notes a target campaign to the competition's "male Marlboro smokers ages 13–24."

A 1997 survey of 534 teens by *USA Today* revealed the following:

Ad	Have Seen Ad	Liked Ad
Joe Camel	95%	65%
Marlboro Man	94%	44%
Budweiser Frogs	99%	92%

Marlboro was the brand smoked by most teens in the survey. The survey found 28% of teens between ages 13 and 18 smoke—an increase of 4% since 1991. In 1987, Camels were the cigarette of choice for 3% of teenagers when Joe Camel debuted. By 1993, the figure had climbed to 16%.

In early 1990, the Federal Trade Commission (FTC) began an investigation of RJR and its Joe Camel ads to determine whether underage smokers were illegally targeted by the 10-year Joe Camel Campaign. The FTC had dismissed a complaint in 1994, but did not have the benefits of the newly-discovered internal memos.

By late 1997, RJR began phasing out Joe Camel. New Camel ads feature men and women in their 20s, with a healthy look, in clubs and swimming pools with just a dromedary logo somewhere in the ad. Joe continued as a youth icon. A "Save Joe Camel" web site developed and Joe Camel paraphernalia brought top dollar. A Joe Camel shower curtain sold for $200. RJR also vowed not to feature the Joe Camel character on non-tobacco items such as T-shirts. The cost of the abandonment was estimated at $250 million.

Philip Morris proposed its own plan to halt youth smoking in 1996 which includes no vending machine ads, no billboard ads, no tobacco ads in magazines with 15% or more of youth subscribers, and limits on sponsorships to events (rodeos, motor sports) where 75% or more of attendees are adults.

It was also in 1997 that the combined pressure from Congress, the state attorneys general, and ongoing class action suits produced what came to be known as "the tobacco settlement" (see case 6.11 for more details). The tobacco settlement in all of its various forms bars outdoor advertising, the use of human images (Marlboro man) and cartoon characters, and vending-machine sales. This portion of the settlement was advocated by those who were concerned about teen-agers and their attraction to cigarettes via these ads and their availability in machines.

Discussion Questions

1. Suppose you were the executive in charge of marketing for R. J. Reynolds. Would you have recommended an alternative to the Joe Camel character? What if RJR insisted on the Joe Camel ad?
2. Suppose you work with a pension fund that has a large investment in RJR. Would you consider selling your RJR holdings?

3. Do you agree with the statement that identification of the logo does not equate with smoking or with smoking Camels? Do regulators agree? Did the Joe Camel ads generate market growth?
4. What effect will RJR's voluntary action have on the regulatory trend?
5. Anti-tobacco activist Alan Blum said, "This business of saying 'Oh, my God, they went after kids' is ex post facto rationalization for not having done anything. It's not as if we on the do-good side didn't know that." Is he right?

CASE 5.2: THE SEXIST BEER ADS

It came from Tustin, California—Nude Beer. The label on the bottle of the new beer bore a photo of a bare-breasted blonde woman, and the advertising campaign included plans for showing a new bare-breasted model each month on the label. But entrepreneur William H. Boam, formerly a commercial photographer, ran into opposition to his application for approval for his new beer's label from the California Department of Alcohol Beverage Control and the U.S. Bureau of Alcohol, Tobacco and Firearms (BATF).

The California regulators referred to the label as "blatant and obnoxious" and "contrary to public welfare and morals." Boam responded: "They can try to stop me, but they are not going to win. This is a fun product. It's not obscene. It's like having a six-pack of *Playboy*."[14]

A BATF regulation provides that packaging for malt beverages "shall not contain any statement, design, device or representation which is obscene." The U.S. Brewers Association's advertising guidelines provide that beer advertising "should not include risque material, suggestive double entendres, 'cheesecake,' or any other material that might be considered even slightly lewd or obscene."

Boam said "It's just a good-looking gal on a good-tasting beer. Society should not be so uptight about nudity. It's not filthy." Boam planned other marketing tools, including Nude Beer Nuts with a model on the label wearing only a cowboy hat and boots. He was also considering nude males "for the girls."

Molson Canadian, a Canadian beer, ran a series of advertisements in its "Canadian Wildlife" campaign featuring a scantily clad woman called "The Rare Long-Haired Fox." Canadian women complained about the ads to Ontario's Consumer and Commercial Relations Minister, Peter Kormos. Kormos announced that the ads were sexist and inappropriate and that his administration would enact strict regulations. Kormos was forced to resign the day after his announcement of regulations because he had appeared in a beefcake pose in the newspaper. However, the Canadian government moved forward to regulate beer advertisements with content guidelines on sex, race, and class.

Discussion Questions

1. Don't all ads with attractive women in them have a sexist overtone?
2. Is it possible to regulate sexism in ads?

---

14. Ruth Stroud, "Brown Bag Needed for Nude Beer?" *Advertising Age*, 18 October 1982, 38.

3. Is nudity in alcohol advertising appropriate?
4. Won't every ad be objectionable to someone?
5. Should First Amendment protections exclude regulation of ad content (other than misrepresentation)?

Case 5.3: Alcohol Advertising: The College Focus

The mix is unquestionably there. Alcohol ads mix youth, fun, and enticing activities like scuba diving and skiing. Anheuser-Busch's Bud Light ads have Spuds MacKenzie, the "Party Animal" dog. Stroh's has its Swedish Bikini Team. Beer companies sponsor large promotions of their products on the beaches during college spring break.[15]

In 1991, then-U.S. Surgeon General Antonia Novello asked the industry to voluntarily cut ads that attract minors. Novello stated, "I must call for industry's voluntary elimination of the types of alcohol advertising that appeal to youth on the bases of certain life-style appeals, sexual appeals, sports appeal, or risky activities, as well as advertising with the more blatant youth appeals of cartoon characters and youth slang."[16] A 1991 survey revealed that 10.6 million of the 20.7 million students in grades seven through twelve had had at least one drink in the last year.[17] Of the drinking group, 8 million drank weekly, 5.4 million had drinking binges and one-half million had five or more drinks in a row at least once a week.[18]

Industry officials maintain that they are very active in and financially supportive of programs for alcohol-use education, including Mothers against Drunk Driving.

Anheuser-Busch spends $20 million of its $260 million ad budget on a campaign that features the slogan "Know when to say when." Miller Brewing Company runs a thirty-second television ad with the slogan "Think when you drink" as part of the $8 million per year it spends to promote responsible drinking.

During spring breaks in 1991 and 1992, Miller and Anheuser-Busch did not use their multistory inflatable beer cans on popular beaches in Florida, Texas, and Mexico. In Daytona Beach, Florida, Miller put billboards along the highways with the slogan "Good beer is properly aged. You should be too." Miller's manager for alcohol and consumer issues, John Shafer, explained, "It's just good business sense to make sure we're on the right side of these issues."[19]

Patricia Taylor, a director at the Center for Science in the Public Interest, responded to the efforts by saying: "The beer companies are spending hundreds of millions every year to present a very positive image of drinking. That overwhelms all attempts to talk about the other side of the issue."[20]

Novello ordered new studies of the link between alcohol advertising and underage drinking. She also urged the industry to drop advertising meant to appeal to

---

15. The industry promoted products with multi-story inflatable beer cans. Jeffrey Zbar, "Spring Break" Inflatable Beer Bottles Gone but Other Marketers Move In," *Advertising Age*, 1 April 1991, 16.

16. Hilary Sout, "Surgeon General Wants to Age Alcohol Ads," *Wall Street Journal*, 5 November 1991, B1.

17. Julia Flynn Siler, "It Isn't Miller Time Yet, and This Bud's Not for You," *Business Week*, 24 June 1991, 52.

18. Ibid.

19. Ibid.

20. Ibid.

young people.[21] Anheuser-Busch created a campaign with ads in trade magazines and posters for stores to remind retailers not to sell beer to underage buyers. Novello responded, "These ads may be a stronger influence on students than they realize."[22]

Late in 1996, Anheuser-Busch announced that it would stop advertising its beer on MTV. Anheuser-Busch spent $534 million on advertising in 1995, with MTV spending equaling $2 million of that total budget. However, televison is known as the best method for reaching Generation X buyers. The ads were shifted to VH1. Coors has never advertised on MTV, stating "we don't like to walk the fine line." Miller Brewing Company continues its MTV ads.

In 1998, the American Academy of Pediatrics and the American Public Health Association joined together to launch a campaign to ask Anheuser-Busch to stop using frogs, lizards and other amphibians in its ads. The posters for these two groups trace beer ads from Spuds MacKenzie to Frank and Louis, the lizards, and ask, "Fed up with beer ads that look like cartoons?" The posters liken the animals to Joe Camel. The two groups will also run a presentation to shareholders at Anheuser-Busch's 1998 annual meeting. They will be joined by Mothers Against Drunk Driving, the Marin Institute and the Center on Alcohol Advertising.

Anheuser-Busch issued a response to the campaign noting that drunk-driving fatalities involving teens and underage drinking have both declined since 1982, and that Anheuser-Busch has spent $200 million since that time on education programs designed to halt underage drinking. Also, Anheuser-Busch did voluntarily abandon, in 1997, the frogs that refrained "Bud-weis-er."

Discussion Questions

1. Suppose you were an officer of a brewery whose advertising campaign targets young adults (18–21). Would you change the campaign?
2. Wouldn't your ads appeal to various groups regardless of their focus?
3. Would it be censorship for the government to control the content of your ads?
4. Are campaigns on responsible drinking sufficient?
5. Do beer companies' ads attempt to encourage underage people to drink?

Case 5.4: The Obligation to Screen? The Obligation to Reject—Soldier of Fortune Classifieds[23]

Soldier of Fortune (SOF) is a national magazine focused on guns and military clothing and aimed at "professional adventurers." In its large classified advertising section, individuals and companies offer guns, gun-related products, gun and equipment repairs, employment opportunities, and personal services.

21. Stuart Elliott, "A Rising Tide of Rhetoric over Warnings on Alcohol," *New York Times*, 2 April 1992, D18.

22. Ibid.

23. Adapted from M. Jennings, *Legal Environment of Business*, 2d ed. PWS Kent, Boston: 1991, 229–31.

Some of the classified ads printed between 1975, the magazine's debut, and 1984 offered services under such titles as "Mercenary for Hire," "Bounty Hunter," "High-Risk Contracts," "Dirty Work," "Mechanic," and "Do Anything, Anywhere at the Right Price." During this period, *SOF* ran 2,000 classified ads, about three dozen of which had titles like these.

Various media, including the Associated Press, United Press International, *Rocky Mountain News*, *Denver Post*, *Time*, and *Newsweek*, reported links between *SOF* classified ads and crimes or criminal plots. These connections were made directly to five specific *SOF* ads and alleged with four others. Law enforcement officials contacted *SOF* staffers in investigating two crimes linked to personal service ads in the magazine.

Nature of *SOF Ads*

Dr. Park Dietz, a forensic psychiatrist, concluded from his study of the ads that the average *SOF* subscriber—a male who owns camouflage clothing and more than one gun—would understand some phrases in *SOF's* classified ads as solicitations for illegal activity given the ads' context. At that time, *SOF* contained display ads for semiautomatic rifles and books with titles such as *How to Kill*, along with articles on "Harassing the Bear, New Afghan Tactics Stall Soviet Victory," "Pipestone Canyon, Summertime in 'Nam and the Dyin' Was Easy," and "Night Raiders on Russia's Border."

Dietz suggested that the *SOF* personal service ads carry the connotation of criminal activity because of the nature of the magazine. He noted that the same ads would not carry that connotation if they appeared in *Esquire* or *Vanity Fair*.

The Hearn Ad

In September, October, and November of 1984, *SOF* ran the following ad:

> EX-MARINES-67–69 'Nam Vets, Ex-DI, weapons specialist—jungle warfare, pilot, M.E., high risk assignments, U.S. or overseas. [Phone number]

"Ex-DI" means ex-drill instructor; "M.E." means multiengine planes; and "high risk assignments" means work as a bodyguard or security specialist.

The ad was placed by John Wayne Hearn, who said he wanted to recruit Vietnam veterans for work as bodyguards and security men for executives. Hearn's partner said they also hoped to train troops for South American countries. Hearn said he did not place the ad with an intent to solicit criminal employment but that 90 percent of the responses to the ad sought his participation in illegal activities, such as beatings, kidnappings, jailbreaks, bombings, and murders. His only lawful inquiry was from a Lebanese oil conglomerate seeking bodyguards; Hearn received a commission to place seven men with it.

Robert Black contacted Hearn through the *SOF* ad. Between 1982 and 1984, Black had asked at least four friends or coworkers in Bryan, Texas, to kill his wife, Sandra Black, or help him kill her. Initially, Black discussed bodyguard work with Hearn, then their conversations focused on Black's gun collection. In October 1984, Hearn traveled to Texas from his Atlanta home to see Black's collection. During the visit, Black told Hearn his plans for murdering his wife. After Hearn returned to Atlanta, Black repeatedly called him. In a conversation with Debbie Bannister,

Hearn's girlfriend, Black offered Hearn $10,000 to kill Black's wife. Bannister then communicated the offer to Hearn.

Hearn had no previous criminal record, but on January 6, 1985, he killed Bannister's sister. On February 2, he murdered Bannister's husband, and nineteen days later, he killed Sandra Black. He was convicted of the murders and sentenced to concurrent life terms.

The Victims' Suit against SOF

Sandra Black's mother, Marjorie Eimann, and her son, Gary Wayne Black, sued *SOF* for negligence in publishing Hearn's ad. The trial court awarded Eimann and Black $9.4 million in damages.

An appellate court reversed the decision, saying:

> Given the pervasiveness of advertising in our society and the important role it plays, we decline to impose on publishers the obligation to reject all ambiguous advertisements for products or services that might pose a threat of harm. The burden on a publisher to avoid liability from suits of this type is too great.

Other Cases of Ad Liability

SOF was sued again over a classified ad after Douglas Norwood was ambushed, assaulted, shot, and finally killed by a car bomb late in 1985. Each of his assailants had been hired through the following *SOF* ads:

> GUN FOR HIRE: 37-year-old professional mercenary desires jobs. Vietnam Veteran. Discreet and very private. Bodyguard, courier, and other special skills. All jobs considered. [Phone number]
>
> GUN FOR HIRE: Nam sniper instructor. SWAT. Pistol, rifle, security specialist, bodyguard, courier plus. All jobs considered. Privacy guaranteed. Mike [Phone number].

The case was settled out of court in 1987.

In another case, Richard Braun was shot and killed outside his Atlanta home by an experienced mercenary, Richard Savage, who had been hired by Braun's business associate, Bruce Gastwirth, through an ad in *Soldier of Fortune*. Savage's ad began with the words "Gun for Hire." Braun's sons sued the magazine and were awarded $4.3 million. The amount was later reduced in a settlement of the case.

The Association of Newspaper Classified Advertising Managers, Inc. (ANCAM) has the following policy:

> Advertisements containing statements that injure the health of readers, directly or indirectly, are not acceptable.

Another ANCAM section provides:

> Any advertisement fostering the evasion or violation of any law or making a direct or indirect offer of any article or service that violates a city, state or federal statute is unacceptable.

Discussion Questions

1. Assume that you are *SOF's* new director of display and classified advertising. You know *SOF* was relieved of any liability for Sandra Black's death, so it is not obligated to check or reject ads. Your conscience, however, remains troubled as you review ads with such language as "high-risk assignment" and "bounty hunter." As you think about the Black case, you rationalize that Hearn was on a murder spree and Black was simply a victim of his sudden violence. On the other hand, Hearn would never have known Black if his classified ad had not brought a call from Robert Black. Further, only five to ten ads of over a total of 2,000 classifieds have resulted in crimes or criminal plots. You discuss this dilemma over lunch with your senior staff member, who responds: "Yes, but we could have prevented those crimes by not running the ads."

Screening the ads will take time, private detectives, and an assumption of liability the law does not require you to make. Will you change *SOF's* ad policy? Will you conduct ad background checks?

2. Does this dilemma present conflicting moral standards?
3. To whom do you owe your loyalty in making your decision?
4. Should *SOF* feel morally responsible for Sandra Black's death?
5. Is the appellate court's decision not to impose liability on *SOF* an application of utilitarianism?
6. Should the decision on advertising policy be different after Sandra Black's murder from its policy before?
7. William L. Prosser, a legal scholar, has stated, "Nearly all human acts . . . carry some recognizable possibility of harm to another." Why do we allow recovery for some of those harmful acts and not others?
8. *Soldier of Fortune* stopped accepting personal service ads in 1986. Is that an appropriate and ethical resolution?

CASE 5.5: AGGRESSIVE MARKETING OF PRESCRIPTION DRUGS: FORMS OF DIRECT SALES

A national television advertising campaign began in April 1993 (during CBS-TV's "60 Minutes") on the signs of clinical depression and the importance of obtaining help. Ads on the same topic appeared in the *New York Times* and *Parade* magazine. The campaign was run by the National Mental Health Association, but the $3 to $4 million cost of the campaign was paid by Eli Lilly & Company, the manufacturer of Prozac, the top-selling antidepressant drug in the world. Lilly also gave the mental health association a $500,000 grant to help identify people who are suffering from depression and need treatment.

The ads did not mention Prozac, but they did note Eli Lilly's financing. An Eli Lilly spokesman said, "It isn't a campaign to promote Prozac. It's a campaign to promote awareness." Dr. Sidney Wolfe, head of the Public Citizen Health Research Group, disagreed:

> The money is given to try to curry favor with groups so they don't resist or oppose things happening with a drug. Or they become *de facto* advocates for a drug. If Lilly is doing this out of the goodness of its heart, why does it have to have its name there? They don't want to be anonymous and that's what the problem is.

In defense of its donation and the ads, Lilly responded that "These programs save lives and aren't promoting any one specific product." The mental health association said, "We are working in partnership with corporate America to disseminate messages of hope and help to the American people."

Discussion Questions

1. Does it matter that Eli Lilly enjoys increased sales as a result of the campaign?
2. Does a pharmaceutical company suppress opposition by making these donations?
3. Do nonprofit organizations compromise their independence by accepting funding from pharmaceutical manufacturers?

Other companies go beyond the "infommercial" approach of Eli Lilly and market their prescription products directly to consumers. For example, Genentech, Inc., has so successfully marketed its growth hormone (protropin/hutropin) for children that the drug is sold to 14,000 patients in the United States—twice the number estimated to have the medical condition that would warrant its use. Genentech's top sales executive was indicted on charges of bribing a Minneapolis physician to prescribe the growth hormone more often. A total of $224,000 was funneled to the physician in the form of research grants and consulting fees.

Genentech sales employees have entered restricted patient areas and scattered literature among patients on Genentech's products. Further, Genentech pays doctors and nurses to contribute information to its registry on patients that describes illnesses and how they were treated; the registry is limited to patients who have been treated with Genentech drugs.

Upjohn, the manufacturer of the antibaldness drug Rogaine, offers "free, private hair-loss consultation" with a doctor in its ads. Generally, the doctor produces a Rogaine prescription. Schering-Plough handed out $5 coupons for its antihistamine, Claritin, which customers could redeem by having their doctors prescribe the drug.

The Food and Drug Administration (FDA) has been policing excessive advertising claims with fines and injunctions, but in 1993, pharmaceutical companies spent over $200 million on ads in everything from the *New Yorker* to *Popular Mechanics*. Edwin P. Maynard, past president of the American College of Physicians and former chairman of its ethics committee, said of the manufacturers: "They are taking the route of advertising directly to this vulnerable population." From 1996 to 1997, ad spending by pharmaceuticals for their prescription drugs increased 90%.

In 1997, the FDA liberalized its policy on direct advertising and issued new regulations permitting companies to advertise specific products without the scrolling addendum of warnings and side effects. The FDA established as its goal "realistic standards" for the companies as well as a desire to promote greater consumer awareness of prescription drugs.

In 1998, the increase is expected to be up 60% to $1.6 billion per year.

Discussion Questions

1. Do users of prescription drugs require more information than ads in the popular media can convey?
2. Are pharmaceutical firms appealing to a vulnerable population?
3. Do the ads create conflicts between physicians and patients?
4. What do you think will occur in ads for these prescription drugs? Could all parties, physicians and patients, benefit from more information?

Section B
Appropriation
of Others' Ideas

When does an idea belong to someone else? Laws on patents and copyrights afford protection in some cases, but other situations are too close to call-or are they?

Case 5.6: Ragu Thick and Zesty

Ragu Foods, Inc., has been the leading seller of prepared spaghetti sauce in the United States since 1972. By 1973, Ragu held over 60 percent of the market. Late in that year, Hunt-Wesson Foods, Inc., decided to enter the market with "Prima Salsa" spaghetti sauce. After extensive marketing and taste studies, Hunt's introduced its sauce in 1976 using the slogan "Extra Thick and Zesty."

Just before Hunt's launched "Prima Salsa," Ragu introduced a new sauce called "Ragu Extra Thick and Zesty." Ragu's advertising campaign used a photo similar to Hunt's of a ladle of sauce being poured over noodles. Ragu's sauce was thickened with starch, whereas Hunt's used a longer cooking process. The label on the Ragu sauce did not make this distinction clear.

Hunt's executives claimed the introduction of the Ragu sauce appropriated all their work and research and created product confusion in consumers' minds.

Ragu maintained that its product was simply a response to competition and good business strategy. Hunt's claimed there can be no competition because of Ragu's domination of the market, which was 65 percent in 1975. Hunt's felt Ragu's methods are unfair.

In 1990, Ragu introduced a sauce called "Ragu Fresh Italian." The Food and Drug Administration (FDA) cited Ragu for six violations of federal labeling law that centered on the word *fresh*. FDA regulations prohibit the use of "fresh" if chemical or heat processing is used. Ragu acknowledged using heat processing but maintained "fresh" is part of a trademark, not a description.

In 1993, Campbell Soup introduced its Prego sauce with comparison ads that depicted Ragu as runny. Ragu sued Campbell for these "misleading ads" since Campbell did not use Ragu's Thick & Chunky sauce to compare.

At the end of 1993, Ragu sauces had 36.2 percent of this $1.1 billion market (down from 50 percent in 1992), while Prego had 26.3 percent (up from 20 percent).

Discussion Questions

1. Was Ragu just an aggressive competitor, or did it appropriate ideas or mislead?
2. Are any moral standards violated by Ragu's conduct in these campaigns?
3. Would you feel comfortable with the "Prima Salsa" name if you were a marketing executive with Ragu? Or with the use of the term "fresh"?
4. Is product confusion a fair method of competition?
5. Aren't companies free to meet the market with their product lines?

CASE 5.7: THE LITTLE INTERMITTENT WINDSHIELD WIPER AND ITS LITTLE INVENTOR

Robert W. Kearns obtained a patent for his first intermittent car windshield wiper system in 1967. During the 1970s, intermittent wiper systems began appearing on the cars of major U.S. and Japanese automakers. Kearns received no money for the use of these systems. The automakers maintained that the idea was an obvious one and it was only a matter of time before their engineers developed the same type of system. They also claimed that their systems differed from Kearns's in design and function.

Kearns filed suit against Ford, General Motors, Chrysler, Fiat, Toyota, and other Japanese auto manufacturers. He had planned to open his own firm to supply the intermittent windshield washer systems to all automakers but was unable to do so after the companies manufactured the systems in-house.

In November 1990, Kearns settled his case with Ford Motor Company for $10.2 million, which amounted to thirty cents per car Ford sold with the intermittent wiper systems. In June 1992, a jury awarded Kearns $11.3 million in damages from Chrysler, or about ninety cents per car, for Chrysler's infringement of Kearns's patent. Chrysler had sold 12,564,107 vehicles with the device. Kearns had originally asked for damages ranging from $3 to $30 per car, or $37.7 to $377 million, based on the treble damage provisions of the patent infringement laws.

Kearns still has suits pending against the other car companies. He spent $4 million in legal fees in the Ford case and expects to spend $5.5 million on the case against Chrysler, which announced it will appeal the "unreasonable and excessive" verdict.

Kearns said his success should be an inspiration for other inventors because it proves they can win against large corporations that have used others' ideas without reimbursement.

Discussion Questions

1. Is it ethical to use an idea based on the risk analysis that the owner of that idea simply cannot afford to litigate the matter?

2. Why was the intermittent wiper system so important to the car makers?
3. Could Kearns have done anything further to protect himself?
4. If you were an executive with one of the car companies still in litigation with Kearns, would you settle the case? Why or why not?

CASE 5.8: V-A-N-N-A: IT BELONGS TO ME

Samsung Electronics ran an advertising campaign that had a letter-turning blonde robot dressed in a red evening dress, complete with diamond bracelet and necklace. The ad was a takeoff on Vanna White's role of turning letters for contestants on television's "Wheel of Fortune." White filed suit alleging that Samsung's use of the "Robo Vanna" was an appropriation of her image and a taking of her creative output. Samsung maintained there was no appropriation because the ads were a takeoff on "Wheel of Fortune."

Discussion Questions

1. Has something been taken without compensation in this case?
2. Is Samsung taking advantage of "Wheel of Fortune" and Vanna White?
3. One advertising law expert has stated, "I wish these people would take a joke." Is the takeoff satire or appropriation?
4. Should Samsung have sought permission to run its ads?

CASE 5.9: UNHAPPY CAMPERS AND COPYRIGHTS

Children at camps around the country in the summer of 1996 were not able to dance the "Macarena" except in utter silence. Their usual oldies dances will not be held this year. The American Society of Composers, Authors & Publishers (ASCAP) notified camps and the organizations that sponsor camps (such as the Boy Scouts of America and the Girls Scouts USA) that they would be required to pay the licensing fees if they used any of the 4,000,000 copyrighted songs written or published by any of the 68,000 members of ASCAP.

The fees for use of the songs have exceeded the budgets of many of the camps. One camp that operates only during the day charges its campers $44 per week. ASCAP wanted $591 for the season for the camp's use of songs such as "Edelweiss" (from "The Sound of Music") and "This Land is Your Land." ASCAP demanded fees for even singing the songs around the camp fire. ASCAP's letters to the camps reminded the directors of the possible penalties of $5,000 and up to 6 days in jail and threatened lawsuits for any infringement of the rights of ASCAP members. Luckily, "Kumbaya" is not owned by an ASCAP member.

Several camp directors wrote and asked for a special program that would allow the camps a discount for the use of the songs. Many of the camps are not run as for-profit businesses but rather include camps such as those for children with cancer and AIDS.

Discussion Questions

1. Why does ASCAP work so diligently to enforce its rights and collect the fees for its members' songs?
2. What risks does ASCAP run if the camps continue to use the songs without payment of the licensing fees?
3. What ethical and social responsibility issues do you see with respect to those camps that are strictly non-profit operations?
4. Can you think of a compromise that would protect ASCAP members' rights but still offer the camps a reasonable chance to use the songs?
5. What would you do if you were an ASCAP member and owned the rights to a song a camp wished to use?

SECTION C
PRODUCT PRICING

What price is fair? Is a fair price always the most customers are willing to pay? Should businesses give special discounts to nonprofit buyers?

CASE 5.10: CATERERS AND THE DUPLICATION OF OVERHEAD RECOVERY

Carts, Candies and Caviar, Inc., (CCC) is a Phoenix, Arizona, caterer. CCC has enjoyed nearly exponential growth since it was founded in 1974 by Cindy Callstone. With sales over $1 million for 1991, Cindy was looking at a bright future but realized she needed financial planning assistance. In 1992, Cindy took on two senior business students from local universities as interns. They were to develop a plan for financing CCC's expansion, including the construction of new kitchen facilities.

The two students, Vera Dickerson and Ralph Dunn, were given full access to CCC's books, records, and contracts. In the course of their review, Vera and Ralph discovered what Vera called "interesting business practices" in billing. For example, Cindy billed all of her computer time to all "cost-plus" customers. These customers had contracts in which they agreed to pay all catering costs plus a certain percentage profit for CCC. In one month, Cindy recovered all of her computer time from fifteen customers.

Cindy billed full "kitchen time" to the same cost-plus customers. Kitchen time is an overhead amount for kitchen facilities computed on a per day or per hour basis. For example, if a dinner preparation takes a full day, Cindy bills the customer for one-thirtieth of the monthly cost of her kitchen facilities. However, it would be rare for Cindy to devote the kitchen solely to one customer. In many cases, the same dinner is prepared simultaneously for eight to ten customers. All the customers would be billed for a full day.

Cindy also has negotiated discount arrangements with soda vendors. For example, for every catered event where she uses Sparkle Soda, Sparkle gives her a 15 percent discount because it views the event as advertising. Cindy does not reflect the 15 percent discount in her billing. Vera found some instances where the customer chose its soda vendor and paid the vendor directly, but Cindy's bill to those customers still included charges for soda. When Vera asked Cindy about these bills for soda, Cindy replied: "If they catch it, we'll pay them back; otherwise, don't worry about it. This is just the way things are done in this business."

After they reviewed the financial records, Vera and Ralph met to discuss their proposed financial strategy. Vera began by commenting, "She's ripping off the customers, and they don't even know it!" Ralph responded, "Look, my uncle is in the catering business. They all operate this way. They get as much into the bill as they can. Maybe the customers will catch it. If they do, you admit the mistake and refund it. If they don't, you make more money. It's no big deal. And besides, look how successful she is. No one is crying 'foul!' They're just giving her more business."

Discussion Questions

1. Evaluate all of Cindy's billing practices from an accounting perspective.
2. Evaluate all of Cindy's billing practices from an ethical perspective.
3. Cindy claims she is just following industry practice. Is this a proper moral standard for her operation?
4. Could Cindy's practices prove costly in the future?
5. If you were Vera, what would you do?

CASE 5.11: PHARMACEUTICALS: ETHICAL PRICING OF LIFE-SAVING CURES

Senators David Pryor of Arkansas and William Cohen of Maine did not mince words. In a hearing on prescription drugs, the two accused drug manufacturers of "price gouging . . . to pad already skyrocketing profit levels." They cited a 6.4 percent increase for prescription drugs in 1992 when prices in other goods rose only 1.5 percent.

Both senators proposed price controls for the industry, but nine major drug companies pledged to Congress to hold their price increases to the overall rate of inflation. With the pledge, the price of the stock of all the drug manufacturers fell to a 13-month low.

The executives for the companies argue that drug price increases:

> are essential to finance the development of important new drugs, which the industry contends may each cost more than $200 million to bring to market. Innovative drugs for cardiovascular and digestive tract diseases, for example, have helped millions of Americans to avert expensive surgery and related hospital costs.

Public sentiment is that the increase in prices cannot continue and that the companies take advantage of people who need prescription drugs, particularly the elderly. In 1996, the National Heart Savers Association launched a campaign against Merck alleging that it broke its pledge to hold drug price increases to the overall rate of inflation (CPI). The group targeted Mevacor and Zocor, claiming Merck's price increases were 144% of the 1995 CPI for Mevacor and 146% for Zocor. The organization then offered to sell the drug in larger doses that patients could cut in half and then take.

Discussion Questions

1. Is there a moral responsibility to keep prescription drug prices as low as possible?
2. What is the responsibility of the drug manufacturers to their shareholders?
3. Are the drug manufacturers, by agreeing to limit increases, attempting to avoid full price regulation?
4. Is self-regulation of pricing in the best interests of all?
5. Are the price increase campaigns a conflict of interest?

CASE 5.12: SALOMON BROTHERS AND BOND PRICING

Before the summer of 1991, Salomon Brothers, an investment banking firm founded in 1911, was the most powerful dealer on Wall Street in the $2.3 trillion U.S. government bond market.

Bond market regulations prohibit any firm from acquiring more than 35 percent of the Treasury notes and bonds at government auctions. This "35 percent rule," as it is known, exists to prevent one firm from buying enough of the market to unilaterally dictate the prices of the instruments.

On August 9, 1991, Salomon announced it was suspending two managing directors, Paul Mozer and Thomas Murphy, along with two other employees, for violations of the 35 percent rule. Mozer had been so publicly critical of the 35% rule that it was often referred to as "the Mozer rule."

The suspension led to the discovery of several other problems involving the rule. In December 1990, Salomon bought 35 percent of an $8.5 billion four-year-note Treasury auction item and also submitted, through a customer, another $1 billion bid on the same notes. The $1 billion was really for Salomon, which ended up with 46 percent of the offering. Salomon had placed a "squeeze" on the market; huge distortions in supply caused by Salomon forced the payment of high prices.

In February 1991, Mozer had a customer, Mercury Asset Management, a branch of S. G. Warburg, place a $1 billion order for thirty-year Treasury bonds. Mozer meant the order to be bogus to surprise a new trader at Salomon Brothers. However, the deal went through and was booked to Salomon. Rigged bids were discovered in three Treasury auctions during 1991.

At the Treasury auction on May 22, 1991, Salomon Brothers bought nearly 90 percent of the two-year-note instruments valued at $12.26 billion through hedge funds, or large partnerships. Prices for the instruments skyrocketed as a result. Salomon denied there was any collusion with the hedge funds, but a government investigation was launched.

The result of Salomon's cornering of the Treasury market was that small bond-trading housing and commercial banks experienced substantial losses—$100 million from the May auction alone. A Texas Christian University MBA graduate, Michael Irelan, was fired from Boatmen's National Bank in St. Louis when he lost $400,000 in the Salomon May "squeeze." "I liked my job and believe I had become a good, sound trader," Ireland said. "But now, who knows if I will be able to do this again."[24]

Hickey Securities, Inc., lost several million dollars in the May "squeeze," and its investors defected, causing its assets to fall from $100 to $30 million in four months.

Richard Breeden, chairman of the SEC, said that there were not just a few bad apples in the Treasury market but the structure of the market was wrong. "It's very important that we . . . take a cold, hard look at: Do the intermediaries, the people who stand behind the Treasury and the ultimate purchasers of these bonds, have too much power?"[25] For some time, primary dealers like Salomon had been advising the Treasury on how to run the market. The dealers could corner the market as follows:

1. The firm puts in a bid for its maximum 35 percent share of the government bonds being auctioned. To ensure that the bid is accepted, it is made slightly above the going price of the bonds already being quoted in the "when-issued" market.
2. The firm simultaneously puts in a bid, at a similarly high price, for more bonds on behalf of its major customers.
3. The bids are accepted by the Treasury Department.
4. In a prearranged transaction, the firm purchases at cost the bonds it bought on behalf of its customers. When the firm has enough bonds to control the supply, it has cornered the market.
5. When other bond dealers want to buy the bonds, perhaps to cover short positions (bonds they sold that they did not own), the firm can name its price.[26]

Up until the trading scandal broke, Salomon had the top profits of all the Wall Street firms: $451 million for the first half of 1991. After the scandal broke, Salomon's stock went from $36 per share in August to $23 by the end of September, a 30 percent drop.

Clients of Salomon began looking elsewhere. By mid-September, Maryland's $13 billion state pension fund was talking with Goldman Sachs and other firms. Salomon sold $40 billion in securities between May 1991 and September 1991, reducing its assets to $105 billion.

Salomon's accounting reserves for litigation by Treasury investors, Salomon shareholders, and competitors were estimated at $1 billion, or one-third of Salomon's net worth. Salomon took a conservative $200 million reserve in October, with the resulting reduction in earnings in what was otherwise a banner year.

Warren E. Buffet, whose firm owned $700 million in Salomon convertible shares, was named interim chairman of the dealer in August 1991. He went before the House Subcommittee on Telecommunications and Finance and confirmed misdeeds

24. Constance Mitchell, "Salomon's 'Squeeze' in May Auction Left Many Players Reeling," *Wall Street Journal*, 31 October 1991, A10.

25. David Wessel, "Treasury and the Fed Have Long Caved in to 'Primary Dealer,'" *Wall Street Journal*, 25 September 1991, A7.

26. Gary Weiss, et al., "The Salomon Shocker: How Bad Will It Get?" *Business Week*, 26 August 1991, 54–57.

by the firm. His testimony indicated Salomon had $10.6 billion, or 94 percent, of the May 1991 Treasury-note auction. Buffet's steps were viewed favorably by prosecutors. "The unquestionably substantial steps taken by Salomon inevitably reduce the government's need to punish," commented Bruce Baird, the prosecutor in the Drexel Burnham Lambert, Inc., junk bond case.[27]

In May 1992, Salomon settled with the SEC for a $290 million penalty and a two-month suspension from trading.[28] Drexel Burnham Lambert had paid $600 million in penalties in 1989 for its junk bond activities. Former Treasury secretary William E. Simon commenting on Salomon's fine, stated, "It's an absolutely startling number. If I understood the infractions, this is an extremely severe penalty against the firm and will most certainly send a message to Wall Street that infractions are going to be dealt with in very harsh ways."[29] No criminal charges were brought against the firm, but four former senior officials were charged with violations of securities laws in Treasury auctions during the 1989–1991 period. Their settlement with the SEC included "six-figure" fines and varying-length prohibitions on securities brokerage employment.

One who settled his case with the SEC is John H. Gutfreund, the former chairman of Salomon. He resigned his 38-year tenure with Salomon when the scandal erupted. His limousine, palatial office, and attentive subordinates are gone. He now has a modest, three-room office and a part-time secretary. He is shunned by many friends and colleagues. He has paid a $100,000 fine to the SEC and agreed to a permanent prohibition on becoming a chairman or chief executive of a securities firm. Mrs. Gutfreund says his activities have been curtailed, and she finds it "so sad to see him stymied." Gutfreund notes that his role at Salomon was "not a small mistake, in retrospect."

In early 1993, Salomon Brothers settled claims with thirty-nine states on the bond trading. As part of the settlement, Salomon agreed to pay $4 million, with half of the settlement going to a special fund to fight fraud and abuse in the brokerage industry.

Most civil suits by investors against Salomon in federal court and arbitration have been settled..

While Congress is considering restructuring the auction market, the Treasury has changed how the auction operates; it now requires verification of large bids and actual receipt of bonds.

Two years after the SEC settlement, Salomon continued to struggle to regain its reputation. It remained on Standard & Poor's credit watch. In the last quarter of 1992, Salomon's profits were down 93 percent. For the year, its profits had plummeted 74 percent. Its underwritings placed it fourth among the Wall Street brokerage houses; it held less than 10 percent of the market. Perhaps its greatest loss was that of executive talent. One senior officer observed, "We lost good people we didn't want to lose. Those good people had experience, relationships and experience in the business. And those things are not going to be rebuilt in a day even if you hire somebody good from the outside."

---

27. Michael Galen, "Salomon: Honesty Is the Gutsiest Policy," *Business Week*, 16 September 1991, 100.

28. One hundred million dollars of the fine was tax-deductible. "Salomon Gets Break on Its Fine," *USA Today*, 30 September 1992, 1B.

29. Michael Siconolfi, Laurie P. Cohen, Kevin G. Salwen. "Salomon Is Breathing Easier after Accepting Huge Fine in Scandal," *Wall Street Journal*, 21 May 1992, A1.

From 1992 to 1994, Salomon's return on equity was less than the other Wall Street trading firms. By the end of 1994, Salomon had slipped to seventh place among the Wall Street firms in terms of numbers of debt and equity offering. Losses in 1994 totaled $399 million, and the problems of the firm, from trading losses to accounting snafus to potential rating downgrades, continued to mount.

In 1995, Salomon's earnings level did recover somewhat in the third quarter, but in 1996, its earnings dropped by 60% by the third quarter. Warren Buffett has described this investment in Salomon of nearly nine years as just a "scratch single."

Discussion Questions

1. Was Salomon's conduct harmful to others?
2. What factors contributed to Salomon's illegal activity?
3. Was the SEC penalty sufficient?
4. Why didn't someone disclose Salomon's practices before the congressional hearings resulted?
5. Can people like Michael Irelan ever be adequately compensated for the losses they suffered through Salomon's actions?
6. In mid-1992, Salomon named Charles Williams, a well-known Wall Street troubleshooter, as its chief of fixed-income compliance. Salomon was said to want "suspenders on top of belts" in its compliance units. Williams reportedly received a $200,000 pay package. Is this the cost of ethics or the price of ethical violations?
7. When Warren Buffett took over temporarily as chairman of Salomon, he made the following statement:

   > Contemplating any business act, an employee should ask himself whether he would be willing to see it immediately described by an informed and critical reporter on the front page of his local paper, there to be read by his spouse, children and friends. At Salomon we simply want no part of any activities that pass legal tests but that we, as citizens, would find offensive.

   Is this a good ethical test for business conduct?
8. Would Gutfreund make the same choices today, given his post-Salomon circumstances?

CASE 5.13: ARCHER DANIELS MIDLAND: A GIANT IN GRAIN

When the Justice Department raided the offices of Archer Daniels Midland (ADM) on June 26, 1995 to search for records related to its investigation of ADM and its competitors for possible violations of federal antitrust laws, an employee in a photo store in Decatur, Illinois (the home of ADM) said, "ADM will probably get a slap on the wrist and that will be the end of it. If I got caught doing that, I'd go to jail. It is scary to think of a company being that powerful."

Between that June day and October 20, 1995, ADM's stock price slid 6.5%. ADM, a grain-processing company was eventually charged with price fixing for two corn-derived products: lysine, a feed supplement for cattle; and citric acid. The Justice Department was tipped off to the ADM conduct in 1992 by an ADM executive, Mark E. Whitacre. Whitacre continued to work for ADM while serving as a government informant. Mr. Whitacre's undercover work resulted in guilty pleas by three Asian companies in 1995. It was revealed during evidentiary hearings that Mr. Whiteacre "selectively recorded" the conversations. Whitacre eventually agreed to plead guilty to two felonies in August, 1995. The felonies were evasion of income tax and failure to disclose compensation to shareholders. When Mr. Whitacre's role with federal investigators was disclosed, ADM charged that the conspiracy was Whitacre's doing and that he had embezzled the gains from the conspiracy from ADM.

On Wednesday, October 16, 1996, ADM pleaded guilty to charges that it had fixed prices. As part of the plea agreement, ADM agreed to pay $100 million in fines and to cooperate with the government in its continuing investigation. Outraged shareholders staged a revolt at the October 17, 1996 shareholder meeting. James E. Burton, chief executive officer of the California Public Employees Retirement System, stated, "The $100 million fine is shareholder assets that are being squandered to pay for criminal activity that never should have occurred. Where was the board of directors?"

Two days after the board meeting, the ADM board accepted the resignation of Michael D. Andreas, the vice chairman of ADM and son of ADM's chairman, and Terrance Wilson, the head of ADM's corn-processing division. ADM board member Brian Mulroney, the former Prime Minister of Canada, stated upon departure from the meeting, "They no longer work here."

On December 3, 1996, three officers of ADM were indicted for conspiracy in fixing prices on lysine, including Terrance Wilson and Michael Andreas. Two Japanese executives were also indicted on conspiracy charges.

Discussion Questions

1. What criminal violations do you think occurred? What ethical violations occurred?
2. Do you agree with Mr. Burton's statement?
3. Who is responsible for the conduct that lead to the guilty plea? Was it best for ADM to plead guilty?
4. What do you think of Mr. Whitacre's undercover work? Would you have done the same thing and worked for the government?
5. Do you agree with the photo employee's statement? Did ADM get just a slap on the wrist?

Section D
Competitors,
The Playing
Field and
Competition

Case 5.14: Slotting: Facilitation, Costs or Bribery

Finding "Bearwiches" on the cookie shelf in your grocery store will be a daunting task. Locating some "Frookies," a new line of fat-free, sugarless cookies, will take you on a journey through various aisles in the store, and you may find them at knee level in the health foods section. You can find packaged Lee's Ice Cream from Baltimore in Saudi Arabia, and South Korea, but it will not be found on the grocery store shelves in Baltimore. The difficulty with finding these items is not that they are not good products. The manufacturers of these products cannot afford to buy shelf space. The shelf space in grocery stores is not awarded on the basis of consumer demand for Bearwiches or Frookies. Shelf space in grocery stores is awarded on the basis of the manufacturer's willingness to pay "slotting" fees. If manufacturers pay, they are given a space on the grocer's shelf. If the slotting fees are not paid, the product is not sold by the grocer.

Slotting fees are fees manufacturers pay to retailers in order to obtain retail shelf space.[30] The practice has been common in the retail grocery industry since 1987. The origins of slotting fees are unclear with different parties in the food chain offering various explanations. Retailers claim slotting was started by manufacturers with the fees paid to retailers as an inducement to secure shelf space. Another

---

30. "Slotting fees" actually pertain to obtaining space in the grocer's warehouse. "Shelf fees," which are fees for placement on the shelf are also charged by some grocery retailers.

theory of origin offered by retailers is that manufacturers use slotting fees to curtail market entrants. If a manufacturer buys more space with additional fees, the market can be controlled by existing manufacturers. Manufacturers claim slotting was started by retail grocers as a means of covering the bookkeeping and warehousing costs of the introduction of a new product. However, two things are clear. First, the practice of affiliated fees for sale is expanding to other industries. The retail book industry, particularly the large chains, now demands fees from publishers for shelf slots and displays for their books. In malls, developers/landlords now demand sums as large as $50,000 from tenants or prospective tenants before a lease can be negotiated or renegotiated. These fees for a position in the mall are referred to as "key money" or "negative allowances." In certain areas, home builders are demanding "access fees" or "marketing premiums" from appliance makers and other residential construction suppliers for use of their products in the builders' developments. In the computer software industry, the packaging of software programs with computers ensures sales and requires a fee. Even the display of programs in electronic stores is subject to a fee. The second clearly evolving trend in affiliated fees is that the practice is inconsistent and the purposes of the fees are unknown. Fees differ from manufacturer to manufacturer, from product to product and from retailer to retailer.

How Slotting Works

Food manufacturers produce over 10,000 new products each year. However, store shelf space remains fixed. Because profit margins at grocery stores hover at very narrow levels of only one to two percent of sales,[31] additional shelf space would not increase profits nor produce guaranteed returns from the new products displayed there. Additionally, grocers must assume the risk of allocating shelf space to a new product that would not sell at a level sufficient to provide even the narrow margins. Retail grocers must absorb the cost of warehousing the product, accounting for it in inventory, barcoding it and eventually stocking the shelves with it.[32] In many cases, particularly where the manufacturer is a small company, there has been little or no advertising of the product and the retail grocer must also incur the cost of advertising the product in some way or offer in-store coupons to entice customer purchases. To the retail grocer, the introduction of a new product and the allocation of precious shelf space is a high-cost risk. There are no guarantees that a new product will garner sales, and there is the downside of the loss of revenue from whatever product is displaced by the new product. To retail grocers, a slotting fee is a means of insulation from the risk of new product introduction and a means of advance recoupment of costs.

Within some retail grocery chains, slotting fees represent the net profits for the organization. Similar to the rental car industry in which earnings come from renters' fees for insurance, car seats and additional driver coverage, some retail grocers' profits come not from the sales of food but from the fees manufacturers pay for access.

---

31. Costs in the retail grocery industry are relatively fixed and cannot be readily reduced. Union wages and other unmanageable cost elements preclude effective efforts at increasing profit margins. Further, competition from the "club" stores (Costs, Sam's Club, Price Club) is intense.

32. The cost of shelving is that of the labor and materials involved in simply changing the shelf sign. Shelf fees are typically a minimal amount such as $50.

The level and nature of slotting fees vary significantly. Some retailers have a flat fee of $5000 per product for introduction. Other retailers have a graduated fee schedule tied to the shelf space location. Eye-level slots cost more than the knee or ground level slots. The prime spaces at the ends of grocery aisles bring premium slotting fees since those spaces virtually insure customer attention.[33] Other stores require that a "kill fee" be paid when a product does not sell. One supermarket chain requires $500 just for a manufacturer to make an appointment to present a new product. Some retailers will not accept a new product even with a slotting fee. Small businesses often incur the cost of product development only to be unable to place the product with grocery stores.

Some stores charge a slotting fee, an additional fee if the product is new, and a "failure fee" on new products to cover the losses if the product fails to sell. A new fee, called the "staying fee," has also developed. A staying fee is an annual rent fee that prevents the retailer from giving a manufacturer's product slot to someone else. Some manufacturers offer to buy out the produce in existing space in order to make room for their product. A 1988 survey found that 70% of all grocery retailers charge slotting fees with one retail store disclosing that its $15-per-store per product slotting fees bring in an additional $50 million in revenue each year.[34] Examples of various slotting fees paid and documented are found in Table 1. The most typical slotting fee for a new product to be placed with a grocery retailer was $10,000. Slotting fees do not typically come down over time, even if the product sells well. At the retail level for CD-Rom sales, the producers pay a 20% fee per shipment, regardless of whether their product is in demand.

TABLE I
Slotting Fees: Amounts and Terms

Payor	Amount	Terms	Payee
Truzzolino Pizza Roll	$25,000	Chain-Wide	Safeway
Old Capital Microwave Popcorn	$86,000	Chain-Wide for $172,000 of Popcorn	Shoprite Stores
United Brands	$375,000	Frozen Fruit Juicebars	New York City Area Stores
Apple & Eve	$150,000	Fruit Punch Product	Limited Stores in Northeast
Frookies	50¢ per box (Increased Price from $1.79 to $2.29)	Sugar-Free Cookies	100 Stores Various
Frito-Lay	$100,000	New Product	Each Grocery Store Chain
Lee's Ice Cream	$25,000 per flavor	Ice Cream	Each Grocery

33. Referred to as "prime real estate" in the industry, slotting fees follow a graduated schedule for the locations. Amounts vary according to aisle space. Bread slotting fees are $500-$1000 per bread-type. Ice cream, with one small segment in frozen foods brings $25,000 per flavor.

34. No convenience store chains charge slotting fees. However, convenience stores do not warehouse inventory. Manufacturers deliver directly to the convenience stores (Gibson).

The Legal Issues Surrounding Slotting

The chairman of the board of a small food manufacturer in Ohio wrote to his Congressman and described slotting fees in this way: "This is nothing but a device to extort money from packers and squeeze all the independent and smaller processors off the shelves and out of business. We believe this is the most flagrant restraint of trade device yet conceived".

It is possible that a slotting fee might fall under the legally prohibited conduct of commercial bribery. However, for a successful prosecution for payment of a bribe, the conduct required must be that in which funds are paid by a seller to a buyer solely for the purpose of acquiring a contract or business opportunity (in the case of slotting, a space on the shelf). As noted earlier, however, the reality is that there are costs associated with awarding an item shelf space. If the funds are simply received by the retailer and used for general operating expenses which include advertising, bookkeeping and warehousing, then the notion that a slotting fee is commercial bribery does not fit within the actus reus, or the required conduct, for criminal prosecution.[35]

Regardless of legalities, the use of slotting fees creates an atmosphere of confusion. It is unclear how slotting payments are made and where the payments are reported. Many small business owners report that the payments they make to grocery retailers must be made in cash. Some owners report that payments are made in cash to both the chain and to individual store managers. The atmospheric result is that there are large amounts of cash changing hands among sellers, managers and purchasers. The former CEO of Harvest Foods, a food retailer in the South, has been indicted on charges of bribery and other related offenses for the alleged receipt of hundreds of thousands of dollars in cash for slotting fees.

Because slotting fees are non-uniform and even non-universal, it is impossible to understand how the fee structure works, how much the fees should be, and whether the fees are actually related to, the costs incurred by retailers in getting a new product to the shelf. The secretive and inconsistent nature of slotting fees and their payment in cash creates an atmosphere similar to that in drug trade.[36] Market entry rights are unclear, fees change, not everyone is permitted to buy into the system and the use and declaration of revenues is unknown. In at least four reports on the practice of slotting fees, parties on both sides referred to slotting as the grocery industry's "dirty little secret:" Cost recoupment, the public airing of the fees, and public, accounting disclosures are non-existent for slotting fees. The secrecy of the fees and the industry's unwillingness to discuss or disclose them is problematic for manufacturers.

From the cost figures offered in Table 1, it is safe to conclude that slotting fees could make market entry prohibitive for many small companies. In some instances, fees have gone beyond the initial slotting costs with some grocery

---

35. Again, it is important to note that a retailer may also charge an "advertising fee."

36. The authors could find only three manufacturers willing to discuss their personal experiences with slotting fees or industry practices. Retribution (i.e., denial of retail access) was cited as the reason for their reluctance. These three manufacturers spoke on condition of anonymity. Two other manufacturers, Richard Worth (Frookies) and Scott Garfield (Lee's Ice Cream) have been public in their discussion of slotting fees. Grocery retailers referred all questions to legal counsel or corporate officers who declined to be interviewed.

chains now demanding up to $40,000 per year for a company to maintain just a square foot of retail space for its product. Even some of the larger companies have difficulty competing because of the large fees. Frito-Lay recently purchased Anheuser Busch's Eagle Snacks after Anheuser had spent over $500 million trying to increase its 17% market share. Frito-Lay now holds 55% of the snack market and pays the largest slotting fees in the grocery industry. Borden ended its foray into the snack market in 1995, and barely survived before it did so. Nearly 30 regional snack companies have gone out of business in the last three years. A vice-president of Clover Club Foods, a Utah-based snack company, believes Frito-Lay's goal is to be the only salted-snack food company in the country. The Independent Baker's Association has described the current situation with slotting fees as being "out of control".

Discussion Questions

1. Are slotting fees a means of allocating risk?
2. What possible employee temptations exist?
3. Would a schedule of fees help?
4. Are slotting fees ethical?

CASE 5.15: MR. GATES: GENIUS AND FIERCE COMPETITOR

The profit for Microsoft Corporation was $3.5 billion for fiscal 1997. Founder Bill Gates was able to capture approximately 90% of the PC market. While many argue Mr. Gates' market share is primarily the result of building a better mouse trap, the Compaq Computer Co. sees Microsoft's market conquest slightly differently. In the spring of 1996, Compaq notified Microsoft that it intended to replace Microsoft's Explorer (Internet access program) with Microsoft's chief competitor's program, Netscape.

Shortly after the notification, Compaq was notified by Microsoft that its Windows 95 licensing agreement was terminated. A follow-up letter offered restoration of licensing if Compaq restored the Explorer program to its Presarios within 60 days. Compaq did so and got the licensing back.

The U.S. Justice Department brought an action seeking to hold Microsoft in contempt for violating an earlier order on "coercion by a dominant company in a way that distorts competition." The 1995 order prohibited Microsoft from tying the sale of one product to the sale of another, as was proposed to Compaq.

Microsoft maintains Explorer is part of an integrated product which they can force buyers to take. However, Netscape maintains that Explorer is produced, advertised and sold separately as a stand-alone product.

A judge issued a $1 million per day fine after a hearing on the alleged violation of tying by Microsoft. A second hearing produced an order precluding Microsoft from forcing PC makers to install Explorer.

Microsoft continued its sales practices pointing to language in the consent decree that reads Microsoft "shall not be construed to prohibit Microsoft from developing integrated products." Microsoft endured the fines until January 1998, when Microsoft agreed to a settlement under which it will not require PC makers to take Explorer. Shortly after the settlement, the Justice Department announced a new antitrust investigation based on allegations of collusion.

Microsoft is poised to introduce Windows 98 and has undertaken a public relations campaign to underscore the market and share price impact if it is not permitted to proceed with Windows 98 sales.

Discussion Questions

1. Is Microsoft just competing?
2. Is there anything unethical about tying product sales?
3. What free market issues exist here?

UNIT SIX
BUSINESS
AND ITS PRODUCT

"A bad reputation is like a hangover. It takes a while to get rid of and it makes everything else hurt."

James Preston
Former CEO, Avon

Quality, safety, service, and social responsibility—customers want these elements in a product and a company. Does the profit motive interfere with these traits?

SECTION A
CONTRACT RELATIONS

The law of contracts is detailed, but ethical discussions center on the fairness of treatment and the balance of the agreement.

CASE 6.1: INTEL AND PENTIUM: WHAT TO DO WHEN THE CHIPS ARE DOWN

A joke about Intel's Pentium chip (source unknown) circulated on the Internet:

Top Ten Reasons to Buy a Pentium-Equipped Computer

10. Your current computer is too accurate.
9. You want to get into the *Guinness Book of World Records* as "owner of most expensive paperweight."
8. Math errors add zest to life.
7. You need an alibi for the IRS.
6. You want to see what all the fuss is about.
5. You've always wondered what it would be like to be a plaintiff.
4. The "Intel Inside" logo matches your decor perfectly.
3. You no longer have to worry about CPU overheating.
2. You got a great deal from the Jet Propulsion Laboratory.
   And, the number one reason to buy a Pentium-equipped computer: It'll probably work.

Intel, which makes components used in 80 percent of all personal computers sold, introduced the powerful Pentium chip in 1993. The firm spent $1 billion developing the chip, while the cost of producing it is estimated to be between $50 and $150 each. Intel shipped 4 million of the chips to computer manufacturers, including IBM.

In July 1994, Intel discovered a flaw in the "floating-point unit" of the chip, which is the section that completes complex calculations quickly.

The flaw caused errors in division calculations involving numbers with more than eight digits to the right of the decimal, such as in this type of equation:

$$\frac{4,195,835}{3,145,727} \times 3,145,727 = 4,195,835$$

Pentium-equipped computers computed the answer, in error, as 4,195,579. Before introducing the Pentium chip, Intel ran 1 trillion tests on it. The company calculated that the Pentium chip would produce an error once every 27,000 years, making the chance of an average user getting an error one in 9 billion.

In November, Thomas Nicely, a mathematician at Lynchburg College in Virginia, discovered the Pentium flaw. On Thanksgiving Day 1994, Intel publicly acknowledged the flaw in the Pentium chip, and the next day, its stock fell from 65 1/8 to 63 7/8 . Intel stated that the problem had been corrected but flawed chips were still being shipped because a three-month production schedule was just ending. The firm initially offered to replace the chips but only for users who must run complicated calculations as part of their jobs. The replacement offer carried numerous conditions.

On December 12, 1994, IBM announced that it would stop all shipments of its personal computers because its own tests indicated that Intel had underrepresented the extent of the Pentium flaw. IBM's tests concluded that computer users working on spreadsheets for as little as fifteen minutes per day could produce a mistake every twenty-four days. Intel's CEO Andrew Grove called IBM's reaction "unwarranted." No other computer manufacturer adopted IBM's position. IBM's chief of its personal computing division, G. Richard Thoman, emphasized that IBM had little choice: "It is absolutely critical for this industry to grow, that people trust that our products work right." Following the IBM announcement, Intel's stock price dropped 6.5 percent, and trading had to be halted temporarily.

On December 20, 1994, Grove announced that Intel would replace all Pentium chips:

> We were dealing with a consumer community that was upset with us. That they were upset with us—it has finally dawned on us—is because we were telling them what's good for them. . . . I think we insulted them.

Replacing the chips could cost up to $360 million. Intel offered to send owners a new chip that they could install or to have service firms replace chips for customers who were uncomfortable doing it themselves.

Robert Sombric, the data processing manager for the city of Portsmouth, New Hampshire, found Intel's decision to go on selling flawed chips for months inexcusable: "I treat the city's money just as if it were my own. And I'm telling you: I wouldn't buy one of these things right now until we really know the truth about it."

Following the replacement announcement, Intel's stock rose $3.44 to $61.25. One market strategist praised the replacement program: "It's about time. It's very clear they were fighting a losing battle, both in public relations as well as user confidence."

Grove responded that Intel's delay in offering replacements was based on concerns about precedent. "If we live by an uncompromising standard that demands perfection, it will be bad for everybody," he said. He also acknowledged that Intel had agreed to sell the flawed Pentium chips to a jewelry manufacturer.

By December 16, 1994, ten lawsuits in three states involving eighteen law firms had been filed against Intel for the faulty chips. While the suits progressed, replacement demands were minimal. Intel's internal employee newsletter had a 1 April 1995 edition that spoofed the infamous chip. A form required customers with Pentium chips to submit a 5000-word essay on "Why My Pentium Should Be Replaced."

In 1997, Intel launched two new products: Pentium Pro and Pentium II and a new potential bug, again affecting only intensive engineering and scientific mathematical operations, was uncovered. Intel, however, published the list of bugs with technical information and remedies for both of the new processors. One analyst commented on the new approach, "They have learned a lot since then. You can't approach the consumer market with an engineering mindset."

In September, 1997, the Federal Trade Commission (FTC) began a broad antitrust inquiry into Intel and whether its practices constituted monopolization. One practice alleged is tying new products to customers' exclusive purchase of existing products. Another practice alleged is "disciplining" customers who cross over to other chip suppliers by cutting off their Intel supply.

Discussion Questions

1. Should Intel have disclosed the flaw in the Pentium chip when it first discovered it in July 1994?
2. Should Intel have issued an immediate recall?
3. Was it ethical to offer limited replacement of the chip?
4. Discuss the long-term damage to Intel.
5. Assume that you are an Intel manager invited to the 1994 post-Thanksgiving meeting on how to respond to the public revelation of the flawed chips. You believe the failure to offer replacements will damage the company over the long term. Further, you feel strongly that providing a replacement is a balanced and ethical thing to do. However, CEO Grove disagrees. How would you persuade him to offer replacements to all purchasers?
6. If you could not persuade Grove to replace the chips, would you stay at the company?
7. Has the Pentium incident caused long-term damage to the computer industry?
8. Consider the following analysis (from "Intel Eats Crow, Replaces Pentium." *Mesa Tribune*, 21 December 1994, F1.):

   Regarding your article "Bare Knuckles at Big Blue" (News: Analysis & Commentary, Dec. 26), future generations of business school students will study Intel Corp.'s response to the problems with the Pentium chip as a classic case study in how to transform a technical problem into a public-relations nightmare.
   Intel's five-point plan consisted of:
   1) Initially deny that the problem exists;
   2) When irrefutable evidence is presented that the problem exists, downplay its significance;
   3) Agree to only replace items for people who can demonstrate extreme hardship;
   4) Continue running your current ad campaign extolling the virtues of the product as if nothing has happened;
   5) Count the short-term profits.

   List other companies discussed in this book or in other readings that followed this same five-point pattern.
9. Do you think Intel's dominance is due exclusively to innovation and quality?

CASE 6.2: HIDDEN CAR RENTAL FEES

During the 1980s, there were six major players in the global rental car market:

Share	(in billions)
Hertz	$4.0
Avis	3.2
Budget	2.5
National	2.5
Alamo	0.6
Dollar	0.5
Other	2.5[1]

Customers are often perplexed by the variety of rates and additional charges they face when they go to rent a car. All the national firms have daily, weekend, and weekly rates. Some firms offer unlimited free mileage, while others offer 100 free miles with a charge for each additional mile.

Extra charges may be made for a second driver, a child seat, remote dropoff, and insurance, including collision/damage waiver (CDW), liability, personal effects, and personal accident coverage. A National Car Rental customer in Boston who paid nine dollars a day on top of the sixty-dollar-per-day rental fee in 1987 said, "It's expensive, but I figure you get in a crack-up and you're going to get nailed if you don't have it."[2]

In 1988, regulatory and legislative bodies began taking on car rental practices. Some states took the position that rental car agents should be licensed as insurance agents. In August 1988, a U.S. district court in New York ordered Hertz Corporation to refund $13 million to customers after the company pleaded guilty to criminal charges in connection with overcharging customers to repair vehicles that had been damaged but for which there was no CDW.

On September 4, 1988, the National Association of Attorneys General appointed a task force headed by Kansas Attorney General Bob Stephan to study deceptive and unfair practices in the car rental industry.

In August 1988, the FTC cited both large and small companies for using deceptive practices in advertising. Clinton Krislov, a Chicago lawyer who represented consumers in class-actions lawsuits against rental agencies in Chicago and Des Moines, observed:

> This is sort of like trying to judge an ugly contest among frogs. There are, I suppose, some pockets of honesty in this business, but. . . . [3]

The FTC also proposed a regulation that would require the use of a standard rental contract and disclosure in all ads of full rental charges, including those for gas, collision protection, and repairs. The regulation would also limit charges for collisions and theft to $100.

---

1. Matthew L. Wald, "Hertz to New York: Pay More," *New York Times*, 19 January 1992, F10.

2. Corie Brown, "Cracking Down on a Costly Car-Rental Option," *Business Week*, 30 November 1987, 135.

3. Alex Taylor, III, "Why Car Rentals Drive You Nuts," *Fortune*, 31 August 1987, 74.

Some renters who refused CDW had been told no cars were available. Others had $1,000 to $3,000 frozen on their credit cards because they did not take CDW.

In 1989, several states considered legislation to ban CDWs. California passed a law that limited the waiver fee to nine dollars per day and required disclosure to the customer about its purposes (including disclosure in ads). New York and Illinois limited charges for car damage to $100 and $200, respectively, which effectively eliminated the need for most renters to buy CDW.

CDW is the money-maker for the smaller rental agencies, which offer lower base rental rates and make their profits through such extras as CDW. These companies maintain that without CDW, which 90 percent of their customers take, they could not compete or survive, and prices would have to go up. Indeed, by 1992, prices at all car rental companies had risen an average of 12 percent.

In 1992, the FTC charged Dollar Rent-A-Car Systems, Inc., and Value Rent-A-Car, Inc., with failure to fully disclose information on charges to customers. Both Dollar and Value settled with the FTC in 1993 by agreeing to disclose more information in their ads.

Under greater scrutiny and regulatory supervision, the companies began implementing new strategies to increase earnings. For example, companies either refuse to rent to or levy a surcharge of ten to fifteen dollars a day on drivers between the ages of twenty-one and twenty-five. National screens potential renters in New York City and Florida for driving-while-intoxciated (DWI) convictions or suspended or revoked licenses. Some firms charge an additional twenty-five dollars for more than one driver and have raised dropoff and refueling fees.

In 1995, Avis and Hertz reinstated mileage charges for certain renters in certain areas in an attempt to recoup costs which doubled from 1992–1995 after manufacturers refused to buy back the rental cars. In 1997, Budget began charging $30–$100 for no-shows on their reservations. A ban on under age 25 drivers is in effect in the industry, with the exception of New York where a judge has ruled such age-based distinctions to be a form of discrimination.

The industry underwent a period of restructuring with Dollar and Thrifty combining into one publicly-held company, Dollar Thrifty. National and Alamo are now owned by Republic Industries.

In 1996, Enterprise Rent-A-Car became the nation's largest rental car company, focusing not on airports, but on small towns and the need for rentals when the family car is in the shop. Enterprise holds 20% of the $15 billion U.S. market. The price of an Enterprise rental is 30% below Avis or Hertz, and most of the company's fees are paid by warranty policies or insurance coverage (in the case of an accident).

Discussion Questions

1. Assume you are the public affairs vice president for one of the top six rental car companies. Would you change any of your policies with respect to CDW?
2. Would you change your advertising to disclose CDW charges?
3. Would you instruct your counter agents to explain that the CDW coverage may be duplicative?
4. Would you change any of the other extra charges typical in the industry (that is, would you revamp your pricing policy)? Would such a change hurt or help your ability to compete?

5. Do you see practices in this industry that regulators may tackle in the future? Would you voluntarily change any of these practices?
6. Is it significant that Enterprise, with its different charges, captured the market?

___

CASE 6.3: THINNING DIET INDUSTRY

Oprah Winfrey started a diet craze when she appeared on her television show in 1988 in her size-ten Calvin Klein jeans and boasted of losing sixty-seven pounds by using Sandoz Nutrition Corporation's Optifast Program. The preventive medicine center at Philadelphia's Graduate Hospital got 500 calls about Optifast the day of Oprah's announcement. Since then, the diet industry has grown 15 percent per year with total annual revenues topping $3 billion. The major competitors are:

Weight Watchers International	$ 1.3 billion
Nutri/System, Inc.	$764 million
Diet Center, Inc.	$275 million
Thompson Medical Company (Slim-Fast)	$260 million
Sandoz Nutrition (Optifast)	$120 million

Diet programs are sold through celebrity endorsements and before-and-after ads. Lynn Redgrave has represented Weight Watchers, Susan St. James has appeared for Diet Center, and Christina Ferrara, Tommy Lasorda, Kathie Lee Gifford, and others have endorsed Slim-Fast and Ultra Slim-Fast. Nutri/System has relied on radio disc jockeys to use its programs and then tell listeners about their weight losses.

The CEO of Weight Watchers likened the diet craze to the excesses of the 1980s on Wall Street: everything is more and more extreme. By mid-year 1990, Representative Ron Wyden of Oregon, chair of the House Small Business Subcommittee, asked industry representatives to explain their hard-sell tactics. Wyden's hearings revealed that fully 90 percent of those who lose weight rapidly on the quick-loss programs regain the lost weight and often more within two years. Wyden asked why employees of these programs were referred to as weight loss specialists when in fact they had no expertise and were really sales personnel. Weight Watchers CEO Charles Berger testified:

> Without touching on the issue of greed, some companies in our field have over-promised quick weight loss. And the promises have grown increasingly excessive.[4]

Just before the House hearings, nineteen women sued Nutri/System and Jenny Craig, Inc., in Dade County (Miami), Florida, for gallbladder damage allegedly caused by the programs' diets. Seventeen of the women had had their gallbladders removed after participating in the Nutri/System program, even though they had no previous diagnosis of gallbladder difficulties.

In response to the suits and in the hearings, Nutri/System stated that obese people are vulnerable to a variety of ailments, including gallbladder disease. The

___

4. Julie Johnson, "Bringing Sanity to the Diet Craze," *Time*, 21 May 1990, 74.

company labeled the suits "without merit" and "a carefully orchestrated" campaign by the lawyers for the nineteen women.

Nutri/System was forced into Chapter 11 bankruptcy but emerged in 1993 under new ownership and a new weight loss philosophy that includes encouraging the use of exercise equipment in its facilities.

A marketing consultant has observed about the diet industry:

> There is such a market for faddish nutritional services that even if you lose some customers you'll get new ones. To some extent in this industry, a lot more depends on how good your marketing is than your product.[5]

In 1991, the Federal Trade Commission charged Optifast 70, Medifast 70 and Ultrafast with making marketing claims that were deceptive and "unsubstantiated hype." The agency called the statement "you'll have all you need to control your weight for the rest of your life" unsubstantiated. The FTC also announced it was investigating other diet programs. Representative Wyden said the FTC's complaints against the three companies were only "the tail of the elephant; the real test is whether these standards will be applied throughout the industry."[6]

By mid-1992, the FTC completed its investigation of misleading advertising by more than a dozen diet chains and promulgated guidelines for such advertising. Before-and-after testimonials must include pictures of typical clients, not just the most successful ones, and claims of keeping the weight off must be documented. The FTC's guidelines were the result of the National Institutes of Health's findings that virtually all dieters regain two-thirds of their weight within a year and all of it within five years.

As the FTC was promulgating these rules, the Food and Drug Administration announced that it would decide whether phenylpropanolamine, an amphetamine-like stimulant, could continue to be used in appetite-suppressant products, such as Acutrim and Dexatrim. Further, lawsuits based in product liability on the inherent dangers of these diet pills (including wrongful death actions) are pending around the country.

Meanwhile, Oprah Winfrey announced that she would never again use a liquid diet, and an Alabama jury awarded $15 million to the mother of a twenty-three-year-old bride-to-be who died of heart failure after losing twenty-one pounds in six weeks under the supervision of the Physicians' Weight Loss Center.

Several sociological issues surround weight loss. Susie Orbach, author of *Fat Is a Feminist Issue*, observes that 50 million Americans begin diets every year: "When I started working in this field 22 years ago, eating problems affected a limited group, women in their 30s and 40s. Now, we know from studies that girls of 9 and women of 60 are all obsessed with the way they look."[7]

The top two companies in the diet industry—Jenny Craig and Weight Watchers—were cited by the FTC in October 1993 for falsely advertising the success of their programs. Three other companies (Diet Center, Nutri/System, and Physi-

---

5. Alix Freedman and Udayan Gupta, "Lawsuits May Trim Diet Firms," *Wall Street Journal*, 23 March 1990, B1.

6. Jeanne Saddler, "FTC Targets Thin Claims of Liquid Diets," *Wall Street Journal*, 17 October 1991, B1, B6.

7. Larry Armstrong and Maria Mallory, "The Diet Business Starts Sweating," *Business Week*, 22 June 1992, 32–33.

cians' Weight Loss Centers of America) settled with the FTC by agreeing to: 1) not misrepresent program performance in ads; 2) gather and make available supporting data; and 3) include disclosures that most weight loss is temporary and say whether a testimonial is typical or not.

The New York City Department of Consumer Affairs was the first in the nation to issue "truth-in-dieting" regulations for diet centers, violations of which carry a $500 fine:

1. Centers must post a prominent Weight-Loss Consumer Bill of Rights sign in every room where a sales presentation is made. The sign informs consumers there may be serious health problems associated with rapid weight loss and that only lifestyle changes, such as healthy eating and exercise, promote permanent weight loss.

2. All centers must also give every potential client a palm-size Consumer Bill of Rights card.

3. All centers must inform potential clients of hidden costs of products or laboratory tests that may be part of the program.

4. All centers must tell dieters the expected duration of the program.

The FTC actions against false advertising led to a 15 percent reduction in diet industry revenues in 1994.

In 1997, just as the industry was recovering, the American Society of Bariatric Physicians released a list of its concerns about the industry's usage of obesity drugs such as Redux and fen-Phen along with promises of permanent weight loss. The presence of the new prescription obesity drugs produced new weight-loss clinics focusing entirely on the pills and prescriptions with a total of 18 million monthly prescriptions in 1996 given, in many cases, not to the clinically obese, but those seeking to lose five to ten pounds.

A 1997 study found the presence of heart valve damage among users of fen-Phen and the FDA withdrew the diet drugs from the market. Those who had been using the diet drugs began litigation. National class action suits began.

Diet centers relying on the two drugs have also been named in the litigation and many, based solely on the prescription approach, have closed. Customers who have become plaintiffs are complaining about the lack of warnings given to them by these diet centers.

In early 1998, a new study of 1,072 people, sponsored by the parent company of the manufacturers of Redux and Pondimin, found only a 6.5% to 7.3% rate of heart valve problems, in patients who took the drugs as opposed to a 4.5% rate in patients who took the dummy pill. A cardiologist labeled the difference in rates "not statistically significant." However, the FDA ban remained and the litigation continued.

Discussion Questions

1. Assume that you get a part-time job as a "weight counselor" with a quick-weight-loss program. Would you have any ethical constraints in performing your job?

2. Don't people just want to lose weight quickly? What if you told them they would gain it back and face health risks but they decided to go forward anyway? Would you and your product be adhering to a proper moral stan-

anyway? Would you and your product be adhering to a proper moral standard of full disclosure and freedom of choice?

3. Does the diet industry make money from temporary motivation? Or does the diet industry only provide temporary motivation?

4. Are the weight-loss ads misleading?

5. Weight Watchers, which posted a $50 million loss in 1994, has begun a new program emphasizing health foods, heart disease prevention, and exercise. Will this type of program avoid the ethical issues of rapid-weight-loss programs?

6. Given the Redux and fen-Phen problems, what can be safely concluded about the diet industry? What would be an ethical approach to running a weight-loss clinic?

7. Do you think there is a conflict with the 1998 study's sponsorship? What precautions should those professors conducting the study take?

CASE 6.4: THE SURE SALE OF THE PAPER BAGS[8]

Smith-Scharff Paper, a Missouri distributor of paper products, had done business with P. N. Hirsch, a subsidiary of Interco Inc., since 1947.

Smith-Scharff supplied Hirsch with paper bags bearing the P. N. Hirsch logo. The distributor ordered the bags from a supplier in quantities that were based on Hirsch's historical sales and kept a supply on hand to meet Hirsch's demand.

The relationship was nearly continuous from 1947 to 1983, except for one year during the 1950s or '60s. During this interruption, Hirsch bought all the bags Smith-Scharff had on hand before it switched to another distributor.

In 1983, P. N. Hirsch was liquidated, and Dollar General purchased its retail outlets. When Arthur L. Scharff, the president of Smith-Scharff, learned of the sale, he wrote to Bernard Mayer, the president of P. N. Hirsch, to demand assurance that the Hirsch bags that Smith-Scharff had on hand would be purchased.

Mayer assured Scharff that P. N. Hirsch would honor all commitments and that the company's integrity should not be questioned. At that time, Smith-Scharff had a $65,000 supply of Hirsch bags. Scharff sent Mayer a bill for that amount.

Hirsch paid $45,000, leaving Smith-Scharff with $20,000 in bags. The distributor then sued Hirsch for the balance.

Hirsch responded that the claim required a written contract, which did not exist. Smith-Scharff said it had relied on an ongoing business relationship in providing the specially manufactured bags that could not be used by or sold to anyone else.

Discussion Questions

1. Were any moral standards violated by either party?

2. Did Smith-Scharff's reliance on its relationship with Hirsch give rise to ethical commitments?

---

8. Adapted from Marianne Jennings, *Business: Its Legal, Ethical and Global Environment*, 4th ed. Cincinnati: ITP (1997), 488–489.

3. What did Mayer mean when he stated that P. N. Hirsch's integrity should not be questioned?
4. Could Smith-Scharff have used the bags in some other way?
5. Do ethical obligations arise even when the legal requirements for a contract are not met?

CASE 6.5: THE CLUTTERED APPLE POWDER[9]

Schulze and Burch Biscuit Company uses dehydrated apple powder to make strawberry and blueberry Toastettes, sold by Nabisco.

E. Edward Park, Schulze and Burch's director of procurement, entered into negotiations to buy apple powder with Rudolph Brady, a broker for Tree Top, Inc., a producer of apple juice, sauce, and other products. Apple powder is a by-product of Tree Top's juice production.

Park and Brady successfully negotiated nine contracts for apple powder. The Schulze and Burch's purchase order contained on its front the following statement that limited the terms of the apple powder contracts to those expressed in the purchase order:

IMPORTANT: The fulfillment of this order or any part of it obligates the Seller to abide by the terms, conditions and instructions on both sides of this order. Additional or substitute terms will not become part of this contract unless expressly accepted by Buyer; Seller's acceptance is limited to the terms of this order, and no contract will be formed except on these terms.

In each of the nine contracts, Brady sent back Tree Top's confirmation, which included the following statement requiring contract disputes be submitted to arbitration:

Seller guarantees to conform to the national pure food laws. All disputes under this transaction shall be arbitrated in the usual manner. This confirmation shall be subordinate to more formal contract, when and if such contract is executed. In the absence of such contract, this confirmation represents the contract of the parties. If incorrect, please advise immediately.

Park and Brady never discussed either of these clauses during the course of their nine-contract relationship.

In the course of the last contract, Schulze and Burch said that the apple powder was "cluttered" with stems and wood splinters that clogged Schulze and Burch's machinery. The clogging shut down the production line and caused financial losses for Schulze and Burch.

When Schulze and Burch complained to the supplier, Tree Top said that under the terms of its confirmation, Schulze and Burch had to submit the matter to arbitration. Schulze and Burch sued Tree Top to recover its income losses and other damages caused by the cluttered powder.

---

9. Adapted from Marianne Jennings, *Business: Its Legal, Ethical and Global Environment*, 4th ed. Cincinnati: ITP (1997), 492–493.

Discussion Questions

1. Did the parties really understand the terms of their agreement?
2. Does it matter whether arbitration is required? Shouldn't Tree Top correct the problems caused by the cluttered apple powder?
3. Are legal technicalities interfering with resolving the problem of a defective product and the buyer's resulting losses?
4. Should Tree Top offer to remedy the problem?
5. Suppose Tree Top had no legal obligation to provide clutter-free powder. Does it have an ethical obligation to do so?

CASE 6.6: SEARS AND HIGH-COST AUTO REPAIRS

In 1991, the California Department of Consumer Affairs began investigating Sears Auto Repair Centers. Sears's automotive unit, with 850 repair shops nationwide, generated 9 percent of the merchandise group's $19.4 billion in revenues; it was one of the fastest-growing and most profitable divisions of Sears over the previous two years.

In the California investigation, agents posed as customers at thirty-three of the seventy-two Sears automotive repair shops located from Los Angeles to Sacramento. They found that they were overcharged 90 percent of the time by an average of $223. In the first phase of the investigation, the agents took thirty-eight cars with worn-out brakes but no other mechanical problems to twenty-seven Sears shops from December 1990 to December 1991. In thirty-four of the cases, the agents were told that their cars needed additional work. At the Sears shop in Concord, a San Francisco suburb, the agent was overcharged $585 to replace the front brake pads, front and rear springs, and control-arm bushings. Sears advertised brake jobs at prices of $48 and $58.

In the second phase of the investigation, Sears was notified of the investigation and ten shops were targeted. In seven of those cases, the agents were overcharged. No springs and shocks were sold in these cases, but the average overcharge was $100 per agent.

Up until 1990, Sears had paid its repair center service advisors by the hour rather than by the amount of work. But in February 1990, Sears instituted an incentive compensation policy under which employees were paid based on the amount of repairs customers authorized. Service advisors also had to meet sales quotas on specific auto parts; those who did not meet the quotas often had their hours reduced or were assigned to work in other departments in the Sears stores. California regulators said the number of consumer complaints they received about Sears shops increased dramatically after the commission structure was implemented.

The California Department of Consumer Affairs charged all seventy-two Sears automotive shops in the state with fraud, false advertising, and failure to clearly state parts and labor on invoices.

Jim Conran, the director of the consumer affairs department, stated:

This is a flagrant breach of the trust and confidence the people of California have placed in Sears for generations. Sears has used trust as a marketing tool, and we don't believe they've lived up to that trust. The violation of the faith that was placed in Sears cannot be allowed to continue, and for past violations of law, a penalty must be paid.[10]

Dick Schenkkan, a San Francisco lawyer representing Sears, charged that Conran issued the complaint in response to bipartisan legislative efforts to cut his agency's funding because of a state budget crunch and claimed, "He is garnering as much publicity as he can as quickly as he can. If you wanted to embark on a massive publicity campaign to demonstrate how aggressive you are and how much need there is for your services in the state, what better target than a big, respected business that would guarantee massive press coverage?"[11]

Richard Kessel, the executive director of the New York State Consumer Protection Board, stated that he also had "some real problems" with Sear's policy of paying people by commission. "If that's the policy," Kessel said, "that in my mind could certainly lead to abuses in car repairs."[12]

Immediately following the issuing of the California complaint, Sears said that the state's investigation was "very seriously flawed and simply does not support the allegations. The service we recommend and the work we perform are in accordance with the highest industry standards."[13]

It then ran the the following ad:

With over two million automotive customers serviced last year in California alone, mistakes may have occurred. However, Sears wants you to know that we would never intentionally violate the trust customers have shown in our company for 105 years.

Ten days after the complaint was announced, the chairman of Sears, Edward A. Brennan, announced that Sears was eliminating the commission-based pay structure for employees who propose auto repairs. He conceded that the pay structure may have created an environment in which mistakes were made because of rigid attention to goals. Brennan announced the compensation system would be replaced with one in which customer satisfaction would now be the primary factor in determining service personnel rewards, shifting the emphasis away from quantity to quality. An outside firm would be hired to conduct unannounced shopping audits of Sears auto centers to be certain the hard sells were eliminated. Further, Brennan said, the sales quotas on parts would be discontinued. While he did not admit to any scheme to recommend unnecessary repairs, he emphasized that the system encouraged mistakes and he accepted full responsibility for the policies. "The buck stops with me," he said.[14]

Sears auto repair customers filed class action lawsuits in California, and a New Jersey undercover investigation produced similar findings of overcharging. New Jersey officials found that 100 percent of the Sears stores in its investigation recommended unneeded work compared to 16 percent of stores not owned by Sears. On June 25, 1992, Sears ran a full-page ad in all major newspapers throughout the country. The ad, a letter signed by Brennan, had the following text:

---

10. Lawrence M. Fisher, "Accusation of Fraud at Sears," *New York Times*, 12 June 1992, C2, C12.

11. Ibid.

12. Ibid.

13. Tung Yin, "Sears Is Accused of Billing Fraud at Auto Centers," *Wall Street Journal*, 12 June 1992, B1.

14. Gregory A. Patterson, "Sears' Brennan Accepts Blame for Auto Flap," *Wall Street Journal*, 23 June 1992, B1.

An Open Letter to Sears Customers:

You may have heard recent allegations that some Sears Auto Centers in California and New Jersey have sold customers parts and services they didn't need. We take such charges very seriously, because they strike at the core of our company—our reputation for trust and integrity.

We are confident that our Auto Center customers' satisfaction rate is among the highest in the industry. But after an extensive review, we have concluded that our incentive compensation and goal-setting program inadvertently created an environment in which mistakes have occurred. We are moving quickly and aggressively to eliminate that environment.

To guard against such things happening in the future, we're taking significant action:

We have eliminated incentive compensation and goal-setting systems for automotive service advisors—the folks who diagnose problems and recommend repairs to you. We have replaced these practices with a new non-commission program designed to achieve even higher levels of customer satisfaction. Rewards will now be based on customer satisfaction.

We're augmenting our own quality control efforts by retaining an independent organization to conduct ongoing, unannounced "shopping audits" of our automotive services to ensure that company policies are being met.

We have written to all state attorneys general, inviting them to compare our auto repair standards and practices with those of their states in order to determine whether differences exist.

And we are helping to organize and fund a joint industry-consumer-government effort to review current auto repair practices and recommend uniform industry standards.

We're taking these actions so you'll continue to come to Sears with complete confidence. However, one thing we will never change is our commitment to customer safety. Our policy of preventive maintenance—recommending replacement of worn parts before they fail—has been criticized by the California Bureau of Automotive Repair as constituting unneeded repairs. We don't see it that way. We recommend preventive maintenance because that's what our customers want, and because it makes for safer cars on the road. In fact, 75 percent of the consumers we talked to in a nationwide survey last weekend told us that auto repair centers should recommend replacement parts for preventive maintenance. As always, no work will ever be performed without your approval.

We understand that when your car needs service, you look for, above all, someone you can trust. And when trust is at stake, you can't merely react, we must overreact.

We at Sears are totally committed to maintaining your confidence. You have my word on it.

Ed Brennan
Chairman and Chief Executive Officer
Sears, Roebuck and Co.

On September 2, 1992, Sears agreed to pay $8 million to resolve the consumer affairs agency claims on overcharging in California. The $8 million included reimbursement costs, new employee training, and coupons for discounts at the service center. Another $15 million in fines was paid in 41 other states to settle class-action suits.

In December 1992, Sears fired John T. Lundegard, the director of its automotive operations, a $3 billion per year portion of its business. Sears indicated that Lundegard's termination was not related to the controversy surrounding the auto centers.

Sears recorded a net loss of $3.9 billion despite $52.3 billion in sales in 1992—the worst performance ever by the retailer in its 108-year history and its first loss since 1933. Its Allstate Insurance division was reeling from damage claims for Hurricane Andrew in the Gulf Coast and Hurricane Iniki in Hawaii ($1.25 billion). Auto center revenue dropped $80 million in the last quarter of 1992, and Sears paid out a total of $27 million to settle state overcharging claims. Moody's downgraded Sears debt following the loss announcement.

In 1994, Sears partially reinstated its sales-incentive practices in its auto centers. Service advisors must earn at least 40 percent of their total pay in commissions on the sale and installation of tires, batteries, shock absorbers, and struts. Not included on commission are brakes and front-end alignments (the core of the 1992 problems). Earnings in auto centers have not yet returned to pre-1992 levels.

Discussion Questions

1. What temptations did the employee compensation system present?
2. If you had been a service advisor, would you have felt comfortable recommending repairs that were not immediately necessary but would be eventually?
3. What will the complaints cost Sears, regardless of their eventual disposition?
4. Did Brennan acknowledge moral responsibility for the overcharges?
5. Does it matter whether the overcharges were intentional or part of business incentives?
6. A public relations expert has said of the Sears debacle: "Don't make the Sears mistake. When responding to a crisis, tell the public what happened and why. Apologize with no crossed fingers. Then say what you're going to do to make sure it doesn't happen again." What are the ethical standards in this public relations formula?
7. What will be the likely results of the incentive reinstatement?
8. There are some who have expressed concerns about the ethical culture at Sears. While incentive systems may have created the auto center fraud problems, consider the following dilemmas involving Sears since the time of its auto center fraud cases:

   - Montgomery Ward obtained an order from a federal court prohibiting Sears from hiring employees away from Wards as it works its way through Chapter 11 bankruptcy. The order was based on an e-mail sent from Sears' regional vice president, Mary Conway, in which Sears managers are instructed to "be predatory" about hiring away Montgomery Ward managers.
   - A class-action civil suit was filed in Atlanta against Sears by consumers who allege that Sears sold them used batteries as new. One of the plaintiffs in the suit alleges that an investigator purchased 100 "new" batteries from Sears in 1995 (in 32 states) and that 78 of them showed signs of previous usage. A Sears internal auto-center document explains that the high allowances the centers must give customers on returns of batteries cuts into profits and induces the sale of used batteries to compensate. (Sears denies the allegation and attributes it to disgruntled former employees

and not understanding that a nick does not necessarily mean a battery is used.)

- Sears admitted to "flawed legal judgment" when it made repayment agreements with its credit card customers who were already in bankruptcy, a practice in violation of creditors' rights and priorities. Sears agreed to refund the amounts collected but still faces possible penalties of $5,000 each for the 2,700 customers who were put into the program. Sears warned the refunds could have a "material effect" on earnings. The announcement caused a price of stock drop of 3 7/8. Sears included the following notice to its credit card customers:

> NOTICE: If you previously filed for personal bankruptcy under Chapter 7 and entered into a reaffirmation agreement with Sears, you may be a member of a Settlement Class in a proposed class action settlement. For information, please call 1-800-529-4500. There are deadlines as early as October 8, 1997 applicable to the settlement.

Sears has, nonetheless, from 1991–1997 been a real Wall Street performer, increasing sales, revenues and net profits. What do you believe creates Sears' culture? Is Sears a testimonial that ethics don't matter? In 1997, Sears' stock price and earnings fell. What lesson is there here?

CASE 6.7: MAGAZINE CONTESTS: THE DISCLOSURE OF ODDS

Investigations of American Family Publishers and Publishers Clearing House center around the mailings sent by the companies that include the term "finalist" on the envelope and whether the materials state clearly enough that "no purchase is required." The "finalist" notification is mailed with subscription information for the purchase of subscriptions to magazines. Most people (99%) who send in their entries do order magazines.

Three states are investigating Publishers Clearing House and American Family Publishers is under investigation in 21 states. The Florida Attorney General has filed suit against Publishers Clearing House as well as Ed McMahon and Dick Clark, their celebrity spokespersons, for deceptive practices.

One mailing from American Family Publishers includes the following:

So please accept our invitation as soon as you receive it. Once you do, you'll experience the thrill of winning—and that's guaranteed.

The investigation in the various states revealed that many senior citizens were subscribing to between 20 and 30 magazines with the hope of collecting prizes they believed were theirs. Some of the language used in the 200 million mailings included the following:

John Doe, it's down to a 2 person race for $11,000,000—you and one other person in —— (state's name placed here) were issued one of two winning numbers.

We have reserved an $11,000,000 sum in your name.

Are you willing to risk letting your alternative take it all?

These statements were in bold while disclaimers establishing that the win was not all that certain were in fine print. The language in bold caused many to buy yet another subscription with the hope of winning.

American Family Publishers (the company with the mailings that read "YOU MAY ALREADY BE A WINNER" on the outside of the envelope) agreed to pay $1.25 million to settle allegations in 32 states plus the District of Columbia regarding deceptive sales practices. Lawsuits against Dick Clark and Ed McMahon, the spokesman for the company, are still pending in three states.

The settlement also requires American Family to establish a toll-free telephone number for information requests as well as a Web site. Consumers must also be given information about getting off American Family mailing lists. Finally, American Home must stop using two mail addresses for the entries. Those who were simply entering the contest were instructed to use one address, while those who were subscribing and entering were told to send their envelope to another address. The two-address system led many to believe that an accompanying subscription was a key in collecting the prize described in the bold print.

Discussion Questions

1. Do you think there was deception in any of the practices?
2. What is the role of regulators in this situation?
3. Have the companies taken advantage of potential customers?

Section B
Product Safety

Only a manufacturer knows the results of its safety tests on a product. Only the manufacturer can correct defects or recall dangerous products. The decision to act on safety tests or recall a product is costly. The only "earnings" on recalls are the preservation of the company's reputation.

Case 6.8: Tylenol: The Product Safety

On December 21, 1994, the *Journal of the American Medical Association* published the results of a five-and-one-half-year study showing that moderate overdoses of acetaminophen (known most widely by the brand name Tylenol) led to liver damage in ten patients. The damage occurred even in patients who did not drink and was most pronounced in those who did drink or had not been eating. Further, the study by Dr. David Whitcomb at the University of Pittsburgh medical school found that taking one pill of acetaminophen per day for a year may double the risk of kidney failure.

The American Association of Poison Control Centers for 1996 show 31,511 cases of inappropriate exposure to pediatric acetaminophen products. There were minor effects in 631 children and life threatening permanent effects in six. Adult deaths from overexposure are put at 100, more than cocaine deaths (hospital statistics are not included).

Tylenol is a stunning source of revenue for McNeil and Johnson & Johnson with revenue of $1.3 billion per years. In 1993, acetaminophen accounted for 48 percent of the total $2.9 billion in sales of all over-the-counter drugs. Tylenol (made by McNeil Consumer Products, a division of Johnson & Johnson) made up 70 percent of all acetaminophen sales. Advil's total sales, the next in amount, trail at less than $400,000,000.

Plaintiffs, who claim they are victims of overdose and the lack of effective warnings, in lawsuits have not been successful against Johnson & Johnson. The product labels, before current modification read "Gentle on an infant's stomach," and Tylenol's ad slogan was, "Nothing's safer."

238

Patients combining Tylenol with alcohol has produced 200 cases of liver damage in the past 20 years with fatality in 20% of those cases. The level of alcohol among these cases was multiple drinks every day.

In 1997, Tylenol added a new label to its infant Tylenol, "Taking more than the recommended dose . . . could cause serious health risks," because of liver damage in children.

Discussion Questions

1. If you were a manufacturer of acetaminophen, how would you respond to the study? What action would you take?
2. How would you handle the litigation?
3. Did the warning take too long?

CASE 6.9: FORD AND ITS PINTO

The Pinto's Development

In 1968, Ford began designing a subcompact automobile that ultimately became the Pinto. Lee Iacocca, then a Ford vice president, conceived the project and was its moving force. Ford's objective was to build a car weighing 2,000 pounds or less to sell for no more than $2,000. At that time, prices for gasoline were increasing, and the American auto industry was losing competitive ground to the small vehicles of Japanese and German manufacturers.

Ordinarily, automakers conduct marketing surveys and preliminary engineering before styling a new line. With the Pinto, however, styling dictated engineering design to a greater degree than usual because it was a rush project. Among the decisions dictated by styling was the placement of the fuel tank. The preferred practice in Europe and Japan was to locate the gas tank over the rear axle in subcompacts because a small vehicle has less "crush space" between the rear axle and the bumper than larger cars. The Pinto's styling, however, required the tank to be placed behind the rear axle, leaving only nine to ten inches of "crush space"—far less than in any other American automobile or Ford overseas subcompact. In addition, the Pinto's bumper was little more than a chrome strip, less substantial than the bumper of any other American car produced then or later. The Pinto's rear structure also lacked reinforcing longitudinal side members, known as "hat sections," and horizontal cross members running between them, such as were found in cars of larger unitized construction and in all automobiles produced by Ford's overseas operations. The absence of the reinforcing members rendered the Pinto less crush-resistant than other vehicles. Finally, the Pinto's differential housing had an exposed flange and bolt heads. These protrusions were sufficient to puncture a gas tank driven forward against the differential by a rear impact.

Pinto prototypes were built and tested. Mechanical prototypes duplicated mechanical features of the design but not its appearance, while engineering prototypes were true duplicates of the design car. Ford tested these prototypes, as well as two production Pintos, to determine the integrity of the fuel system in rear-end accidents. It also tested to see if the Pinto would meet a proposed federal regulation requiring all automobiles manufactured in 1972 to be able to withstand a twenty-mile-per-hour fixed-barrier impact and those made after January 1, 1973, to withstand a thirty-mile-per-hour fixed-barrier impact without significant fuel spillage.

The crash tests revealed that the Pinto's fuel system as designed could not meet the proposed twenty-mile-per-hour standard. When mechanical prototypes were struck from the rear with a moving barrier at twenty-one miles per hour, the fuel tanks were driven forward and punctured, causing fuel leakage in excess of the standard prescribed by the proposed regulation. A production Pinto crashed at twenty-one miles per hour into a fixed barrier resulted in the fuel neck being torn from the gas tank and the tank being punctured by a bolt head on the differential housing. In at least one test, spilled fuel entered the driver's compartment through gaps resulting from the separation of the seams joining the rear wheel wells to the floor pan. The seam separation was caused by the lack of reinforcement in the rear structure and insufficient welds of the wheel wells to the floor pan.

Ford tested other vehicles, including modified or reinforced mechanical Pinto prototypes, that proved safe at speeds at which the Pinto failed. Vehicles in which rubber bladders had been installed in the tank and were then crashed into fixed barriers at twenty-one miles per hour had no leakage from punctures in the gas tank. Vehicles with fuel tanks installed above rather than behind the rear axle passed the fuel system integrity test at thirty-one miles per hour against a fixed barrier. A Pinto with two longitudinal hat sections added to firm up the rear structure passed a twenty-mile-per-hour fixed-barrier test with no fuel leakage.

When a prototype failed the fuel system integrity test, the standard of care in the industry was to redesign and retest it. The vulnerability of the production Pinto's fuel tank at speeds of twenty and thirty miles per hour in fixed-barrier tests could have been remedied inexpensively, but Ford produced and sold the Pinto without doing anything to fix the defects. Among the design changes that could have been made were: side and cross members at $2.40 and $1.80 per car, respectively; a shock-absorbent "flak suit" to protect the tank at $4; a tank within a tank and placement of the tank over the axle at $5.08 to $5.79; a nylon bladder within the tank at $5.25 to $8; placement of the tank over the axle surrounded with a protective barrier at $9.59 per car; imposition of a protective shield between the differential housing and the tank at $2.35; improvement and reinforcement of the bumper at $2.60; and addition of eight inches of crush space at a cost of $6.40. Equipping the car with a reinforced rear structure, smooth axle, improved bumper, and additional crush space at a total of $15.30 would have made the fuel tank safe when hit from the rear by a vehicle the size of a Ford Galaxie. If, in addition, a bladder or tank within a tank had been used or if the tank had been protected with a shield, the tank would have been safe in a rear-end collision of forty to forty-five miles per hour. If the tank had been located over the rear axle, it would have been safe in a rear impact at fifty miles per hour or more.

The feasibility study for the Pinto was conducted under the supervision of Robert Alexander, vice president of car engineering. Ford's Product Planning Committee, whose members included Lee Iacocca, Alexander, and Harold MacDonald, Ford's group vice president of car engineering, approved the Pinto's concept and made the decision to go forward with the project. During the course of the project, regular product review meetings were held that were chaired by MacDonald and attended by Alexander. As the Pinto approached actual production, the engineers responsible for the components of the project "signed off" to their immediate supervisors, who in turn "signed off" to their superiors, and so on up the chain of command until the entire project was approved for release by Alexander, MacDonald, and ultimately, Iacocca. The Pinto crash tests results were known to these decision-makers when they decided to go forward with production.

Analysis of the Gas Tank Issues

Harley Copp, a former Ford engineer and executive in charge of the crash testing program, testified that when the highest level of Ford's management decided to produce the Pinto, they knew that the gas tank was vulnerable to puncture and rupture at low rear-impact speeds, which created a significant risk of death or injury from fire, and that the problem could be fixed for a nominal cost. He testified that management's decision was based on the cost savings that Ford would incur from omitting or delaying implementing the remedies.

Other evidence corroborated Copp's testimony. At an April 1971 product review meeting chaired by MacDonald, a report by Ford engineers on the financial impact of a proposed federal standard on fuel system integrity and the cost savings that would accrue from deferring even minimal "fixes" of the Pinto was discussed. It is reasonable to infer that the report was prepared for and known to Ford officials in policy-making positions.

Finally, Copp testified to having conversations in late 1968 or early 1969 with the chief assistant research engineer in charge of cost-weight evaluation of the Pinto and later with the chief chassis engineer in charge of crash testing the early prototype. In these conversations, both men expressed concern to Copp about the integrity of the Pinto's fuel system and complained about management's unwillingness to deviate from the design if the change would cost money. Tables 5–1 and 5–2 show the estimated costs of design modification.

Calendar Year	Sales (1,000)	Estimated Unit Cost ($)	Estimated Total Cost ($ million)	Present Value of Estimated Costs in 1970 ($ million)
1970	76	8.00	.608	.608
1971	328	8.00	2.624	2.385
1972	287	8.00	2.296	1.897
1973	268	8.00	2.144	1.611
1974	192	8.00	1.536	1.049
1975	170	8.00	1.360	.844
1976	106	8.00	.848	.479
		Total		8.873

TABLE 5-1
Costs of the 1970 Potential Design Modification Strategy: Low Estimate[15]

15. *Automotive News,* Almanac Issues for 1971–1979 (Detroit: Slocum Publishing Company, 1971, and Marketing Services, 1972–1979).

TABLE 5-2
Costs of the 1970
Potential Design
Modification Strategy:
High Estimate

Calendar Year	Sales (1,000)	Estimated Unit Cost ($)	Estimated Total Cost ($ million)	Present Value of Estimated Costs in 1970 ($ million)
1970	76	18.66	1.418	1.418
1971	328	18.66	6.120	5.564
1972	287	18.66	5.355	4.425
1973	268	18.66	5.001	3.757
1974	192	18.66	3.583	2.447
1975	170	18.66	3.172	1.969
1976	106	18.66	1.978	1.116
	Total			20.696

J. C. Echold, Ford's director of automotive safety, studied the issue of gas tank design in anticipation of government regulations requiring modification. His study, "Fatalities Associated with Crash Induced Fuel Leakage and Fires," included the following cost-benefit analysis:

> The total benefit is shown to be just under $50 million, while the associated cost is $137 million. Thus, the cost is almost three times the benefits, even using a number of highly favorable benefit assumptions.[16]

Benefits

Savings–180 burn deaths, 180 serious burn injuries, 2,100 burned vehicles.
Unit cost–$200,000 per death, $67,000 per injury, $700 per vehicle.
Total Benefits–(180 x $200,000) + (180 x $67,000) + (2,100 x $700) = $49.15 million

Costs

Sales–11 million cars, 1.5 million light trucks
Unit cost–$11 per car, $11 per truck
Total costs–(11,000,000 x $11) + (1,500,000 x $11) = $137 million

Ford's unit cost of $200,000 for one life was based on a National Highway Traffic Safety Administration calculation developed as follows:

---

16. Ralph Drayton, "One Manufacturer's Approach to Automobile Safety Standards," *CTLA News* 8 February 1968, 11.

Component	1971 Costs
Future productivity losses	
Direct	$132,000
Indirect	41,300
Medical costs	
Hospital	700
Other	425
Property damage	1,500
Insurance administration	4,700
Legal and court	3,000
Employer losses	1,000
Victim's pain and suffering	10,000
Funeral	900
Assets (lost consumption)	5,000
Miscellaneous accident cost	200
Total Per Fatality	$200,725[17]

A Gas Tank Tragedy

In November 1971, Mr. and Mrs. Gray purchased a 1972 Pinto hatchback manufactured by Ford in October 1971. The Grays had trouble with the car from the outset. During the first few months of ownership, they had to return the car to the dealer for repairs a number of times. The problems included excessive gas and oil consumption, down-shifting of the automatic transmission, lack of power, and occasional stalling. It was later learned that the stalling and excessive fuel consumption were caused by a heavy carburetor float.

On May 28, 1972, Mrs. Gray, accompanied by thirteen-year-old Richard Grimshaw, set out in the Pinto from Anaheim for Barstow to meet Mr. Gray. The Pinto was then six months old and had been driven approximately 3,000 miles. Mrs. Gray stopped in San Bernadino for gasoline, then got back onto Interstate 15 and proceeded toward Barstow at sixty to sixty-five miles per hour. As she approached the Route 30 off ramp where traffic was congested, she moved from the outside fast lane into the middle lane. The Pinto then suddenly stalled and coasted to a halt. It was later established that the carburetor float had become so saturated with gasoline that it sank, opening the float chamber and causing the engine to flood. The driver of the vehicle immediately behind Mrs. Gray's car was able to swerve and pass it, but the driver of a 1962 Ford Galaxie was unable to avoid hitting the Pinto. The Galaxie had been traveling from fifty to fifty-five miles per hour but had slowed to between twenty-eight and thirty-seven miles per hour at the time of impact.

The Pinto burst into flames that engulfed its interior. According to one expert, the impact of the Galaxie had driven the Pinto's gas tank forward and caused it to be punctured by the flange or one of the bolts on the differential housing so that

---

17. Mark Dowie, "Pinto Madness," *Mother Jones*, September/October 1977, 28.

fuel sprayed from the punctured tank and entered the passenger compartment through gaps opening between the rear wheel well sections and the floor pan. By the time the Pinto came to rest after the collision, both occupants had been seriously burned. When they emerged from the vehicle, their clothing was almost completely burned off. Mrs. Gray died a few days later of congestive heart failure as a result of the burns. Grimshaw survived, only through heroic medical measures. He underwent numerous and extensive surgeries and skin grafts, some occurring over the ten years after the collision. He lost parts of several fingers on his left hand and his left ear, and his face required many skin grafts.[18]

Aftermath of the Pinto: Criminal and Civil Liability

As Ford continued to litigate Mrs. Gray's lawsuit and thousands of other rear-impact Pinto suits, damages reaching $6 million had been awarded to plaintiffs by 1980. In 1979, Indiana filed criminal charges against Ford for reckless homicide. The indictment appears below:

State v. Ford Motor Co.
Indictment in Four Counts Charging Three Counts of Reckless Homicide, a Class D Felony, and One Count of Criminal Recklessness, a Class A Misdemeanor
No. 5324 (1979)
Indiana Superior Court, Elkhart County, Indiana

The Grand Jurors of Elkhart County, State of Indiana, being first duly sworn upon their oaths do present and say:

Count I

That Ford Motor Company, a corporation, on or about the 10th day of August, 1978, in the County of Elkhart, State of Indiana, did then and there through the acts and omissions of its agents and employees acting within the scope of their authority with said corporation recklessly cause the death of Judy Ann Ulrich, a human being, to-wit: that the Ford Motor Company, a corporation, did recklessly authorize and approve the design, and did recklessly design and manufacture a certain 1973 Pinto automobile, Serial Number F3T10X298722F, in such a manner as would likely cause said automobile to flame and burn upon rear-end impact; and the said Ford Motor Company permitted said Pinto automobile to remain upon the highways and roadways of Elkhart County, State of Indiana, to-wit: U.S. Highway Number 33, in said County and State; and the said Ford Motor Company did fail to repair and modify said Pinto automobile; and thereafter on said date as a proximate contributing cause of said reckless disregard for the safety of other persons within said automobile, including, the said Judy Ann Ulrich, a rear-end impact involving said Pinto automobile did occur creating fire and flame which did then and there and thereby inflict mortal injuries upon the said Judy Ann Ulrich, and the said Judy Ann Ulrich did then languish and die by incineration in Allen County, State of Indiana, on or about the 11th day of August, 1978.

And so the Grand Jurors aforesaid, upon their oaths aforesaid, do say and charge that the said Ford Motor Company, a corporation, did recklessly cause the death of the said Judy Ann Ulrich, a human being, in the manner and form aforesaid, and contrary to the form of the statutes in such cases made and provided, to-wit: Burns Indiana Statutes, Indiana Code Section 35-42-1-5; and against the peace and dignity of the State of Indiana.

---

18. Adapted from *Grimshaw v. Ford Motor Co.*, 174 Cal. Rptr. 348 (1981).

Counts II and III

P [Counts II and III repeat the allegations of Count I as to the deaths of Donna M. Ulrich and Lynn M. Ulrich, respectively.]

Count IV

That Ford Motor Company, a corporation, on or about the 10th day of August, 1978, and diverse days prior thereto, in the County of Elkhart, State of Indiana, did through the acts and omissions of its agents and employees acting within the scope of their authority with said corporation, recklessly create a substantial risk of bodily injury to the persons of Judy Ann Ulrich, Donna M. Ulrich and Lynn M. Ulrich, human beings, and each of them, to-wit: that the Ford Motor Company, a corporation, did recklessly permit a certain 1973 Pinto automobile, Serial Number F3T10X298722F, designed and manufactured by the said Ford Motor Company to remain upon the highways and roadways of Elkhart County, State of Indiana, to-wit: U.S. Highway Number 33 in said County and State; and said Pinto automobile being recklessly designed and manufactured in such a manner as would likely cause said automobile to flame and burn upon rear-end impact; and that the said Ford Motor Company had a legal duty to warn the general public and certain occupants of said Pinto automobile, namely: Judy Ann Ulrich, Donna M. Ulrich and Lynn M. Ulrich of the dangerous tendency of said Pinto automobile to flame and burn upon rear-end impact; and the said Ford Motor Company did fail to repair and modify said Pinto automobile; and that as a proximate contributing cause of said Ford Motor Company's acts, omissions and reckless disregard for the safety of other persons within said Pinto automobile, including the said Judy Ann Ulrich, Donna M. Ulrich and Lynn M. Ulrich, a rear-end impact involving said Pinto automobile did occur on or about August 10, 1978, in Elkhart County, Indiana, creating fire and flame which did then and there and thereby inflict bodily injury upon the persons of the said Judy Ann Ulrich, Donna M. Ulrich and Lynn M. Ulrich, human beings, and each of them.

And so the Grand Jurors aforesaid, upon their oaths aforesaid, do say and charge that the said Ford Motor Company, a corporation, did recklessly create a substantial risk of bodily injury to the persons of Judy Ann Ulrich, Donna M. Ulrich and Lynn M. Ulrich, human beings, and each of them, in the manner and form aforesaid, and contrary to the form of the Statutes in such cases made and provided, to-wit: Burns Indiana Statutes, Indiana Code Section 35-42-2-2, and against the peace and dignity of the State of Indiana.

A true bill.

Discussion Questions

1. Calculate the total cost if all the "fixes" for the Pinto gas tank problem had been done.
2. What was management's position on the fixes?
3. Who was responsible for Grimshaw's injury? Would Copp have moral responsibility for the accident, death, and injuries involving Mrs. Gray's Pinto?
4. Did the Pinto design violate any laws?
5. Was Ford simply answering a public demand for a small, fuel-efficient, and inexpensive auto?
6. Don't all automobiles present the potential for injuries? Do we assume risks in driving and buying an automobile?
7. If you had held Copp's position, what would you have done differently?

8. The Pinto has become a popular stock car on the racing circuit. Recalled Pintos can be purchased for $50 from junkyards. Should Ford be concerned about such use?

9. In 1996, Ford issued a recall on 8.7 million vehicles because a joint investigation with NHTSA revealed the ignition in certain cars could short circuit and cause a fire. Ford ran full-page ads in major newspapers. The ad from the *Wall Street Journal*, May 8, 1996, B7, is reproduced below:

T.J. Wagner   Ford Motor Company
Vice President   Dearborn, MI 48121
Customer Communication & Satisfaction

To Our Ford, Lincoln and Mercury Owners:

As I am sure you have read, Ford Motor Company recently announced a program to voluntarily recall 8.7 million vehicles to replace ignition switches. You should know that at the time we announced the recall, the actual number of complaints which may be related to the ignition switch in question was less than two hundredths of one percent of that total. We regret the inconvenience this has caused the customers who have placed their trust in our products.

Q: *What happened?*
A: Following an intensive investigation in cooperation with the U.S. National Highway Traffic Safety Administration and Transport Canada, we determined that the ignition switch in a very small percentage of certain models could develop a short circuit–creating the potential for overheating, smoke, and possibly fire in the steering column of the vehicle. The factors that contribute to this are a manufacturing process change to the ignition switch in combination with the electrical load through the switch.

Q: *What vehicles are affected by this voluntary recall?*
A: The following model year vehicles are affected:

- 1988 Ford EXP.
- 1988–1990 Ford Escort.
- 1988–1992 Ford Mustang, Thunderbird, Tempo, and Mercury Cougar and Topaz.
- 1993 Ford Mustang, Thunderbird, Tempo, and Mercury Cougar and Topaz models built prior to October 1992.
- 1988–1989 Ford Crown Victoria, Mercury Grand Marquis and Lincoln Town Car.
- 1988–1991 Ford Aerostar, Ford Bronco full-size sport utility and Ford F-Series light truck.

Q: *What should I do?*
A: If you own one of these vehicles, you will receive a letter from us instructing you take your vehicle to the Ford or Lincoln/Mercury dealer of your choice and have the switch replaced free of charge. However, you do not have to wait for our letter. You may contact your dealer and arrange to have the switch replaced immediately if you choose, free of charge.

Q: *How long will it take?*
A: The repair procedure should take about one hour. But please contact your dealer in advance to schedule a time that is convenient for you.

Q: *What if I need additional help?*

A: You may contact your dealer anytime, or call our Ford Ignition Switch Recall Customer Information Line at 1-800-323-8400.

We're in business because people believe in or products. We make improvements because we believe we can make our products better. And at times we'll take a major step like this to make sure that people who buy a Ford, Lincoln or Mercury vehicle know that they bought more than a vehicle, they bought a company and a dealer organization that stands behind the cars and trucks they build and sell. This is our *Quality is Job 1* promise to you. Thank you for your patience and support.

Has Ford had a cultural change on product safety?

CASE 6.10: A TOY TO DIE FOR

Larami Corporation developed 1992's hottest toy, the Super Soaker. The high-pressure, high-volume squirt gun came in several sizes and fired powerful shots of liquid up to fifty feet away. Larami held 70 percent of the market because of its patented air compression system.

The Super Soaker and similar toys not only proved to be popular, they proved to be deadly. Young people loaded them with not only water, but bleach, ammonia, and urine. A fifteen-year-old Boston boy was killed and two others wounded in battles with these new-age squirt guns loaded not with water but household chemicals. Larami issued a one-page expression of sympathy for the family of the Boston boy and added that violence and misuse of the gun are things "we cannot control."

Boston's mayor, Raymond Flynn, asked retailers to stop selling the gun. A bill was introduced in the Michigan legislature to outlaw the large squirt guns. Woolworth's and Bradlee's pulled the toys from their shelves, and the Sharper Image catalog issued a statement saying it would donate all profits from the sales of the Super Soaker in Boston to charity. A toy industry analyst noted that putting a "Banned in Boston" sticker on the squirt guns may be the best way to sell more of them.

Discussion Questions

1. Should Larami go out of business in response to the death and injuries caused by the guns?
2. Should Larami halt production of the gun?
3. Should Larami control the availability of the gun in certain areas?
4. Should toy stores pull the best-selling water guns from their shelves?
5. Is Larami morally responsible for the death of the Boston boy and the injuries to the others?

CASE 6.11: THE TOBACCO INDUSTRY

The tobacco industry today faces several major legal and political issues, including litigation by smokers who have developed cancer and other tobacco-related illnesses, increasing concern about tobacco advertisements, the exposure of non-smokers to lung disease through passive smoke, antismoking ordinances, a pending Congressional settlement of class action litigation in exchange for various programs and taxes, and large investors divesting themselves of tobacco company stocks in the name of their ethical commitments.

Since the 1965 ban on television advertising of tobacco products and the ongoing surgeon general reports on the effects of smoking and secondary smoke, tobacco companies have been faced with increasing challenges with regard to product marketing. Norway and Finland outlawed all forms of tobacco ads in the 1970s, and Canada's ban on them took effect in January 1989.

To keep the market alive in the United States, tobacco firms offer over 300 brands of cigarettes that are somehow different by being slimmer, microfiltered or glitzier. R. J. Reynolds (RJR) came under fire in early 1990 for attempting to introduce "Uptown," a cigarette geared to African-American smokers. Only 30.5 percent of white males smoke compared to 39 percent of black males. RJR withdrew its test market plans for "Uptown" in the Philadelphia area after intense public pressure and a harsh attack by Louis W. Sullivan, then-Secretary of Health and Human Services, who noted that "Uptown's message is more disease, more suffering and more death for a group already bearing more than its share of smoking-related illness and mortality."[19]

Sullivan based his remarks on a study that showed blacks have a lung cancer rate 58 percent higher than whites. A Baltimore survey showed that while smoking and drinking ads make up 20 percent of billboard advertising in white communities, they comprise 78 percent in black neighborhoods.[20]

RJR responded to the criticisms by saying that it intended only to be upfront about its intentions: "We're an honest company. What do you say when the audience is going to be predominantly black?"[21]

Then, in February 1990, RJR announced plans to introduce "Dakota," a cigarette aimed at young, poorly educated white women, referred to as "virile females." Eighteen to twenty-four-year-old women are the only group of Americans whose rate of smoking is increasing. The Dakota advertising campaign focuses on favorite pastimes of these women, including: "cruising," "partying," "hot-rod shows," and "tractor pulls."[22]

Subsequent U.S. Surgeon Generals have focused on the youth-targeted messages of Joe Camel (see Case 5.1).

In spite of aggressive marketing, sales figures for the tobacco industry look worse than ever. Sales volume has been declining since 1988 although Third World markets are growing, with sales in those nations responsible for nearly 50 percent of tobacco companies' profits.

---

19. Michael Quinn, "Don't Aim That Pack at Us," *Time*, 29 January 1990, 60.

20. "RJR Takes 'Uptown' Ad out of Pack," *Mesa Tribune*, 20 January 1990, A9.

21. James R. Schifman, "Uptown's Fall Bodes Ill for Niche Brands," *Wall Street Journal*, 22 January 1990, B1.

22. "Cigarette's Target: The 'Virile' Female," *Arizona Republic*, 17 February 1990, A6.

Aggressive action by antismoking groups has significantly affected legislation and investors. During his tenure, Health and Human Services Secretary Sullivan proposed that states enact laws banning cigarette machines on college and university campuses to protect minors. In 1988, California voters passed an initiative adding a twenty-five cents-per-pack tax to cigarettes to fund a $28.6 million antismoking campaign targeting teens. In 1996, Arizona imposed a tax with the revenue to be used for a teen antismoking campaign.

A group called the Tobacco Divestment Group has urged universities to sell their tobacco stock holdings, refuse gifts from tobacco companies, and prohibit tobacco company sponsorship of campus events. In May 1990, then-Harvard President Derek Bok announced that the university had sold its tobacco holdings. Bok said Harvard was motivated "by a desire not to be associated as a shareholder with companies engaged in significant sales of products that create a substantial and unjustified risk of harm to other human beings."[23] Twenty two percent of TIAA-CREF beneficiaries voted in 1996 to divest their fund of all tobacco holdings. In 1998, Sara Lee divested itself of its tobacco subsidiary pursuant to demands from shareholders and the public alike. City University of New York also divested itself of $3.5 million in tobacco stocks. Johns Hopkins University sold its tobacco company holdings because the investments "undermine its efforts to fight cancer."[24]

In April 1990, the issue of passive smoking assumed a prominent position when the Environmental Protection Agency released a study showing that "passive" smoking causes 3,800 lung cancer deaths each year. "Passive smoking" is inhaling smoke generated by others smoking.[25] The April 1990 EPA study demonstrating a link between higher cancer rates and exposure to secondary smoke offered a new liability theory for nonsmokers. The American Heart Association has recommended that second-hand smoke be treated as an environmental toxin and be banned from offices and public places. Dr. Homayoun Kazemi, a physician who helped prepare the American Heart Association's position, stated, "In terms of carcinogenicity, there is nothing even close. The second-closest (environmental) cause of lung cancer would be asbestos."[26]

The industry was also experiencing setbacks in litigation. In 1989, Tony Cipollone recovered $400,000 in compensatory damages for the death of his wife, Rose, who had had lung cancer but continued to smoke. Cipollone based his case on the theory that at the time his wife became addicted to tobacco, there were inadequate warnings on cigarettes and ads enticed her to smoke by portraying it as safe and embraced by the medical profession.[27] One ad had praised L & M cigarettes as "Just What the Doctor Ordered."[28] In 1992, the Supreme Court upheld the verdict on the grounds that the companies failed to warn of the possible dangers of smoking. The verdicts in other tobacco product liability cases vacillate between victories

---

23. Kathleen Deveny and Joseph Pereira, "Tobacco Stakes Sold by Harvard," *Wall Street Journal*, 24 May 1990, B1.

24. "University Drops Tobacco Stocks," *Mesa Tribune*, 23 February 1991, A6.

25. Barbara Rosewicz and Albert R. Karr, "Smoking Curbs Get a New Life from EPA Plan," *Wall Street Journal*, 25 June 1990, B1.

26. "Heart Group Urges Ban on Secondhand Smoke," *Mesa Tribune*, 11 June 1992, A1, A6.

27. Stephen Koepp, "Tobacco's First Loss," *Time*, 27 June 1988, 49–50.

28. Lawrence Tell and Scot Ticer, 'A Pothole in Tobacco Road," *Business Week*, 27 June 1988, 32, *Cipollone v. Liggett Group, Inc.*, 505 U.S. 504 (1992).

and defeats for the industry, but the suits continue with new legal bases as more dangers are uncovered in new studies.[29]

A 1992 study linked mothers' smoking more than one pack of cigarettes a day to serious behavior problems in their children. Another 1992 study confirmed the hazards of passive smoke and resulted in congressional hearings on the issue

During the 1990s, 26 state attorneys general brought suit against the tobacco companies seeking recoupment of their states' public funds expended for the healthcare and treatment of indigent smokers (Medicaid recovery suits).

At the same time this state litigation was emerging, Jeffrey Nesbitt, a long-time Washington insider, began raising the regulatory issue of tobacco as an unregulated product that was a killer. Following the loss of his father to lung cancer in 1991, Mr. Nesbitt began developing consensus within the agency where he had worked since 1989, the Food and Drug Administration (FDA), to take regulatory steps. By 1994, he had developed information and an approach to regulation that centered around underage smokers. Dr. David Kessler, the head of the FDA, enlisted the support of the White House and began a campaign to regulate sale and advertising of tobacco to minors.

Also in 1994, Dr. Jeffrey Wigand, a former researcher with Brown & Williamson Tobacco Corp., came forward after seven tobacco industry executives testified, in an enormously contentious hearing before Congress, that they didn't believe nicotine was addictive. The executives testified as follows:

"I, too, believe that nicotine is not addictive."
—Donald S. Johnston, American Tobacco

"I believe that nicotine is not addictive."
—Thomas E. Sandefur, Jr., Brown & Williamson

"I believe that nicotine is not addictive."
—Edward A. Horrigan, Jr., Liggett Group

"The data that we have been able to see has all been statistical data that has not convinced me that smoking causes death."
—Andrew H. Tisch, Lorillard Tobacco

"Oral tobacco has not been established as a cause of oral cancer."
—Joseph Taddeo, U.S. Tobacco

"Cigarettes and nicotine clearly do not meet the classic definition of addiction."
—James W. Johnston, R.J. Reynolds

"Philip Morris does not manipulate nor independently control the level of nicotine."
—William I. Campbell, Philip Morris

Dr. Wigand made a public disclosure that the companies relied on nicotine addiction. Indeed, Dr. Wigand was attacked with a 500-page dossier on his personal life that was released to the public. Dr. Wigand's information was revealed publicly on ABC TV's "Day One" news program and Philip Morris filed a $10 billion suit against ABC. ABC settled the suit with an apology for its statement that companies "add significant amounts of nicotine from outside sources."

---

29. William Glaberson and Pete Engardio, "A Jury Takes Tobacco Companies off the Hook–for Now," *Business Week*, 13 January 1986, 32; *see also*, Smart, "It Takes More than Black Robes to Scare Tobacco Companies," *Business Week*, 8 April 1991, 34.

Dr. Wigand was kept from television interviews because of a clause in his employment agreement that prohibited disclosure of company proprietary information after his departure from the company.

In 1995, upon the advice of political consultant Dick Morris, President Clinton took on the tobacco issue, and had a turning popularity point in the 1996 presidential campaign when his opponent, Bob Dole, publicly expressed doubts about nicotine's addictiveness.

In August, 1996, a Florida case brought by Grady Carter brought the tobacco industry its first loss in a case based solely on product liability[30]—the jury awarded Carter $750,000 from Brown & Williamson.

By early 1997, the Liggett Group, smallest of the U.S. tobacco companies (1.9% of the market), broke rank with the other companies, and agreed to a settlement of litigation pending in 22 of the 26 states. Bennett LeBow, the CEO of Liggett, agreed to pay 25% of its pretax profit for the next 25 years to a fund to be used to aid legal efforts against the tobacco industry. Liggett agreed to place warnings on cigarette packs that they are addictive.

In mid-1997, the tobacco companies, facing the suits by attorneys general, private lawsuits around the country, and a class action lawsuit in Florida by flight attendants based on cancer caused by exposure to second-hand smoke, came to the negotiating table.

A deal was reached with the following provisions:

- Tobacco companies will pay $368 billion. Money will go to health care for children, medical care for indigent citizens with tobacco-related illnesses, anti-smoking education, free stop-smoking classes and to finance state stings on retailers. Part of this pact is punitive, for past wrongs and misconduct.
- Food and Drug Administration will regulate nicotine, but not ban it until 2009, and then only with Congress' approval.
- FDA must approve any new ingredients added to tobacco.
- No advertising on outdoor billboards, at sports venues or on the Internet.
- Human images or cartoon characters cannot be used in tobacco advertising.
- Larger and stronger wording printed on cigarette packages, including SMOKING CAN KILL YOU.
- Under-age tobacco use must drop by 30 percent in five years, 50 percent in seven years and 60 percent in 10 years.
- No more cigarettes sold in vending machines.
- No smoking in most public places and workplaces, except some restaurants and bars.
- No smoking in fast-food and similar restaurants frequented by children.
- Tobacco companies must fund a massive anti-smoking advertising campaign, but will have no say in its content.
- Sick smokers can still sue for actual damages, but can collect punitive damages only on future wrongdoing.
- All class-action suits against tobacco companies are banned.

With the Congressional session that began in January 1998, debate over the approval of the tobacco settlement was ongoing and intense. It was during this time that documents revealing tobacco companies' intentions to court younger

---

30. The *Cipollone* case was unique in that recovery was based on the misleading nature of the ads and the failure to warn of dangers rather than just the inherent danger of cigarettes as a product.

smokers were revealed and produced outrage that translated to some members of Congress proposing greater penalties. Also, in February 1998, documents revealed that R.J. Reynolds apparently altered nicotine delivery to smokers in order to increase the "kick" of its Winston brand.

While debate was ongoing, the tobacco industry agreed to a $15 billion settlement in a Texas product liability suit with the $15 billion to be paid over 25 years to reimburse the state for treating smoking-related illnesses.

In late January, 1998, the Justice Department announced it was launching an antitrust investigation of the tobacco companies for alleged price collusion.

The April, 1998, Congressional version of the settlement required tobacco companies to do the following:

- Pay $516 billion over 25 years to settle legal claims and finance antismoking campaigns (the cost of this plank would be passed on to buyers with a $1.10 price per pack increase)
- Ban on billboard ads
- Ban on sponsorships where at least 75% of event attenders are not 18 or above

Despite mounting pressure, RJR CEO, Steven Goldstone, on April 8, 1998, rejected the Congressional proposal for a tobacco settlement and promised to fight any efforts by the federal government to raise tobacco prices and restrict tobacco advertising. The industry announced with its rejection of the settlement a campaign focusing on the issues of "coercion" and "Big-Brother-type" Congress. Congress still had the authority to raise prices and authorize the FDA to regulate or ban tobacco, but First Amendment protections would preclude its banishment of billboards and sponsorships (the ad restriction components). An industry-united full-page ad read as follows:

We Agreed to Change the Way We Do Business . . . Not To Go Out of Business[31]

Last June, our industry agreed to historic concessions that would change forever the way tobacco products are made, marketed and sold in this country.

While we are still committed to change, regrettably we believe the political process has ended any prospect for achieving a rational, comprehensive tobacco solution. Instead of mounting the kind of massive and sustained assault on underage tobacco use that the politicians all say they favor, Congress is now considering legislation that is not only unconstitutional, but also would:

- Impose half a *trillion* dollars in new taxes on the American people.
- Allow an unelected federal agency to make it illegal for adults to buy tobacco products.
- Create a black market in tobacco products.
- Establish 17 new federal bureaucracies.
- Devastate the tobacco industry and cost thousands of jobs among retailers, wholesalers, distributors, growers and others.

For our employees and the millions of Americans who use our products and work with the industry, we must oppose this effort. We agreed to fundamental change in the way we do business, but we cannot agree to changes that would put us out of business.

Philip Morris Incorporated • R.J. Reynolds Tobacco Company
Brown & Williamson Tobacco Corporation
Lorillard Tobacco Company • United States Tobacco Company

---

31. From *USA Today*, 10 April 1998, 7A.

Discussion Questions

1. In his testimony in the Minnesota trial to recover Medicaid costs, Geoffrey Bible, chairman and CEO of Philip Morris said, "I think we have a duty to make as safe a product as it possibly could," and "[We have] a duty to make the public aware of risk factors." Is this a company's moral or legal responsibility?

2. Are there any differences between the "Uptown" and "Dakota" marketing strategies and other consumer-oriented marketing?

3. Is it moral for tobacco companies to sell their products?

4. Evaluate the postures of Harvard, Johns Hopkins, NYU, and Sara Lee in divesting themselves of tobacco company stock.

5. Evaluate the 1994 testimony of the executives on the addictiveness of nicotine. In 1997, the executives recanted that testimony. Was there an ethical breach? A moral responsibility?

6. Is freedom of choice an issue in the sale of tobacco? Is it an issue in advertising tobacco products?

7. Americans smoke 1 billion cigarettes per day. Fifteen billion cigarettes re smoked around the world each day. Philip Morris's earnings are $30 billion per year. Tobacco companies are at the top of any list of profitability. What impact will the proposed settlement have? Economically, is it wise? Ethically, will it accomplish anything?

8. Evaluate the issue of passive smoke. Are the rights of nonsmokers violated by the presence of smoke? Is this issue still emerging?

CASE 6.12: ATVs: DANGER ON WHEELS

Honda Motor Company, Ltd.; Yamaha Motor Company, Ltd.; Suzuki Motors Company, Ltd.; Kawasaki Heavy Industries, Ltd.; and Polaris Industries all made various types of motorcycles and all-terrain vehicles (ATVs) during the late 1970s and 1980s. Honda was the leading seller of ATVs, offering a full range of three-wheel models. It even made a very small three-wheel ATV for children ages four through ten that it advertised at the height of the market in the mid-1980s. The fat-wheeled vehicles that look like large tricycles were advertised as able to conquer all land surfaces with great ease. Suzuki's ads said its ATV would "embarrass the wind."

The ATV was introduced in 1977 by Honda; several other manufacturers entered the market in the following year. Yamaha and Kawasaki ATVs were larger in size and motor capacity and carried higher price tags than Honda's.

In 1978, based on a complaint from the National Association of Emergency Room Physicians (NAERP) and the American Neurological Society (ANS), the Consumer Product Safety Commission began investigating ATVs and their use and misuse. The commission's reports, which incorporated information from NAERP and ANS, found that:

1. ATV accidents were increasing dramatically:[32]

---

32. Daniel B. Moskowitz, "Why ATVs Could Land in a Heap of Trouble," *Business Week*, 30 November 1987, 38. The numbers do vary in press releases and according to various groups.

	ATV-Related Emergency Room Admissions	Deaths from ATV Accidents
1982	8,600	26
1983	26,900	85
1984	63,900	153
1985	85,900	246
1986	86,400	268

Of all the fatalities over the five-year period, 165 involved children ages eleven and younger, while 47 percent of the total involved children ages sixteen and younger.

2. Of all ATV-related injuries, 90 percent involved people under the age of thirty and 70 percent involved those under the age of eighteen.

3. In some areas, ATV-related injuries accounted for 45 percent of all emergency care on weekends.

4. Ninety percent of all injuries happened to experienced ATV riders (those who had logged more than twenty-five hours of riding time).

5. Leg injuries were common, with spiral fractures being the most frequent form.

6. Many injuries requiring emergency care were leg burns caused by riders holding their legs too close to ATV engines.

Dr. Ralph R. Fine, codirector of the National Spinal Cord Injury Statistical Center, testified before a House committee about his concerns: "We were seeing a disproportionate number of spinal cord injuries resulting from three wheeler or ATV crashes. These are dangerously deceptive, deceptively dangerous vehicles."[33]

Honda was aware of the report and submitted a study to the Consumer Product Safety Commission that showed the accidents with injuries happened when ATVs were misused. Referred to in the Honda report as "hotdogging," misuse included driving too fast, climbing hills at ninety-degree angles, going through rapidly moving water, and using ramps for jumping.

Between 1982 and 1986, there were more than 50,000 ATV-related injuries. By 1986, 2.1 million ATVs at an average price of $2,000 each were in use. Between 1982 and 1988, 858 people were killed in ATV accidents, many of them young children. A Consumer Product Safety Commission report concluded, "Children under 12 years of age are unable to operate any size ATV safely."[34] State attorneys general began efforts to regulate ATV use in 1986. Texas Assistant Attorney General Stephen Gardner stated, "These are killer machines. They should not be allowed."[35] The CPSC tried to have the industry sales to sixteen-year-olds and younger banned, but was unsuccessful.

After the report, Yamaha introduced a four-wheel ATV, including one model with two seats. Yamaha also undertook a dealer education program and issued an instruction manual with the vehicles to encourage responsible operation.

Roy Janson of the American All-Terrain Vehicle Association, a subsidiary of the American Motorcyclist Association, stated at congressional hearings on ATVs:

---

33. "Public Safety: All-Terrain Vehicles," *National Safety and Health News*, August 1985, 78–80.

34. Randolph Schmid, "Safety Panel Tackles All-Terrain Cycle Issue," *Phoenix Gazette*, 19 November 1986, A14.

35. Daniel B. Moskowitz, "Why ATVs Could Land in a Heap of Trouble," *Business Week*, 30 November 1987, 38.

Problems result primarily from how a vehicle is used rather than from its design. When ATVs are used as intended, they present no unreasonable risk to their operators. The major problems related to three-wheel ATV injuries are the failure of users to wear proper safety equipment while operating ATVs and using these vehicles in areas not recommended for ATV recreation. User education and information programs are clearly the most effective means for addressing the problems relating to misuse.[36]

In 1980, major nationally franchised rental centers ceased renting ATVs because of liability concerns.

In 1986, the Consumer Product Safety Commission published proposed ATV regulations that included these key provisions:

1. No ATVs below certain size limits would be manufactured. ATV riders would have to weigh at least 100 pounds and be at least sixteen years old.
2. All ATVs would have four wheels.
3. All manufacturers would undertake educational ad campaigns on the use and dangers of ATVs. No promotional advertising would be permitted in any media form.

While the proposed regulations were being debated, ATV accidents continued to climb steadily. Of particular concern was the marked increase in severe injuries, such as spinal cord and head injuries, to children six to ten years of age. At the same time, some manufacturers continued to provide studies to the Consumer Product Safety Commission indicating misuse, not design, was the primary cause of ATV accidents.

By 1987, the Association of Trial Lawyers of America had established a clearinghouse for the exchange of information on ATV claims, and over 400 lawsuits had been filed. Three-fourths of the suits were being settled for a typical payment of $1 million.

Because of increased, widely publicized objections from consumer groups, as well as a call for action from the American Academy of Pediatrics, the commission recalled three-wheel ATVs in May 1988 and halted their manufacture. Meanwhile, manufacturers accelerated production of four-wheel vehicles. After judicial review of the commission's order and agreements were reached with the five manufacturers, the commission withdrew the recall but successfully implemented the ban on future sales.

Some consumer groups, however, still felt a recall was necessary. James Florio, a Congressman from New Jersey, said, "How can anyone truly concerned with safety in effect say "tough luck' to people who currently own these unsafe vehicles?"[37]

However, the manufacturers did agree to take the following steps:

Offer cash incentives to encourage owners of ATVs purchased after December 30, 1987, to enroll in training programs.

Revise warning labels and owner's manuals to outline the dangers of vehicle operation.

Set up a consumer telephone hotline.

Restrict sales of ATVs with engine displacements greater than ninety cubic centimeters displacement (CCD) to people sixteen years or older; children under twelve years would not be permitted to operate vehicles with engines greater than seventy CCD.

---

36. "Public Safety," 79.
37. "Outlawing a Three-Wheeler," *Time*, 11 January 1988, 59.

Scrap a provision in the preliminary agreement that would have required ATV purchasers to sign a form acknowledging the risks of operating the vehicle.[38]

Honda sent out the following "Safety Alert" to owners of its ATVs in January 1988:

The Consumer Product Safety Commission has concluded that all-terrain vehicles (ATVs) may present a risk of death or severe injury in certain circumstances. While accidents may occur for many reasons:

Over 900 people, including many children, have died in accidents associated with ATVs since 1982.

Many people have become severely paralyzed or suffered severe internal injuries as a result of accidents associated with ATVs.

Thousands of people have been treated in hospital emergency rooms every month for injuries received while riding an ATV.

Because of this, the United States government has filed a lawsuit against all manufacturers and distributors of ATVs asking the court to declare that ATVs are hazardous and to order the manufacturers and distributors to take actions to protect ATV riders. The distributors, while contesting the validity of the allegations made by the government, are presently engaged in discussions with the government to resolve these issues without litigation.

You should be aware that an ATV is not a toy and may be dangerous to operate. An ATV handles different from other vehicles, including motorcycles and cars. According to the Consumer Product Safety Commission, at ATV can roll over on the rider or violently throw the rider without warning, and even hitting a small rock, bump, or hole at low speed can upset the ATV.

To avoid death or severe personal injury:
Never drive an ATV without proper instruction. *Take a training course.* Beginning drivers should receive training from a certified instructor. . . .

Never lend your ATV to anyone who has not taken a training course or has not been driving an ATV for at least a year.

Always follow these age recommendations:

A child under 12 years old should never drive an ATVwith engine size 70 CCD or greater.

A child under 16 years old should never drive an ATV with engine size greater than 90 CCD.

Never allow a child under 16 years old to drive an ATV without adult supervision. Children need to be observed carefully because not all children have the strength, size, skills, or judgment needed to drive an ATV safely.

Never drive an ATV after consuming alcohol or drugs.

Never carry a passenger on an ATV; carrying a passenger may upset the balance of the ATV and may cause it to go out of control.

Never drive an ATV on pavement. The vehicle is not designed to be used on paved surfaces and may be difficult to control.

Never drive an ATV on a public road, even a dirt or gravel one, because you may not be able to avoid colliding with other vehicles. Also, driving on a public road with an ATV may be against the law.

Never attempt to do "wheelies," jumps, or other stunts.

---

38. Matt DeLorenzo, "ATV Companies Agree to Warn, Train Owners," *Automotive News*, 21 March 1988, 58.

Never drive an ATV without a good helmet and goggles. You should also wear boots, gloves, heavy trousers, and a long-sleeve shirt.

Never drive an ATV at excessive speeds.

Always be extremely careful when driving an ATV, especially when approaching hills, turns, and obstacles and when driving on unfamiliar or rough terrain.

Always read the owner's manual carefully and follow the operating procedures described.

Discussion Questions

1. Is the ATV too dangerous to be sold?
2. Are the warnings and the ban on future ATV sales sufficient?
3. If you were in marketing for one of the five firms, could you continue your sales efforts?
4. Should the three-wheel ATV have been recalled?
5. Is the cost of a recall just too high?

CASE 6.13: TYLENOL: THE PRODUCT RESCUE

In 1982, twenty-three-year-old Diane Elsroth died after taking a Tylenol capsule laced with cyanide. Within five days of her death, seven more people died from taking tainted Tylenol purchased from stores in the Chicago area.

Tylenol generated $525 million per year for McNeil Consumer Products, Inc., a subsidiary of Johnson & Johnson. The capsule form of the pain reliever represented 30 percent of Tylenol sales. McNeil's marketing studies indicated that consumers found the capsules easy to swallow and believed, without substantiation, that Tylenol in capsule form worked faster than Tylenol tablets.

The capsules' design, however, meant they could be taken apart, tainted, and then restored to the packaging without evidence of tampering. After the Chicago poisonings, which were never solved, McNeil and Johnson & Johnson executives were told at a meeting that processes for sealing the capsules had been greatly improved, but no one could give the assurance that they were tamperproof.

The executives realized that abandoning the capsule would give their competitors, Bristol-Myers (Excedrin) and American Home Products (Anacin), a market advantage, plus the cost would be $150 million just for 1982. Jim Burke, CEO of Johnson & Johnson, told the others that without a tamperproof package for the capsules, they would risk the survival of not only Tylenol but Johnson & Johnson. The executives decided to abandon the capsule.

Frank Young, a Food and Drug Administration commissioner, stated at the time, "This is a matter of Johnson & Johnson's own business judgment, and represents a responsible action under tough circumstances."[39]

Johnson & Johnson quickly developed "caplets"—tablets in the shape of a capsule, then offered consumers a coupon for a bottle of the new caplets if they turned in their capsules. Within five days of the announcement of the capsule recall and caplets offer, 200,000 consumers had responded. Johnson & Johnson had eliminated

---

39. "Drug Firm Pulls All Its Capsules off the Market," *Arizona Republic*, 18 February 1986, A2.

a key product in its line—one that customers clearly preferred—in the interest of safety. Otto Lerbinger of Boston University's College of Communication cited Johnson & Johnson as a "model of corporate social responsibility for its actions."[40]

President Ronald Reagan, addressing a group of business executives, said, "Jim Burke, of Johnson & Johnson, you have our deepest admiration. In recent days you have lived up to the very highest ideals of corporate responsibility and grace under pressure."[41]

Within one year of the Tylenol poisonings, Johnson & Johnson regained its 40 percent market share for Tylenol.

Discussion Questions

1. Was the risk small that there would be other poisonings of Tylenol capsules?
2. Were the shareholders' interests ignored in the decision to take a $150 million dollar write-off and a possible loss of $525 million in annual sales by abandoning the capsules?
3. Suppose that you were a Tylenol competitor. Would you have continued selling your capsules?
4. Was Burke's action a long-term decision? Did it take into account the interests of all stakeholders?
5. What financial arguments could be made against the decision to abandon the capsule?
6. Were the risks appropriately balanced in this case?
7. Following the poisonings, the federal government developed packaging regulations for nonprescription drugs. Should manufacturers have developed the tamperproof packaging on their own?
8. General Robert Wood Johnson, the CEO of Johnson & Johnson from 1932 to 1963, wrote a credo for his company that states the company's first responsibility is to the people who use its products and services; the second responsibility is to its employees; the third to the community and its environment; and the fourth to the stockholders. Johnson and his successors have believed that if the credo's first three responsibilities are met, the stockholders will be well served. Does Johnson & Johnson follow its credo?

---

40. Pat Guy and Clifford Glickman, "J & J Uses Candor in Crisis," *USA Today*, 12 February 1986, 2B.
41. "The Tylenol Rescue," *Newsweek*, 3 March 1986, 52.

Section C
Product Quality

Quality is a management buzz word. Managing for total quality is how product quality is ensured.

Case 6.14: Preventable Potholes

Ed Dietrich owns Gerty's Gravel, a highway construction firm. Before going on his own, Dietrich spent fifteen years working for another firm where he learned that U.S. highways have a life expectancy of only twenty years and consist of three layers. Layer one, the bottom, is two to six feet of compacted original soil; layer two is twelve inches of concrete; and the final layer is four inches of asphalt.

In contrast, European highways are expected to last forty years and have six layers: five to six feet of backfilled new soil on the bottom; four inches of asphalt separation; ten inches of gravel drainage; ten inches of concrete; four to six inches of asphalt base; and, finally, three inches of special asphalt.

Dietrich also discovered that European asphalt firms spend up to twenty times that of U.S. firms on research and development. For example, in France, a firm has discovered that road life can be doubled by adding a polymer similar to shredded Tupperware to the asphalt; the cost is 8 percent more than standard asphalt.

Dietrich's business strategy is to build roads in the European style, including adding the French polymer. His costs, however, will be 25 to 30 percent higher than that of competitors that build in the traditional U.S. way. Dietrich also faces the problem that state and local governments award contracts to the lowest bidder, even though the work may be sloppy and the materials less than top quality.

Dietrich could win as many projects as he wants if he ignores the European technology and builds roads the way they have been built in the United States since the 1950s. Dietrich tells his road supervisor, Matt Cochran:

> The U.S. roads are a mess. The latest figures from the Federal Highway Administration are that 52 percent of our interstate highways and other major roads are rated "low fair" or rutted, cracked and unfit for high-speed travel. That translates to a cost of $120

billion a year for resulting accidents and congestion. I want to build the right kinds of roads, but I'll never get this business going if I don't underbid. Believe me, I know all the tricks of getting the prices down. I can outbid anyone. But the road won't last.

A provision requiring contractors to guarantee their roads was eliminated in a highway bill passed by Congress in 1991; the Associated General Contractors objected that road warranties would just invite litigation.

Cochran responds to Dietrich, "Just build the roads. You don't have to give a guarantee. It's what they want—roads, quick and cheap. Besides, who's really hurt by a few potholes here and there?"

Discussion Questions

1. Would it bother you to build cheap roads if you knew how to build better ones?
2. You are not legally required to give a guarantee. Does it bother you to sell a shoddy product?
3. Will Dietrich have difficulty running a business built on underbidding at the expense of quality?
4. Could Dietrich find a market niche for his firm based on his dilemma?
5. Do the builders of shoddy roads have moral responsibility for injuries and accidents caused when the roads deteriorate in a few years?

CASE 6.15: GENERIC CONSULTING

Towers Perrin, an international management consulting firm, had created a diversity consulting division to help companies deal with issues of diversity in the work force. The credo for this Towers Perrin division was, "Prescription without diagnosis is malpractice." Towers Perrin would not recommend a diversity plan for a company without first studying its structure, demographics, industry, etc.

Towers Perrin had contracts for diversity consulting with Nissan USA and Thomson Consumer Electronics, a French-based electronics firm. Both companies paid over $100,000 for a 105-page report and recommendation. The reports are very similar and have, in many instances, identical language despite the differences between the two companies in products, structure, location, and work force.

In fact, Towers Perrin furnished the following advice to Thomson Consumer Electronics, Inc.; Nissan Motor Co. U.S.A.; Harris Bank in Chicago; Midwest Power, now MidAmerican Energy Co.; and large subsidiaries of Westinghouse Electric Corp., Bechtel Group, Inc. and Wackenhut Corp.

- Separate the concept of Affirmative Action from that of managing diversity.
- Rely primarily on established formal media so that diversity becomes viewed as an integral on-going process.
- Carefully define both internal and external audience. All management and supervisory levels should receive messages first as their buy-in is essential.
- Ensure that all leaders and managers understand that diversity communication must be continual and constant. Message repetition is essential.

- Develop clear and simple messages related to work/life that have the same meaning for the receiver as they do for the sender.
- As the Diversity Strategy process becomes more integral to [the client's] culture, messages can become more subtle and subliminal.
- Incorporate diversity training in management leadership training.
- Incorporate diversity training perspectives in the implementation of the new performance management process.
- Establish management accountability for effective performance management of diverse employees.
- Further develop the informal mentoring process to become more formal and inclusive.
- Effectively tie high-visibility developmental assignments and promotional activities to the accountability for embracing and managing diversity.
- Create and use diversity-based behavioral competencies as prerequisites for managerial and leadership assignments.
- Use the diversity strategy to invite more creativity and employee empowerment.
- Focus on flexibility in approaches to work, policies, and procedures to help eliminate the artificial barriers to empowerment.
- Emphasize diversity in succession planning.
- Emphasize diversity in all promotional activities.
- Cluster and communicate diversity benefits under the work/life banner.
- Experiment with highly flexible pilot work arrangements and evaluate their effectiveness.

NOTE: There are minor wording differences in the reports for Harris Bank and Midwest Power. For example, in the second recommendation, above, the word "primarily" is omitted.

Discussion Questions

1. What risk does Tower Perrin run by issuing two such similar reports?
2. Will this nationally-reported story affect Towers Perrin's business?

SECTION D
CUSTOMER PRIVACY

How much should businesses know about you? Should they give your name to other firms for direct-mail advertising?

CASE 6.16: CREDIT CARD AND BUYING PRIVACY

A consumer's name can be sold for as little as $35 and as much as $200. Credit card users' names and purchases are grouped, regrouped, sold, and resold to companies interested in targeting them because of their income, buying habits, or location. Without these lists of names, direct marketers are forced to use a shotgun approach that may or may not bring results. But if a marketer knows you own a luxury car, you are a good target for car alarm marketing. If the marketer knows you buy clothes via catalog purchases, you are a good target for a new clothing catalog. American Express, for example, breaks its card holders into six spending tiers based on card use, including "Rodeo Drive Chic," "Fifth Avenue Sophisticated," "Fashion Conscious," and "Value Seeker." The lists are then used in sales promotions by Saks Fifth Avenue, American Airlines, Hertz and Marriott Hotels.

As technology has improved, the ability to collect and refine lists of potential customers has grown. Lotus developed a CD-ROM database called MarketPlace that listed consumers but withdrew it after receiving 30,000 letters and calls from people who did not want to be on it. Lotus also received objections from the American Civil Liberties Union and Computer Professionals for Social Responsibility. A recent survey by Equifax, one of the country's top three credit reporting agencies, found that 76 percent of the public feel that the sale of personal information about income, home ownership, and credit history is unacceptable.

Steve Toman, chairman of the Direct Marketers Association, warned in 1988 that information businesses have to be psychologically and financially prepared to defend themselves and their product. He warned that "strict laws in the areas of privacy and ethics could virtually put us out of business."[42]

In California, the Personal Information Integrity Act that passed in 1994 required firms to notify individuals within seven days each time information about them was collected or transmitted. Based on the right of correction established by the federal Consumer Credit Reporting Act, the legislation allows consumers a chance to correct the information collected about them. The requirements of the Act probably triple the costs of the data collection firms and will force most direct-mail houses out of business.

Information businesses are attempting to regulate themselves. Equifax is experimenting with a database of people who agree to offer information that will be used for direct-mail marketing in exchange for $250 per year in discounts on products for which they are targeted. Equifax no longer sells lists drawn from its confidential credit files to direct-mail firms because it believes such sales to be "morally wrong."

New York's Attorney General Robert Adams, an advocate for the rights of credit card users, stated: "A consumer who pays with a credit card is entitled to as much privacy as one who pays with cash or check. Credit card holders should not unknowingly have their spending patterns and life-styles analyzed and categorized for the use of merchants fishing for prospects."[43]

Adams's office and American Express Company entered into an agreement by which American Express will notify customers that their names could be sold for marketing purposes and give them the option of being excluded from marketing efforts. As part of the agreement, American Express acknowledged that it was using information about card holders' life-styles and spending habits to engage in joint marketing efforts with merchants.

The House Banking Committee scrapped a measure to bar credit bureaus from selling private financial data to direct marketers, but the Federal Trade Commission continues to call the practice illegal. However, proposed amendments to the Fair Credit Reporting Act would require credit bureaus to give consumers the right to opt out of lists that will be used by marketers.

Discussion Questions

1. Is using credit card information for marketing "morally wrong"?
2. Is there a difference between a credit reporting agency selling consumer information and a credit card company selling it?
3. What about the rights of people who do not feel their privacy is violated and would welcome the targeted marketing efforts? How are they affected?
4. Is selling the lists illegal?
5. Should information firms voluntarily impose restrictions on or develop standard procedures for selling lists of names?

42. "Privacy and Ethics Issues Affect List Industry," *Direct Marketing News*, October 1988, 8.

43. Peter Pae, "American Express Discloses It Gives Merchants Data on Cardholders' Habits," *Wall Street Journal*, 14 May 1992, B4.

UNIT SEVEN
BUSINESS AND ITS
STAKEHOLDERS

The decisions of a business affect many people, especially those who have a stake in the continuing profitable operation of the business. Examining the interests of its stakeholders before reaching a decision in an ethical dilemma can be an effective tool for strategic planning.

SECTION A
SHAREHOLDERS' INTERESTS

The interests of shareholders and the interests of management are not always the same. Whose interest should prevail?

CASE 7.1: ICE-T, THE *BODY COUNT* ALBUM, AND SHAREHOLDER UPRISINGS

Ice-T (Tracy Morrow), a black rap artist signed under the Time Warner label, released an album called *Body Count* in 1992 that contained a controversial song, "Cop Killer." The lyrics included: "I've got my twelve-gauge sawed-off . . . I'm 'bout to dust some cops off . . . die, pig, die."

The song set off a storm of protest from law enforcement groups. At the annual meeting of Time Warner at the Beverly Wilshire Hotel, 1,100 shareholders, as well as police representatives and their spokesman, Charlton Heston, denounced Time Warner executives in a five-hour session on the album and its content. Heston noted that the compact disc had been shipped to radio stations in small replicas of body bags. One police officer said the company had "lost its moral compass, or never had it." Others said that Time Warner seemed to cultivate these types of artists. One shareholder claimed that Time Warner was always "pushing the envelope" with its artists, such as Madonna with her "sex" book, and its products, such as the film *The Last Temptation of Christ*, which drew large protests from religious groups. Another shareholder pointed out that Gerald Levin, Time Warner president, promised a stuttering-awareness group that the cartoon character Porky Pig would be changed after they made far less vocal protests.

Levin responded that the album would not be pulled. He defended it as "depicting the despair and anger that hang in the air of every American inner city, not advocating attacks on police." Levin announced Time Warner would sponsor a TV forum for artists, law enforcement officials, and others to discuss such topics as racism and free speech. At the meeting, Levin also announced a four-for-one stock split and a 12 percent increase in Time Warner's dividend.

The protests continued after the meeting. Philadelphia's municipal pension fund decided to sell $1.6 million in Time Warner holdings to protest the Ice-T song. Said Louis J. Campione, a police officer and member of the city's Board of Pensions and Retirement, "It's fine that somebody would express their opinions, but we don't have to support it."

Several CEOs responded to Levin's and Time Warner's support of the song.[1] Roger Salquist, CEO of Calgene, Inc., noted:

> I'm outraged. I think the concept of free speech has been perverted. It's anti-American, it's antihumanity, and there is no excuse for it.
>
> I hope it kills them. It's certainly not something I tolerate, and I find their behavior offensive as a corporation.
>
> If you can increase sales with controversy without harming people, that's one thing. [But Time-Warner's decision to support Ice-T] is outside the bounds of what I consider acceptable behavior and decency in this country.

David Geffen, chairmen of Geffen Records, who refused to release Geto Boys records because of lyrics, said:

> The question is not about business, it is about responsibility. Should someone make money by advocating the murder of policemen? To say that this whole issue is not about profit is silly. It certainly is not about artistic freedom.
>
> If the album were about language, sex or drugs, there are people on both sides of these issues. But when it comes down to murder, I don't think there is any part of society that approves of it.... I wish [Time Warner] would show some sensitivity by donating the profits to a fund for wounded policemen.

Jerry Greenfield, co-founder of Ben & Jerry's Homemade, Inc., responded that "songs like "Cop Killer" aren't constructive, but we as a society need to look at what we've created. I don't condone cop killing. [But] to reach a more just and equitable society everyone's voice must be heard."

Neal Fox, CEO of A. Sulka & Company (an apparel retailer owned by Luxco Investments), said:

> As a businessperson, my inclination is to say that Time Warner management has to be consistent. Once you've decided to get behind this product and support it, you can't express feelings of censorship. They didn't have recourse.
>
> Also, they are defending flag and country for the industry. If they bend to pressures regarding the material, it opens a Pandora's box for all creative work being done in the entertainment industry.
>
> On a personal basis, I abhor the concept, but on a corporate basis, I understand their reasoning.

John W. Hatsopoulos, executive vice president of Thermo Electron Corporation, had this to say:

> I think the fact that a major U.S. corporation would almost encourage kids to attack the police force is horrible. Time Warner is a huge corporation. That they would encourage something like this for a few bucks.... You know about yelling fire in a crowded theater.
>
> I was so upset I was looking at [Thermo Electron's] pension plan to see if we owned any Time-Warner stock [in order to sell it]. But we don't own any.

---

1. Reprinted with permission of *The Wall Street Journal* © 1992 Dow Jones & Company, Inc. All rights reserved.

Bud Konheim, CEO of Nicole Miller, Ltd., weighed in with:

I don't think that people in the media can say that advertising influences consumers to buy cars or shirts, and then argue that violence on television or in music has no impact. The idea of media is to influence people's minds, and if you are inciting people to riot, it's very dangerous.

It's also disappointing that they chose to defend themselves. It was a knee-jerk reaction instead of seizing the role to assert moral leadership. They had a great opportunity. Unfortunately, I don't think they will pay for this decision because there is already so much dust in people's eyes.

George Sanborn, CEO of Sanborn, Inc., said: "Would you release the album if it said, 'Kill a Jew or bash a fag'? I think we all know what the answer would be. They're doing it to make money."

Mark Nathanson, CEO of Falcon Cable Systems Company, responded: "If you aren't happy with the product, you don't have to buy it. I might not like what [someone like Ice-T] has to say, but I would vigorously defend his right to express his viewpoint."

Stoney M. Stubbs, Jr., chairman of Frozen Food Express Industries, Inc., commented: "The more attention these types of things get, the better the products sell. I don't particularly approve of the way they play on people's emotions, but from a business standpoint [Time Warner is] probably going to make some money off it. They're protecting the people that make them the money . . . the artists."

Despite the flap over the album, sales were less than spectacular. It reached number 32 on the Billboard Top 200 album chart and sold 300,000 copies.

On June 29, 1992, Levin defended Time Warner's position in the *Wall Street Journal*:

Time Warner is determined to be a global force for encouraging the confrontation of ideas. We know that profits are the source of our strength and independence, of our ability to produce and distribute the work of our artists and writers, but we won't retreat in the face of threats of boycotts or political grandstanding. In the short run, cutting and running would be the surest and safest way to put this controversy behind us and get on with our business. But in the long run, it would be a destructive precedent. It would be a signal to all the artists and journalists inside and outside Time Warner that if they wish to be heard, then they must tailor their minds and souls to fit the reigning orthodoxies.

In the weeks and months ahead, Time Warner intends to use the debate engendered by the uproar over this one song to create a forum in which we can bring together the different sides in this controversy. We will invest in fostering the open discussion of the violent tensions that Ice-T's music has exposed.

We're under no illusions. We know all the wounds can't be healed by such a process or all the bitterness—on both sides—talked out of existence. But we believe that the future of our country—indeed, of our world—is contained in the commitment to truth and free expression, in the refusal to run away.[2]

By August 1992, protests against the song had grown and sales suffered. Ice-T made the decision himself to withdraw "Cop Killer" from the *Body Count* album. Time Warner asked music stores to exchange the *Body Count* CDs for ones without "Cop Killer." Some store owners refused, saying there were much worse records.

---

2. Reprinted with permission of *The Wall Street Journal* © 1992 Dow Jones & Company, Inc. All rights reserved.

Former Geto Boys member, Willie D., said Ice-T's free speech rights were violated. "We're living in a communist country and everyone's afraid to say it," he said.

Following the flap over the song, the Time Warner board met to establish general company policies to bar distribution of music deemed inappropriate. By February 1993, Time Warner and Ice-T agreed that Ice-T would leave the Time Warner label because of "creative differences." The split came after Time Warner executives objected to Ice-T's proposed cover for his new album, which showed black men attacking whites.

By May 1993, Time Warner's board was steering the company into more family-oriented entertainment. It began its transition with the 1993 release of such movies as *Dennis the Menace*, *Free Willy*, and *The Secret Garden*.

In June 1995, presidential candidate, Senator Robert Dole, pointed to Time Warner's rap albums and movies as societal problems. Public outcry against Time Warner resulted.

In June, 1995, C. DeLores Tucker, 67, and head of the National Political Congress of Black Women handed Chairman of Time Warner, Michael J. Fuchs, the following lyrics from a Time Warner label recording:

> Her body's beautiful,
> so I'm thinkin' rape.
> Grabbed the bitch by her mouth,
> slam her down on the couch.
> She begged in a low voice:
> "Please don't kill me."
> I slit her throat
> and watch her shake like on TV.
>   —Geto Boys, *Mind of a Lunatic*

and asked Mr. Fuchs the following, "Read this out loud. I'll give you $100 to read it." Mr. Fuchs declined.

Mrs. Tucker was joined by William Bennett, a GOP activist and former Education Secretary. Mrs. Tucker believes Time Warner is "pimping pornography to children for the almighty dollar. Corporations need to understand: What does it profit a corporation to gain the world but lose its soul? That's the real bottom line."

In June, 1995, following Mrs. Tucker's national campaign, Time Warner fired Doug Morris, the chairman of domestic music operations. By July, Morris and Time Warner were in litigation. Morris had been a defender of gangsta rap music and had acquired the Interscope label that produced albums for Tupac Shakur and Snoop Doggy Dogg. Mr. Fuchs said the termination had nothing to do with the rap controversy.

Rap accounts for less than 10 percent of total sales in the record industry. Total sales are about $12 billion with rock music bringing in $4 billion of the sales. Some retail chains, including Wal-Mart refuse to carry the gangsta rap albums and some radio stations refuse to play the songs. The songs cited included the following:

> "I'd rather use my gun 'cause I get the money quicker . . . got them in the frame–Bang! Bang! . . . blowing [expletive] to the moon."
>   —Tupac Shakur, "Strugglin"

These lyrics contain slang expressions for using a AK-47 machine gun to murder a police officer:

"It's 1-8-7 on a [expletive] cop . . . so what the [expletive] does a nigger like you gotta say? Got to take trip to the MIA and serve your ass with a [expletive] AK.
—Snoop Doggy Dogg, "Tha' Shiznit"

Discussion Questions

1. Was Ice-T's song an exercise of free speech or sensationalism for profit?
2. Would you have taken Levin's position?
3. Is Time Warner morally responsible for its artists?
4. Does screening lyrics set a dangerous precedent?
5. Would shareholder objections influence your response to such a controversy?
6. What was Time Warner's purpose in firing Morris? By November 1995, Time-Warner's Levin fired Michael Fuchs. What message is there for executives in controversial products?

CASE 7.2: COMPENSATION-FUELED DISHONESTY: FRAUD TO GET RESULTS

Joseph Jett earned his Harvard master's degree in business administration in 1987.[3] Dismissed from his first post-degree job at CS First Boston, he then worked for Morgan Stanley but was laid off in the post-1980s Wall Street cutbacks. Despite his lack of experience in government securities, Jett was hired in 1991 by Kidder Peabody & Company to work in the government bonds section of its fixed-income department.

The fixed-income department was headed by Edward A. Cerullo, an exceptionally bright, hands-off manager who emphasized profits and was credited with turning Kidder around following the late-1980s insider trading scandals. Some fixed-income traders so feared telling Cerullo of losses that they underreported their profits at certain times so that they would have reserves to cover any future losses.

At the time of Cerullo's tenure and Jett's employment, Kidder Peabody was owned by General Electric (GE), which had purchased it in 1986 for $602 million. To establish Kidder as a Wall Street force, GE poured $1 billion into the firm and had begun to see a return only from 1991 to 1994. In 1992, GE had tried to sell Kidder to Smith Barney, Harris Upham & Company, but the sale fell through when Smith Barney learned of the extent of Kidder's mortgage-backed bond inventory.

Jett's initial performance in the bonds section was poor: he lost money. Fellow traders recalled Jett's first months on the job as demonstrating his lack of knowledge; some questioned whether Jett should have been hired at all. Even when Jett began earning profits, his reputation remained mediocre. "I don't think he knew the market. He made mistakes a rookie would make," said a former Kidder trader who worked in the 750-member fixed-income section with Jett.

Hugh Bush, a trader at Kidder, raised questions when he examined Jett's trades. In April 1992, Bush accused Jett of "mismarking" or misrecording trading positions, an illegal practice. Bush's allegations were never investigated, and he was fired within a month.

---

3. Because of a balance on his tuition bill, he did not receive his degree until 1994. In June 1994, he paid the balance due on his tuition, and Harvard processed his degree.

In 1991, Linda LaPrade sued Kidder, claiming that she was terminated as a vice president when she brought illegal trading to the attention of Cerullo. She also claimed she was told to increase allotments from government agency security issuers by "any means necessary."

Also in 1991, the National Association of Securities Dealers (NASD) fined Kidder and Cerullo $5,000 for conduct by one of Kidder's bond traders, Ira Saferstein, who profited from a customer error.[4]

During this same period, Jett's profits bulged to 20 percent of the fixed-income group's total, and he was made head of the government bond department. Jett's profits, however, did not exist. Jett had taken advantage of an accounting loophole at Kidder that enabled him to earn a $9 million bonus for 1993 alone. The fictitious profits were posted through an accounting system that separated out the interest portion of the bond. Jett captured the profit on the "strip" (the interest portion of the bond) before it was reconstituted or turned back into the original bond. Kidder's system recognized profits on the date that the reconstituted bond was entered into the system. The result was that over two and one-half years, Jett generated $350 million in fictitious profits. When the scheme was uncovered by auditors in April 1994, GE had to take a $210 million write-off in its second quarter.

On April 17, 1994, Jett was fired, his bonus and accounts frozen, and the SEC began an investigation. Kidder hired Gary G. Lynch, a lawyer and former head of enforcement at the SEC, to conduct an inquiry into the losses and Jett's conduct.

As Lynch's inquiry progressed and the SEC stepped in, the casualties at Kidder began and continued in a steady stream:

June 22, 1994: GE fired Kidder CEO Michael Carpenter.

July 14, 1994: Kidder's brokerage chief, Michael Kechner, quit.

July 22, 1994: Cerullo quit.

August 4, 1994: Kidder fired three additional trading managers.

In December 1994, GE sold Kidder to Paine Webber for $670 million. The sale required GE to take a $917 million loss on the value of Kidder's assets and a $500 million write-off for the fourth quarter of 1994. GE's income dropped 48 percent for the quarter or about 45 cents per share. About half of Kidder Peabody's 5,000 employees would be laid off following completion of the deal.

A group of GE shareholders sued GE for the loss in share value resulting from the Kidder problems, the write-off, and the subsequent sale of Kidder for a loss.

Lynch determined that Jett acted alone: "The obvious motive for this effort was to achieve a degree of recognition and compensation that had previously eluded Jett in his professional career." Lynch added that the fraud was not detected because Jett's immediate supervisors did not understand the nature of his trading activities. Their failure to review trade tickets allowed Jett to perpetrate his fraud. Lynch concluded with what he called a simple message: "You have to understand *how* people are making money."

When the logistics of the fraud were explained, GE Chairman John F. Welch, Jr., said, "It's a pity that this ever happened. Jett could have made $2 to 3 million honestly."

---

4. Cerullo said of the Saferstein incident, "The guy did something we told him not to. He did it again, and we fired him on the spot. He did the trade, and I got smacked."

Mr. Jett did file a $25 million libel suit against Kidder, Peabody and its lawyers and officers. However, the papers were not served on any of the defendants perhaps because such litigation would permit unlimited discovery and questioning of Mr. Jett.

In early January 1996, the SEC filed civil administrative charges against Jett. Mr. Jett responded by saying, "I am completely innocent of these charges against me— I will not allow people to condemn me wrongly."

Edward Cerullo was charged with the failure to supervise. Mr. Cerullo settled and agreed to a one-year suspension as well as a fine of $50,000.

Mr. Jett decided to fight the charges and said, "Kidder and GE have taken my name and dragged it through the mud. They have robbed me of two of the most productive years of my life." Mr. Jett gave up his apartment and has lived with friends. Kidder permitted him to take $150,000 he had in his retirement account, and he has worked hauling furniture for $8 per hour. Mr. Jett says he gave $2 million of the money to his parents. In late 1996, a panel of NASD arbitrators agreed to release $1 million from Jett's brokerage account that had been frozen.

In a 1996 interview on CBS's *60 Minutes*, Gary Lynch was asked if there was any chance Mr. Jett was innocent. Mr. Lynch responded, "There's no chance." However, *Business Week* did produce an opinion piece on Joseph Jett and referred to the SEC case as "flimsy."

At Mr. Jett's June 1996 hearing, he testified, using his computer diary, that management knew about his bond-trading strategy. The alleged scheme was one of using government strips or securities that were created by peeling away and repackaging the interest payments on 30-year government bonds. One expert explained it as changing $1 into four quarters. There is a change in structure, but there are no revenues, and Mr. Jett was booking the changes as revenues.

Following Mr. Jett's hearing, the SEC filed a brief in the matter accusing Mr. Jett of introducing "bogus diary entries" from his computer. Mr. Jett had introduced 20 diary entries at his hearing to show management knowledge. However, only 5 of those entries matched entries retrieved from the master computer files of Kidder and obtained by the SEC. The matter remains pending.

Discussion Questions

1. An executive noted that Wall Street firms "have become victims of compensation schemes resulting in outrageously high salaries and bonuses. It brings out the worst in people who have any worst in them." Are compensation schemes responsible for poor ethical choices? Does a firm establish an ethical tone or culture with its compensation system? Should the jump in revenues from Jett's unit from 6% to 27% have triggered an investigation?

2. Cerullo earned an estimated $20 million in compensation during the time of Jett's alleged scam. In other words, he enjoyed increased compensation if Jett did well.

   Consider this rap song, "Requiem Rap at Kidder P Blow," that circulated around Kidder during its final pre-sale days:

   > Big Boss and Joe went skiing in the snow:
   > He said, Joe, what you're doing, don't wanna know;
   > But, keep on doing it, doing it though,

'Cause I am the Main Man at Kidder P Blow.
 . . . Then one month Kidder P took a double blow;
Joe's profits were phony, the Man said so;
And the Fed jacked rates so the economy'd slow;
April was the cruelest month at Kidder P Blow.
 . . . GE aimed all the blame at Ed Curello
He was the man who'd let the boys go.
To Joe and the V-Man he never said no.
'Twas the worst of times at Kidder P Blow.

Jett maintains his supervisors knew what he was doing, directed his trading, and used the profits to deflect scrutiny from Kidder's mortgage bond problems. Even if his supervisors did not know, did they not want to know? Is it an ethical violation to ignore signals?

3. What parts of the GE-Kidder culture and circumstances contributed to the "do what is necessary" ethical posture?

4. Why were Bush's and LaPrade's allegations so readily dismissed? Why were they fired?

5. Lynch's report concluded that the attitude in the Kidder bond department was "never question success," and that no one was willing to ask hard questions about Jett's ever-increasing profits. Were other employees enjoying the success too much? What ethical breaches did they commit by ignoring the implausibility of the success?

6. Lynch's report noted that some Kidder employees had questions about Jett's trading but "were reluctant or unsure how to report their concerns despite the existence of legal and compliance departments and an ombudsman." What could Kidder Peabody have done to eliminate such hesitancy?

7. List all the lives affected and harm resulting from Jett's conduct.

SECTION B
EXECUTIVE SALARIES

How much is too much? Should shareholders have the right to control the amount paid to executives?

CASE 7.3: LEVELS OF EXECUTIVE COMPENSATION: HOW MUCH SHOULD THE BOSS MAKE?

Pay levels for executives have been increasing rapidly since 1980. Sibson & Company data show that between 1980 and 1990, the average cash compensation for CEOs grew over 160 percent.[5] At the same time, the average hourly wage paid to nonsupervisory manufacturing employees did not keep pace with inflation. CEOs in United States-based companies earn 363 times more than the average employee, while Japanese CEOs earn only 16 times more.[6]

Honda Motor Company paid its top thirty-six officers about $10.2 million total in 1990. Nissan Motor Company paid even less in 1990 to its forty-eight officers. Because of Japan's 65 percent tax rate, the highest-paid officers would have brought home less than $150,000. By contrast, Lee Iacocca, CEO of Chrysler, had direct compensation of $4.65 million during the same period, in addition to 62,500 shares of Chrysler stock valued at $718,000. Compensation to other executives included:

COMPANY	CEO	PAY (For 1997)[7]
Travelers Group	Sanford Weill	$230,725,000
Coca-Cola Co.	Roberto Goizueta	111,832,000
Healthsouth	Richard Scrushy	106,790,000

5. Jeffrey Birnbaum, "From Quayle to Clinton, Politicians Are Pouncing on the Hot Issue of Top Executives' Hefty Salaries," *Wall Street Journal*, 15 January 1991, A16.

6. Jill Abramson and Christopher J. Chipello, "High Pay of CEOs Traveling with Bush Touches a Nerve in Asia," *Wall Street Journal*, 30 December 1991, A1.

7. Jennifer Reingold, Richard A. Melcher, and Gary McWilliams, "Executive Pay," *Business Week*, 20 April 1998, 64–65.

Occidental Petroleum	Ray Irani	101,505,000
Nabors Industries	Eugene Isenberg	84,547,000
Cadence Design Systems	Joseph Costello	66,842,000
Intel	Andrew Grove	52,214,000
HBO & Co.	Charles McCall	51,409,000
Morgan Stanley Dean Witter	Philip Purcell	50,807,000
Monsanto	Robert Shapiro	49,326,000
General Electric	John Welch	39,894,000
American Express	Harvey Golub	33,457,000
Health Mgmt. Associates	William Schoen	30,945,000
Bristol-Myers Squibb	Charles Heimbold	29,211,000
Providian Financial	Shailesh Mehta	28,365,000
Allied Signal	Lawrence Bossidy	28,237,000
Pfizer	William Steere	28,120,000
America Online	Stephen Case	26,913,000
Travelers Property Casualty	Robert Lipp	26,301,000
Colgate-Palmolive	Reuben Mark	25,390,000

The levels of CEO compensation have outraged large institutional investors and small shareholders. Shareholder proposals calling for reform in the setting of executive pay were submitted at the 1997 annual meetings of forty-three companies. The New York City Employees Retirement System, for example, proposed through its 259,328 shares of Reebok that executive compensation be established by an independent panel. Said Elizabeth Holztman, a trustee of the New York system, "It is unconscionable to have sky-high executive compensation that is not related to long-term corporate performance."[8]

The California Public Employee Retirement System (Calpers) released a list of executives and their pay in twelve high-profile companies for 1991 in an attempt to pressure management of the firms into reform. Calpers had tried to negotiate privately with the firms but was rebuffed in some cases. Calpers spokesman Richard H. Koppes stated "This year, the kinder and gentler approach doesn't seem to be working. That's why we released the names."[9]

Some shareholders have pointed out conflicts of interest in board compensation committees: CEOs from other firms are members of the board, and lawyers whose firms furnish the bulk of the company's legal services sit on the committee that determines the compensation of the CEO—the same person who hires the law firm. Management consultant Graef Crystal explained, "It's a cozy you-scratch-my-back-I'll-scratch-yours arrangement. If you're a CEO, you don't want Mother Teresa or the Sisters of Charity on your compensation committee."[10]

Stanley C. Gault, chairman of Goodyear Tire & Rubber Company, has joined with the shareholders in their complaints: "The American public is tired of seeing executives make many, many millions of dollars a year when the stock price goes down, the dividends are cut, and the book value is reduced."[11] Some executives have initiated reform in their compensation system out of fear of new federal regulations. On the other hand, others, such as the late Roberto C. Goizueta of Coca-Cola, continue to defend their compensation: "Our stock outperformed the other

8. "Reebok Comes under Fire for Executive Pay," *Wall Street Journal*, 21 March 1991, G1.

9. Ibid.

10. Thomas McCarroll, "The Shareholders Strike Back," *Time*, 4 May 1992, 46–47.

11. John Byrne, Dean Foust, and Lois Therriem, "Executive Pay," *Business Week*, 30 March 1992, 52.

twenty-nine stocks in the Dow industrial average in the past decade. The end result has been the creation of $50 billion of additional wealth for the share owners of our company in the same time period."[12] Goizueta's defense of his compensation at the annual shareholders' meeting met with applause.

Ben & Jerry's Homemade, Inc., the Vermont ice cream manufacturer, once limited its CEO pay to seven times the average worker's salary. Herman Miller, a Fortune 500 company, limits its CEO's pay—salary and bonus—to twenty times the average employee paycheck, which was $28,000 in 1991. The average CEO compensation in the other Fortune 500 companies is 117 times the salary of the average worker. Max DePress, a member of Herman Miller's founding family and chairman of the company's board, said, "People have to think about the common good. Our CEO and senior officers make good competitive salaries when the performance is there."[13] Miller's nonunionized plant workers support the plan, he said: "This is a fair and equitable way to pay. . . . If they tried to revoke it, people would speak out."[14]

James O'Toole, executive director of the leadership institute at the University of Southern California, said the Herman Miller plan should be the model others follow, "instead of the bad examples of the 1980s. The purpose of the corporation is much broader than meeting the needs of stock speculators or the power needs of top managers."[15]

In 1992, a bill was passed by Congress that limits the ability of companies to deduct CEO compensation from their taxes as a means of controlling increases. The bill puts an upper limit of $1,000,000 on such tax deductions. At the same time, the SEC passed new rules and formats for disclosing of executive compensation in annual proxy materials. Boards have also begun to act on the issue. Compensation committees comprised only of outside directors exist at 80 percent of the institutions surveyed by Dow Jones. These committees are hiring independent consultants to advise them on compensation issues.

Several issues surround executive pay:

1. Many executives are rewarded for the increase in their companies' share prices although the share prices have increased largely due to the bull market and not because of the efforts of the management team;
2. Shareholders continue to make proposals as part of the proxy materials regarding the formulas used for executive compensation; and
3. Regulation of executive pay is still progressing. To date the SEC mandates disclosure of the pay of the top five executives in a company, the means and information used by the human resources committee of the company's to establish pay levels, and the comparative performance of the company.

---

12. Jerry Schwartz, "Coke's Chairman Defends $86 Million Pay and Bonus," *New York Times*, 16 April 1992, C1.

13. Jacqueline Mitchell, "Herman Miller Links Worker-CEO Pay," *Wall Street Journal*, 7 May 1992, B1.

14. Ibid.

15. Ibid.

Discussion Questions

1. So long as a company is performing and providing a return to investors and growth in the value of their investment, should executive compensation be an issue?
2. The compensation of executives is largely a deductible business expense. Are U.S. taxpayers subsidizing the large CEO salaries?
3. Should CEO pay be tied to workers' compensation?
4. Should CEO pay be tied to company performance?
5. Who should establish executive pay rates?
6. Should institutional investors and other shareholders have input on executive compensation?
7. Do directors who work for the company as consultants or lawyers have conflicts of interest in setting executive compensation?
8. Would government regulation of executive pay interfere with the free enterprise system?

SECTION C
CORPORATE
CONTRIBUTIONS

Many businesses look to help communities by supporting various nonprofit organizations. But what happens when community members disagree about the value or values of the nonprofit organization?

CASE 7.4: THE BOY SCOUTS OF AMERICA, US WEST, AND GAY RIGHTS

The Boy Scouts of American (BSA), founded in 1910, relies on private support from individuals, foundations, and corporations. The Scout oath is:

On my honor, I will do my best:
To do my duty to God and my Country,
To obey the Scout Law.
To help other people at all times.
To keep myself physically strong,
Mentally awake, and morally straight.

The BSA's policy of refusing to admit gays as members or as troop leaders was challenged in a lawsuit filed in Los Angeles by a gay man whose application to become a scoutmaster was rejected. BSA also faced legal challenges over its policies against admitting women and atheists. Because of its policies, the San Francisco United Way withdrew a $9,000 contribution to BSA, and the city's board of education banned BSA activities on school property during school hours.

US West, the largest corporation headquartered in Colorado, has annual revenues of $9.7 billion and 14,000 of its 53,000 employees in the state. The company's charitable foundation gave $300,000 to BSA in Colorado in 1990 and 1991. US West's philanthropic giving concentrates on early childhood development pro-

West's philanthropic giving concentrates on early childhood development programs, rural economic development, and American Indian tribal colleges.

In response to employees' questions about BSA admittance policies, US West called for a review of its foundation's contributions to the organization. An internal memo from the firm's public relations board called BSA policies "particularly troubling . . . in light of US West's values around pluralism and diversity."[16] The board recommended that the foundation "review its giving practices, working to align its funding decisions with its own policies and with US West's values."[17]

The US West foundation decided to continue to support BSA and released the following statement: "There is no litmus test we can apply to every organization we fund on every issue. We do not have to agree with everything an organization espouses in order to support the good it does overall."[18]

Jim Tuller, treasurer of the Employee Association of Gays and Lesbians at US West, responded, "There's a profound sense of disappointment. I'm surprised they made the decision so quickly. I think this was a political hot potato and the company, perhaps, reacted to their switchboard lighting up."[19] Sue Anderson, director of the Gay and Lesbian Community Center in Denver, noted, "It's unfortunate they claim to back gay and lesbian employees, but at the same time support an organization that actively works against them. It really sets a confusing standard."[20]

Bill Kephart, director of the Denver BSA Council noted, "We're pleased. You have to appreciate, [that] it's been a very delicate situation for us. US West is an important sponsor for us. We respect that; at the same time, we need to stand firm in our position."[21]

BSA continued to face publicity and legal challenges. In 1998, James Dale, a Rutgers University student and former Eagle Scout, won his New Jersey litigation that sought his reinstatement as a Scout leader. BSA had ousted him after it learned he was gay.

Tim Curran, another gay rights activist, lost a similar suit in California for his reinstatement.

Discussion Questions

1. Was US West's decision to give money to the BSA inconsistent with its corporate commitment to plurality and diversity?
2. Should a corporation be free to choose whom it donates to?
3. Will public outcry serve to restrict corporate giving?
4. In mid-1992, Levi Strauss & Company decided to end its financial support ($40,000 to $80,000 annually) to the BSA because the organization's exclusion of homosexuals was "at odds" with the company's "core values." Levi Strauss said it "could not fund any organization that discriminates on the

---

16. Adriel Bettelheim, "Scout Aid May Be Cut," *Denver Post*, 31 October 1991, 1A.

17. Ibid.

18. Adriel Bettelheim, "US West Won't End Boy Scout Aid," *Denver Post*, 7 November 1991, 1A, 16A.

19. Ibid.

20. Ibid.

21. Price Colman, "US West to Keep Funding Boy Scouts," *Rocky Mountain News*, 7 November 1991, 55.

basis of sexual orientation and religious beliefs."[22] Rev. Donald Wildmon, a Methodist minister, responded, "The fact that they would penalize the Boy Scouts for refusing to accept openly practicing homosexuals as scoutmasters shows they no longer want the business of a majority of Americans."[23] Should Levi Strauss and other firms be able to use their donation clout to dictate the policies of their donees?

CASE 7.5: DAYTON-HUDSON AND ITS CONTRIBUTIONS TO PLANNED PARENTHOOD

Dayton-Hudson Corporation is a multistate department store chain. In 1990, its charitable foundation gave $18,000 to Planned Parenthood and other contributions to Children's Home Society, the Association for the Advancement of Young Women, and the Young Women's Christian Association. It had contributed to Planned Parenthood for twenty-two years.

Antiabortion groups have vocally criticized corporate foundations that support Planned Parenthood and have persuaded J.C. Penney Company and American Telephone and Telegraph to stop their contributions to the organization. After Pioneer Hi-Bred International's foundation gave $25,000 to Planned Parenthood of Greater Iowa for rural clinics that did not perform abortions, Midwest farmers began circulating a flyer headlined, "Is Pioneer Hi-Bred Pro-Abortion?" CEO Thomas Urban canceled the donation, saying, "We were blackmailed, but you can't put the core business at risk."[24] When antiabortion groups raised their objections with the Dayton-Hudson foundation, the foundation board decided to halt its contributions to Planned Parenthood.

Prochoice supporters responded strongly by boycotting Dayton-Hudson stores, writing letters to newspaper editors, and closing charge accounts. Pickets appeared outside Dayton-Hudson stores and cut up their charge cards for media cameras.

A trustee for the New York City Employees Retirement System, which owned 438,290 Dayton shares, commented: "By antagonizing consumers, they've threatened the value of our investment."[25]

Dayton-Hudson decided to resume its funding of Planned Parenthood, even though antiabortion groups announced plans to boycott the company's stores.

Discussion Questions

1. Is there any way for a corporation to meet all demands in formulating policies on philanthropic giving?

22. Woody Hochswender, "Boy Scouts Learn Levis Don't Fit," *New York Times*, 5 June 1992, A12.

23. Ibid.

24. Richard Gibson, "Boycott Drive Against Pioneer Hi-Bred Shows Perils of Corporate Philanthropy," *Wall Street Journal*, 10 June 1992, B1.

25. Kevin Kelly, "Dayton-Hudson Finds There's No Graceful Way to Flip-Flop," *Business Week*, 24 September 1990, 50.

2. Should contributions be considered simply an extension of marketing and made accordingly?
3. Should contributions be consistent with the firm's culture and values?
4. Is giving in to objections to certain donations by special-interest groups ethical?

Case 7.6: Giving and Spending the United Way

The United Way, which evolved from the local community chests of the 1920s, is a national organization that funnels funding to charities through a payroll-deduction system.

Ninety percent of all charitable payroll deductions in 1991 were for the United Way. This system, however, has been criticized as coercive. Bonuses, for example, were offered for achieving 100 percent employee participation. Betty Beene, president of United Way of Tristate (New York, New Jersey, and Connecticut), commented, "If participation is 100 percent, it means someone has been coerced."[26] Tristate discontinued the bonuses and arm-twisting.

United Way's system of spending also came under fire through the actions of William Aramony, president of the United Way from 1970 to 1992. During his tenure, United Way receipts grew from $787 million in 1970 to $3 billion in 1990. But some of Aramony's effects on the organization were less positive.

In early 1992, the *Washington Post* reported that Aramony:

Was paid $463,000 per year.

Flew first class on commercial airlines.

Spent $20,000 in one year for limousines.

Used the Concorde for trans-Atlantic flights.

The article also revealed that one of the taxable spin-off companies Aramony had created to provide travel and bulk purchasing for United Way chapters had bought a $430,000 condominium in Manhattan and a $125,000 apartment in Coral Gables, Florida, for his use. Another spin-off had hired Aramony's son, Robert Aramony, as its president.

When Aramony's expenses and salary became public, Stanley C. Gault, chairman of Goodyear Tire & Rubber Company, asked, "Where was the board? The outside auditors?"[27] Aramony resigned after fifteen chapters of the United Way threatened to withhold their annual dues to the national office.

Said Robert O. Bothwell, executive director of the National Committee for Responsive Philanthropy, "I think it is obscene that he is making that kind of salary and asking people who are making $10,000 a year to give 5 percent of their income."[28]

In August 1992, the United Way board of directors hired Elaine Chao, the Peace Corps director, to replace William Aramony at a salary of $195,000, with no

---

26. Susan Garland, "Keeping a Sharper Eye on Those who Pass the Hat," *Business Week*, 16 March 1992, 39.

27. Ibid.

28. Felicity Barringer, "United Way Head Is Forced Out in a Furor Over His Lavish Style," *New York Times*, 28 February 1992, A1.

perks.[29] She reduced staff from 275 to 185 and borrowed $1.5 million to compensate for a decline in donations. By 1995, United Way donations had still not returned to their 1991 $3.2 billion.

In September 1994, William Aramony and two other United Way officers, including the chief financial officer, were indicted by a federal grand jury for conspiracy, mail fraud, and tax fraud. The indictment alleged the three officers diverted more than $2.74 million of United Way funds to purchase an apartment in New York City for $383,000, interior decorating for $72,000, a condominium, vacations, and a lifetime pass on American Airlines. In addition, $80,000 of United Way funds were paid to Aramony's girlfriend, a 1986 high school graduate, for consulting, even though she did no work.

On April 3, 1995, Aramony was found guilty of twenty-five counts of fraud, conspiracy, and money laundering. Two other United Way executives were also convicted.

By April, 1998, donation levels were still not completely reinstated and relationships between local chapters and the national organization were often strained. United Way's donation fell 11 percent since 1991 while overall charitable giving was up 9 percent.

Discussion Questions

1. Was there anything unethical about Aramony's expenditures?
2. Was the board responsible for the expenditures?
3. Is the perception as important as the acts themselves?
4. If Aramony were a CEO of a for-profit firm, would your answers change?
5. What obstacles did Chao face as she assumed the United Way helm?

---

29. Desda Moss, "Peace Corps Director to Head United Way," *USA Today*, 27 August 1992, 6A; Sabra Chartrand, "Head of Peace Corps Named United Way President," *New York Times*, 27 August 1992, A8.

SECTION D
SOCIAL ISSUES

Should business spending and product decisions take into account social goals and impact? Is spending by businesses to solve social problems necessary or a misuse of funds?

CASE 7.7: THE CHICAGO INNER-CITY SCHOOL EXPERIMENT

A group of Chicago businesses pooled funds to create a privately owned and operated elementary school in a Chicago inner-city neighborhood because of their concerns about the quality of education. Observing that American businesses spend $4 to $5 billion annually in training just to bring their workers to very basic skill levels, these businesses determined that they would help improve public education. They incorporated business notions on pay and accountability in the most challenging environment—an inner-city school.

The school is free for neighborhood children ages two to twelve. At the school, students get breakfast, lunch, and snacks, as well as after-school care.

Teachers in the school are paid 10 percent more than their public school counterparts. The school is run like a private corporation, and the administrators and teachers understand that a lack of improvement in the students can result in termination of employment.

If it achieves its goals, this project could be a model for other schools. The founders of this Chicago experiment believe the future success of their businesses lies in the skills of their employees.

Discussion Questions

1. Would Milton Friedman support the school founders' endeavor as a proper use of shareholder funds?

2. A shareholder of one of the businesses has protested: "Why are my funds being used for an inner-city school? We have taxes for that. I invested in a distribution firm, not an education firm. Your job is to earn my dividend, not spend it on things you think are important."

If you were the director of shareholder relations for the firm, how would you respond to the shareholder?

CASE 7.8: ROCK MUSIC WARNING LABELS

In the summer of 1985, Tipper Gore, the wife of then-Senator Albert Gore of Tennessee, and Susan Baker, the wife of former U.S. Treasury Secretary James Baker, formed a citizens' group called the Parents Resource Music Center (PMRC). The group's concern was that rock music advocates "aggressive and hostile rebellion, the abuse of drugs and alcohol, irresponsible sexuality, sexual perversions, violence and involvement in the occult." Gore began the group after she listened to the song "Darling Nikki" from her eleven-year-old daughter's *Purple Rain* album by Prince. The song is about a girl masturbating as she looks at a magazine. Gore then discovered Sheena Easton singing about "genital arousal," Judas Priest singing about oral sex at gunpoint, and the following lyrics in Motley Crue's top-selling *Shout at the Devil* album: "\. . . now I'm killing you. . . . Watch your face turning blue."

PMRC's strategy was to work with record companies to reach a mutually agreeable solution to the problem. PMRC met with the Recording Industry Association of America to request a ratings system for records, similar to that used for movies, and a requirement that printed lyrics be included with all records so that disc jockeys would know what they are sending out over the airwaves. In the first month after PMRC was organized, it received over 10,000 letters of support and inquiry. PMRC maintains a database with the following information:

Teenagers listen to their music four to six hours per day for a total of 10,000 hours between grades seven and twelve.

Of all violent crimes, 70 percent are committed by youths under the age of seventeen.

Teenage suicide has increased by 300 percent since 1955.

U.S. teenage pregnancy rates are the highest in the world.

When PMRC failed to reach an agreement with the record industry, congressional hearings were held on a proposed bill to require labeling on records. Susan Baker and Tipper Gore testified, as did musicians Frank Zappa, former member of the Mothers of Invention, and Dee Snider of Twisted Sister. Zappa stated, "Putting labels on albums is the equivalent of treating dandruff by decapitation."

Though nothing came of the hearings, by 1990, bills were pending in thirty-five state legislatures to require labeling of records. PMRC backed state groups lobbying for the legislation. In Arizona, a reporter for *New Times* asked a sponsor of a labeling bill, Senator Jan Brewer, to read some of the objectionable lyrics. The reporter recorded the reading, set it to music, and played the tape over the speakers in the Capitol.

In May 1990, with the state legislative debates on the label requirements still in progress, the Recording Industry Association of America introduced a uniform label for albums with explicit lyrics and expressed hope that its voluntary use by industry members would halt the passage of legislation. The black-and-white label appears in the lower right-hand corner of the album and reads: "Parental Advisory—Explicit Lyrics." The label is to be used on albums with lyrics relating to sex, violence, suicide, drug abuse, bigotry, or satanic worship. Use of the label is the decision of the record company and the artist.

The PMRC and the National Parent and Teacher Association endorsed the warning system and asked state legislators to consider dropping proposed label legislation.

Controversy continued to surround rock music lyrics. In the summer of 1990, parents of a teenager who committed suicide sued the rock group Judas Priest, alleging that its lyrics resulted in murderous mind control and the death of their son. Their subliminal persuasion argument was unsuccessful.

By 1995, the record industry's then 10-year-old warning label program was reviewed with the conclusion that parents don't know what the explicit-lyrics stickers are. A meeting between the Recording Industry Association of America and the National Association of Recording Merchandisers resulted in new plans to help the system work better. The provisions include:

- Display signs in stores explaining the "Parental Advisory Explicit Lyrics" logo.
- Ensure that record companies use the correct size (1-inch by ½-inch) and placement (lower right) on the record's permanent packaging.
- Alert reviewers of each record's sticker status.
- Encourage inclusion of a record's warning label in ads and promotional materials.

The attention to gangsta rap music (see case 7.1) also resulted in increased attention to lyrics. Recording company MCA was targeted in 1996 for marketing "death and degradation." MCA refused to make changes other than complying with warning labels and called Mr. William Bennett, a former secretary of Education and author, a "warden of morality." Wal-Mart continued to refuse to stock explicit lyric music.

In late November 1997, the Senate began exploring the effects of music on children. One parent testified that his 15-year-old son committed suicide after listening to the Marilyn Manson album, "Antichrist Superstar." The Senate is considering warning labels on albums for violence, death and drugs.

Discussion Questions

1. What are the ethical issues in the production of songs with explicit lyrics?
2. Will voluntary regulation work for the recording industry?
3. If you were a record producer, would your company sign artists who sing explicit lyrics?
4. If you were a record producer, would you feel an obligation to do more than put a warning label on albums with explicit lyrics?

5. You have just been informed that a teenager committed suicide while listening to the music of one of the artists your company produces. The music suggested suicide as an alternative to unhappiness. Would you feel morally responsible for the suicide? Should the artist feel morally responsible?

CASE 7.9: THE MOMMY DOLL

Villy Nielsen, APS, a Danish toy company, introduced the Mommy-To-Be doll in the United States. The doll, named Judith, looks like it is pregnant. When its belly is removed, a baby is revealed inside that can be popped out. Once the baby is removed, the doll's original stomach pops into place. The new stomach is flat and instantly restores Judith's youthful figure.

Teenage girls are intrigued by the doll, and call it "neat." However, Diane Welsh, the president of the New York chapter of the National Organization for Women, stated, "A doll that magically becomes pregnant and unpregnant is an irresponsible toy. We need to understand having a child is a very serious business. We have enough unwanted children in this world."[30]

Mommy-To-Be comes with Charles, her husband, and baby accessories. An eleven-year-old shopper said of the doll, "I don't think she looks like a mommy. . . . She looks like a teenager."[31]

Discussion Questions

1. Is the doll a socially responsible toy?
2. Would you carry the doll if you owned a toy store?
3. Would you want your children to have the doll?

CASE 7.10: THE TOYS PARENTS AND TEACHERS HATE

Kenner Products, Inc., a subsidiary of Hasbro, Inc., developed a line of forty action figures called Savage Mondo Blitzers. The figures carried such names as Knight to Dismember, Snot Shot, Barf Bucket, Puke Shooter, Butt Kicker, Projectile Vomit, Eye Pus, and Kiss My Bat.

During test marketing of the toys, actual sales were double what Kenner had expected.

> The catalog copy for the toys read: "Parents will hate 'em, teachers will despise 'em, but Savage Mondo Blitzers will be the latest rage with kids."

Teachers and students wrote to the company to protest the toys, and parent-teacher groups moved to organize boycotts against Kenner and Hasbro.

---

30. "Mommy Doll Makes Birth a Snap," *Mesa Tribune*, 9 May 1992, A7.
31. Ibid.

Kenner said the toys were intended to be "wacky, irreverent, and humorous."[32]

A toy buyer commented, "If parents let their kids watch MTV, they're certainly going to allow them to play with Mondo Blitzers."[33]

Discussion Questions

1. Suppose that you are the marketing director for Kenner. The test market results for Savage Mondo Blitzers tell you that you have a "slam dunk" in terms of the line's success. Nonetheless, the toys disgust you with their reference to psychotic killers and bodily functions. Would you be able to continue marketing the line? Would you feel Kenner was exploiting children with these toys?

2. Suppose that you are a toy store owner. Would you have any ethical reservations about selling this line of toys?

3. If you were the children's TV ad director for a local TV station, would you have any ethical reservations about running Savage Mondo Blitzer ads?

CASE 7.11: BEAVIS, BUTT-HEAD, AND MTV

Beavis and Butt-head are two cartoon caricatures of teenage boys who speak in monosyllables with no inflection and tend to create mischief. During a good portion of the show, which provides commentary on rock videos, Beavis and Butt-head burn and destroy things. In October 1993, the mother of a five-year-old boy who started a fire that killed his sister attributed the child's actions to Beavis and Butt-head's burning of things.

In one episode of the "Beavis and Butt-head Show," one of the characters set fire to the other's hair by igniting spray from an aerosol can. Fire Chief Stan Crosley of Sidney, Ohio, said that his unit was called to put out a house fire started by three girls trying the same trick.

After these incidents, MTV moved the show from 7 to 10:30 P.M. and included the following disclaimer:

> Beavis and Butt-head are not role models. They're not even human. They're cartoons. Some of the things they do would cause a real person to get hurt, expelled, arrested, possibly deported. To put it another way: Don't try this at home.

Discussion Questions

1. Is MTV responsible for the fires, death, and injury?
2. What responsibility do parents have to monitor their children's TV watching?
3. Did MTV do enough by moving the show and issuing the disclaimer?

---

32. Joseph Pereira, "We've Not Mentioned the Worst, and They're Selling Them to Kids," *Wall Street Journal*, 28 February 1992, B1.

33. Ibid.

4. What purposes, if any, does the "Beavis and Butt-head Show" serve beyond raising MTV's ratings?
5. Would you advertise your youth-oriented product on "The Beavis and Butt-head Show"?

CASE 7.12: SHOCK JOCK: HOWARD STERN

"Shock Jock" Howard Stern's radio talk show, which originates at Infinity Broadcasting Corporation's flagship New York station, is number one in its time slot in New York, Philadelphia, Los Angeles, Boston, and several other cities. A total of 20 million listeners tune in each week. Stern is known for his banter that borders on, and occasionally is, indecent. His on-the-air routines involve such subjects as "Butt Bongo" and "Lesbian Dial-a-Date." Infinity has been fined $1.67 million by the Federal Communications Commission (FCC) for Stern's material that allegedly violated federal on-the-air decency standards. Since the fines have not deterred the violations, one commissioner has cited ongoing complaints as the basis for conducting an FCC hearing into whether Infinity's licenses for its eleven stations should be revoked.

Stern's book, *Private Parts*, published by Simon & Schuster in October 1993, had such chapter titles as "Yes, I am Fartman"; Stern appears semi-clothed on the cover. Twelve days after its release, the book was in its seventh printing, having sold more than 1 million copies.

Mr. Stern has enjoyed continued success with his 1997 critically acclaimed movie, *Private Parts* and a new 1998 CBS television contract.

Discussion Questions

1. Does Infinity have an obligation to monitor and control Stern?
2. Does Simon & Schuster have an obligation to establish editorial standards?
3. Are shareholders of Infinity or Simon & Schuster concerned about standards of decency, given Stern's success?
4. Would you publish Stern's book? Would you hire him as a radio talent?

CASE 7.13: RETAILERS AND WEAPONS: SELF-IMPOSED BANS

In October 1993, a court ordered Kmart Corporation to pay $12.5 million to Deborah Kitchen, who was left a quadriplegic after her boyfriend, Thomas Knapp, shot her point-blank in the neck with a rifle he purchased at Kmart. The trial records show he was so drunk at the time of purchase that he could not legibly complete the federal firearms forms, so a clerk did it for him. The family of a couple slain by their schizophrenic son with a .38 caliber handgun he had purchased at Wal-Mart sued Wal-Mart in December 1993.

By the end of 1993, both Wal-Mart and Kmart announced they would no longer sell any guns at their retail stores. Firearm sales for the two discounters totaled $158 million. A Wal-Mart spokesman said, "A majority of our customers tell us

$158 million. A Wal-Mart spokesman said, "A majority of our customers tell us they would prefer not to shop in a retail store that sells handguns."

Both retailers were the last to stop selling guns. Montgomery Ward and Sears, Roebuck stopped in 1981; Ward's felt the sales were too problematic, and Sears cited burdensome paperwork.

In September 1994, a thirteen-year-old boy was fatally shot by a police officer in the stairwell of a New York City housing project because he was carrying a toy gun the officer assumed to be real. A similar incident occurred when another officer shot and wounded a 16-year-old youth who was also carrying just a toy gun.

By October 1994, both Kay-Bee Toy Stores and Toys 'R' Us announced that they would no longer carry realistic-looking military- or police-style weapons. They would sell only brightly colored, oversized toy guns or those with logos or decals that clearly distinguish them from real weapons.

Said Ann Iverson, president and CEO of Kay-Bee, which has a chain of 1,100 stores nationwide, "This step is just a part of Kay-Bee's strategy to re-evaluate our merchandise mix and address what families need today in terms of fun, safe, and developmentally sound toys." Toy guns represent 2 percent of Kay-Bee's inventory.

CEO Michael Goldstein of Toys 'R' Us has led an industry initiative to eliminate the realistic-looking guns. He said, "The issue is the potential harm that these products pose to children and others. We believe that by taking this step we can help raise awareness and encourage manufacturers and other retailers to join us in this effort."

A Toys 'R' Us shopper commented, "If it saves a couple kids' lives, I think it's a good thing. Actually, it's a courageous move. They're going to lose business."

Discussion Questions

1. Are the Kmart and Wal-Mart decisions on gun sales rooted in ethics or potential liability?
2. Do retailers have a potential liability in selling toy guns?
3. Did the ban on realistic toy weapons earn publicity for the toy store chains? Do you believe that was partially their motivation? Consider the following comment by a spokeswoman for Target, which has never carried the realistic-looking guns: "The only guns we have are neon plastic toy guns. We cater to the family, and we don't really consider realistic toy guns to be a family toy."
4. If you were a toy retailer, would you carry realistic-looking toy guns?
5. If you were a retailer, would you sell guns? If no retailers sell guns, have consumers lost a fundamental constitutional right?

CASE 7.14: "IT MAY BE IMMORAL BUT NOT ILLEGAL. THE BOTTOM LINE IS MONEY."

"Sylvia Daniel of Ducktown, Tennessee, is known as "Machine Gun Mama" and the "First Lady of Firearms." She still sells machine guns outlawed under President Ronald Reagan in 1986 because they were made before the ban went into effect. In 1985, she sold them for $185; now, she sells them for $3,000. She and her husband specialize in selling weapons by finding loopholes in gun control laws. Wayne Daniel said, "If there is a dollar to be made, make it. It may be immoral but not illegal. The bottom line is money. This is a legal business."

The Daniels sell their semiautomatic M-11/9 pistol nationwide. An agent of the Bureau of Alcohol, Tobacco and Firearms noted that this weapon is good for only two things: the firing range and killing. Sylvia Daniel agreed, but added, "It's not the gun, it's the people. We sell to federally licensed dealers. They sell it to you. Did you take it home and put it under your bed and your son got it and killed with it? Is that my fault? I know kids are killed every day. But the problem is not the gun. . . . It's not about gun control. It's about crime control."

The Daniels also sell a "Mac-in-a-sack" for $160, which consists of fifty-two parts for the M-11/9. Excluded are the barrel and frame where the serial number would be, so buyers can make guns with no serial number. The Daniels also sell a briefcase that holds a Mac and has a switch to fire the pistol. The ATF labels the briefcase, one of the Daniels' best-sellers, an assassination device.

Discussion Questions

1. Describe the Daniels' ethical standards.
2. Are the Daniels persuasive in disclaiming responsibility for what guns do?
3. Aren't the Daniels just fulfilling a market need?
4. Could you work for the Daniels?

Section E
Public Disclosure
and Relations

Every business sooner or later has a public relations crisis. Some crises result from poor ethical choices; others spring from events no business can control. But in many business crises, the public must have information. How forthcoming should a business be? Is full disclosure best? How important is being certain the facts are correct?

7.15 E. Coli, Jack-in-the-Box and Cooking Temperatures

On January 11, 1993, young Michael Nole and his family ate dinner at a Jack-in-the-Box restaurant in Tacoma, Washington, where Michael enjoyed his $2.69 "Kid's Meal." The next day, Michael was admitted to Children's Hospital and Medical Center in Seattle with severe stomach cramps and bloody diarrhea. Several days later, Michael died of kidney and heart failure.

At the same time, 300 other people in Idaho, Nevada, and Washington who had eaten at Jack-in-the-Box restaurants were poisoned with E. coli bacteria, the cause of Michael's death. By the end of the outbreak, over 600 people nation-wide were affected.

Jack-in-the-Box, based in San Diego, was not in the best financial health, having just restructured $501 million in debt. The outbreak of poisonings came at a difficult time for the company.

Federal guidelines require that meat be cooked at 140 degrees Fahrenheit. Jack-in-the-Box followed those guidelines. In May 1992 and September 1992, the state of Washington notified all restaurants, including Jack-in-the-Box, of new regulations requiring hamburgers to be cooked at 155 degrees Fahrenheit. The change would increase restaurants' costs because cooking at 155 degrees slows delivery of food to customers and increases energy costs.

At a news conference one week after the poisonings, Jack-in-the-Box president Robert J. Nugent criticized state authorities for not notifying the company of the 155-degree rule. A week later, the company found the notifications, which it had misplaced, and issued a statement.

After the Jack-in-the-Box poisonings, the federal government recommended that all states increase their cooking temperature requirements to 155 degrees. Burger King cooks at 160 degrees, Hardee's, Wendy's, and Taco Bell at 165 degrees. The U.S. Agriculture Department also changed its meat inspection standards.

The poisonings cut sales at Jack-in-the-Box by 20 percent. Three store managers were laid off, and the company's plan to build five new restaurants was put on hold until sales picked up. Jack-in-the-Box scrapped 20,000 pounds of hamburger patties produced at meat plants where the bacteria was suspected to have originated. It also changed meat suppliers and added extra meat inspections of its own at an expected cost of $2 million a year.

Consumer groups advocated a 160-degree internal temperature for cooking and a requirement that the meat no longer be pink or red inside.

A class action law suit brought by plaintiffs with minor E-Coli effects was settled for $12 million. Two other suits, brought on behalf of children who went into comas, were settled for $3 million and $15.6 million respectively.

Discussion Questions

1. In 1993 Jack-in-the-Box adopted tougher standards for its meat suppliers than those required by the federal government so that suppliers test more frequently for E-Coli. Could Jack-in-the-Box have done more after the outbreak occurred?

2. The link between cooking at 155 degrees and the destruction of E.coli bacteria has been publicly known for five years. The federal Centers for Disease Control tests showed Jack-in-the-Box hamburgers were cooked at 120 degrees. Should Jack-in-the-Box have increased cooking temperatures voluntarily and sooner?

3. What does the misplacement of the state health department notices on cooking temperature say about the culture at Jack-in-the-Box?

4. Are there moral issues involved in deciding what temperature to cook meat at?

5. A plaintiff's lawyer praised Jack-in-the-Box saying, "They paid out in a way that made everybody walking away from the settlement table think they had been treated fairly." What do we learn about the company from this statement?

CASE 7.16: "DATELINE NBC": PICK UP GM FROM THE GM PICKUP STORY

On its "Dateline NBC" program, NBC News reported on safety issues involving sidesaddle gas tanks on General Motors (GM) trucks manufactured between 1973 and 1987. The report included a videotape of a staged crash conducted by NBC News and its consultants. A fire erupted when a car struck the side of a GM truck, and the NBC correspondent reported that the gas tank had ruptured.

Furious over the "Dateline NBC" report, GM alleged the crash shown involved a truck rigged with model rocket engines and sued NBC for defamation.

NBC News president Michael Gartner admitted that "sparking devices" were used but maintained the report was still fair and accurate.

GM's information on the tests came from an Indiana journalist who had learned of the test rigging from local firefighters who had helped at the test site. A videotape of the crash shot by a firefighter and still pictures taken by his girlfriend clearly showed white smoke coming from the rockets affixed to the underside of the truck before the crash. Based on the photos, GM searched area junkyards and found the test truck with its gas cap tossed in its bed, along with the duct tape used to attach the explosives.

The fuel tanks had been kept by the firm NBC hired to do the tests, the Institute for Safety Analysis. This firm supplies plaintiffs' expert witnesses in crash cases.

NBC officials maintained the rocket engines were taped to the truck but denied they sparked the fire. The broadcaster did agree to apologize, however. The apology was read on "Dateline NBC" by anchors Jane Pauley and Stone Phillips:

> We deeply regret that we included the inappropriate demonstration in our "Dateline" report.
>
> We apologize to our viewers and to General Motors.
>
> We acknowledge the placing of the incendiary devices was a bad idea from start to finish.
>
> The GM truck gas tank was not punctured by the collision, although "Dateline" said it was in its report.
>
> This unscientific demonstration was not representative of an actual side impact collision.

NBC's Gartner resigned following the apology, and the reporter and producers of the story were fired. NBC agreed to pay GM for the cost of its investigation and its legal fees.

Discussion Questions

1. Why did NBC embellish the staged accident?
2. Is it significant that outsiders disclosed that the test was rigged?
3. Even if the rockets did not cause the explosion, was it ethical to use them?
4. Did the firm hired by NBC to stage the accident have a conflict of interest?
5. If you were an NBC employee at the scene of the staging, what would you have done?

UNIT EIGHT
BUSINESS AND
GOVERNMENT

Businesses are regulated by government agencies, but they also provide goods and services to those same agencies. Unique ethical dilemmas arise on both sides when the private and public sectors cross.

Section A
Government Employees

"I want a society that is based on truth. That means no longer hiding what we used to hide."

Boris Yeltsin

Dishonesty by government officials and employees not only costs us money, it undermines our faith in their integrity and that of our public institutions. Ethical breaches by government employees have far-reaching effects because they are so public.

—Michael Josephson

Case 8.1: A Club in My Name

The Keds Corporation paid $7.2 million to the fifty state attorneys general to settle a complaint that the shoemaker had engaged in price fixing involving several lines of Keds' girls and womens shoes. The attorneys general each received a portion of the $7.2 million and had agreed to give the money to charities. Most donated the funds to Boys and Girls Clubs in their states.

Arizona's attorney general, Grant Woods, donated his state's share, $85,500, to the Mesa Boys and Girls Club, which used the money to help build a $3 million clubhouse that it then named after Woods.

A state representative noted:

It is a very good cause and I support the Boys and Girls Club, but that is not the point. The money is public money. It is not [Woods's] money.

My point is that no agency or director should be able to direct money to any specific personal cause or for personal use.

Discussion Questions

1. What issues of propriety are raised?
2. Is it bad form to raise ethical issues when all the money went to charity?
3. How could the state representative's reaction have been anticipated?

Case 8.2: The Fireman and His Family

Robert "Hoot" Gibson served with the Phoenix Fire Department for nearly four decades. He was serving as deputy chief when he retired immediately after a four-month investigation revealed the following:

- holiday pay of $5,000 to employees who had not actually worked those holidays;
- three employees were permitted to store their pontoon boat at a city property;
- Design 10, a company owned by Gibson's wife and three children, had the contract for clothing sales to the fire department;
- Gibson's son was hired to open the department's print shop; and
- Relatives of Gibson and other employees were hired as temporary employees without going through standard hiring procedures.

Discussion Questions

1. What ethical breaches could you see in this conduct?
2. What tests could have been applied to prevent these decisions from being made?

Case 8.3: The Censured and Resigning Council Member

The following chronology details the actions of Mr. Jim Stapley, a former member of the Mesa City Council.

March 1994
- Stapley printed a photograph of him and former President Reagan in a campaign brochure for the City Council primary election. The photo was taken with a cardboard cutout of the former president, however.

April 1996
- Councilwoman Joan Payne leaked word of a 15-month-old memo to the city manager in which she accused Stapley of putting his hand on her knee during a helicopter ride and of mailing her pornographic material. She asked the city manager to order Stapley to stay away from her.

In response, Stapley issued his own memo a few days later, saying that Payne touched his knee.

May 1997

■ Stapley called a Mesa justice of the peace about an eviction case proceeding against his son William. The case was later transferred to another Mesa Justice Court, but the judge said the two actions were not related.

June 1997

■ Stapley sought to have disorderly conduct charges dropped against Lee Watkins, a friend and political ally. In addition, Stapley sought to have the city prosecutor fired. The council voted to censure Stapley after this incident, minutes after a measure to oust him failed by two votes.

July 1997

■ Stapley filed a lawsuit against Payne, saying she defamed him in two radio appearances by calling him a "pervert in polyester" and a "racist." The suit was settled in October. Terms were not made public.

August 1997

■ Stapley possibly violated his censure by placing several calls to Mesa Fire-fighters Union President Chris Medrea about a $1,000 donation the union made to Payne's legal defense fund, established after Stapley sued her for defamation. Stapley said he feels he didn't violate the censure because he was contacting Medrea in his role with the union, not as a city firefighter.

October 1997

■ A memo surfaced in which Stapley was accused of impersonating a Pinal County sheriff's detective at a Florence courthouse in February 1995. Police records say Stapley flashed a police badge and said he was a detective when he visited the clerk's office at Pinal County Superior Court. He was looking for a search warrant affidavit on a narcotics case involving his son, Kenneth.

■ Stapley circulated petitions at a meeting attended by city employees. The action may have been unethical, since city policy forbids candidates to ask city employees to sign petitions in city buildings on city time.

Following the October 1997 impersonation, Mr. Stapley resigned.

Discussion Questions

1. What ethical breaches do you feel occurred?
2. What impact would Mr. Stapley's conduct have on employees?
3. Would Mr. Stapley's involvement affect the wheels of justice?
4. Do you think employees would be comfortable complaining?

CASE 8.4: IRS EMPLOYEES AND SENSITIVE DATA

In 1997, the IRS disciplined hundreds of employees for using agency computers and records to browse through the tax records of friends, relatives and celebrities. The IRS fired 23 employees, disciplined 349 and provided counseling for 472.

During 1996 and 1997, the IRS investigated 1,515 cases of "snooping" among its 102,000 employees. Half of the employees have computer access to taxpayer returns.

Those employees who were counseled said they did not believe that what they did was wrong nor that there would be any sanctions for doing it. The law is not violated by "snooping", it is violated only if the information is disclosed to others.

Discussion Questions

1. What is so bad about snooping?
2. Should the law be the only standard?
3. What if the snooping was used only for clues to help in litigation?

SECTION B GOVERNMENT CONTRACTS

The existence of unlimited sources of funds often is used to justify behavior. In government contracts, the supply of funds seems endless, and the competition is stiff. These benefits and pressures often cause poor resolutions of ethical dilemmas. Pay particular attention to the impact of media coverage in the cases.

CASE 8.5: STANFORD UNIVERSITY AND GOVERNMENT OVERHEAD PAYMENTS

Included in government research grants to universities are indirect cost payments designed to compensate for the researchers' use of the schools' facilities.

Stanford University received approximately $240 million in federal research funds annually. About $75 million went to actual research, while Stanford billed the federal government $85 million, or 20 percent of its operating budget for its overhead. The rest of the research funds went toward employee benefits. An audit of Stanford's research program in 1990 by U.S. Navy accountant Paul Biddle revealed that the school billed the government for a $3,000 cedar-lined closet in president Donald Kennedy's home (Hoover House), $2,000 for flowers, $2,500 for refurbishing a grand piano, $7,000 in bedsheets and table linens, a $4,000 reception for trustees following Kennedy's 1987 wedding, and $184,000 in depreciation for a seventy-two-foot yacht as part of the indirect costs for federally funded research.

In response to the audit, Stanford withdrew requests for reimbursement totaling $1.35 million as unallowable and inappropriate costs. Stanford's federal funds were cut by $18 million per year.

Kennedy issued the following statements as the funding crisis evolved:

December 18, 1990: What was intended as government policy to build the capacity of universities through reimbursement of indirect costs leads to payments that are all too easily misunderstood.

Therefore, we will be reexamining our policies in an effort to avoid any confusion that might result.

At the same time, it is important to recognize that the items currently questioned, taken together, have an insignificant impact on Stanford's indirect-cost rate. . . .

Moreover, Stanford routinely charges the government less than our full indirect costs precisely to allow for errors and disallowances.

—*From a university statement*

January 14, 1991: We certainly ought to prune anything that isn't allowable—there isn't any question about that. But we're extending that examination to things that, although we believe are perfectly allowable, don't strike people as reasonable.

I don't care whether it's flowers, or dinners and receptions, or whether it's washing the table linen after it's been used, or buying an antique here or there, or refinishing a piano when its finish gets crappy, or repairing a closet and refinishing it—all those are investments in a university facility that serves a whole array of functions.

—*From an interview with the Stanford Daily*

January 23, 1991: Because acute public attention on these items threatens to over-shadow the more important and fundamental issue of the support of federally sponsored research, Stanford is voluntarily withdrawing all general administration costs for operation of Hoover House claimed for the fiscal years since 1981. For those same years, we are also voluntarily withdrawing all such costs claimed for the operations of two other university-owned facilities.

—*From a university statement*

February 19, 1991: I am troubled by costs that are perfectly appropriate as university expenditures and lawful under the government rules but I believe ought not be charged to the taxpayer. I should have been more alert to this policy issue, and I should have insisted on more intensive review of these transactions.

—*From remarks to alumni*

March 23, 1991: Our obligation is not to do all the law permits, but to do what is right. Technical legality is not the guiding principle. Even in matters as arcane as government cost accounting, we must figure out what is appropriate and act accordingly. Over the years, we have not hesitated to reject numerous lawful and attractive business proposals, gifts, and even federal grants because they came with conditions we thought would be inappropriate for Stanford. Yet, with respect to indirect-cost recovery, we pursued what was permissible under the rules, without applying our customary standard of what is proper. . . .

The expenses for Hoover House—antique furniture, flowers, cedar closets—should have been excluded, and they weren't. That the amounts involved were relatively small is fortunate, but it doesn't excuse us. In our testimony before the subcommittee I did deal with this issue, but I obviously wasn't clear enough. I explained that we were removing Hoover House and some similar accounts from the cost pools that drew indirect-cost recovery because they plainly included inappropriate items. What came out in the papers was that Stanford removed the costs because it was forced to, not because it was wrong. . . . That is not so. To repeat, the allocation of these expenses to indirect-cost pools is inappropriate, regardless of its propriety under the law.

—*From remarks to alumni*[1]

1. Karen Grassmuch, "What Happened at Stanford: Key Mistakes at Crucial Times in a Battle with the Government over Research Costs," *Chronicle of Higher Education*, 15 May 1991, A26.

By July 1991, Kennedy announced his resignation, effective August 1992, stating, "It is very difficult . . . for a person identified with a problem to be a spokesman for its solution."[2] Gerhard Casper, who was hired as Stanford's new president, said, "I just want this to remain one of the great universities in the world. I ask that we question what we are doing every day." Kennedy remains at Stanford, teaching biology.

Discussion Questions

1. Did Kennedy's ethics evolve during the crisis? Contrast his March 23, 1991, ethical posture with his December 18, 1990, assessment.
2. Is legal behavior always ethical behavior?
3. Do Casper's remarks reflect an ethical formula for Stanford's operations?

CASE 8.6: THE DEGREES-FOR-GRANTS PROGRAM

Walter Frost was a professor of aerospace-related sciences at the University of Tennessee Space Institute. The specialized campus for graduate aerospace studies is in Tullahoma, 135 miles from the University of Tennessee's main campus in Knoxville. It is next to an Air Force Base and fifty miles from a large Army base and missile command center in Huntsville, Alabama.

Frost's work on wind shear and other flight hazards interested the National Aeronautics and Space Administration (NASA). In 1975, Frost established FWG Associates, Inc., a for-profit research firm to which the University of Tennessee gave cheap office space in a research park. From 1981 to 1991, FWG earned $5.2 million from NASA on contracts. FWG also had contracts with the Army. Frost was doing very well, he drove a Porsche or Cadillac and hosted Christmas parties with dinner for one hundred at Nashville's Opryland Hotel.

A number of NASA, Army, and other federal government employees became students of Frost in the master's and doctoral degree programs at the university. Leon Felkins, an FWG employee, began noticing similarities between drafts of documents FWG was preparing for government contracts and the master's theses and doctoral dissertations being completed by government employees. Felkins charged that Frost "would get paid to do a study for NASA and he would do a study. Then one day the cover sheet on the report would change and it would become someone's dissertation."

For example, Dennis Faulkner, a civilian employee at the U.S. Army Space Center in Huntsville, was awarded a doctorate in May 1990. The following excerpts from an FWG report and Faulkner's dissertation illustrate Felkins's point:

> In addition to the spatial velocity and reflectivity fields of the JAWS microbursts, which were analyzed and reported by Frost, et al. (1985), JAWS data sets also provided turbulence information in the form of radar-measured pulse, wind, and total standard deviations (defined below).
> —"Development of a Microburst Turbulence Model" by H.P. Chang and Walter Frost, March 1987

---

2. "Embattled Stanford President to Quit," *Mesa Tribune*, 30 July 1991, A6.

In addition to the spatial velocity and reflectivity fields of the JAWS microbursts, which were analyzed and reported by Frost, et al. (1985), JAWS data sets also provided turbulence information in the form of radar-measured pulse, wind, and total standard deviations (defined below).
—*Dennis A. Faulkner doctoral dissertation, May 1990*

Peggy Potter, a NASA scientist, earned a master's degree in 1989 from the University after studying under Frost. The following excerpts from an FWG report and her thesis were discovered by university officials:

5.0 CONCLUSIONS

From the data set gathered at VAFB SLC-6 Tower 301 during the period from April 1975 to March 1982 the following concluding remarks may be made:

1. The most prevailing wind directions at Tower 301 are from north, northeast, southwest, and northwest especially in the spring and summer. Over 60 percent of the wind is from north. Significant diurnal variation of wind speeds occurs in the summer and fall months.
—*FWG Associates report to NASA by H.P. Chang and Walter Frost, February 26, 1987*

5.0 CONCLUSIONS

From the data set gathered at VAFB SLC-6 Tower 301 during the period from April 1975 to March 1982 the following concluding remarks are made:

1. The most prevailing wind directions at Tower 301 are from north, northeast, southwest, and northwest especially in the spring and summer over 60 percent of the wind from north. Significant diurnal variation of wind speeds appeared in the summer and fall months.
—*Peggy S. Potter master's thesis, December 1989*[3]

John S. Theon, chief of NASA's Radiation Dynamics and Hydrology Branch in Washington, D.C., entered the Ph.D. program at the Space Institute in 1983 and received his degree eighteen months later with a dissertation on the effects of orography. In 1984, NASA awarded FWG a contract on "Orographic Program Data." Eight pages of diagrams in the FWG reports are the same as diagrams in Theon's dissertation.

Upon the university's discovery of the similarities in FWG work and the theses and dissertations, Frost retired. Two students were asked to return their degrees and one filed a lawsuit against the University of Tennessee.

Discussion Questions

1. Was anyone really harmed by the degrees being awarded?
2. How would you have acted if you had been an FWG employee and knew of the similarities?

---

3. If you were an Army engineer with the opportunity to easily earn a Ph.D., would you have accepted the FWG work as your dissertation?
4. Is there a conflict of interest with the institute and the university?
5. Isn't all business based on the notion of quid pro quo?

CASE 8.7: CASINO LEASES AND THE COUNTY SUPERVISOR

Yvonne Atkinson Gates, the chairman of the Clark County, Nevada, Commission, an elected office, also operated her own daiquiri business. Many of the new and expanding hotels in Clark County, where Las Vegas is located, have retail space available for shops and restaurants. Ms. Atkinson Gates, as a commissioner, makes decisions on whether proposed hotels and expansions will be approved.

Ms. Atkinson Gates was alleged to have approached executives from five casinos about leasing space for her daiquiri franchises. Ms. Atkinson Gates acknowledges the contacts but that they "were made in passing and cannot be considered solicitations." She acknowledged actually seeking an arrangement with MGM Grand Resorts.

Sheldon Adelson, the chairman of Las Vegas Sands, Inc. said, "I was shocked, absolutely shocked that Yvonne would come to me directly. I felt she was pressuring me to agree. And when I didn't, I think she went out of her way to vote against my project." Adelson wanted to build a Sands Venetian Mall, but his proposal was not approved by the commission.

The state Ethics Commission is investigating Ms. Atkinson Gates' conduct with her daiquiri business.

Discussion Questions

1. Is there a conflict in Ms. Atkinson Gates' solicitations?
2. How should she handle the business solicitations?
3. What conclusions did Mr. Adelson draw? Is he justified?
4. Ms. Atkinson Gates says she is a silent partner. Does this status help?

CASE 8.8: BIDS, EMPLOYEES AND CONFLICTS

The state of Arizona awarded the contract for indemnity insurance for the state's 55,000 employees to Intergroup of Arizona. An investigation by the Attorney General's office found that the Department of Administration, the agency responsible for reviewing bids and awarding contracts, permitted a state employee who is the wife of an Intergroup executive, to make key decisions about the insurance bids and the process.

By the time the investigation was completed, the contract had been awarded.

Discussion Question

1. What problems do you see with the process?
2. Why do you think no one said anything until the investigation was conducted?
3. How will Intergroup fare in the next round of contract bids?

Section C
Government
Responsibilities

How careful must government be with our money? The accountability of government employees for managing funds and resources is a critical area of focus in ethics.

Case 8.9: Orange County: Derivative Capital of the United States

On December 6, 1994, Orange County, California, filed for bankruptcy protection. The chairman of the Orange County Board of Supervisors said the step was necessary to prevent local agencies from withdrawing their funds from the county's investment fund of $7.5 billion, which might force a fire sale of the fund's assets.

The investment pool had substantial holdings in risky financial instruments known as derivatives (see Case 4.6 for more information) that would provide returns only if interest rates continued to fall. Interest rates rose, and Orange County had large debts from borrowing to invest in derivatives. As a result, the county could not pay its creditors and its investment pool lost $2.5 billion. The investments had been masterminded by County Treasurer Robert Citron.

Twelve different brokerage houses were left with loans to Orange County that might not be repaid. The announcement of the county's bankruptcy caused the stock market to plunge fifty points. Litigation is pending by school districts and other government entities against the brokers who handled the derivatives sales. Hiring was frozen in the county, and many people with disabilities whose funds were in the Orange County investment pool could not withdraw their money because of the bankruptcy.

Discussion Questions

1. Should government investment decisions be based on factors different from those used in making private investment decisions?
2. List all the groups of people affected by the losses in Orange County.
3. What impact will Orange County's bankruptcy have on the ability of other government entities to sell their bonds?
4. Would you invest your own money in derivatives?
5. Should Orange County voters and investment pool participants have been given more information on the risk?
6. Should brokers who made the investment be held liable for advising Orange County to purchase unsuitable securities for its funds?

CASE 8.10: CARS AND CONFLICTS

Maricopa County supervisors, Mary Rose Wilcox and Ed King (elected officials), turned in their county cars that they had been taking home with them. King's chief administrator also turned in his car. County policy is that employees may check out cars but should not drive them home without prior authorization, which is given only for night hearings or activities and next-day trips where distance to a car pick-up at the motor pool makes it time prohibitive.

Their use of vehicles was revealed in a public meeting by another supervisor who said it was "feeding off the taxpayers and sending the wrong message to county employees."

Discussion Questions

1. Mrs. Wilcox apologized and said, "Sometimes, you get so immersed in things that you don't see what's right. I made a mistake, and for that, I'm sorry." What could have helped her see the issue?
2. What operational dangers for government agencies arise when elected officials don't follow the rules?

SOURCES

Sources for Case 2.1

Frisby, Michael K., and Bruce Ingersoll. "First Lady Turned $1,000 Investment Into a $98,000 Profit, Records Show." *Wall Street Journal*, 30 March 1994, A1.

"Hillary in the Pits." *Wall Street Journal*, 30 March 1994, A18.

Ingersoll, Bruce. "Agriculture Chief's Handling of Chicken Industry Revives Questions About Clinton's Ties to Tyson." *Wall Street Journal*, 17 March 1994, A16.

"O Tempora! O Mores!" *Wall Street Journal*, 21 March 1994, A18.

Sources for Case 2.3

Burton, Thomas M. "Doctor-Owned Labs Earn Lavish Profits In a Captive Market." *Wall Street Journal*, 1 March 1989, A1, A6.

Burton, Thomas M. "Doctors May Refer Patients to Labs Owned by Doctors, Doctors' Group Says." *Wall Street Journal*, 24 June 1992, B6.

Sources for Case 2.6

"Asides." *Wall Street Journal*, 30 December 1997, A10.

Behar, Richard. "On Fresh Ground." *Time*, 26 December 1994, 111.

Behar, Richard, and Michael Kramer. "Something Smells Fowl." *Time*, 17 October 1994, 42–44.

Benedetto, Richard. "Calls Ethics Accusations Distracting." *USA Today*, 4 October 1994, 1A.

Benedetto, Richard. "A Personnel Loss for Clinton." *USA Today*, 4 October 1994, 3A.

Cauchon, Dennis. "Millionaire Tyson Stretches Political Limits." *USA Today*, 5 October 1994, 4A.

Clark, Kim. "Tough Times for the Chicken King." *Fortune*, 28 October 1996, 88–97.

Eastland, Terry. "How Justice Tried to Stop Smaltz." *Wall Street Journal*, 22 December 1997, A19.

"Espy Quits with Push from Clinton." *Arizona Republic*, 4 October 1994, A1, A9.

"Espy to Court." *USA Today*, 11 September 1997, 6A.

Fields, Gary and Tom Squiteri. "Tough Term Is Warning in Intern Scandal." *USA Today*, 19 March 1998, 1A.

Godrey, John. "Tyson Foods is Fined $6 Million." *Washington Times*, 11 January 1998, 1, 22.

Ingersoll, Bruce. "Agriculture Chief's Handling of Chicken Industry Revives Questions About Clinton's Ties to Tyson." *Wall Street Journal*, 17 March 1994, A16.

Ingersoll, Bruce. "Espy Case Figure, John Hemmingson, Is Indicted Again." *Wall Street Journal*, 7 August 1996, B2.

Ingersoll, Bruce. "Espy Inquiry Focuses on Mystery Memo to Learn If Coverup Occurred Over Industry Favoritism." *Wall Street Journal*, 16 January 1995, A14.

Ingersoll, Bruce. "Former Lobbyist for Sun-Diamond Gets Split Decision in Trial on Aiding Espys." *Wall Street Journal*, 26 November 1997, B2.

Ingersoll, Bruce. "Lobbyist for Tyson Indicted in Espy Probe." *Wall Street Journal*, 18 September 1996, B5.

Ingersoll, Bruce. "Sun-Diamond Gets Find of $1.5 Million in Espy Affair." *Wall Street Journal*, 14 May 1997, B7.

Ingersoll, Bruce and Jeffrey H. Birnbaum. "Agriculture Secretary Espy Resigns Under Pressure From the White House." *Wall Street Journal*, 4 October 1994, A3.

Johnston, David. "Agriculture Chief Quits as Scrutiny of Conduct Grows." *New York Times*, 4 October 1994, A1, A11.

Nichols, Bill. "Espy's Once-Promising Political Career Probably Over." *USA Today*, 28 August 1997, 4A.

Nichols, Bill. "Ex-Cabinet Member Indicted." *USA Today*, 28 August 1997, 1A.

Novak, Viveca. "The Peril of Prosecutorial Passion." *Time*, 16 June 1997, 42.

Seper, Jerry. "Illegal Gifts, Cover-Up Charged in Espy Indictment." *Washington Times*, 7 September 1997, 11.

Seper, Jerry. "Judge OK's Tyson Foods' Plea Deal." *Washington Times*, 25 January 1998, 10.

Seper, Jerry. "Lobbyist for Tyson Indicted." *Washington Times*, 12 October 1997, 7.

Seper, Jerry. "Payments to Espy Brother Bring Big Fine." *Washington Times*, 25 January 1998, 10.

Seper, Jerry. "Tyson Foods is Names a Target in Espy Investigation." *Washington Times*, 6 July 1997, 8.

Stout, David. "Inquiry on Espy Leads to Indictment of Former Chief Aide." *New York Times*, 23 April 1997, A12.

Sources For Case 2.9

Starkman, Dean. "Five Brokers Indicted for Insider Trades Linked to Ex-Morgan Stanley Officer." *Wall Street Journal*, 23 December 1997, B9.

Starkman, Dean. "Three Indicted for Insider Trading Tied to Ex-Morgan Stanley Aide." *Wall Street Journal*, 25 November 1997, B2.

Truell, Peter. "An Employee on Wall Street is Arrested." *New York Times*, 7 November 1997, C8.

Truell, Peter. "Lessons of Boesky and Milken Go Unheeded in Fraud Case." *New York Times*, 26 November 1997, C1, C10.

Truell, Peter. "Sparring for Pieces of the Wall Street Action." *New York Times*, 26 December 1997, C1, C2.

Sources for Case 2.10

Carley, William M. "Secret Suit: What Did He Know?" *Wall Street Journal*, 19 January 1988, B1, B8.

"Judge Sets Michigan Venue for GM Suit Against VW." *Wall Street Journal*, 18 October 1996, B5.

Maremont, Mark and Joseph Pereira. "Engineer Indicted on Charges He Stole Trade Secrets on Gillette Shaving System." *Wall Street Journal*, 26 September 1997, B2.

"Non Compete Clauses are Serious." *Wall Street Journal*, 10 December 1996, A1.

Sources for Case 2.11

Fuchsberg, Gilbert. "Harvard Has Some Crimson Faces Over a Lesson in Practical Politics." *Wall Street Journal*, Apr. 9, 1992, B1.

"Harvard Student Rigging Election Must Write Paper." *Wall Street Journal*, April 24, 1992, A3.

Source for Case 2.12

Barry, Dan. "Cheating Hearts and Lying Resumes." *New York Times*, 14 December 1997, WK1, WK4.

Source for Cases 2.13 and 2.14

Jennings, Marianne. "How Ethical Are You?" *Business Credit*, April 1992, 32–33.

Sources for Case 2.15

Johnson, Kirk. "Connecticut Lawmakers Legalize Radar Detectors." *New York Times*, 23 June 1992, A6.

"U.S. Acts to Ban Radar Detectors in Big Trucks." *New York Times*, 12 November 1993, A1, A16.

Source for Case 2.16

Shellenbarger, Sue. "How to Look Like a Workaholic While Still Having a Life." *Wall Street Journal*, 28 December 1994, B1.

Source for Case 2.17

Crawford Rehabilitation Services, Inv. v. Weissman, 1997 WL 304917 (Colo. 1997).

Sources for Case 3.1

Cohen, Cynthia. "Perils of Partnership Reviews: Lessons from Price Waterhouse v. Hopkins." *Labor Law Journal* (October 1991): 677–82.

Interview with Ann Hopkins, 18 June 1993.

"More Women Become Partners in Accounting." *Wall Street Journal*, 10 August 1993: B1.

Price Waterhouse v. Hopkins, 490 U.S. 228 (1989).

Sources for Case 3.2

Kennen, William, Jr. "Handwriting Analysis—What Can It Tell You?" *Sales and Marketing Management* (April 1990): 44–47.

Sackheim, Kathryn K. *Handwriting Analysis and the Employee Selection Process.* Westport, Conn.: Quorum Books, 1990.

Source for Case 3.4

Stout, Hilary. "Paying Workers for Good Health Habits Catches On as a Way to Cut Medical Costs." *Wall Street Journal,* 26 November 1991, B1, B5.

Sources for Case 3.5

Castro, Janice, et al. "Battling the Enemy Within." *Time,* 17 March 1986: 52–61.

Eisen, Jerry. "Companies Increase Use of Testing to Determine Dishonesty, Drug Use." *Arizona Business Gazette,* 29 February 1988, 13.

Gary, Roderick. "Drugs in the Workplace." *Arizona Daily Star,* 8 January 1989, F1, F5.

Hess, David. "Drug Tests Urged in Jobs Dealing With Public Trust." *Arizona Republic,* 19 August 1986, A1.

Sources for Case 3.6

Behar, Richard. "Who's Reading Your E-Mail?" *Fortune,* 3 February 1997, 57–70.

Bulkeley, William M. "Voice Mail May Let Competitors Dial 'E' for Espionage." *Wall Street Journal,* 28 September 1993, B1, B9.

Couch, Mark P. "E-Mail Can Return to Haunt Employers, Workers." *Mesa Tribune,* 2 February 1997, E1, E5.

Garza, Christina E. "The Touchy Ethics of Corporate Anthropology." *Business Week,* 30 September 1991, 78.

Jacobson, David C., et al. "Peril of the E-Mail Trail." *National Law Journal,* 16 January 1995, C1, C22.

Rothfeder, Jeffrey, et al. "Is Your Boss Spying on You?" *Business Week,* 15 January 1990, 74–75.

Source for Case 3.7

Lane, Randall. "Nice Guys Finish First." *Forbes,* 16 December 1996, 236–242.

Source for Case 3.8

Graff, James L. and Andrea Sachs. "It Was a Joke!" *Time,* 28 July 1997, 62.

Sources for Case 3.9

Blum, Andrew. "Hooter Suit Lawyer Faces Ethics Complaint." *National Law Journal,* 15 November 1993: 13.

Gibson, Richard. "Hooters Tries to Do Good Works By Selling Lots of Chicken Wings." *Wall Street Journal*, 8 February 1995, B1.

Source for Case 3.10

International Union v. Johnson Controls, Inc., 499 U.S. 187 (1991).

Sources for Case 3.11

de Lisser, Eleena and Benjamin A. Holden. "Denny's Begins Repairing Its Image—and Its Attitude." *Wall Street Journal*, 11 March 1994, B1, B3.

"Denny's Settles Bias Case." *Arizona Republic*, 29 May 1994, A12.

Hawkins, Chuck. "Denny's: The Stain That Isn't Coming Out." *Business Week*, 28 June 1993, 98–99.

Jones, Del. "Denny's Checks Smaller Than Plaintiffs Expected." *USA Today*, 12 December 1995, 1B.

Rice, Faye. "Denny's Changes Its Spots." *Fortune*, 13 May 1996, 133–140.

Thomas, Emory. "Denny's Shines Its Bad Image With New Deal." *Wall Street Journal*, 9 November 1994, B1, B7.

Walker, Blair S. "Denny's, NAACP Sign $1 Billion Pact." *USA Today*, 2 July 1993, 1B.

Sources for Case 3.12

Donovan, Karen. "Is Texaco's Counsel Really Independent?" *National Law Journal*, 25 November 1996, A6.

Eichenwald, Kurt. "An Unsought Role on a Bigger Stage." *New York Times*, 14 November 1996, C4.

Eichenwald, Kurt. "Blowing the Whistle, and Now Facing the Music." *New York Times*, 16 March 1994, 3–1.

Eichenwald, Kurt. "Ex-Texaco Official Charged with Obstruction of Justice." *New York Times*, 20 November 1996, A1, C4.

Eichenwald, Kurt. "Rights Groups Urge Boycott of Texaco." *New York Times*, 13 November 1996, C1, C6.

Eichenwald, Kurt. "Texaco Executives, On Tape, Discussed Impeding a Bias Suit." *New York Times*, 4 November 1996, A1, C4.

Eichenwald, Kurt. "The Two Faces of Texaco." *New York Times*, 10 November 1996, 3–1, 3–2, 3–10, 3–11.

Eichenwald, Kurt. "U.S. Inquiring Into Texaco's Actions in Suit." *New York Times*, 5 November 1996, C1.

Enrico, Dottie. "Charges of Racism, Sexism Cut Deep." *USA Today*, 12 November 1996, 1B, 2B.

Ewing, Terzah. "Ex-Texaco Official Is Indicted in Case Tied to Bias Suit." *Wall Street Journal*, 30 June 1997, A9.

Firtsch, Peter, Allanna Sullivan, and Rochelle Sharp. "Texaco to Pay $176.1 Million in Boas Suit." *Wall Street Journal*, 18 November 1996, A3–A4.

Herbert, Bob. "Shell Oil's Own Little Problem." *New York Times*, 22 November 1996, A15.

Jenkins, Holman W., Jr. "Texaco Ransoms Its Image for $176 Million." *Wall Street Journal*, 26 November 1996, A19.

Jones, Del. "Jackson Calls for Boycott of Texaco." *USA Today*, 13 November 1996, 1A.

Jones, Del and Ellen Neuborne. "Texaco Settles Bias Lawsuit." *USA Today*, 18 November 1996, B1.

Neuborne, Ellen. "Ex-Texaco Exec Accused of Obstruction." *USA Today*, 20 November 1996, A1.

Neuborne, Ellen. "Texaco Tapes Show Companies Have a Way to Go." *USA Today*, 5 November 1996, 1C.

"Portrait of a Company Behaving Badly." Bari-Ellen Roberts' excerpts from her book with *Time* reporter Jack E. White, *Roberts v. Texaco*, as excerpted in *Time*, 16 March 1998, 47–51.

Powers, Lenita and Kathy Balog. "Texaco Boycott Low Key, But Worries Some." *USA Today*, 14 November 1996, 1B.

"Texaco Names First Black Woman." *USA Today*, 8 July 1997, 2B.

"Texaco to Pay $176 Million to End Bias Suit." *Arizona Republic*, 16 November 1996, A1–A2.

Sources for Case 3.13

Dowd, Maureen. "Civil Rights Siren." *New York Times*, 24 December 1997, A13.

Oldenburg, Ann. "Actress Fired for Being Pregnant Wins Lawsuit." *USA Today*, 23 December 1997, 1D.

Oldenburg, Ann. "'Hurt' Spelling Says Tylo's Pregnancy Wasn't Issue." *USA Today*, 26 December 1997, 1D.

Source for Case 3.14

Granser v. Box Tree South, Ltd., 623 NYS2d 977 (Sup Ct 1994).

Sources for Case 3.15

Carley, William M. "Don't Read This! There is Stuff Here That's Confidential." *Wall Street Journal*, 7 April 1997, A1, A8.

"Noncompete Clauses are Serious." *Wall Street Journal*, 10 December 1996, A1.

Source for Case 3.16

Haller, Vera. "Baby Juice Scam Nets Executives Fine, Prison Time." *Mesa Tribune*, 17 June 1988, A10.

Sources for Case 3.17

Bloom, Michael A. "Key in New Era Settlement." *National Law Journal*, 15 July 1996, A4.

Carton, Barbara. "Unlikely Hero: A Persistent Accountant Brought New Era's Problems to Light." *Wall Street Journal*, 19 May 1995, B1, B10.

Davis, Ann. "Charity's Troubles Put Dechert in Bind." *National Law Journal*, 29 May 1995, A6.

Gerlin, Andrea. "Among the Few Given Money by New Era, Many See Blessings in Giving It Back." *Wall Street Journal*, 20 June 1995, B1, B10.

Lambert, Wade. "Trustee in New Era Bankruptcy May Pursue 'Donations.'" *Wall Street Journal*, 22 May 1995, B3.

Secklow, Steve. "A New Era Consultant Lured Rich Donors Over Pancakes, Prayers." *Wall Street Journal*, 2 June 1995, A1, A4.

Secklow, Steve. "How New Era's Boss Led Rich and Gullible Into a Web of Deceit." *Wall Street Journal*, 19 May 1995, A1, A5.

Secklow, Steve. "New Era's Bennett Gets 12-Year Sentence." *Wall Street Journal*, 23 September 1997, B13.

Secklow, Steve. "Prudential Securities Agrees to Settle New Era Suits by Paying $18 Million." *Wall Street Journal*, 18 November 1996, A4.

Secklow, Steve. "Retired Judge Will Sort Out New Era Mess." *Wall Street Journal*, 29 June 1995, B1, B16.

Secklow, Steve and Joseph Rebello. "IRS is Studying Whether New Era's Donors Committed Fraud on Deductions." *Wall Street Journal*, 24 May 1995, A3.

Slobodzian, Joseph. "New Era Founder Says: God Made Him Do It." *National Law Journal*, 17 March 1997, A9.

Wulf, Steve. "Too Good to Be True." *Time*, 29 May 1995, 34.

Sources for Case 3.18

Alexander, Keith. "Judy: Dow Chemical 'Negligent'." *USA Today*, 19 August 1997, 1A.

Blakeslee, Sandra. "Lawyers Say Dow Study Saw Implant Danger." *New York Times*, 7 April 1994, A1, A9.

Bossert, Rex. "Breast Implant Suits: A Bankruptcy Matter?" *National Law Journal*, 14 April 1997, A1, A24.

Burton, Thomas M. "3M, Four Others Join Implant Settlement." *Wall Street Journal*, 12 April 1994, B8.

Burton, Thomas M., "Dow Chemical, for First Time, Is Found Liable in a Trial Over Breast Implants," *Wall Street Journal*, 16 February 1995, B8.

Burton, Thomas M. "Dow Chemical Wins Victory on Suit Site." *Wall Street Journal*, 12 May 1997, B10.

Burton, Thomas M. "Dow Corning Moves to Quit Chapter 11." *Wall Street Journal*, 3 December 1996, A3.

Burton, Thomas M. "Frequency of Reoperations for Women with Breast Implants Put at Nearly 25%." *Wall Street Journal*, 6 March 1997, B6.

Burton, Thomas M. "Silicone-Implant Plaintiffs to Propose Dow Corning Pay as Much as $3.8 Billion." *Wall Street Journal*, 10 March 1998, B9.

Byrne, John A. "Informed Consent." *Business Week*, 2 October 1995, 104–117.

Carey, John. "Breast-Implant Cases: Let the Science Testify." *Business Week*, 16 December 1996, 40.

"Dow Corning Prevails in Breast Implant Suit." *National Law Journal*, 26 September 1994, B2.

Edwards, Tamala M. "Sleights of Silicone." *Time*, 1 September 1997, 64.

Hopkins v. Dow Corning Corp., 1994 WL 460 325 (9th Cir. 1994).

In re Dow Corning, 86 F.3d 493 (1996).

Nocera, Joseph. "The Reversal of Fortune on Implants." *Fortune*, 29 September 1997, 28–29.

Taylor, Gary. "Implant Plaintiffs Reach Into a Deep Pocket." *National Law Journal*, 23 January 1995, A8.

Taylor, Gary, "Jurors Fault Dow Units on Implants," *National Law Journal*, 27 February 1995, A1.

Source for Case 3.19

Personal interview with John M. Gravitt, 24 June 1993.

Sources for Case 3.20

Hammonds, Keith H. "Lotus Opens a Door for Gay Partners," *Business Week*, 4 November 1991, 80, 85.

Neuborne, Ellen. "One in 10 Firms Extend Benefits to Life Partners." *USA Today*, 24 January 1997, 1B.

Sources for Case 3.21

Ballinger, Jeff and Claes Olsson. *Beyond the Swoosh: The Struggle of Indonesians Making Nike Shoes*, ICDA/Global Publications Foundations, Uppsala Sweden 1997.

Canedy, Dana. "Peering Into the Shadows of Corporate Dealings." *New York Times*, 25 March 1997, C1, C6.

Deane, Daniela. "Senators to Hear of Slave Labor on U.S. Soil." *USA Today*, 31 March 1998, 9A.

Frandsen, Jon. "Chinese Labor Practices Assailed." *The Mesa Tribune*, 19 March 1998, B2.

Gibbs, Nancy. "Suffer the Little Children." *Time*, 26 March 1990, 18.

Herbert, Bob. "Brutality in Vietnam." *New York Times*, 28 March 1997, A19.

King, Sharon R. "Flying the Swoosh and Stripes." *New York Times*, 19 March 1998, C1, C6.

Landler, Mark. "Reversing Course, Levi Strauss Will Expand Its Output in China." *New York Times*, 9 April 1998, C1.

Lowry, Tom and Bill Beyers. "Earnings Woes Trip Nike; Layoffs Loom." *USA Today*, 25 February 1998, 1B.

McCormick, John and Marc Levinson. "The Supply Police." *Newsweek*, 15 February 1993, 48–49.

Mitchell, Russell and Michael O'Neal, "Managing by Values."*Business Week*, 1 August 1994, 40–52.

Myerson, Allen R. "In Principle, a Case For More 'Sweatshops.'" *New York Times*, 22 June 1997, E5.

Neuborne, Ellen. "Nike to Take a Hit in Labor Report." *USA Today*, 27 March 1997, 1A.

Nichols, Martha. "Third-World Families at Work: Child Labor or Child Care?" *Harvard Business Review*, January–February 1993, 12–23.

"Nike Refuses to 'Just Do It.'" *Business Ethics*, Jan/Feb 1998, 8.

"Nike Tries to Quell Exploitation Charges." *Wall Street Journal*, 25 June 1997, A16.

"Nike's Workers in Third World Abused, Report Says." *Arizona Republic*, 28 March 1997, A10.

Richards, Bill. "Tripped Up By Too Many Shoes, Nike Regroups." *Wall Street Journal*, 3 March 1998, B1, B15.

Seller, Patricia. "Four Reasons Nike's Not Cool." *Fortune*, 30 March 1998, 26–28.

"Slave Labor." *Fortune*, 9 December 1996, 12.

"Susie Tompkins." *Business Ethics*, January/February 1995, 21–23.

Zachary, G. Pascal. "Levi Tries to Make Sure Contract Plants in Asia Treat Workers Well."*Wall Street Journal*, 28 July 1994, A1, A5.

Sources for Case 4.1

Baquet, Dean. "Tips on BCCI Flowed Freely for Years." *New York Times*, 27 August 1992, C1, C4.

Baquet, Dean, and Jeff Gerth. "Lawmaker's Defense of BCCI Went Beyond Speech in Senate." *New York Times*, 26 August 1992, A1.

Barrett, Paul. "Justice Agency, Which Let BCCI Out of Its Grip, Is Now Under Fire from Critics in Both Parties." *Wall Street Journal*, 1 August 1991, A14.

"BCCI Hits Home." *Time*, 20 July 1992, 17.

"BCCI Opening." *Wall Street Journal*, 5 September 1995, A14.

"BCCI: The Never-Ending Story." *The Banker*, January 1992, 4.

"The BCCI Trail." *The Economist*, 27 July 1991, 13–14.

Beaty, Jonathan and Sam C. Gwynne. "The Dirtiest Bank of All," *Time*, 29 July 1991, 42–45.

Beaty, Jonathan, and Sam C. Gwynne. "The Riyadh Connection." *Time*, 10 August 1992, 40–41.

Beaty, Jonathan, and Sam C. Gwynne. "Is That All There Is?" *Time*, 30 December 1991, 59.

Berkman, Harvey. "Lawsuit Names BCCI Lawyers." *National Law Journal*, 25 July 1994, A4.

"Clark Clifford, Law Partner Indicted in BCCI Fraud." *Mesa Tribune*, 30 July 1992, A1.

Demick, Barbara. "Clifford Indicted in Bank Fraud." *Arizona Republic*, 30 July 1992, A1, A7.

Dwyer, Paula. "What Clifford and Altman Did Wrong." *Business Week*, 30 September 1991, 30.

Frankel, Bruce. "Pair Deny BCCI Charges." *USA Today*, 30 July 1992, 2A.

Gwynne, Sam C. "Innocent as Charged." *Time*, 30 August 1993, 34.

Kuttner, Robert. "Controlling the Climate That Let BCCI Bloom." *Business Week*, 29 July 1991, 16.

"Long Arm of the Law." *Time*, 13 July 1992, 18.

Prokesch, Steven. "Regulators Agree on Rules to Prevent More BCCI's." *New York Times*, 7 July 1992, C1, C4.

Puente, Maria. "Sen. Hatch Defends His Defense of BCCI." *USA Today*, 27 August 1992, 6A.

"That BCCI Can of Worms." *The Banker*, 19 August 1991, 4.

Truell, Peter, and Thomas Petzinger Jr. "Clifford, Altman Indicted in BCCI Case." *Wall Street Journal*, 30 July 1992, A2.

Sources for Case 4.2

Marshall, Steve. "Overcharges Force New Rx in Fla. Hospitals." *USA Today*, 6 July 1992, 1A.

Rundle, Rhonda. "How Doctors Boost Bills by Misrepresenting the Work They Do." *Wall Street Journal*, 6 December 1989, A1.

Winslow, Ron. "Medicare Tries to Save With One-Fee Billing for Some Operations." *Wall Street Journal*, 10 June 1992, A1, A5.

Sources for Case 4.3

Findlay, Steven. "3 Executives From Hospital Chain Indicted." *USA Today*, 31 July 1997, 1A.

Lagnado, Lucette. "Columbia/HCA Warns of Profit Decline." *Wall Street Journal*, 10 September 1997, A3.

Lagnado, Lucette. "Ex-Manager Describes the Profit-Driven Life Inside Columbia/HCA." *Wall Street Journal*, 30 May 1997, A1, A6.

Myerson, Allen R. "The Battle For Hearts and Tonsils." *New York Times*, 7 October 1997, C1, C4.

Woodyard, Chris. "Affidavit: Columbia Covered Up Medicare Error." *USA Today*, 8 October 1997, 3B.

Woodyard, Chris. "Columbia/HCA Lawsuits Plague Stock Holdings." *USA Today*, 20 August 1997, 3B.

Woodyard, Chris. "FBI Alleges Systemic Fraud at Columbia." *USA Today*, 7 October 1997, 1B.

Sources for Case 4.4

"Internal Probe Underway by Directors at MiniScribe." *Electronic News*, 29 May 1989, 19.

"ITT Qume Chief Named President at MiniScribe." *Electronic News*, 5 November 1984, 20–21.

Pollack, Andrew. "The $550 Million Verdict." *The New York Times*, 9 February 1992, C2.

Pollack, Andrew. "Large Award in MiniScribe Fraud Suit." *The New York Times*, 5 February 1992, C1.

Schneider, Michelle. "MiniScribe Execs Rigged Huge Fraud, Audit Says." *Rocky Mountain News*, 12 September 1989, 1B–2B.

Sleeth, Peter. "Audit to Compound MiniScribe's Troubles." *The Denver Post*, 6 August 1989, 1H–7H.

Sleeth, Peter. "MiniScribe Details 'Massive Fraud.'" *The Denver Post*, 12 September 1989, 1C, 4C.

Sleeth, Peter. "MiniScribe Stock Plunges 36%." *The Denver Post*, 13 September 1989, 1D.

Zipper, Stuart. "Filings Reveal MiniScribe Struggle." *Electronic News*, 15 January 1990, 38, 40.

Zipper, Stuart. "MiniScribe Seeks Chapter 11 Sale of Firm for $160M." *Electronic News*, 8 January 1990, 1, 54.

Sources for Case 4.5

Anders, George. "Phar-Mor Scandal Clouds Corporate Partners." *Wall Street Journal*, 6 August 1992, C1, C19.

Ansberry, Clare. "Phar-Mor's Problems May Give Boost to Rest of Drug Discount Industry." *Wall Street Journal*, 6 August 1992, A4.

Coleman, Calmetta Y. "Phar-Mor's Haft Agrees to Quit His Position." *Wall Street Journal*, 25 August 1997, B7.

Freudenheim, Milt. "Phar-Mor and Its Ex-Auditor Clash on Fraud Case." *New York Times*, 6 August 1992, C3.

Freudenheim, Milt. "Phar-Mor Says Profit Was Faked." *New York Times*, 5 August 1992, C1, C4.

"Hard Pills to Swallow." *Time*, 17 August 1992, 16.

"Monus, Co-Founder of Phar-Mor, Gets a 20-Year Sentence." *Wall Street Journal*, 4 December 1995, B8.

Murray, Matt. "Phar-Mor to Merge with Shopko Stores." *Wall Street Journal*, 10 September 1996, A3.

Murray, Matt. "Wounded Phar-Mor Found a Healer in Antonio Alvarez." *Wall Street Journal*, 26 May 1995, B1.

"Phar-Mor Dismisses 2 More." *New York Times*, 7 August 1992, C4.

"Phar-Mor, Inc. Plan for Reorganization Is Cleared by Judge." *Wall Street Journal*, 30 August 1995, A8.

Schiller, Zachary. "Wait A Minute—Phar-Mor Is Still Kicking." *Business Week*, 8 March 1993, 60, 61.

Stern, Gabriella. "Chicanery at Phar-Mor Ran Deep, Close Look at Discounter Shows." *Wall Street Journal*, 20 January 1994, A1, A4.

Stern, Gabriella. "Phar-Mor, Embattled Chain, Is Trying to Stem Panic Among Vendors, Lenders." *Wall Street Journal*, 12 August 1992, A3.

Stern, Gabriella. "Phar-Mor Fiasco Puts Shapira in Hot Seat." *Wall Street Journal*, 7 August 1992, B1.

Stern, Gabriella. "Phar-Mor Hires President, Shuffles Its Top Executives." *Wall Street Journal*, 5 February 1993, B2.

Stern, Gabriella, and Clare Ansberry. "A Founder Embezzles Millions for Basketball, Phar-Mor Chain Says." *Wall Street Journal*, 5 August 1992, A1, A8.

"2 New Plans for Phar-Mor in Revamping." *New York Times*, 25 April 1995, C2.

Williger, Stephen D. "Phar-Mor—A Lesson in Fraud." *Wall Street Journal*, 28 March 1994, A14.

Sources for Case 4.6

Antilla, Susan. "P & G Sees Charge on Derivatives." *New York Times*, 13 April 1994, C1, C16.

"Britain's Barings PLC Bets on Derivatives—and the Cost Is Dear." *Wall Street Journal*, 27 February 1995, A1, A6.

Colarusso, Dan. "Picking Up the Shattered Pieces of a Lifetime of Saving." *New York Times*, 1 September 1996, F3.

Craig, David. "Week's Hunt for Barings Trader Ends."*USA Today*, 3 March 1995, 1B, 2B.

Donovan, Karen. "Mutual Funds Confront Lawsuits over Derivatives." *National Law Journal*, 7 November 1994, A1, A24.

Donovan, Karen. "SEC, Lawyers Spar over Derivatives Restrictions." *National Law Journal*, 20 March 1995, B1, B2.

Dwyer, Paula, et al. "The Lesson from Barings' Straits." *Business Week*, 13 March 1995, 30–32.

Greenwald, John. "Derivatives Slump; Losers Go to Court." *National Law Journal*, 7 November 1994, A1, A24.

Holland, Kelly. "Derivatives: Alive, but Oh So Boring." *Business Week*, 30 January 1995, 76–77.

Itansell, Saul. "Piper Jaffray Agrees to Pay $70 Million." *New York Times*, 16 February 1995, C3.

Lipin, Steven. "Bankers Trust Say P&G Deal Wasn't Unique." *Wall Street Journal*, 22 November 1994, C1, C20.

MacDonald, Elizabeth. "FASB Moving Ahead on Rule on Derivatives." *Wall Street Journal*, 17 July 1997, A7.

Murray, Matt, and Paulette Thomas. "After the Fall: Fingers Point and Heads Roll." *Wall Street Journal*, 23 December 1994, B1, B4.

Pollack, Andrew. "First Boston to Pay Fine in Orange County Bond Offering." *New York Times*, 30 January 1998, C1, C6.

"The Sound of Pips Squeaking." *The Economist*, 23 November 1996, 91.

"Survey Reports on Derivative Usage." *Deloitte & Touche Review*, 13 May 1996, 1.

Sources for Case 4.7

Maremont, Mark. "Bausch & Lomb's Board Puts on Its Glasses." *Business Week*, 6 November 1995, 41.

Maremont, Mark. "Blind Ambition." *Business Week*, 23 October 1995, 78–92.

Maremont, Mark. "Judgment Day at Bausch & Lomb." *Business Week*, 25 December 1995, 39.

Norris, Floyd. "Bausch & Lomb and SEC Settle Dispute on '93 Profits." *New York Times*, 18 November 1997, C2.

Norton, Erile. "CEO Gill to Retire From Bausch & Lomb; Carpenter Is Seen As Possible Successor." *Wall Street Journal*, 14 December 1995, B3.

Sources for Case 4.8

"Baridis Acquaintance Pleads Guilty of Insider Trading." *Wall Street Journal*, December 26, 1997, B5

Donovan, Karen. "Levitt Speech Raises Insider Questions." *National Law Journal*, March 16, 1998, B1.

Lowry, Tom and Thor Valdmanis. "Four charged with passing merger tips totaling $1.8 million." *USA TODAY*, April 2, 1998, 1B

Morrow, David. "Insider Traders in White Coats." *New York Times*, April 11, 1998, B1, B5

Rynecki, David and Tom Lowry, "Damaged reputation puts exchange information on defensive." *USA TODAY*, March 2, 1998, 1B, 2B

SEC v. Mervyn Cooper and Kenneth E. Rottenberg, No. 95–8535 (C.D. Cal. 1995)

Starkman, Dean. "Five Brokers Indicted for Insider Trades Linked to Ex-Morgan Stanley Officer," *Wall Street Journal*, December 23, 1997, B9

Starkman, Dean. "Three Indicted for Insider Trading Tied to Ex-Morgan Stanley Aide." *Wall Street Journal*, Nov. 26, 1997, B2.

Starkman, Dean, "Ex-Salomon Investment Banker Charged." *Wall Street Journal*, April 2, 1998, B16

Truell, Peter. "An Employee on Wall St. Is Arrested." *New York Times*, Nov. 7, 1997, C8

Sources for Case 4.9

Cohen, Laurie P. and Amy Stevens. "Dan Dorfman's Woes Mount as Investigators Widen Criminal Probe." *Wall Street Journal*, 16 February 1996, A1, A7.

Reilly, Patrick M. "Money Fires Dan Dorfman For Not Divulging Sources." *Wall Street Journal*, 4 January 1996, B1, B6.

Schroeder, Michael. "Losing *Money*." *Business Week*, 15 January 1996, 40.

Sources for Case 4.10

Bailey, Jeff and Scott Kilman. "Here's What's Driving Some Lenders Crazy: Borrowers Who Think." *Wall Street Journal*, 20 February 1998, A1.

Darlin, Damon. "The Newest American Entitlement." *Forbes*, 8 September 1997, 113.

Dugas, Christine. "Credit Card Delinquencies Near Record." *USA Today*, 18 September 1997, B1.

Dugas, Christine. "Non-Mortgage Debts Top Income for Millions." *USA Today*, 2 October 1997, B1.

O'Brien, Timothy L. "Giving Credit Where Debt is Due." *New York Times*, 14 December 1997, 14.

Waddell, Fred. "Easy Credit: A Wall Around the Poor." *New York Times*, 15 February 1998, BU12.

Woodyard, Chris. "Fast-Food Stores Slowly Turning to Credit Cards." *USA Today*, 2 July 1997, 1B.

Sources for Case 4.12

"Outlawing a Three-Wheeler." *Time*, 11 January 1988, 59.

"The Price of a Good Night's Sleep." *New York Times*, 26 January 1992, E9.

Source for Case 4.13

Holden, Ted, and Jennifer Wiener. "Revenge of the 'Office Ladies'" *Business Week*, 13 July 1992, 42–43.

Sources for Case 4.16

Brink, Susan, et al. "Optimistic Field Work." *U.S. News & World Report*, 29 March 1993, 63.

Brodeur, Paul. "How Many Cancers Will It Take?" *New Yorker*, 7 December 1992, 106–119.

Levy, Doug. "Power Lines' Link to Brain Cancer." *USA Today*, 11 January 1995, 1D.

Park, Robert L. "Power Line Paranoia." *New York Times*, 13 November 1996, A19.

Savitz, David A. and Dana P. Loomis. "Magnetic Field Exposure in Relation to Leukemia and Brain Cancer Mortality Among Electric Utility Workers." *American Journal of Epidemiology*, 141 (2) 123–134 (1995).

Sternberg, Steve. "Power Lines Not a Cancer Risk for Kids." *USA Today*, 3–6 July 1997, 1A.

"Utility Wins Power-Line Cancer Suit," *Arizona Republic*, 1 May 1993, A23.

Sources for Case 4.17

Clements, Michael. "Domino's Detours 30-Minute Guarantee." *USA Today*, 22 December 1993, 1A.

Mattiace, Peter. "Suit Asks Domino's Pizza Be Pulled From Fast Lane." *Arizona Republic*, 1 December 1990, A1, A7.

Miller, Krystal, and Richard Gibson. "Domino's Stops Promising Pizza in 30 Minutes." *Wall Street Journal*, 22 December 1993, B1, B3.

Sources for Case 4.18

Bernstein, Aaron. "Who Says Job Anxiety Is Easing?" *Business Week*, 7 April 1997, 38.

Deutsch, Claudia H. "Kodak to Lay Off 10,000 Employees in a 10% Cutback." *New York Times*, 12 November 1997, A1, C4.

THE DOWNSIZING OF AMERICA, *New York Times*, 1996 Times Books.

"Intel Cuts 1,100 in Chandler Division." *Mesa Tribune*, 13 January 1998, A1, A4.

"J. Crew Dismisses 10% of Work Force." *New York Times*, 14 January 1998, C2.

Maynard, Micheline. "GM Plans to Unload Plants, 42,000 Jobs." *USA Today*, 17 November 1997, 1B.

Sources for Case 4.20

Bennet, James. "G.M. Settles Suit over Plant Closing." *New York Times*, 15 April 1994, C3.

Bryant, Adam. "Swinging the G.M. Ax: Which Plants Are Next?" *New York Times*, 10 November 1992, C1.

Hayes, Arthur S. "Concerns Find It Harder to Leave Town after Receiving Tax Breaks." *Wall Street Journal*, 1 March 1993, B10.

Leven, Doron P. "Court Backs G.M. on Plant Closing." *New York Times*, 5 August 1993, C4.

Leven, Doron P. "Judge Blocks Plan by G.M. to Close a Plant in Michigan." *New York Times*, 10 February 1993, C1, C5.

Treece, James B. "The Plants That GM Will Probably Padlock." *Business Week*, 14 December 1992, 34–35.

Woodruff, David, and Zachary Schiller. "Smart Step for a Wobbly Giant." *Business Week*, 7 December 1992, 38.

Sources for Case 4.21

Jennings, Marianne M. "Aaron Feuerstein—An Odd CEO." *Business: Its Legal, Ethical and Global Environment*, 1997.

Wulf, Steve. "The Glow From a Fire. ' *Time*, 8 January 1996, 49.

Sources for Case 4.22

Chandler, Susan. "An Empty Chair at Herman Miller." *Business Week*, 24 July 1996, 44.

Upbin, Bruce. "A Touch of Schizophrenia." *Forbes*, 7 July 1997, 57–59.

Sources for Case 4.24

Dietrich, Bill. "Is Oil-Spill Skipper a Fall Guy?" *Arizona Republic*, 28 January 1990, A2.

"Exxon Labeled No. 1 in Bungling a Crisis." *Arizona Republic*, 24 March 1990, A8.

"Exxon, Lloyd's Agree to Valdez Settlement." *Wall Street Journal*, 1 November 1996, B2.

"Exxon Stops the Flow." *Time*, 25 March 1992, 51.

"Exxon to Pay $1.1 Billion in Spill." *Arizona Republic*, 13 March 1991, A3.

Foster, David. "Oily Legacy." *Mesa Tribune*, 18 March 1990, D1.

Galen, Michele, and Vicky Cahan. "Getting Ready for Exxon vs. Practically Everybody." *Business Week*, 25 September 1989, 190–92.

Galen, Michele, and Vicky Cahan. "The Legal Reef Ahead for Exxon." *Business Week*, 12 March 1990, 39.

Hayes, Arthur S., and Milo Geyelin. "Oil Spill Trial Yields $2.5 Million." *Wall Street Journal*, 11 September 1991, B2.

Kangmine, Linda, and Carol Castaneda. "For Alaska, Tide Has Changed." *USA Today*, 14 June 1994, 3A.

"Like Punch in Gut: Exxon Skipper Talks." *Arizona Republic*, 25 March 1990, A1, A12.

McCoy, Charles. "Exxon Reaches $1.15 Billion Spill Pact That Resembles Earlier Failed Accord." *Wall Street Journal*, 1 October 1991, A3.

McCoy, Charles and Peter Fritsch. "Legal Experts Surprised by Exxon Deals With Fish Processors in Valdez Case." *Wall Street Journal*, 14 June 1996, B5.

Marshall, Steve. "Jury Rules Exxon Must Pay $287 Million to Alaska Fishermen." *USA Today*, 12 August 1994, 3A.

"Native Americans Awarded $9.7 Million from Exxon." *National Law Journal*, 10 October 1994, A19.

"Nice Work, Joe." *Time*, 4 December 1989, 48.

"Paying up for the Exxon Valdez." *Time*, 8 August 1994, 18.

Rempel, William C. "Exxon Captain Acquitted." *Arizona Republic*, 23 March 1990, A1.

Rubin, Julia. "Exxon Submits Final Oil-Spill Cleanup Plan." *Burlington Vermont Free Press*, 28 April 1990, 2A.

Satchell, Michael, and Betsy Carpenter. "A Disaster That Wasn't." *U.S. News & World Report*, 18 September 1989, 60–69.

Schneider, Keith. "Jury Finds Exxon Acted Recklessly in Valdez Oil Spill." *New York Times*, 14 June 1994, A1, A8.

Schneider, Keith. "$20 Million Settlement in Exxon Case." *New York Times*, 26 July 1994, A8.

Solomon, Caleb. "Exxon Attacks Scientific Views of Valdez Spill." *Wall Street Journal*, 15 April 1993, B1, B10.

Solomon, Caleb, "Exxon's Real Problem: Many of Its Oil Fields Are Old and Declining." *Wall Street Journal*, 19 September 1994, A1, A6.

Solomon, Caleb. "Jury to Weigh Exxon's Actions in Spill." *Wall Street Journal*, 7 June 1994, B5.

Sullivan, Allanna. "Exxon Begins Final Defense in Valdez Spill." *Wall Street Journal*, 2 May 1994, B1, B3.

Sullivan, Allanna, and Arthur S. Hayes. "Exxon's Plea Bargaining." *Wall Street Journal*, 21 February 1990, B8.

Treaster, Joseph B. "With Insurers' Payment, Exxon Says Valdez Case Is Ended." *New York Times*, 1 November 1996, C3.

Tyson, Rae. "Valdez Cleanup Is Skin Deep." *USA Today*, 22 March 1994, 3A.

Welles, Chris. "Exxon's Future: What Has Larry Rawl Wrought?" *Business Week*, 2 April 1990, 72–76.

Sources for Case 4.25

Crossen, Cynthia. "How 'Tactical Research' Muddied Diaper Debate." *Wall Street Journal*, 17 May 1994, B1.

Deard, Betty. "Disposable Diapers Are Challenged." *Arizona Republic*, 29 May 1989, A1.

Deveny, Kathleen. "States Mull Rash of Diaper Regulations." *Wall Street Journal*, 15 June 1990, B1.

Schiller, Zachary. "Turning Pampers into Plant Food?" *Business Week*, 22 October 1990, 38.

Sources for Case 4.26

Gerlin, Andrea. "How a Penney Buyer Made up to $1.5 Million on Vendors' Kickbacks."*Wall Street Journal*, 7 February 1995, A1, A18.

Gerlin, Andrea. "J.C. Penney Ex-Employee Sentenced to Jail." *Wall Street Journal*, 28 August 1995, A9.

Sources for Case 4.27

"A Big Honda Dealer Is Indicted in Federal Bribery Case." *New York Times*, 5 December 1996, C4.

Bennet, James. "Guilty Plea in Honda Bribery Case." *New York Times*, 8 February 1995, C1, C8.

Bennet, James. "Corruption Called Broad in Honda Case." *New York Times*, 4 April 1995, C1, C6.

"Dealers Given Right to Sue Honda Over Bribery Scheme." *Arizona Republic*, 31 August 1996, A8.

"Honda Execs Guilty in Bribery Scheme." *USA Today*, 2 June 1995, 1B.

"Honda Sentence." *USA Today*, 28 August 1995, 1B.

Sources for Case 5.1

Beatty, Sally Goll. "Marlboro's Billboard Man May Soon Ride Into the Sunset." *Wall Street Journal*, 1 July 1997, B1, B6.

Boot, Max. "Turning a Camel Into a Scapegoat." *Wall Street Journal*, 4 June 1997, A19.

Burger, Katrina. "Joe Cashes In." *Forbes*, 11 August 1997, 39.

Dagnoli, Judann. "RJR Aims New Ads at Young Smokers." *Advertising Age*, 11 July 1988, 2–3.

Geyelin, Milo. "Reynolds Aimed Specifically to Lure Young Smokers Years Ago, Data Suggest." *Wall Street Journal*, 15 January 1998, A4.

Horovitz, Bruce and Doug Levy. "Tobacco Firms Try to Sow Seeds of Self-Regulation." *USA Today*, 16 May 1996, 1B, 2B.

Horovitz, Bruce and Melanie Wells. "How Ad Images Shape Habits." *USA Today*, Jan. 31–Feb. 2, 1997, 1A, 2A.

Hwang, Suein L., Timothy Noah and Laurie McGinley. "Philip Morris Has Its Own Youth-Smoking Plan." *Wall Street Journal*, 16 May 1996, B1, B4.

Ingersoll, Bruce. "Joe Camel Ads Illegally Target Kids, FTC Says." *Wall Street Journal*, 29 May 1997, B1, B8.

"Joe Camel Shills to Kids." *USA Today*, 2 June 1997, 12A.

Kline, Alan. "Joe Camel is One Species the Government Wants Extinct." *Washington Times*, 8 June 1997, 10.

Levy, Doug. "Blowing Smoke?" *USA Today*, 15 January 1998, 1B, 2B.

Levy, Doug and Melanie Wells. "Papers: RJR Did Court Teens." *USA Today*, 15 January 1998, 1A, 1B.

Lippert, Barbara. "Camel's Old Joe Poses the Question: What Is Sexy?" *Adweek's Marketing Week*, 3 October 1988, 55.

Mallory, Maria. "That's One Angry Camel." *Business Week*, 7 March 1994, 94, 95.

"March against Smoking Joe." *Arizona Republic*, 22 June 1992, A3.

Martinez, Barbara. "Antismoking Ads Aim to Gross Out Teens." *Wall Street Journal*, 31 March 1997, B1. B5.

Meier, Barry. "Tobacco Executives Wax Penitent Before House Panel in Hopes of Preserving Accord." *New York Times*, 30 January 1998, A15.

Rausch, Gary. "Tobacco Firms Unite to Curb Teen Smoking." *Mesa Tribune*, 24 June 1991, B1, B6.

Shapiro, Eben. "FTC Staff Recommends Ban of Joe Camel Campaign." *Wall Street Journal*, 11 August 1993, B1, B8.

"Smokin' Joe Camel Near His Last Gasp." *Time*, 9 June 1997, 47.

Wells, Melanie and Chris Woodyard. "FTC Says Joe Camel Tobacco Icon Targeted Young." *USA Today*, 29 May 1991, 1A.

White, Anna. "Joe Camel's World Tour." *New York Times*, 23 April 1997, A21.

Source for Case 5.2

Koeppel, Dan. "Molson and Labatt's Ignite a Backlash." *Adweek's Marketing Week*, 8 April 1991, 6.

Sources for Case 5.3

Balu, Rekha. "Anheuser-Busch Amphibian Ads Called Cold-Blooded by Doctors." *Wall Street Journal*, 10 April 1998, B6.

Buck, Rinker. "Ode to Miller Beer." *Adweek's Marketing Week*, 27 May 1991, 16.

Colford, Steven W. "FTC May Crash Beer Promos' Campus Party." *Advertising Age*, 25 March 1991, 3–4.

Horovitz, Bruce. "Brewer to Stop Ads on MTV." *USA Today*, 23 December 1996, 1A.

Wells, Melanie. "Budweiser Frogs Will be Put Out to Pasture." *USA Today*, 14 January 1997, 1B, 8B.

Yang, Catherine and Stan Crock. "The Spirited Brawl Ahead Over Liquor Ads on TV." *Business Week*, 16 December 1996, 47.

Sources for Case 5.4

Eimann v. Soldier of Fortune Magazine, Inc., 880 F.2d 830 (5th Cir. 1989).

"Military Magazine Gets Jury Judgment Reduced." *Wall Street Journal*, 1 March 1993, B3.

Norwood v. Soldier of Fortune Magazine, Inc., 651 F.Supp. 1397 (W.D. Ark. 1987).

Tomlinson, Don. "Choosing Social Responsibility over Law: The *Soldier of Fortune* Classified Advertising Cases." *Business & Professional Ethics Journal* 9 (1990): 79–96.

Sources for Case 5.5

Gutfeld, Rose. "FDA Attacks Drug Makers' Ads to Doctors." *Wall Street Journal*, 3 August 1993, B1, B6.

Ingersoll, Bruce and Yumiko Ono. "FDA to Clear the Way for Blitz of TV Drug Ads." *Wall Street Journal*, 8 August 1997, B1.

Jenkins, Holman W. "Is Advertising the New Wonder Drug?" *Wall Street Journal*, 25 March 1998, A23.

King, Ralph T., Jr. "In Marketing of Drugs, Genentech Tests Limits of What Is Acceptable." *Wall Street Journal*, 10 January 1995, A1, A14.

Ono, Yumiko. "Prescription Drug Makers Heighten Hard-Sell Tactics." *Wall Street Journal*, 29 August 1994, B1, B4.

Tanouye, Elyse. "Critics See Self-Interest in Lilly's Funding of Ads Telling the Depressed to Get Help." *Wall Street Journal*, 15 April 1993, B1, B6.

Weber, Joseph, and John Carey. "Drug Ads: A Prescription for Controversy." *Business Week*, 18 January 1993, 58, 60.

Sources for Case 5.6

"Critics Take Apart Label of Ragu a Word at a Time." *Arizona Republic*, 2 May 1990, A7.

Hunt-Wesson Foods, Inc. v. Ragu Foods, Inc., 627 F.2d 919 (9th Cir. 1980).

Rejtman, Jack. "Spaghetti Sauce Spat between Prego, Ragu Is Set to Thicken." *Wall Street Journal*, 4 August 1993, B5.

Source for Case 5.7

"Chrysler Told to Pay Inventor $11.3 Million." *New York Times*, 12 June 1992, C3.

Source for Case 5.8

"Do You Vanna Dance with Lawyers?" *Business Week*, 18 October 1993, 8.

Sources for Case 5.11

"Freudenheim, Milt. "Future Clouded as Drug Makers and Stocks Fall." *New York Times*, 4 February 1993, C1, C15.

Heart-Saver Ad, *New York Times*, 23 July 1996, A16.

"Prescription Drug Makers Accused of Gouging Public." *Arizona Republic*, 4 February 1993, A3.

Sources for Case 5.12

Baumohl, Bernard. "Swaggering into Trouble." *Time*, 26 August 1991, 41.

Cohen, Laurie P. "Ex-Salomon Trader Supplied Information to Prosecutors." *Wall Street Journal*, 28 May 1992, C1.

Cohen, Laurie P. "Gone From Salomon 16 Months, Gutfreund Finds Life Frustrating." *Wall Street Journal*, 4 December 1992, A1, A4.

Eichenwald, Kurt. "Former Top Salomon Officers Settle Bid Case." *New York Times*, 4 December 1992, C1.

Eichenwald, Kurt. "Outside Lawyer Appointed General Counsel at Salomon." *New York Times*, 2 September 1992, C3.

Eichenwald, Kurt. "Salomon Still Struggling to Diversify Its Business." *New York Times*, 8 September 1992, C1, C4.

Eichenwald, Kurt. "Two Sued by SEC in Bidding Scandal at Salomon Bros." *New York Times*, 3 December 1992, C1, C2.

Gilpin, Kenneth. "Salomon Profit Drops 93% in Quarter." *New York Times*, 23 October 1992, C1.

Gilpin, Kenneth N. "Salomon Reports Surprising Earnings Drop of Nearly 60%." *New York Times*, 23 October 1996, C5.

Hertzberg, Daniel, and Laurie P. Cohen. "Scandal Is Fading Away for Salomon, but Not for Trader Paul Mozer." *Wall Street Journal*, 7 August 1992, A1.

Labaton, Steven. "Wall Street Opposing Bond Rules." *New York Times*, 1 June 1991, C1.

Loomis, Carol. "Warren Buffett's Wild Ride at Salomon." *Fortune*, 27 October 1997, 114–132.

McNamee, Mike. "The Judgment of Salomon: An Anticlimax." *Business Week*, 1 June 1992, 106.

Moses, Jonathan M. "Ruling Leaves Salomon Scandal Claims on Two Fronts." *Wall Street Journal*, 17 December 1992, B10.

Power, William. "Salomon's Big Loss Could Well Become Goldman Sach's Gain." *Wall Street Journal*, 10 September 1991, A1, A8.

"The Salomon Scandal in Bondage." *Economist*, 14 September 1991, 92–93.

"Salomon: The SEC Points Its Finger." *Business Week*, 14 December 1992, 46.

"Salomon Settlement." *USA Today*, 7 January 1993, 1D.

Salwen, Kevin. "Salomon's Dealer Role Is Supported." *Wall Street Journal*, 27 September 1991, C1, C17.

Salwen, Kevin. "House Panel Seeks to Amend Securities Bill." *Wall Street Journal*, 7 August 1992, A5.

Salwen, Kevin, and John Connor. "SEC Mulls Penalties for Street." *Wall Street Journal*, 2 October 1991, C1.

Salwen, Kevin, and Tom Herman. "Freddie Mac Fines Firms for Inflated Orders." *Wall Street Journal*, 4 October 1991, C1.

Salwen, Kevin G., and Jonathan M. Moses. "SEC Sues Ex-Trader at Salomon." *Wall Street Journal*, 3 December 1992, C1.

Siconolfi, Michael. "Salomon Names Charles Williams a Compliance Chief." *Wall Street Journal*, 16 June 1992, B14.

Siconolfi, Michael. "Scandal at Salomon Leaves Its Mark on the Bottom Line." *Wall Street Journal*, 7 February 1992, C1.

Spiro, Leah Nathans. "The Bomb Shelter Salomon Built." *Business Week*, 9 September 1991, 78–80.

Spiro, Leah Nathans, "Turmoil at Salomon," *Business Week*, 1 May 1995, 144–54.

"The Judgment of Salomon." *The Economist*, 21 September 1996, 75–76.

Weiss, Gary. "Behind the Happy Talk at Salomon." *Business Week*, 11 November 1991, 150–52.

Weiss, Gary. "Clearing the Wreckage." *Business Week*, 2 September, 1991, 66–68.

Weiss, Gary, et al. "How Bad Will It Get?" *Business Week*, 7 October 1991, 122–24.

Sources for Case 5.13

"ADM Still Doesn't Get It." *Fortune*, 11 November 1996, 30–31.

Armstrong, Larry. "All Roads Lead to ADM." *Business Week*, 23 September 1996, 42–43.

Burton, Thomas M. "Former ADM Executive Mark Whitacre Pleads Guilty to Embezzling $9 Million." *Wall Street Journal*, 13 October 1997, B12.

Eichenwald, Kurt. "Archer Daniels Midland to Pay a $100 Million Fine in Pricing Case." *New York Times*, 15 October 1996, A1, C3.

Eichenwald, Kurt. "Informant Said to Agree to Plea Deal." *New York Times*, 27 September 1995, C1, C3.

Eichenwald, Kurt. "Judge Lets Archer Tapes Be Admitted." *New York Times*, 17 April 1998, C6.

Eichenwald, Kurt. "2 Executives Step Down at Archer Daniels." *New York Times*, 18 October 1996, C1, C4.

Kilman, Scott. "Ajinomoto Pleads Guilty to Conspiring With ADM, Others to Fix Lysine Price." *Wall Street Journal*, 15 November 1996, A18.

Sources for Case 5.14

Excerpted and adapted from: Aalberts, Robert J. and Marianne M. Jennings. "The Ethics of Slotting: Is this Bribery, Facilitation Marketing or Just Plain Competition?" Forthcoming: *Journal of Business Ethics*, 1998.

Aalberts, R. J. and L. Lynn Judd. "Slotting in the Retail Grocery Business: Does It

Violate the Public Policy Goal of Protecting Business Against Price Discrimination?" *DePaul Law Review* 40, 1991, 397–416.

Deloitte Touche: 1997, Questions a Stockholders' Meeting.

Fiser, J. "Do Businesses Have Moral Obligations Beyond What the Law Requires?" *Journal of Business Ethics*, April 1996, 457–468.

Foreign Corrupt Practices Act: 1997, 15 U.S.C. § 78m(b).

Friedman, M. "The Social Responsibility of Business is to Increase it Profits." *The New York Times Magazine*, 13 September 1970, 32–33, 122–126.

Gibson, R. "Supermarkets Demand Food Firms' Payments Just to Get on the Shelf." *Wall Street Journal*, 1 November 1988, A1 and A14.

Grand Union v. FTC, 300 F.2d 92 (2d Cir. 1962).

Greenstein, J. "Battle for Shelf Space Puts Publishers in Financial Bind." *Video Business* 15(26), 1995, 42.

Greenwald, J. "Frito-Lay Under Snack Attack." *Time*, 30 June 1996, 62–63.

Hetrick, Ross. "Ice Cream Firm Frozen." *Baltimore Sun*, 25 September 1995, 13C.

Interviews with manufacturers and retailers conducted from 1995–1997. The authors pledged anonymity to these sources.

Laczniak, G. "Business Ethics: A Managers' Primer." *Business*, 23–29 January 1983.

"Policy Hearings Shift Focus to FTC Impact on Small Business." *BNA Antitrust and Trade Regulation Report* 69 (1738), 1995, 581.

Ross, B. "Money Talks *20/20*." 10 November 1995, Transcript #1545.

Somervill, Sean. "High Price of Shelf Space." *Baltimore Sun*, 10, 1996, 4D.

Sources for Case 5.15

Bank, David and John R. Wilke. "Microsoft and Justice End a Skirmish, Yet War Could Escalate." *Wall Street Journal*, 23 January 1998, A1, A6.

Krantz, Michael. "Will Reno Brake Windows." *Time*, 3 November 1997, 76–78.

Lohr, Steve. "Court Is Not Where They'd Like to Go Today." *New York Times*, 18 January 1998, WK5.

Wilke, John R. "Microsoft Subject of New Antritrust Probe." *Wall Street Journal*, 24 April 19998, A2.

Sources for Case 6.1

Carlton, Jim, and Stephen Kreider Yoder. "Humble Pie: Intel to Replace Its Pentium Chips." *Wall Street Journal*, 21 December 1994, B1, B9.

Carlton, Jim, and Scott McCartney. "Corporations Await More Information; Will Consumers Balk?" *Wall Street Journal*, 14 December 1994, B1, B5.

Castro, Janice. "When the Chips Are Down." *Time*, 26 December 1994, 126.

"Intel Eats Crow, Replaces Pentiums." *Mesa Tribune*, 21 December 1994, F1.

"Intel's PC Dominance Draws Scrutiny." *Wall Street Journal*, 25 September 1997, A3.

Kim, James. "Intel Proactive With Potential Buy." *USA Today*, 6 May 1997, 1B.

Ortiz, Catalina. "Intel to Replace Flawed Pentium Chips." *Arizona Republic*, 21 December 1994, A1, A8.

Overstreet, James. "Pentium Jokes Fly, but Sales Stay Strong." *USA Today*, 7 December 1994, 1B.

Port, Otis. "A Chip on Your Shoulder—or Your Cuffs." *Business Week*, 23 January 1995, 8.

Ramstad, Evan. "Pentium: a Cautionary Tale." *Arizona Republic*, 21 December 1994, C1.

Sager, Ira, and Robert D. Hof. "Bare Knuckles at Big Blue." *Business Week*, 26 December 1994, 60-62.

Schmitt, Richard B. "Flurry of Lawsuits Filed against Intel over Pentium Flaw." *Wall Street Journal*, 16 December 1994, B3.

Yoder, Stephen Kreider. "The Pentium Proposition: To Buy or Not to Buy." *Wall Street Journal*, 14 December 1994, B1.

Ziegler, Bart, and Don Clark. "Computer Giants' War over Flaw in Pentium Jolts the PC Industry." *Wall Street Journal*, 13 December 1994, A1, A11.

Sources for Case 6.2

Brink, Susan, Edward C. Baig, Steven D. Kaye, Margaret Mannix. "A Pox on Young Drivers." *U.S. News & World Report*, 29 March 1993, 63.

Bryant, Adam. "GM Agrees to Sell Car Rental Unit," *New York Times*, 5 April 1995, C1, C2.

"Car-Rental Firms Make Extra Drivers Costly." *Wall Street Journal*, 10 November 1992, B1.

Dahl, Jonathan. "Rental Counters Reject Drivers without Good Records." *Wall Street Journal*, 23 October 1992, B1.

Dahl, Jonathan, and Christopher Winans. "States, Car-Rental Firms Collide over Damage Waivers." *Wall Street Journal*, 14 August 1989, B1.

Golz, Earl. "Hidden Auto Rental Charges, Fees Can Take You for a Ride." *Mesa Tribune*, 21 February 1989, D1.

Hirsch, James S. "Auto Renters Hit the Brakes on Under-25s." *Wall Street Journal*, 16 March 1993, B1.

Hirsch, James S. "'Do-Not-Rent' Lists Tag Bad Drivers." *Wall Street Journal*, 15 September 1993, B1.

Hirsch, James S. "Rental Car Firms Jack up Their Prices." *Wall Street Journal*, 4 November 1992, B1, B13.

Jacobson, Gianna. "Enterprise's Unconventional Path." *New York Times*, 23 January 1997, C1, C6.

Jones, David. "Illinois Moves to Ban Rental Car Waivers." *National Underwriter*, 11 July 1988, 3, 79.

Katz, Michael. "FTC Forces Car Rental Firms to Reveal All." *Wall Street Journal*, 14 August 1992, B1, B2.

Knox, Noelle. "Cars Available! But With More Strings Attached." *New York Times*, 11 January 1998, BU6.

Miller, Lisa. "Car Rental Industry Promises That Things Will Improve. Really." *Wall Street Journal*, 17 July 1997, A1, A8.

Miller, Lisa. "Young Drivers Can Rent Cars, New York Rules." *Wall Street Journal*, 28 March 1997, B1, B2.

O'Reilly, Brian. "The Rent-A-Car Jocks Who Made Enterprise #1." *Fortune*, 28 October 1996, 126–128.

Rosato, Donna. "Budget Rent-A-Car to Charge No-Shows." *USA Today*, 3 July 1997, 1B.

Taylor, Alex, III. "Why Car Rentals Drive You Nuts." *Fortune*, 31 August 1987, 74.

Wald, Matthew. "Hertz to New York: Pay More." *New York Times*, 19 January 1992, F10.

Wald, Matthew L. "Car-Rental Computers Rejecting High-Risk Drivers." *New York Times*, 9 September 1993, A1, A9.

Wald, Matthew L. "Hertz Ends 'Drop Charges' on One-Way Rentals." *New York Times*, 15 October 1992, C1, C10.

Sources for Case 6.3

Alexander, Keith L. "A Health Kick at Weight Watchers." *Business Week*, 16 January 1995, 36.

Barrett, Amy. "How Can Jenny Craig Keep on Gaining?" *Business Week*, 12 April 1993, 52-53.

"A Bill of Rights for Dieters." *Shape*, November 1993, 30.

Freedman, Alix, and U. Gupta. "Lawsuits May Trim Diet Firms." *Wall Street Journal*, 23 March 1990, B1, B2.

Hellmich, Nanci. "Heart Valve Damage Prompts Withdrawal." *USA Today*, 16 September 1997, 1A.

Hellmich, Nanci. "Withdrawal of Drugs Leaves Dieters in Quandary." *USA Today*, 22 September 1997, 6D.

Hilts, Philip J. "Medicine Remains as Much Art as Science." *New York Times*, 21 September 1997, WK5.

Janofsky, Michael. "Hearing for Franchisees in Nutri/System Buyout." *New York Times*, 11 May 1993, C6.

Johannes, Laura. "New Diet-Drug Data Spark More Controversy." *Wall Street Journal*, 1 October 1997, B1, B12.

Johannes, Laura and Steve Secklow. "Heart-Valve Problem That Felled Diet Pills Had Arisen Previously." *Wall Street Journal*, 11 December 1997, A1.

Johnson, Julie. "Bringing Sanity to the Diet Craze." *Time*, 21 May 1990, 74.

Kolata, Gina. "Companies Recall 2 Top Diet Drugs at F.D.A.'s Urging." *Wall Street Journal*, 16 September 1997, A1.

Langreth, Robert and Laura Johannes. "Redux Diet Pill Receives a Boost in New Study." *Wall Street Journal*, 1 April 1998, B1, B4.

Neuborne, Ellen. "Weight-Loss Programs Going Hungry." *USA Today*, 28 July 1994, 1C, 2C.

O'Neill, Molly. "Five Diet Companies Ask U.S. for Uniform Rules on Ads." *New York Times*, 25 August 1992, C1, C2.

Saddler, Jeanne. "Three Diet Firms Settle False Ad Case; Two Others Vow to Fight FTC Charges." *Wall Street Journal*, 1 October 1993, B8.

Saddler, Jeanne. "Diet Firms' Weight-Loss Claims Are Being Investigated by FTC." *Wall Street Journal*, 26 March 1993, B1, B5.

Schroder, Michael. "The Diet Business Is Getting a Lot Skinnier." *Business Week*, 24 June 1991, 132-34.

Snider, Mike. "FTC Cites Diet Firms for False Claims." *USA Today*, 1 October 1993, 1D.

Snider, Mike. "FTC Weighs Claims of Diet Program Ads." *USA Today*, 26 March 1993, 1D.

Sternberg, Steve. "Study: No Heart Damage From Diet Drug." *USA Today*, 1 April 1998, 1A.

Weber, Joseph. "The Diet Business Takes It on the Chin." *Business Week*, 16 April 1990, 86-87.

Source for Case 6.4

Smith-Scharff Paper v. P.N. Hirsch & Co., 754 S.W.2d 928 (Mo. 1988).

Source for Case 6.5

Schulze and Burch Co. v. Tree Top, Inc., 831 F.2d 709 (7th Cir. 1987).

Sources for Case 6.6

Berner, Robert. "Sears Faces Controversy Over Car Batteries." *Wall Street Journal*, 26 August 1997, B2.

Berner, Robert and JoAnn S. Lublin, "Sears Is Told It Can't Shop for Ward Brass." *Wall Street Journal*, 13 August 1997, B1, B6.

Conlin, Michelle. "Sears: The Turnaround Is For Real." *Forbes*, 15 December 1997.

Feder, Barnaby J. "Sears Post First Loss Since 1933." *New York Times*, 23 October 1992, C1.

Fisher, Lawrence M. "Sears' Auto Centers to Halt Commissions." *New York Times*, 23 June 1992, C1.

Flynn, Julia, Christina Del Valle, Russell Mitchell. "Did Sears Take Other Customers for a Ride?" *Business Week*, 3 August 1992, 24-25.

Fuchsberg, Gilbert. "Sears Reinstates Sales Incentives in Some Centers." *Wall Street Journal*, 7 March 1994, B1.

Healey, James R. "Sears Auto Cuts Commissions." *USA Today*, 23 June 1992, 2B.

Healey, James R. "Shops under Pressure to Boost Profits." *USA Today*, 14 July 1992, 1A.

Miller, James. "Sears Roebuck Expects Loss in Third Period." *Wall Street Journal*, 8 September 1992, A3.

"Open Letter." *Arizona Republic*, 25 June 1992, A9.

Patterson, Gregory A. "Distressed Shoppers, Disaffected Workers Prompt Stores to Alter Sales Commissions." *Wall Street Journal*, 1 July 1992, B1, B4.

Patterson, Gregory A. "Sears Debt of $11 Billion Is Downgraded." *Wall Street Journal*, 11 December 1992, A3.

Read, Nat B. "Sears PR Debacle Shows How Not to Handle a Crisis." *Wall Street Journal*, 11 January 1993, A14.

"Sears Gets Handed a Huge Repair Bill." *Business Week*, 14 September 1992, 38.

"Sears Roebuck Fires Head of Its Auto Unit." *Wall Street Journal*, 21 December 1992, B6.

Steinhauer, Jennifer. "Time to Call a Sears Repairman." *New York Times*, 15 January 1998, B1, B2.

Stevenson, Richard W. "Sears' Crisis: How Did It Do?" *New York Times*, 17 June 1992, C1.

Woodyard, Chris. "Sears to Refund Millions to Bankrupt Customers." *USA Today*, 11–13 April 1997, 1A.

Source for Case 6.7

Loury, Tom. "Settlement Won't End American Family Woes." *USA Today*, 20 March 1998, 1B, 2B.

Sources for Case 6.8

"Acetaminophen Overdoses Linked to Liver Damage." *Mesa Tribune*, 21 December 1994, A12.

Cole, Richard. "Tylenol Agrees to Warning on Labels of Risk to Children." *Arizona Republic*, 19 October 1997, A5.

Easton, Thomas and Stephan Herrera. "J & J's Dirty Little Secret." *Forbes*, 12 January 1998, 42–44.

Levy, Doug. "Acetaminophen Overuse Can Lead to Liver Damage." *USA Today*, 22 December 1994, 1D.

"Second Tylenol Study Links Heavy Use to Kidney Risk." *Arizona Republic*, 22 December 1994, A6.

Sharp, Deborah. "Alcohol-Tylenol Death Goes to Trial in Florida." *USA Today*, 24 March 1997, 3A.

Sources for Case 6.9

Dardis, Rachel, and Claudia Zent. "The Economics of the Pinto Recall." *Journal of Consumer Affairs*, Winter 1982, 261-77.

Patterson, Gregory A. "Downscale Racer: The Pinto Is Junk, But It Sure Is Fast." *Wall Street Journal*, 14 June 1990, A1.

"Who Pays for the Damage?" *Time*, 21 January 1980, 61.

Sources for Case 6.10

Pereira, Joseph. "Toy Maker Faces Dilemma as Water Gun Spurs Violence." *Wall Street Journal*, 11 June 1992, B1, B10.

"Squirt, Squirt, You're Dead." *Time*, 22 June 1992, 35.

Sources for Case 6.11

Bovard, James. "Double-Crossing to Safety." *American Spectator*, January 1995, 24-29.

Cippollone v. Liggett Group, 505 U.S. 504 (1992).

Cox, James. "Decision Unlikely to Snuff Profits." *USA Today*, 25 June 1992, 1B.

Davis, Robert and Doug Levy. "Texas Tobacco Suit Settled for $15 Billion." *USA Today*, 16–18 January 1998, 1A.

Dedman, Bill. "Executive Says He's Uncertain About Tobacco's Harm." *New York Times*, 3 March 1998, A16.

Dorfman, John R. "Will Tobacco Stocks Burn Out or Stay Hot?" *Wall Street Journal*, 29 June 1992, C1.

Elias, Marilyn. "Tying Moms' Smoking to Kids' Behavior." *USA Today*, 9 September 1992, 1D.

Feder, Barnaby J. "Tobacco Foes Jump to Use Admission About Addiction." *New York Times*, 23 March 1997, A17.

France, Mike, Lori Bongiorno, John Carey, Catherine Yang. "Nicotine Fit." *Business Week*, 7 April 1997, 34–36.

Friedman, Alix M. and Suein L. Hwang. "How Seven Individuals With Diverse Motives Halted Tobacco's Wars." *Wall Street Journal*, 11 July 1997, A1, A8.

Geyelin, Milo. "Liability Suits, While Rising, May Not Prevail." *Wall Street Journal*, 26 June 1992, B1.

Geyelin, Milo and Suein L. Hwang. "What Brought Big Tobacco to the Table." *Wall Street Journal*, 18 April 1997, B1, B7.

Hall, Mimi and Susan Page. "RJR Says No to Tobacco Deal." *USA Today*, 9 April 1998, 1A.

Levy, Doug. "Moms' Nicotine Levels Found in Newborns." *USA Today*, 20 March 1997, 1D.

Lowry, Tom. "Liggett Settlement Burns Tobacco Firms." *USA Today*, 21 March 1997, 1B.

Meier, Barry. "Among Cigarette Makers, Old Habits Die Hard." *New York Times*, 7 September 1997, E3.

Meier, Barry. "Cigarette Maker Manipulated Nicotine, Its Records Suggest." *New York Times*, 23 February 1998, A1, A15.

Rodriguez, Eva M. and Jeffrey Taylor. "U.S. Launches Tobacco Antitrust Probe." *Wall Street Journal*, 30 January 1998, A3.

Rosenbaum, David E. "Clinton Pushes for Tighter Regulation of Tobacco." *New York Times*, 16 January 1998, A14.

Snider, Mike. "Passive Smoke Gets New Study." *USA Today*, 21 July 1992, 1D.

Van Voris, Bob. "Latest Tobacco Headache: Flight Attendants' Case." *National Law Journal*, 26 May 1997, A1, A26.

Sources for Case 6.12

"ATV Makers Warned to Halt Sales to Children or Face Ban." *Mesa Tribune*, 2 October 1986, A2.

"ATV Makers Agree to Warnings, Vehicle Ban." *Arizona Business Gazette*, 9 May 1988, Law 3.

Bolger, James. "The High Gravity Risk of ATV's." *Safety & Health*, November 1987, 48-49.

Isley, Alan R. "Industry Is Emphasizing Safety." *USA Today*, 6 November 1986, 1B.

Maynard, Frederick M. "Peril in the Path of All-Terrain Vehicles." *Business and Society Review*, Winter 1987, 48-52.

Riggenbach, Jeff. "Regulation Not Needed; Danger Is Exaggerated." *USA Today*, 6 November 1986, 10A.

"Safety Group Targets Use of ATVs by Young Riders." *Mesa Tribune*, 20 November 1986, A4.

"We Need Regulation of Dangerous ATVs." *USA Today*, 14 November 1986, 10A.

Sources for Case 6.13

Brief History of Johnson & Johnson, 1992. (Company pamphlet.)

"Legacy of Tampering." *Arizona Republic*, 29 September 1992, A1.

Source for Case 6.14

Van Voorst, Bruce. "Why America Has So Many Potholes." *Time*, 4 May 1992, 64-65.

Source for Case 6.15

Blackmon, Douglas. "Consultant's Advice On Diversity Was Anything But Diverse." *Wall Street Journal*, 11 March 1997, A1, A16.

Sources for Case 6.16

Bayor, Leslie. "Equifax Addresses Mail Preferences." *Advertising Age*, 14 January 1991, 21.

Bird, Laura. "Amid Privacy Furor, Lotus Kills a Disk." *AdWeek's Marketing Week*, 28 January 1991, 21.

Coleman, Lynn G. "Biz-to-Biz Software Rises from Grave." *Marketing News*, 2 September 1991, 43.

"Equifax Vows to Get It Right." *Business Week*, 13 July 1992, 38.

Francese, Peter. "What Business Are You In?" *American Demographics*, April 1991, 2.

"Lotus Cancels CD-ROM Project amid Privacy Concerns." *Direct Marketing*, March 1991, 8.

Miller, Cyndee. "Lotus Forced to Cancel New Software Program." *Marketing News*, 18 February 1991, 11.

Oliver, Suzanne L. "You've No Place to Hide." *Forbes*, 29 April 1991, 86-88.

Posch, Robert. "Worst List Threat of the Decade." *Direct Marketing*, March 1988, 124.

Posta, Melissa Della. "California List Business Headed for Extinction?" *Folio*, February 1990, 17.

"Privacy and Ethics Issues Affect List Industry." *Direct Marketing*, October 1988, 8.

Radding, Alan. "Lotus Stirs Research Marketplace." *Advertising Age*, 14 January 1991, 21.

Rappaport, Donn. "Privacy Paranoia: List Owners Need to Regulate Themselves before the Government Docs." *Folio*, October 1990, 101-2.

Ruhe, Linda Savage. "Marketers Hope to Program Buying Habits." *Advertising Age*, 19 July 1984, 44.

Schwartz, Marvin. "List Usage Ethics and Marketing Opportunity in Merge/Purge." *Direct Marketing*, August 1987, 52-56.

"A Tighter Rein on Credit Data for Marketing Urged." *Credit Risk Management Report*, 25 May 1992, 2-3.

Uehling, Mark D. "Here Comes the Perfect Mailing List." *American Demographics*, August 1991, 11-12.

Sources for Case 7.1

Delany, Paul. "Amos 'n Andy in Nikes." *New York Times*, 11 October 1993, A10.

Dunham, Richard S. and Michael Oneal. "Gunning for the Gangstas." *Business Week*, 19 June 1995, 41.

Ehrenreich, Barbara. "Or Is It Creative Freedom?" *Time*, 20 July 1992, 89.

"Facing Continuing Attacks, the Rapper Yanks His Antipolice Anthem." *Time*, 10 August 1992, 23.

Ferguson, Tim W. "Will Sunlight Improve the Taste of Ice-T's Distributor?" *Wall Street Journal*, 21 July 1992, A15.

"Ice-T Cools 'Cop' Song amid Death Threats." *Arizona Republic*, 29 July 1992, A1.

"The Iceman Goeth." *Time*, 8 February 1993, 21.

"Ice-T Ices 'Cop Killer' for Tour." *Mesa Tribune*, 28 July 1992, A2.

"Ice-T, a Rap Performer, to Drop Controversial Song." *Wall Street Journal*, 24 July 1992, B5.

Jones, James, and David Zimmerman. "Not All Will Yank Ice-T LP." *USA Today*, 30 July 1992, 1D.

Kinsley, Michael. "Ice-T: Is the Issue Social Responsibility?" *Time*, 20 July 1992, 88.

Landler, Mark. "Defender of Gangsta Rap Ousted at Warner." *New York Times*, 22 June 1995, A1, C4.

Landler, Mark. "Time Warner Seeks a Delicate Balance in Rap Music Furor." *New York Times*, 5 June 1995, A1, C8.

Lieberman, David. "Time Warner Shifts on Morris Firing." *USA Today*, 6 July 1995, 1B.

Marshall, Steve. "'Cop Killer' Cut Pulled from Album." *USA Today*, 29 July 1992, 1A.

"Protestors Demand That Time Warner Pulls Its *Body Count* Album." *Time*, 27 July 1992, 23.

Roberts, Johnnie L. "Time Warner Directors May Bar Release of Certain Music." *Wall Street Journal*, 24 July 1992, B1, B6.

Strauss, Neil. "Rap's a 10% Slice of the Recording Industry Pie." *New York Times*, 5 June 1995, C8.

"Support, Anger after Ice-T's Move." *USA Today*, 31 July, 1992, 2D.

"Time Warner Shake-Up." *Time*, 27 November 1995, 37.

"Time Warner's Ice-T Defense Is Assailed." *Wall Street Journal*, 23 July 1992, B1, B8.

Woo, Linda. "Flap Fails to Heat Up Ice-T Sales." *Arizona Republic*, 30 July 1992, B1.

Sources for Case 7.2

Arkin, Stanley S. "Should Kidder Advance Jett's Defense Costs?" *National Law Journal*, 10 October 1994, A21, A22.

Carley, William M., Michael Siconolfi, and AmalRumar Naj. "How Will Welch Deal with Kidder Scandal? Problems Keep Coming." *Wall Street Journal*, 3 April 1994, A1, A6.

Cohen, Laurie P., Alix M. Freedman, and William Power. "Kidder's No. 2 Man Comes under Scrutiny in Trading Scandal." *Wall Street Journal*, 2 May 1994, A1, A12.

Donovan, Karen. "For Kidder's Top Lawyer, Caseload Clean-up Looms." *National Law Journal*, 9 January 1995, B1, B2.

Frantz, Douglas, and Sylvia Nasar. "The Ghost in Kidder's Money-Making Machine." *New York Times*, 29 April 1994, C1, C4.

Freedman, Alix M., Laurie P. Cohen, and Michael Siconolfi. "Kidder Bond Traders Came under Fire Well before Jett." *Wall Street Journal*, 6 May 1994, C1, C6.

"GE Stumbles." *USA Today*, 20 January 1995, 4B.

Hansell, Saul. "Kidder Peabody Jolted by Phantom Bond Trades." *New York Times*, 19 April 1994, C1, C13.

"How a Sheepskin Fell through the Cracks." *Business Week*, 6 June 1994, 6.

Kadlec, Daniel, and Eric D. Randall. "Wall Street Ethics Again Face Scrutiny." *USA Today*, 5 August 1994, 1B, 2B.

"Kidder's Jett Testifies That Manager Knew of His Bond Strategy." *Wall Street Journal*, 21 June 1996, B6.

Lowry, Tom. "Former Trader Gets to Tell SEC His Side." *USA Today*, 20 May 1996, 5B.

Lowry, Tom. "Jett Says He Took Heat For Accounting Changes at Kidder." *USA Today*, 20 June 1996, 2B.

Mayer, Martin. "Joe Jett Wins a Round." *Institutional Investor*, Jan. 1997, 8.

Maynard, Michael, and David Craig. "Tarnished Brokerage a Liability." *USA Today*, 18 October 1994, 1B, 2B.

Nasar, Sylvia. "Jett's Kidder Supervisor Breaks His Silence." *New York Times*, 26 July 1994, C1, C14.

Nasar, Sylvia. "Kidder Scandal Tied to Failure of Supervision." *New York Times*, 5 August 1994, A1, C3.

O'Brien, Timothy L. and Michael Siconolfi. "SEC Accuses Jett of Introducing Phony Diary Entries." *Wall Street Journal*, 14 April 1997, B8.

Siconolfi, Michael. "An Employee Fired by Kidder Peabody Casts a Pall of Fear." *Wall Street Journal*, 29 April 1994, A1, A2.

Siconolfi, Michael. "How Kidder, a Tiger in April, Found Itself the Prey by December." *Wall Street Journal*, 29 December 1994, A1, A4.

Siconolfi, Michael. "Report Faults Kidder for Laxness in Jett Case." *Wall Street Journal*, 5 August 1994, C1, C19.

Siconolfi, Michael. "SEC Authority to File Without Quorum Is Questioned in Kidder Peabody Case." *Wall Street Journal*, 8 January 1996, B5.

Siconolfi, Michael. "SEC Is Raising New Red Flag With Jett Case." *Wall Street Journal*, 10 January 1996, A6.

Siconolfi, Michael. "SEC to File Civil Charges in Kidder Scandal." *Wall Street Journal*, 8 January 1996, A3, A4.

Siconolfi, Michael. "With Scandal Report Due Today, Kidder Ousts Another Official." *Wall Street Journal*, 14 August 1994, A1, A4.

Siconolfi, Michael, and Anita Raghavan. "Paine Webber's Main Challenge Is Making Kidder Acquisition Work." *Wall Street Journal*, 18 October 1994, C1, C19.

Spiro, Leah Nathans. "They Said, He Said at Kidder Peabody." *Business Week*, 8 August 1994, 60-62.

Spiro, Leah Nathans. "What Joseph Jett's Defense Will Look Like." *Business Week*, 13 June 1994, 70.

Spiro, Leah Nathans, Elizabeth Lesly, and Tim Smart. "Why Jack Welch Cracked Heads at Kidder." *Business Week*, 4 July 1994, 33.

Weiss, Gary. "The Flimsy Case Against Joseph Jett." *Business Week*, 1 July 1996, 90.

"Will Jett's Suit Fly?" *National Law Journal*, 22 March 1995, A4.

Sources Case 7.3

Becker, Gary. "The Problem Is Not What CEOs Get-It's Getting Them to Go." *Business Week*, 2 March 1992, 18.

Byrne, John. "What, Me Overpaid? CEOs Fight Back." *Business Week*, 4 May 1992, 142-62.

Byrne, John A. "Deliver or Else." *Business Week*, 27 March 1995, 36-38.

Cowan, Alison Leigh. "The Gadfly CEOs Want to Swat." *New York Times*, 2 April 1992, 3:1,6.

Dobrzynski, Judith H. "CEO Pay: Something Should Be Done—But Not by Congress." *Business Week*, 3 February 1992, 29.

"How Sweet It Was." *Time*, 24 February 1992, 42.

Lublin, JoAnn S. "Compensation Panels Get More Assertive, Hiring Consultants and Sparking Clashes." *Wall Street Journal*, 15 July 1992, B1.

Lublin, JoAnn S. "Raking It In." *Wall Street Journal*, 12 April 1995, R1-R15.

Salwen, Kevin G. "Shareholder Proposals on Pay Must Be Aired, SEC to Tell 10 Firms." *Wall Street Journal*, 13 February 1992, A1, A4.

Salwen, Kevin G., and JoAnn S. Lublin. "Giant Investors Flex Their Muscles More at U.S. Corporations." *Wall Street Journal*, 27 April 1992, A1, A8.

Wilke, John R. "Reebok Holders Reject Plan for Panel to Set Salaries, But It Gets Sizable Vote." *Wall Street Journal*, 6 May 1992, A2.

Sources for Case 7.4

"Ex-Eagle Scout Sues Group over Ban on Homosexuals." *New York Times*, 30 July 1992, A12.

Jennings, Marianne. "Gay Leaders." *Deseret News*, 13 April 1998, A4.

Knight, Al. "US West: Give a Lot, Take a Lot." *Denver Post*, 10 November 1991, 5H.

"Scouts' Gay Ban Is Misguided." *Denver Post*, 3 November 1991, 2H.

Source for Case 7.5

Portnoy, Fern. "Corporate Giving Creates Tough Decisions, Fragile Balances." *Denver Business Journal*, 15 November 1991, 15.

Sources for Case 7.6

Allen, Frank E., and Susan Pulliam. "United Way's Rivals Take Aim at Its Practices." *Wall Street Journal*, 6 March 1992, B1, B6.

Barringer, Felicity. "Ex-Chief of United Way Vows to Fight Accusations." *New York Times*, 10 April 1992, A13.

Duffy, Michael. "Charity Begins at Home." *Time*, 9 March 1992, 48.

"Ex-executives of United Way Indicted." *Arizona Republic*, 14 September 1994, A6.

Gitell, Seth. "Your United Way Dollars at Work." *Weekly Standard*, 2 September 1997, 27–29.

Johnston, David Cay. "United Way Faced With Fewer Donors Giving Less Money." *New York Times*, 9 November 1997, A1, A14.

Kinsley, Michael. "Charity Begins with Government." *Time*, 6 April 1992, 74.

Moss, Desda. "Change Is Focus of United Way Meeting." *USA Today*, 19 August 1992, 7A.

Moss, Desda. "Former United Way Chief Charged with Looting Funds." *USA Today*, 14 September 1994, 1A.

Moss, Desda. "United Way's Ex-Chief Guilty of Using Funds," *USA Today*, 14 April 1995, 1A.

Moss, Desda. "USA's Largest Charity Fears Financial Fallout from $2.74 Million Scandal." *USA Today*, 15 September 1994, 4A.

Weiner, Tim. "United Way's Ex-chief Indicted in Theft." *New York Times*, 14 September 1994, A7.

Sources for Case 7.7

Kotlowitz, Alex. "A Businessman Turns His Skills to Aiding Inner-City Schools." *Wall Street Journal*, 25 February 1992, A1, A8.

"Why Business Should Invest in Literacy." *Business Week*, 20 July 1992, 102.

Sources for Case 7.8

Andrews, Robert M. "Records Get Uniform Warning Tag." *Arizona Republic*, 10 May 1990, A1.

Foster, Ed. "Music-Label Bill Shelved." *Arizona Republic*, 24 March 1990, A1.

Gundersen, Edna. "Explicit Lyrics Warning Just Aren't Sticking." *USA Today*, 25 October 1995, 1D.

Henry, William A. "Did the Music Say Do It?" *Time*, 30 July 1990, 65.

Malone, Julia. "Washington Wives Use Influence to Target Sex, Drugs in Rock Music." *Christian Science Monitor*, 23 August 1995, 1, 36.

"MCA 'Peddling Filth,' Critics Say." *Arizona Republic*, 11 December 1996, A7.

"Musicians Mock Senators' Wives at Hearing." *Mesa Tribune*, 20 September 1995, A4.

"Record Firm to Back Stores with Legal Aid." *Mesa Tribune*, 5 June 1990, A2.

Stout, David. "Senate Hearing Is Told Lyrics Led to Suicide." *New York Times*, 7 November 1997, A1.

"Warning: Rock Music Ahead." *Time*, 21 May 1990, 69.

White, Carrie. "Rating Rock Music." *Mesa Tribune*, 12 December 1995, D1.

Sources for Case 7.11

"Beavis and Butt-head Move to Non-Prime Time." *USA Today*, 19 October 1993, 3D.

Gable, Donna. "Fanning the Fire Over 'Beavis.'" *USA Today*, 15 October 1993, 1D.

"Mother Blames MTV Cartoon in Fatal Blaze Started by Son." *Mesa Tribune*, 9 October 1993, A6.

"MTV Cartoon Linked to Fatal Fire." *Arizona Republic*, 9 October 1993, A5.

Stewart, Susan. "Leave It to Beavis?" *Parenting*, February 1994, 57.

USA Today, 22 October 1993, 13A.

Sources for Case 7.12

Anderson, Kurt. "Big Mouths." *Time*, 1 November 1993, 60-66.

"FCC Gets Complaints on 'Shock Jock.'" *Mesa Tribune*, 19 March 1994, A3.

Tilsner, Julie. "From Radio Rage, Raging Best-Sellers." *Business Week*, 1 November 1993, 42.

Sources for Case 7.13

Berger, Loren. "Who's Minding the Gun Counter?" *Business Week*, 25 October 1993, 120-22.

Deters, Barbara. "Two Major Toy Chains Take Steps to Remove Realistic Play Guns." *Arizona Republic*, 15 October 1994, A31, A32.

Gerlin, Andrea. "Wal-Mart Stops Handgun Sales Inside Its Stores." *Wall Street Journal*, 23 December 1993, B1, B8.

Pereira, Joseph, and Barbara Carton, "Toys 'R' Us to Banish Some 'Realistic' Toy Guns." *Wall Street Journal*, 14 October 1994, B1, B9.

Source for Case 7.14

Davis, Robert. "Gun Sales All 'Supply and Demand.'" *USA Today*, 19 April 1994, 1A, 2A.

Sources For Case 7.15

Bayles, Fred. "Meat Safety." *USA Today*, 8 October 1997, 1A.

Bryant, Adam. "Foodmaker Cancels Expansion." *New York Times*, 15 February 1993, C3.

Gibson, Richard, and Scott Kilman. "Tainted Hamburger Incident Heats Up Debate over U.S. Meat-Inspection System." *Wall Street Journal*, 12 February 1993, B1, B7.

Grover, Ronald, Dori Jones Yang, and Laura Holson. "Boxed in at Jack-in-the-Box." *Business Week*, 15 February 1993, 40.

"Jack-in-the-Box Ends E-Coli Suits." *National Law Journal*, 17 November 1997, A8.

Tolchin, Martin. "Clinton Orders Hiring of 160 Meat Inspectors." *New York Times*, 12 February 1993, A11.

Yang, Catherine, and Amy Barrett. "In a Stew over Tainted Meat." *Business Week*, 12 April 1993, 36.

Sources For Case 7.16

Donlon, Brian. "Dateline Producers Fired." *USA Today*, 22 March 1993, 3D.

Donlon, Brian, and Jim Healy. "GM Accepts NBC Apology, Settles Suit." *USA Today*, 10 February 1993, 1A, 2A.

Glaberson, William. "Former Chief of NBC News Finds New Life at Iowa Daily." *New York Times*, 28 March 1994, C1, C6.

Healey, Jane R., and Micheline Maynard. "Behemoths Battle over Mere Minute." *USA Today*, 9 February 1993, 1A, 2A.

Jennings, Marianne. *Business: Its Legal, Ethical and Global Environment*, 3d ed. San Francisco: Wadsworth, 1993: 75-76.

Jensen, Elizabeth. "Some Journalists Join GM in Criticizing NBC's Treatment of Truck-Crash Story." *Wall Street Journal*, 10 February 1993, B1, B8.

Maynard, Micheline. "GM Suit Attacks NBC Report." *USA Today*, 9 February 1993, 1A.

Source for Case 8.1

Mitchell, Kirk. "Mesa Club Got Funds." *Mesa Tribune*, 7 January 1995, A1, A6.

Source for Case 8.2

Fiscus, Chris. "Key Official Forced to Retire." *Arizona Republic*, 18 October 1996, A1, A12.

Sources for Case 8.3

Moeser, Chris. "Stapley Quits Mesa Council." *Mesa Tribune*, 1 November 1997, A1, A4.
Nowicki, Dan. "Council Rebukes Stapley." *Mesa Tribune*, 19 June 1997, A1, A4.
Thomason, Art. "Red Beets Less Luster in Scandal." *Arizona Republic*, 19 June 1997, EV1.

Source for Case 8.4

"IRS Fires 23 Workers Over Data Snooping." *Mesa Tribune*, 9 April 1997, A1.

Sources for Case 8.5

Associated Press. "Stanford's Chief Resigns over Billing Controversy." *Arizona Republic*, 30 July 1991, A8.
Cordes, Colleen. "Universities Review Overhead Charges; Some Alter Policies on President's Home." *Chronicle of Higher Education*, 3 April 1991, A1.
Leatherman, Courtney. "Stanford's Shift in Direction." *Chronicle of Higher Education*, 7 September 1994, A29.
McWilliams, Gary. "Less Gas for the Bunsen Burners." *Business Week*, 20 May 1991, 124-26.
Shao, Maria. "The Cracks in Stanford's Ivory Tower." *Business Week*, 11 March 1991, 64-65.

Source for Case 8.6

Putka, Gary. "A Professor Swapped Degrees for Contracts, University Suspects." *Wall Street Journal*, 12 July, 1991, A1.

Sources for Case 8.7

Green, Susan. "Official Defines Role in Venture." *Las Vegas Review Journal*, 4 October 1997, 1A, 2A.
Green, Susan. "Official Sought Casino Leases." *Las Vegas Review Journal*, 3 October 1997, 1A, 2A.

Source for Case 8.8

Snyder, Jodie. "AG: Insurer Chosen Unfairly." *Arizona Republic*, 2 August 1997, B1, B2.

Sources for Case 8.9

"As Orange County Investments Flop, Kids' Money Is Frozen." *Mesa Tribune*, 10 December 1994, A9.

Coffee, John C. "The Suitability Doctrine Revisited: Can Orange County Sue Its Broker for Recommending the Purchase of Unsuitable Securities for Its Funds?" *National Law Journal*, 16 January 1995, B4, B6.

Craig, David. "Dow Plunges 50 as Investors Skitter." *USA Today*, 9 December 1994, 1B.

Craig, David. "Orange County Freezes Hiring as Markets Feel the Heat." *USA Today*, 9 December 1994, 1A.

Donovan, Karen. "Chapter 9: The Next Page." *National Law Journal*, 26 December 1994, A6.

Greenwald, John. "The California Wipeout." *Time*, 19 December 1994, 55.

Hofmeister, Sallie. "In Rare Move, California County Files for Bankruptcy Protection." *New York Times*, 7 December 1994, C1, C5.

Jereski, Laura. "How a Rescue Mission Failed, Just Barely, in Orange County." *Wall Street Journal*, 22 December 1994, A1, A14.

Jereski, Laura. "Orange County Fund Losses Put at $2.5 Billion." *Wall Street Journal*, 12 December 1994, A3, A5.

Jereski, Laura. "Who Bears Loss Becomes Critical Orange County Issue." *Wall Street Journal*, 10 January 1995, C1.

Johnson, Kevin, and David J. Lynch. "California County Seeks Court Help on Debt." *USA Today*, 7 December 1994, 1A.

Jones, Del. "County Seeks Bankruptcy Protection." *USA Today*, 7 December 1994, 1C, 2C.

Lynch, David J. "How Golden Touch Turned into Crisis." *USA Today*, 23 December 1994, 1B.

Memmott, Mark. "Orange County's Woes Won't Sway Fed's Course." *USA Today*, 8 December 1994, 1B.

"Orange County Fallout Hits Stocks." *Arizona Republic*, 8 December 1994, C3.

"Orange County Seeks Protection under Bankruptcy Law." *Mesa Tribune*, 7 December 1994, A7.

Stevens, Amy. "Attorneys May Share Blame by Not Disclosing Risk in Orange County." *Wall Street Journal*, 16 December 1994, B3.

Taylor, Jeffrey. "Hard-Charging Broker Draws the Spotlight in Orange County Miss." *Wall Street Journal*, 12 December 1994, A1, A7.

Source for Case 8.10

Schwart, David. "2 Supervisors, Aide Turn in County Cars." *Arizona Republic*, 4 May 1994, B1, B5.

BUSINESS DISCIPLINE INDEX

Product/Company/Individuals/ Subject Index

Topic Index